THE
HANDY
FORENSIC
SCIENCE
ANSWER
BOOK

Patricia Barnes-Svarney and
Thomas E. Svarney

**READING CLUES AT THE CRIME
SCENE, CRIME LAB AND IN COURT**

VISIBLE
I N K
PRESS

Detroit

THE HANDY FORENSIC SCIENCE ANSWER BOOK

Most Visible Ink Press books are available at special quantity discounts when purchased in bulk by corporations, organizations, or groups. Customized printings, special imprints, messages, and excerpts can be produced to meet your needs. For more information, contact Special Markets Director, Visible Ink Press, www.visibleink.com, or 734-667-3211.

Managing Editor: Kevin S. Hile
Art Director: Mary Claire Krzewinski
Typesetting: Marco Divita
Proofreaders: Larry Baker and Shoshana Hurwitz
Indexer: Larry Baker

Cover images: Image of Ted Bundy by Mark T. Foley / State Archives of Florida, Florida Memory; all other images, Shutterstock.

Library of Congress Cataloging-in-Publication Data
Names: Barnes–Svarney, Patricia L., author. | Svarney, Thomas E., author.
Title: The handy forensic science answer book / by Patricia Barnes-Svarney and Thomas E. Svarney.
Description: Canton, MI : Visible Ink Press, [2018] | Includes bibliographical references and index. |
Identifiers: LCCN 2018019729 (print) | LCCN 2018021117 (ebook) | ISBN 9781578596812 (ebook) | ISBN 9781578596218 (pbk. : alk. paper)
Subjects: LCSH: Forensic sciences–Miscellanea.
Classification: LCC HV8073 (ebook) | LCC HV8073 .B358 2018 (print) | DDC 363.25–dc23
LC record available at https://lccn.loc.gov/2018019729

10 9 8 7 6 5 4 3 2 1

Printed in the United States of America.

About the Author

Patricia Barnes-Svarney is a science writer. Over the past few decades, she has written or coauthored more than 35 books, including Visible Ink Press' *The Handy Anatomy Answer Book, The Handy Biology Answer Book*, and *The Handy Nutrition Answer Book*. She is the author of *When the Earth Moves: Rogue Earthquakes, Tremors, and Aftershocks*, and she was also the editor/author of the award-winning *New York Public Library Science Desk Reference*.

Thomas E. Svarney is a scientist who has written extensively about the natural world. His books, with Patricia Barnes-Svarney, include Visible Ink Press' *The Handy Anatomy Answer Book, The Handy Biology Answer Book*, and *The Handy Nutrition Answer Book*, and he is also the author of *Skies of Fury: Weather Weirdness around the World* and *The Oryx Guide to Natural History*.

They live in Endicott, New York.

ALSO FROM VISIBLE INK PRESS

The Handy African American History Answer Book
by Jessie Carnie Smith
ISBN: 978-1-57859-452-8

The Handy American Government Answer Book: How Washington, Politics, and Elections Work
by Gina Misiroglu
ISBN: 978-1-57859-639-3

The Handy American History Answer Book
by David L. Hudson Jr.
ISBN: 978-1-57859-471-9

The Handy Anatomy Answer Book, 2nd edition
by Patricia Barnes-Svarney and Thomas E. Svarney
ISBN: 978-1-57859-542-6

The Handy Answer Book for Kids (and Parents), 2nd edition
by Gina Misiroglu
ISBN: 978-1-57859-219-7

The Handy Art History Answer Book
by Madelynn Dickerson
ISBN: 978-1-57859-417-7

The Handy Astronomy Answer Book, 3rd edition
by Charles Liu
ISBN: 978-1-57859-419-1

The Handy Bible Answer Book
by Jennifer Rebecca Prince
ISBN: 978-1-57859-478-8

The Handy Biology Answer Book, 2nd edition
by Patricia Barnes Svarney and Thomas E. Svarney
ISBN: 978-1-57859-490-0

The Handy Boston Answer Book
by Samuel Willard Crompton
ISBN: 978-1-57859-593-8

The Handy California Answer Book
by Kevin S. Hile
ISBN: 978-1-57859-591-4

The Handy Chemistry Answer Book
by Ian C. Stewart and Justin P. Lamont
ISBN: 978-1-57859-374-3

The Handy Christianity Answer Book
by Steve Werner
ISBN: 978-1-57859-686-7

The Handy Civil War Answer Book
by Samuel Willard Crompton
ISBN: 978-1-57859-476-4

The Handy Communication Answer Book
By Lauren Sergy
ISBN: 978-1-57859-587-7

The Handy Diabetes Answer Book
by Patricia Barnes-Svarney and Thomas E. Svarney
ISBN: 978-1-57859-597-6

The Handy Dinosaur Answer Book, 2nd edition
by Patricia Barnes-Svarney and Thomas E. Svarney
ISBN: 978-1-57859-218-0

The Handy English Grammar Answer Book
by Christine A. Hult, Ph.D.
ISBN: 978-1-57859-520-4

The Handy Forensic Science Answer Book: Reading Clues at the Crime Scene, Crime Lab, and in Court
by Patricia Barnes-Svarney and Thomas E. Svarney
ISBN: 978-1-57859-621-8

The Handy Geography Answer Book, 3rd edition
by Paul A. Tucci
ISBN: 978-1-57859-576-1

The Handy Geology Answer Book
by Patricia Barnes-Svarney and Thomas E. Svarney
ISBN: 978-1-57859-156-5

The Handy History Answer Book, 3rd edition
by David L. Hudson, Jr., J.D.
ISBN: 978-1-57859-372-9

The Handy Hockey Answer Book
by Stan Fischler
ISBN: 978-1-57859-513-6

The Handy Investing Answer Book
by Paul A. Tucci
ISBN: 978-1-57859-486-3

The Handy Islam Answer Book
by John Renard, Ph.D.
ISBN: 978-1-57859-510-5

The Handy Law Answer Book
by David L. Hudson, Jr., J.D.
ISBN: 978-1-57859-217-3

The Handy Literature Answer Book
By Daniel S. Burt and Deborah G. Felder
ISBN: 978-1-57859-635-5

The Handy Math Answer Book, 2nd edition
by Patricia Barnes-Svarney and Thomas E.
  Svarney
ISBN: 978-1-57859-373-6

The Handy Military History Answer Book
by Samuel Willard Crompton
ISBN: 978-1-57859-509-9

The Handy Mythology Answer Book
by David A. Leeming, Ph.D.
ISBN: 978-1-57859-475-7

The Handy New York City Answer Book
by Chris Barsanti
ISBN: 978-1-57859-586-0

The Handy Nutrition Answer Book
by Patricia Barnes-Svarney and Thomas E.
  Svarney
ISBN: 978-1-57859-484-9

The Handy Ocean Answer Book
by Patricia Barnes-Svarney and Thomas E.
  Svarney
ISBN: 978-1-57859-063-6

The Handy Pennsylvania Answer Book
by Lawrence W. Baker
ISBN: 978-1-57859-610-2

The Handy Personal Finance Answer Book
by Paul A. Tucci
ISBN: 978-1-57859-322-4

The Handy Philosophy Answer Book
by Naomi Zack, Ph.D.
ISBN: 978-1-57859-226-5

The Handy Physics Answer Book, 2nd edition
By Paul W. Zitzewitz, Ph.D.
ISBN: 978-1-57859-305-7

The Handy Presidents Answer Book, 2nd
  edition
by David L. Hudson
ISB N: 978-1-57859-317-0

The Handy Psychology Answer Book, 2nd
  edition
by Lisa J. Cohen, Ph.D.
ISBN: 978-1-57859-508-2

The Handy Religion Answer Book, 2nd edition
by John Renard, Ph.D.
ISBN: 978-1-57859-379-8

The Handy Science Answer Book, 4th edition
by The Carnegie Library of Pittsburgh
ISBN: 978-1-57859-321-7

The Handy State-by-State Answer Book: Faces,
  Places, and Famous Dates for All Fifty
  States
by Samuel Willard Crompton
ISBN: 978-1-57859-565-5

The Handy Supreme Court Answer Book
by David L Hudson, Jr.
ISBN: 978-1-57859-196-1

The Handy Technology Answer Book
by Naomi E. Balaban and James Bobick
ISBN: 978-1-57859-563-1

The Handy Texas Answer Book
by James L. Haley
ISBN: 978-1-57859-634-8

The Handy Weather Answer Book, 2nd edition
by Kevin S. Hile
ISBN: 978-1-57859-221-0

PLEASE VISIT THE "HANDY ANSWERS" SERIES
WEBSITE AT WWW.HANDYANSWERS.COM.

Acknowledgments

If there is anything we've learned from writing this book it is that the men and women (and yes, even K-9 companions, rescue dogs, and other wild and domestic animals) that deal with any aspect of forensic science are an amazing group. It takes a great deal of patience, knowledge, determination, and discipline to examine, investigate, and interpret what occurs in a crime or accident—much of it done to keep peace in our world.

As always, we'd like to thank Roger Jänecke, our wonderful publisher, who asked us to write what turned out to be a multi-discipline science book. We also thank our editor-without-compare, Kevin Hile, for all his help and suggestions. We'd also like to thank Larry Baker and Shoshana Hurwitz for their proofreading and indexing work. A big thanks to Agnes Birnbaum, our good friend and (patient) agent, who understands not only why and how we write, but that we also need to talk about our cats more often than not, too! You're the best, Agnes. And, of course, thanks to our family and friends (you know who you are), who understand why we sometimes disappear periodically when we're writing.

Finally, and overall, we salute those people who try to understand the intricacies of forensic science, no matter what branch or discipline. To those people—and to those in forensics and law enforcement who have helped us (and others) understand and get through a bunch of traumatic experiences during our time on this planet—we thank you. Keep up the good work.

Table of Contents

Photo Sources

Aude (Wikicommons): p. 33.

Bachrach Studios: p. 98.

Bibliotèque Nationale de France: p. 286.

Ebyabe (Wikicommons): p. 332.

Enzoklop (Wikicommons): p. 187.

Executive Office of the President of the United States: p. 210.

Federal Bureau of Investigation: p. 171.

Florida Memory Project: p. 311.

Olaf Growald: p. 217.

Jplozai (Wikicommons): p. 339.

Library of Congress: pp. 23, 325.

Karl Mumm: p. 134.

National Geographic Society: p. 25.

National Portrait Gallery, London, England: pp. 21, 190.

Mark Pellegrini: p. 235.

PLoS Genetics: p. 185.

Polytec GmbH: p. 207.

Ribelle2289 (Wikicommons): p. 110.

Shutterstock: pp. 3, 5, 6, 10, 11, 15, 36, 40, 43, 45, 48, 50, 52, 57, 60, 62, 64, 67, 69, 74, 77, 78, 80, 83, 85, 88, 92, 94, 97, 100, 102, 104, 107, 108, 112, 114, 116, 118, 120, 127, 129, 132, 142, 144, 147, 148, 151, 153, 154, 157, 163, 166, 176, 180, 182, 194, 196, 201, 202, 205, 213, 214, 219, 225, 227, 231, 239, 241, 243, 246, 248, 250, 253, 255, 258, 260, 265, 276, 277, 280, 281, 290, 292, 300, 319, 345.

Strand Magazine: p. 326.

Karen T. Taylor: p. 139.

University of New Haven: p. 31.

University of Virginia Fine Arts Library: p. 26.

U.S. Department of Defense: p. 315.

White House Historical Association: p. 297.

Public domain: pp. 18 (top and bottom), 19, 28, 89, 136, 191, 199, 230, 267, 271, 302, 304, 308, 309.

Introduction

We live in a world in which humans are most often surrounded by other humans. And among all those contacts, there are people who are not as "above board" as others. Those people and their nefarious ways are the reasons why forensic science has made its way into our culture—and why the field continues to grow and advance.

Most of us have been exposed to certain facets of forensic science. While working on this book, we, the authors, had several forensic events that occurred, including being the first at an accident scene; watching law enforcement go through the scene of an unattended death; and entering a house that had been burglarized. All of them were frightening, but the people involved in law enforcement and forensics were considerate, thorough, and above all, very professional. Their methods and techniques were nothing like what many people see on television or in the movies. (In fact, at the burglary scene, we got an earful about how real life forensic science works versus "CSI-type" shows—and there's a world of difference!)

After writing this book, and after those events, we learned about the difficulties—and the many successes—people encounter in the fields that make up forensic science. We learned (firsthand) many facets of forensics, including how easy it is to contaminate a crime scene, how not every investigation results in a lead, and even how every eyewitness of a crime scene can tell a very different story as to what occurred.

The Handy Forensic Science Answer Book examines this fascinating and complex world of trying to understand accidents, crime, and the criminal. It explains how forensic science came into being and improved over time. It offers a look at how autopsies are carried out (of recent and less recent remains), how forensic investigators seek biological and physical evidence at an accident or crime scene, and the how and why behind all pieces of what is found at a crime scene or accident—from prints and DNA evidence to toolmarks, weapons, and explosive interpretations. It examines the lesser-known investigations, such as documents and cryptanalysis, along with forensic geology and meteorology. It puts everything together, explaining how such forensic information is used in a court, and it even looks at the psychology of the criminal mind, along with examining forensic science's more controversial subjects. It also presents some of the more interesting cases in forensic science, going into detail about some of the more insidious famous and not-so-famous cases.

The latter part of the book gives the reader information about how forensics has been used and examined in the media (nonfiction and fiction). And finally, it offers an extensive list of resources to allow the reader to further examine other forensic ideas.

There is no Sherlock Holmes to deduce a crime or what the criminal is thinking (although it would be nice), and there is no Hercule Poirot to use his "little grey cells" to solve a mystery. Modern forensic scientists, examiners, and investigators do use deduction and their little grey cells, but there is so much more to solving what occurred at a scene—criminal or otherwise. Each piece of evidence is like finding a piece of a puzzle, one that will (and sometimes won't) help to solve a crime, reconstruct an accident, or understand how an item failed. Sometimes the answers are out there; sometimes they are not. But it is often the challenge of finding answers that spur the forensic scientists, analysts, and investigators to continue.

This book is for those people who want to know more about how forensic science works and why it is such an important field, from amateur and armchair detectives to those who may be thinking of choosing forensics as a profession. And you won't need a magnifying glass—just the curiosity to know more about the world of forensic science!

INTRODUCTION TO FORENSIC SCIENCE

DEFINING FORENSIC SCIENCE

What are some general definitions of forensic science?

Forensic science (often abbreviated FS) can generally be defined in several different ways. In the case of the law, it is considered to be any science used for the purposes of the law to gain impartial evidence. (Thus, in general, it is said that any science used for the purposes of the law is termed a forensic science.) According to the Crime Museum, forensic science is also often considered "an argument or discussion used for a legal matter in a court of law," and according to the American Academy of Forensic Sciences, forensic science is called a "necessary tool in the search for the truth in any legal proceeding." Although these definitions are most familiar to those in law-enforcement agencies (mostly associated with a crime) and the courts (associated with evidence in a court of law), forensics can also be thought of as any science used for the purposes of civil disputes or even to protect public health. For example, forensic science methods and analyses can be used in accident investigations, food contamination analysis, or even in forensic anthropological studies.

What is the origin of the word "forensic"?

"Forensic" is from the Latin *forensis*, meaning "of or before the forum." It is also often interpreted as a public discussion or belonging to debate or discussion—a leftover from ancient Roman time (for more about ancient Romans and forensics, see the chapter "The History of Forensic Science").

Are the terms "forensics" and "forensic science" interchangeable?

In today's usage, the terms *forensics* and *forensic science* are pretty much the same thing. The term "forensic" is essentially a synonym for "legal" or "related to the courts";

1

plus, the word is closely related to the scientific field. This is why the terms—including in some dictionaries—are commonly used interchangeably.

Does forensic science only pertain to law-enforcement and criminal cases?

No, not all forensic science is about law-enforcement and prosecution of criminal cases. These ideas have been, no doubt, propagated by certain media for over a century—from books and magazine articles to modern television and movies, and although many of the advances in forensic science have been benefited by criminal case methods and analyses, it also pertains to civil and legal matters, along with determining why certain non-criminal events and actions occur (such as transportation-related accidents).

Why is forensic science considered to be multidisciplinary?

Forensic science is multidisciplinary because no one single science answers all forensic questions, especially in the collection and analysis of evidence. Forensic investigators and experts from many disciplines are needed in order to solve a forensic puzzle—from biology (for example, for an autopsy) to accounting (for example, in a white-collar crime case). In fact, according to the American Academy of Forensic Science, "There is literally no end to the number of disciplines that become 'forensic' by definition," and in the future, they predict that even more specialties will become part of the term "forensic."

What are some of the scientific disciplines used in forensic science?

Many scientific disciplines are used in forensic science. Some examples are biology, geology, pathology, genetics, chemistry, cryptanalysis, psychology, and ballistics, and within these examples are often subfields. For example, in chemistry, a person may be an expert in the analysis of drugs and poisons, while another person may be an expert in the analysis of paints, tools, and other physical items.

What are some scientific fields that are "nonforensic"?

Although many methods and techniques used in forensics are from various scientific fields, some sciences are not as applicable. For example, the term "forensic astronomy" has often been used to describe people who use astronomy to determine ancient constellations, but it is not as well recognized or widely needed as other scientific fields involved in forensic science.

Why are various facets of forensic science often necessary in terms of crime and accidents?

Various facets of forensic science are often needed, especially in terms of crime and accidents, for several reasons. For example, often, a lack of eyewitnesses are present at a crime scene or accident—and if such witnesses are present, many people are unreliable in terms of giving evidence. This is usually because people may be partial to a certain aspect of the crime or person who commits a crime or are subjective in what they wit-

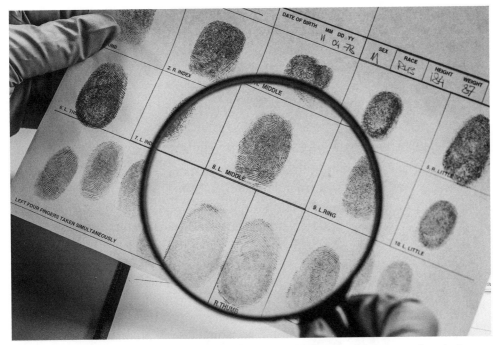

An early discipline of forensic science was the study of fingerprints. Today, crime labs have an extremely diverse array of tools to study evidence at their disposal.

ness. Another reason for needing forensic science is historical—it can often be used to solve "cold cases" that occurred years before.

Why is scientific evidence the best tool to use in forensic science?

Because scientific evidence from forensic methods and analyses cannot "lie," the results are most often impartial and objective—unlike many eyewitnesses' reports or interpretations of events. In most cases, this makes forensic science the best tool to resolve criminal, civil, or other legal matters.

What is deductive versus inductive reasoning in forensics?

Deductive and inductive skills are definitely different, both of which can be used in forensic science. Deductive reasoning is based mainly on science, with the various principles resulting in certain answers. In other words, it moves from the general to the specific. For instance, when applied to DNA analysis in the crime lab, deductive reasoning is based on the known scientific principles of human genetics. This, in turn, allows the forensic expert in DNA analysis to come to certain viable conclusions about a DNA sample. Inductive reasoning is essentially moving from something specific to the general. In other words, it relies on a certain piece of information to determine a broad conclusion about an event, such as where a fire started in a building or where an explosion originated, but

3

because it is not based on exhaustive evidence and because a certain degree of uncertainty is present, inductive reasoning has its limitations. Overall, it is thought that inductive reasoning can often complement deductive reasoning during an investigation.

TERMS IN FORENSIC SCIENCE AND LAW

What is the difference between *cause* of death and *manner* of death?

Cause of death and manner of death are two different things, especially in the eyes of the law. The following gives a brief synopsis of both cause and manner of death:

- *Cause of death*—The cause of death is the main reason why a person died. For example, they may have died from a gunshot wound, spinal trauma from a severe accident, or a heart attack.

- *Manner of death*—The manner of death depends on the reason or reasons (such as a sequence of events or actions) for the death, and in most jurisdictions, it is determined by the medical examiner (or coroner, if no medical examiner is around). For example, most categories include the following (in the United States): natural death (solely by a certain disease and/or natural disease process), an accident (injury when no evidence exists of intent to harm), suicide (injury with intent to cause self-harm or one's own death), homicide (caused by a person to another person with the intent to cause harm, fear, or death; it is interesting to note that a "homicidal manner of death" does not indicate that a criminal act has occurred, as this is determined by the legal process and not by the certifier of death, such as the coroner or medical examiner), undetermined (if inadequate information is available as to the circumstances of death, especially if one manner of death is just as seemingly logical as another; for example, if a person is unconscious with a massive head injury, without knowing the events that took place, it may be hard to determine whether it was due to an accidental fall or a homicidal event), and pending.

What happens if a death is due to a combination of natural and unnatural events?

If a death is due to a combination of natural and unnatural events, the preference is generally given to the non-natural cause. For example, if a person suffers a myocardial infarction (heart attack) while swimming in the ocean, loses consciousness, and drowns, the manner of death is ruled an accident. This is because the person may have had the ability to survive the heart attack if they had been on land. Or, if a natural death is hastened by a bad fall, the manner of death is no longer considered natural but accidental.

How are some deaths interpreted as natural or accidental?

Deaths are interpreted and classified in several ways. For example, deaths due to motor vehicle collisions are considered accidental in manner. Those deaths from the improper use of medical devices or improper therapy (for example, the failure to repair an obvious injury to an artery inflicted during surgery) are considered accidental. Those deaths due to chronic substance abuse, such as hepatic cirrhosis due to alcohol abuse, are usually considered natural.

What is a "cold case"?

The term "cold case" does not actually have a universal definition. In general, most references define a cold case as a crime or accident that has not been fully solved, and although it is not being currently worked on, the investigation remains "open" in case new information emerges, but other definitions exist. For example, according to the National Institute of Justice, the definition of a cold case can vary between agencies. The NIJ defines a cold case as "any whose probative investigative leads have been exhausted." This means that even a case that is only a few months old—not years old—can be considered to be a cold case. The recent interest in cold cases comes not only from the media (most often television programs) but also from advances in DNA technology that allow experts to take a new look at old evidence. (For more about cold cases, see the chapter "In the Crime Lab: Analyzing Older Remains," and for cold cases and DNA, see the chapter "In the Crime Lab: DNA Analysis.")

Do other countries have any "cold cases"?

Yes, "cold cases" are not just investigated in the United States. As to be expected, many criminal cases have never been solved, but in other countries outside of the United States, they are often called "historical" cases.

What is an exhumation?

An exhumation (also called "disinterment") is generally defined as the removal of something buried. It is most often used in terms of human remains. In particular, it is the removal of human remains from a grave or vault for the purpose of an examination, usually to look for evidence in a criminal case (such as a poison that may have been overlooked) or to determine something historically (such as the exhumation of a historical person from the early 1900s to determine whether any foul play was involved in their death).

What is a cadaver versus a corpse?

A cadaver is a dead body and usually refers to a human body after death. Other terms frequently used interchangeably for a dead body are corpse, body, or remains, but some differences exist. A cadaver is a dead

The removal of human remains from a grave— whether a formal or makeshift one—or vault is called an exhumation.

human body used in scientific or medical research. In other words, if a person is dead, they are a corpse, but if someone uses a person's body for research—or even to determine the cause of death from a crime—they are called a cadaver.

What is a crime?

The word "crime" has several definitions. In general, and according to *Merriam-Webster Dictionary*, it is "an act or the commission of an act that is forbidden." It also includes omission of a duty that is commanded by public law. Synonyms include an unlawful or illegal act, a misdeed, a felony, or a misdemeanor (although these terms actually differ in their legal definition).

What is evidence?

Evidence—from the Latin *evidential*, from *evident*, or obvious to the mind or eye—is generally defined as an available body of facts or information indicating whether a belief or proposition is true or valid. In a court of law, it is the data presented to the court or jury relating to facts, in particular to the existence or nonexistence of alleged or disputed facts. This can include such data as those from testimonies from witnesses, records of events, documents, and other such items pertaining to the case and/or objects, such as those found at a crime scene.

What is an eyewitness?

According to most references, an eyewitness is a person who actually sees some act, event, or occurrence and can usually give an account of what happened. This firsthand account is most often useful at crime or accident scenes, although many times, accounts differ from eyewitness to eyewitness, as everyone observes and interprets events differently. (For more about eyewitnesses and testimony, see the chapters "Putting It All Together" and "Controversies in Forensic Science.")

What is a homicide?

A homicide occurs when the death of a person is unlawfully caused by another person. A synonym is the term "murder." In criminal cases, homicide can be further categorized and defined as "justifiable homicide," "first-degree murder," "involuntary manslaughter," and other terms. (For more about the courts, see the chapter "Putting It All Together.")

An eyewitness is a person who was actually at the scene of a crime and was able to see what happened and, hopefully, who did it.

Where did "9-1-1" originate?

In the United States, the dialed numbers "9-1-1" (nine-one-one) are used by the public in order to obtain help during an emergency. In 1967, the President's Commission on Law Enforcement and Administration of Justice recommended that a "single number should be established" nationwide for reporting emergency situations, along with different numbers for each type of emergency. This was deemed too difficult to remember in the various types of emergencies. Thus, in 1968, the 9-1-1 emergency number was established after the Federal Communications Commission met with the American Telephone and Telegraph Company (AT&T) with the intention of creating more useful (and memorable) universal emergency numbers. The number was also chosen as it was never authorized as an office, area, or service code.

It took a while before emergency numbers were established throughout the United States. Only 17 percent of the population had 9-1-1 service in 1976; by 1979, only 27 percent; and by 1987, 50 percent of the population had the emergency service. Today, to date, 96 percent of the country is covered by some type of 9-1-1 service—with even Canada adopting 9-1-1 as the country's emergency numbers. (For more about 9-1-1, see the National Emergency Number Association website at http://www.nena.org.)

Is a homicide the same in every country?

No, other "types" of homicides exist, especially in other countries. For instance, culpable homicide is often a term used in countries such as South Africa and Scotland. For example, in South Africa, "culpable homicide" is equivalent to manslaughter. One example is the South African Olympic sprinter Oscar Pistorius (1986–) who, in 2013, alleged that he mistook his girlfriend Reeva Steenkamp for a house intruder and shot her through the bathroom door. In 2014, he was convicted of manslaughter, as he said he did not intentionally kill her, but his actions were negligent, or culpable homicide. (All murders are culpable homicides, but not all culpable homicides are murder.) In 2016, his conviction on manslaughter was reversed by a higher court—it believed that Pistorius should have known that firing his gun would kill whomever was behind the door—and, as of this writing, he was sentenced to six years in prison for the murder of his girlfriend.

What are terms that indicate a familial relation to a victim and their killer?

Several terms indicate a familial relationship between a victim and their killer. For example, a *parricide* is the killing of a parent or another close relative. A *patricide* is the act of killing one's own father; a *matricide* is the killing of one's own mother. While an *infanticide* describes the murder of a child, *fratricide* and *sororicide* apply to the murder of an adult brother and sister, respectively.

What is a criminalist?

A criminalist has several descriptions. Specifically, it is a broad term that includes several tasks within the field of forensic science. One definition states that criminalists are often called crime scene investigators or lab technicians, who examine the crime or accident scenes' physical evidence to understand possible connections between the scene (and scenes in other places), victims, perpetrators, and offenders. (For more about crime scene investigators, see the chapter "At the Crime Scene: The Crime Site and Investigation Teams.") A criminalist also uses methods to identify physical evidence at a crime or accident scene, which can be applied to linking suspects, objects, and locations as evidence.

What is the difference between a criminalist and a criminologist?

In general, a criminalist is a person who uses their background in the sciences—from chemistry, biology, geology, and other scientific studies—to investigate, analyze, and solve crimes. On the other hand, a criminologist is a person who specializes in sociology or psychiatry and psychology in order to understand the causes and effects of crime on society. (For more about how psychology and psychiatry fit with forensic science, see the chapter "The Criminal Mind.")

DISCIPLINES WITHIN
FORENSIC STUDIES

What are some of the more common disciplines found in association with forensic science?

Many examples exist of disciplines found in association with forensic science. The following lists only a few of the more common disciplines and how they apply to forensics:

- *Digital and Multimedia*—This can include such methods as the analysis of computer records and/or the examination of a surveillance video as evidence (for more about digital media and forensics, see the chapter "Other Forensic Investigations").

- *Jurisprudence*—This discipline, which means studies that pertain to the law, is often used in forensics. For example, expert witnesses and trial lawyers are found in association with forensics within this discipline. (For more about the law, jurisprudence, and forensics, see the chapter "Putting It All Together.")

- *Odontology (Forensic Dentistry)*—Odontology is a discipline that is often used in forensics, especially in terms of personal identification of a victim, such as comparing dental records and a crime victim. It is also used in such forensic analyses as evaluating bite marks. (For more about odontology, see the chapters "In the Crime Lab: Analyzing a Body" and "In the Crime Lab: Trace Evidence.")

> ## What two people are often referred to as the "father of criminalistics"?
>
> Two people have often been called the "father of criminalistics"—both separated by many decades. Austrian criminal jurist and examining magistrate Hans Gustav Adolf Gross (1847–1915) is often called the "father of criminalistics" (or "father of criminal investigation") by many, since in 1893, he wrote a classic text called *Handbuch für Untersuchungsrichter, Polizeibeamte, Gendarmen* (*Handbook for Magistrates, Police Officials, Military Policemen*). It especially emphasized the cross-transfer of evidence, for instance, of soils, fibers, or hair to the victim from the perpetrator. Another person who is often called the "father of criminalistics" is American chemist and forensic scientist Paul Leland Kirk (1902–1970). He established criminology as an academic field and wrote the classic forensic book *Crime Investigation: Physical Evidence and the Police Laboratory*. He was also involved in several famous criminal cases that were decided based on his forensic investigations.

- *Pathology and Biology*—Both pathology and biology are disciplines that are used quite often in forensics. For example, experts who deal with autopsies often have a degree in pathology and are called forensic pathologists (for more about pathology, see the chapter "In the Crime Lab: Analyzing a Body"), and, for example, experts in insects, or forensic entomologists, are often called in to determine how long a discovered body has been exposed to the elements (for more about the use of biology in forensics, see the chapter "At the Crime Scene: Looking for Biological Evidence").

- *Psychiatry and Behavioral Science*—This discipline is often used in terms of a criminal suspect and trial. For example, it is used to determine a person's competence to stand trial and for culpability. (For more about psychology and behavior in forensic science, see the chapter "The Criminal Mind.")

- *Document Analysis*—This discipline is often used in analyses to determine, for example, the authorship of a handwritten document. It is also a discipline that can help in document restoration. (For more about document interpretation in forensics, see the chapter "In the Crime Lab: Questioned Documents and Cryptanalysis.")

Why is toxicology important to forensic science?

Toxicology—from the Greek word *toxikos*, or "poison"—is the study of certain poisons and toxins. In forensic science, toxicologists can determine whether a deceased person died of a poison or toxic substance. It is also used in drug testing of individuals, most often in terms of work, such as jobs for security or when hiring a person for a certain job. (For more details about toxicology, see the chapter "In the Crime Lab: Analyzing a Body.")

Are forensic dentistry and odontology two different things?

No, the two terms are used interchangeably. In fact, odontology is usually referred to as forensic dentistry. This branch of forensics involves the study of teeth, bite marks, and sometimes jaws, especially in the identification of human (or also animal, if applicable) remains—in other words, studies common to dentistry. (For more about how teeth are interpreted in the lab, see the chapter "In the Crime Lab: Analyzing a Body.")

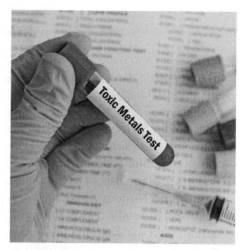

Toxicologists analyze remains to see if someone died of poisoning, toxins in the environment, or drug overdoses. They can also test for drug use in company employees.

How is engineering used in forensic science?

This discipline can be used in a forensic study to investigate accidents or events. It can also be applied in the search for design defects in materials. In forensic science, an engineer may be asked to apply the tools and techniques of science and engineering to civil, criminal, and regulatory issues. For example, they often investigate transportation accidents (such as an air or rail accident), product failures (including those that involve personal injury), environmental contamination (such as those that cause harm to people or the environment), and certain criminal acts and events (such as proving or disproving who was responsible for a traffic accident).

Why are the behavioral sciences, psychology, and psychiatry important to forensic science?

The behavioral sciences, psychology, and psychiatry are important to many facets of forensic science. For example, they can help in legal issues for criminal (for example, to determine whether a person is competent to stand trial) and civil (for example, determining a person's emotional distress caused by a defendant's actions) cases or in such areas as family or domestic relations law (for example, in child custody disputes). (For more about criminal psychology, see the chapter "The Criminal Mind.")

Why is forensic accounting necessary?

In forensic accounting, experts use accounting, auditing, and investigative skills when conducting an investigation (it is often referred to in the media as "white-collar crime"). For example, the companies Enron and WorldCom were both involved with corporate fraud and were exposed with the help of experts in forensic accounting. (For more about forensic accounting, see the chapter "In the Crime Lab: Questioned Documents and Cryptanalysis.")

Does a field exist called music forensics?

Robin Thicke

As the words imply—and, of course, not as well known as criminal forensics—music forensics (or a forensic musicologist) includes seeking evidence for various problems in the music world. For example, experts look for evidence of plagiarism, mainly a duplicate of a certain tune or words in a newer song as compared to one already published. One example occurred in 2013 when a song called "Blurred Lines" came into question. A lawsuit was brought against the creators of the song, Robin Thicke and Pharrell Williams. The singers said that their successful single song was not a duplicate of Marvin Gaye's "Got to Give It Up," but a jury agreed with the Gaye family's claim of duplication. The two were fined almost $7.4 million in damages. The charges were sustained because of the testimony of expert witnesses in musicology in the "Blurred Lines" trial. In particular, the musicologists discovered that eight places in the song had "substantial similarities" to Gaye's original "Got to Give It Up."

How has forensic geology been used in certain investigations?

Forensic geology (also called geoforensics) is the use of rocks, minerals, soils, petroleum products (oil, gas, etc.), and landforms as evidence in a criminal or civil case. For example, experts in forensic geology have aided authorities to find people who steal valuable artifacts from federal lands, such as American Indian objects. Such expertise was also instrumental in solving the mystery of who kidnapped and murdered Adolph Coors (1916–1960), heir to the Coors Beer fortune. When layers of dirt behind the fender of a suspicious vehicle were compared to soil samples from around the Rocky Mountains where Coors was kidnapped, the analyses eventually led to the movements of the car—and, eventually, to the killer Joseph Corbett (1928–2009; he eventually committed suicide). (For more about forensic geology, see the chapter "Other Forensic Investigations.")

What are some aspects of wildlife forensics?

Wildlife forensics has many aspects, and all, as the name implies, have to do with evidence in association with animals. For example, animal tracks and digging at a crime scene may indicate the location of a decaying body. Wildlife experts may also help with such crimes as the theft of cacti from federal lands. (For more about wildlife forensics, see the chapter "Other Forensic Investigations.")

What is food forensics?

Food forensics is the field that specializes in determining food safety and quality issues. It is necessary for several reasons, including consumer safety and to understand a certain food industry's liability—and, often, their reputation as a food supplier. (For more about food forensics, see the chapter "Other Forensic Investigations.")

THE HISTORY OF FORENSIC SCIENCE

THE EARLY YEARS IN FORENSIC SCIENCE (BEFORE 1800 B.C.E.)

When did the concept of forensic science begin?

No one truly knows when the concept of forensic science first began. A form of forensic science probably originated when humans tried to understand why an accident or event occurred. Although it was primitive and did not include a court or other organized group of people, this type of reasoning could have been the start of forensic science.

Where do some historians believe the concept of forensic science originated?

Although not all historians agree on when or what, they all seem to agree that the concept of forensic science originated at some point in China. For example, it is thought that forensic medicine began around the sixth century based on the earliest known mention in an alleged book titled *Ming Yuen Shih Lu* (also seen as *Ming Yuan Shih Lu*), translated as *True Records of the Clarification of Wrongs*, by Chinese physician Hsu Chich-Ts'si (although it is often debated as to the true author of the text, Chich-Ts'si is most often noted). The true contents are also often debated, as the book has since been lost. Another book written in the tenth century, *I Yu Chi* (*Records of Doubtful Criminal Cases*) by Ho Ning, is reported to also have certain early forensic science concepts included.

What book is often cited as the first written account of forensic science?

A book that is often cited as the first (second or third if Hsu Chich-Ts'si's and Ho Ning's books are counted) written account that mentions forensic science—particularly medicine and entomology (the study of insects)—to solve criminal cases was written by criminal court judge Song Ci (1186–1249; his name is often seen as Sung Tz'u or Sung Chee; he is often called the "father of forensic medicine") during the Southern Song Dynasty. It was called *Xi Yuan Ji Lu* (often translated as *Washing Away of Wrongs* or *Collected Cases of Injustice Rectified*). The book offered several cases that Song Ci had heard about or witnessed. In addition, he presented certain ways of determining whether a person's death was caused by murder, suicide, or accident (and explained how to interpret various aspects of an autopsy). For example, he explained how to distinguish between a drowning (water in the lungs) and strangulation death, and, among many other accounts, he offered advice on wound characteristics, poisons, and even some information on what is now called forensic dentistry (or odontology).

What was a law enforcer called in ancient China?

Law enforcers in ancient China were called "prefects," men and women who had limited authority across certain areas and for only for a certain amount of time. The local magistrates (who answered to governors appointed by the emperor) were in charge of their jurisdiction, or prefectures (thus the word "prefects"), including the prefects. The prefects were often in charge of handling investigations (similar to today's police detectives), while subprefects, people under the prefects' authority, were in charge of the law enforcement in their respective regions.

Who were the law enforcers in ancient Athens, Greece?

Law enforcers in ancient Athens, Greece, consisted of three hundred to four hundred (depending on the reference) foreign, publicly owned slaves. (The Greek citizenry found it uncomfortable to accuse each other.) The slaves were reportedly called the Scythian archers, who were brought back to Athens after the naval battle of Salamis (480 B.C.E.). The slaves—called "rod-bearers," their translated name—were used in crowd control, dealing with criminals and prisoners and making arrests. In fact, it is often said that the Scythian archers were the first police force.

Were North American Indian "trackers" some of the first people to practice a kind of forensic science?

Yes, in many ways, North American Indian "trackers"—most were hunters—could be thought of as the first people to practice a kind of forensic science in the Americas. For example, many of them were experts in understanding nature, including weather conditions, animal tracks (including such details as knowing the size, shape, and features of an animal's track), and the cycle of the seasons. Each of these factors helped them in the hunt to reach their prey—much like today's forensic experts who look for evidence, for example, at a crime scene. (For more about modern American Indian trackers, see this chapter.)

How was the word "forensic" used in ancient Rome?

The word "forensic" was often used in ancient Rome in the marketplace, in which many business affairs were carried out through discussion. It was also more commonly used in relation to public affairs, such as those that included Roman governmental debates and actions by courts of law. For example, a criminal charge meant presenting a case before a forum, or a group of public individuals—the loose translation for "forensic"—in which the case would often be decided in favor of the person with the best argument and presentation.

Who were the law enforcers in ancient Roman time?

Unlike a separate police force, the Roman army's task was to provide security in ancient Rome. If more security was needed,

A statue of Augustus Caesar, the first emperor of Rome who also established the Praetorian Guard and "vigiles," who served as both police and firemen.

cities would hire local watchmen. While the army provided a type of law enforcement, the magistrates were the people who investigated crimes.

What did the first Roman emperor establish to protect the citizens of Rome?

The first Roman emperor, Augustus Caesar (63 B.C.E.–14 C.E.; born Gaius Octavius Thurinus and adopted by his great uncle, Julius Caesar; he took on "Augustus Caesar" after he became ruler), was responsible for establishing several "law-enforcement" groups during his reign. For example, he began the Praetorian Guard in 26 B.C.E., a select group of guards who protected him and his surroundings in the city of Rome. Augustus also eventually had over a dozen sectors in Rome protected by squads of men called vigiles or the *Vigiles urbani* ("watchmen of the city") to police areas, catch criminals, and capture runaway slaves. Their tasks also included being the firefighters of the city. (Rome under Augustus was said to have had the world's first fire brigade, established in 6 C.E. after a disastrous fire in the city.) Also, the *Cohorte urbanae* ("urban cohorts") were soldiers who often were used as an antiriot force.

When was the first organized police force created?

Although ancient Athens, Greece, is said to have had the first police force (see above), it is said that the first centrally organized police force was founded in 1667. King Louis XIV sent down a royal edict, registered by the *Parlement* ("Parliament") of Paris, France, on March 15, creating the office of *lieutenant général de police* ("lieutenant general of police"). The chosen lieutenant general was Gabriel Nicolas de la Reynie (see below), who became the head of the Paris police force. According to the edict, the duty of the police force was "ensuring the peace and quiet of the public and of private individuals, purging the city of what may cause disturbances, procuring abundance, and having each and everyone live according to their station and their duties."

Who was Gabriel Nicolas de la Reynie?

The head of the first organized police force in Paris, France, was Gabriel Nicolas de la Reynie (1625–1709). After the royal edict from King Louis XIV in 1667, Reynie restructured and improved the efficiency of the Paris police force and had forty-four *commissaires de police* (police commissioners; by 1709, they were assisted by *inspecteurs de police*, or police inspectors) under his authority. Paris was divided into sixteen districts policed by the commissaires, with each assigned to a specific district. The practice of the Paris police force was eventually extended to the rest of France by a royal edict in October 1699, resulting in the creation of lieutenants general of police (and commissaires) in all the larger French cities and towns.

Who claims to have had the first uniformed policemen in the world?

The claim of the "first uniformed police force" is often debated, but almost all historians agree that it was France that started the "trend." One claim is that Gabriel Nicolas de la Reynie was the founder of the first uniformed police force in 1667 (see above). Another claim is that around a year after the French Revolution in 1800, French military leader and self-proclaimed emperor Napoléon I (and as Napoléon Bonaparte, 1769–1821) reorganized the police forces in several larger cities, calling it the *Préfecture de police* (Prefecture of Police), and in 1829, by government decree—according to today's Paris Prefecture of Police website (at http://www.prefecturedepolice.interieur.gouv.fr/English) —the first uniformed police force in France, known as the *Sergents de ville* ("city sergeants"), was created.

When was the term "detective" first used in a publication?

Some disagree as to when the word "detective" was first used in a publication. According to *The Oxford English Dictionary*, the word "detective" was first used in 1843 as an adjective, not a noun. Also in 1843, *Chambers's Edinburgh Journal* wrote: "...A certain number of intelligent men have been recently selected to form a body called the 'detective police' ... and at times the detective policeman attires himself in the dress of ordinary individuals, or 'plain clothes'...." By the year 1850, William Henry Wills wrote the essay "The modern science of thief-taking," seen in *Old Leaves: Gathered from Household Words* (published in 1860 and mainly a collection of Wills's own ideas about life in the Victorian era) in which he stated, "...To each division of the Metropolitan Force is attached two officers, who are denominated Detectives. Thus the Detective Police, of which we hear so much, consists of only forty-two individuals, whose duty it is to wear no uniform, and to perform the most difficult operations of their craft."

Where did the term "cop" come from in reference to the police?

No one knows where the word "cop" came from in reference to the police. Theories are numerous, including that some of the first police officers in London wore copper buttons on their blue uniforms and were therefore called "coppers," abbreviated as "cops"; in the United States, the copper badges worn by police officers led to the name "coppers," or "cops." Another theory is that officers signing registers during their duty shift would abbreviate their assignment as "Constable on Patrol," or C.O.P. Still another theory is that because the word "cop" meant apprehension or to catch in the mid-1800s and because police officers would apprehend criminals, they were called "coppers," which eventually shortened to "cops." However, like many words that have a long history in English (and other) languages, no one truly knows the real story—or who first used the term.

When did forensic medicine become a "real" science?

It is difficult to determine when forensic medicine became a true science, but many historians believe the Italian physician Fortunatus Fidelis (1550–1630; his name has several different spellings depending on the text) was the first person whose studies led to modern forensic medicine. He wrote *De Relationibus Medicorum* in 1602 (other sources suggest 1598), stressing medical interpretations of victims. For example, he noted several medical ideas about a drowning victim, saying that such an investigation is not difficult as the person would have certain physical characteristics, such as a bloated abdomen and mucus secretion from the nostrils. Another physician also laid the foundation for modern pathology along with Fidelis—Italian physician Paul Zacchias (1584–1659), who is often called the "father of legal medicine," as his book *Quaestiones medico-legales* established the study of legal medicine. He, like Fidelis, also studied the changes that occurred in the human body as a result of disease and death, paving the way for forensic medicine.

When was the word "forensic" first used?

The term "forensic"—translated from Latin as "in open court" or "public"—eventually entered the English language around 1659. Although it had been used in medical writings for many years, it was only when *Merriam-Webster Dictionary* officially recognized and printed the word that it gained its current usage. In modern times, it applies mainly to legal and criminal investigations.

Who was Marcello Malpighi?

In 1686, Italian biologist and physician Marcello Malpighi (1628–1694) mentioned that everyone's fingers had certain ridges, spirals, and loops—what is now known as fingerprints. Even though Malpighi mentioned that the features were important to identify individuals, he did not suggest using fingerprints as evidence in a crime. Malpighi is famous for other contributions to medicine and biology and is often called the "father of microscopic anatomy, histology, physiology, and embryology" by some historians.

Who was Joannes Ernestus Hebenstreit?

Joannes (or Johannes) Ernestus Hebenstreit (1703–1757) was a German physician, naturalist, professor of medicine, and prolific writer, including numerous works that could be applied to medical jurisprudence. For example, he was the author of *Anthropologia Forensis* in 1751 (or 1753, depending on the reference), a treatise on forensic anthropology (for more about the subject, see the chapter "Other Forensic Investigations").

Italian biologist and physician Marcello Malphigi was one of the first to note that people had distinctly individual fingerprints that could be used to identify them.

When was the first documented use of physical matching?

It is thought that the first documented use of physical matching was in 1784 in Lancaster, England. The evidence helped bring to trial and convict John Toms of murdering Edward Culshaw with a pistol. According to records from the time, when Culshaw's body was examined, a pistol wad (or a piece of paper that is crushed in the pistol to secure the balls and powder in the gun's muzzle) was found in Culshaw's head wound. The piece of paper matched perfectly with a ripped newspaper in Toms's pocket. This matching evidence was enough to convict Toms.

Who were Henry and Sir John Fielding?

Although he was a well-known author, Henry Fielding (1707–1754; *The History of Tom Jones, a Foundling*; *Amelia*; and many others) was a magistrate and also the co-founder of the Bow Street Runners in England (their base of operation was on Bow Street, near Covent Garden). In 1749, after the War of Austrian Succession, London

Better known as the novelist of such satirical works as *Tom Jones,* Henry Fielding also started, with his brother, a policing force in England called the Bow Street Runners.

had an alleged crime wave, although some historians believe it may simply have been more reports of crimes in the newspapers. Either way, Fielding created the Bow Street Runners—a group of constables and ex-constables (originally six men) to whom he paid retainers to locate and arrest offenders (and if the government paid a reward for a conviction of a criminal, the Runner could claim the reward).

Henry Fielding's half brother, Sir John Fielding (1721–1780), was the cofounder of the Bow Street Runners. He also was responsible for many reforms in England's criminal justice system and was also called "a pioneer in the treatment of juvenile offenders." Sir John Fielding was appointed as a magistrate in London in the mid-1700s, although he was legally blind (from an accident while in the Navy at age nineteen). It was alleged that he could recognize close to three thousand criminals just by the sound of their voice.

THE 1800s TO EARLY 1900s IN FORENSIC SCIENCE

How did a person's skull fit into criminal evidence in the early 1800s?

The practice of cranioscopy (from the Greek *kranion* [skull] and *scopos* [vision]), or measuring a person's cranium (the largest part of a human skull) to determine a person's personality, especially their mental and moral faculties, was developed by German neuroanatomist and physiologist Franz Joseph Gall (1758–1822; he was also a pioneer in the study of how certain locations in the brain determined various mental functions). He believed that by measuring the skull, he could determine a person's personality traits, character, and even whether they would become a criminal. Cranioscopy was eventually called phrenology (from the Greek *phrenos* [mind] and *logos* [study]) by Gall's German student (and eventually a physician) Johann Gaspar Spurzheim (1776–1832), who wrote extensively about the practice. He also added physiognomy, in which a person's facial characteristics (including expressions) and features could be correlated to their character traits.

Who was Cesare Lombroso?

Italian criminologist Cesare Lombroso (1835–1909) is often referred to as the founder of anthropological criminology, or scientifically linking the nature of a crime with the perpetrator's personality or phys-

Italian physician and criminologist Cesare Lombroso believed that some people were born killers and that certain facial features could betray their true nature.

19

ical characteristics. In particular, he believed that a person's skull and facial features were links to the person's genetic criminal nature. (He also originated the idea that a person can be a "natural-born criminal" and was a proponent of biological determinism.) He divided the features into (depending on the reference) fourteen traits, including whether the person had large jaws; a forward projection of the jaw; a low, sloping forehead; high cheekbones; flattened or upturned nose; handle-shaped ears; hawklike nose or fleshy lips; hard, shifty eyes; scanty beard or baldness; insensitivity to pain; and long arms.

What forensic-oriented books began to appear around the turn of the nineteenth century?

By the early 1800s, several forensic medical books began to be published, mainly by physicians interested in the field of medical jurisprudence. For example, French physician François-Emmanuele (or Emanuel) Fodéré's (1764–1835) multivolume *Traité de médecine légale et d'hygiène publique ou de police de santé* (1813; roughly translated as *Treaty of Forensic Medicine and Public Hygiene or Health Police*) became a standard work of legal medicine for many years. In 1811, French physician Paul (also seen as Pierre) Augustin Olivier Mahon wrote the three-volume work called *Médecine-légale et Police médicale* (*Legal Medicine and Medical Police*), and in 1815, English physician O. W. Bartley wrote *A Treatise on Forensic Medicine, or Medical Jurisprudence*.

Who was Eugène François Vidocq?

French criminal-turned-criminalist Eugène François Vidocq (1775–1857) was not always on the side of the law—and had quite an adventurous life. Initially, after time in the French revolutionary wars and on the streets, he was sued by a person he had beaten and sent to jail for three months, but various criminal circumstances and several escapes led to a much longer jail sentence. After many years of escapes and recaptures, he was apprehended and offered to be an informant for the police (in many ways, he became a "secret agent," using his criminal background in the underworld to gather informa-

When and where were the first municipal police forces in America?

The idea of a central municipal police force was not to develop until the 1830s in America. According to East Kentucky University's Police Studies Department, by 1838, the first American police force was established in Boston, which included both day- and night-duty shifts (although some references state that Philadelphia, in 1833, was first when it organized an independent, twenty-four-hour police force). This was followed by New York City in 1844 (it became the New York City Police Department in 1845), and Albany, New York, and Chicago in 1851. In 1853, New Orleans and Cincinnati organized police forces, and in 1857, Newark, New Jersey (and some references say Philadelphia) established an official police force. By the 1880s, all the major cities in the United States had municipal police forces.

tion). The police recognized his value as an informant, and by 1811, he informally established a detective bureau, the *Brigade de la Sûreté?* of Paris, often referred to as the first detective force in the world. (In 1834, he also started what is often called the first private detective agency called *Le Bureau des Renseignements*.) After the police further realized the value of a civil detective force, it was eventually officially made a security police force in Paris's *Prefecture of Police*.

What contributions did Eugène François Vidocq make to modern criminal investigation?

According to the Vidocq Society, the criminalist Eugène François Vidocq made many contributions that helped establish modern criminal investigation. For example, he was the first to introduce a card-index system as a form of record keeping; added the science of ballistics into police work; is thought to have been the first to make casts of foot and shoe impressions at a crime scene; and was a master of disguise and surveillance.

When and where was the first recorded use of questioned document analysis?

Although François Demelle was the first to publish a scientific treatise about questioned documents in 1609 (a book about handwriting analysis), it took until 1810 for the first recorded use of questioned document analysis. The analysis occurred in Germany—the chemical testing of the ink dye used on what is called the *Konigin Hanschritt* document—and helped develop new ways to determine forged versus authentic documents.

Who was Sir Robert Peel?

A British statesman and twice the prime minister of England, Sir Robert Peel (1788–1850) is often called the "father of British policing." He established London's metropolitan police force based at the short street leading to a courtyard called the Scotland Yard in 1829. He also employed close to one thousand constables in his force and developed what is known as the Peelian Principles, or the ethical requirements that he believed police officers should follow (for more about the Scotland Yard and Peelian Principles, see below).

Who were the "Peelers"?

In England, towns and cities until the eighteenth century were policed by what

British prime minister Sir Robert Peel established London's metropolitan police.

were called "parish constables." Between 1749 and 1839, the Bow Street Runners became the professional law enforcers in Britain, enforcing the decisions of the magistrates (for more about the Bow Street Runners, see this chapter). Around 1829 (the Victorian age), the London police force was created by an act introduced in Parliament by Home Secretary Sir Robert Peel. By 1839, these constables of the London metropolitan police force—nicknamed "Peelers" and then "bobbies" after Peel—had replaced the Bow Street patrols and the River Police (who prevented crime along the Thames River). The Peelers had to follow strict rules, including having to be between five and seven feet tall, having to be age twenty to twenty-seven, having to be fit, and having no history of being in trouble. They also had to wear their uniforms (blue coattails and a tall top hat) on and off the job, work seven days a week, get permission to marry, and, with only one pound pay a week, only received five days (unpaid) a year off for a holiday.

What were the Peelian Principles?

According to several police websites from the United Kingdom, nine Peelian Principles were developed by Sir Robert Peel—or "general instructions" issued to every new police officer from 1829 onward. The principles were as follows (as quoted from several websites):

- The basic mission for the police is to prevent crime and disorder.
- The ability of the police to perform their duties is dependent upon public approval of police actions.
- Police must secure the willing cooperation of the public in voluntary observance of the law to be able to secure and maintain the respect of the public.
- The degree of cooperation of the public that can be secured diminishes proportionately to the necessity of the use of physical force.
- Police seek and preserve public favor [written as "favour" in England] not by pandering to public opinion but by constantly demonstrating absolute impartial service to the law.
- Police use physical force to the extent necessary to secure observance of the law or to restore order only when the exercise of persuasion, advice, and warning is found to be insufficient.
- Police, at all times, should maintain a relationship with the public that gives reality to the historic tradition that the police are the public and the public are the police, the police being only members of the public who are paid to give full-time attention to duties which are incumbent on every citizen in the interests of community welfare and existence.
- Police should always direct their action strictly toward their functions and never appear to usurp the powers of the judiciary.
- The test of police efficiency is the absence of crime and disorder, not the visible evidence of police action in dealing with it.

Who was Jan Evangelista Purkinje?

In 1823, Czech physiologist and anatomist Jan Evangelista Purkinje (1787–1869; also known as John Evangelist Purkinje and Purkynê) published a thesis discussing nine fingerprint patterns based on their geometric patterns (some of which are still mentioned in today's study of fingerprint patterns): arch, tented arch, ulna loop, radial loop, peacock's eye/compound, spiral whorl, elliptical whorl, circular whorl, and double loop/composite. However, like Italian biologist and physician Marcello Malpighi (for more about Malpighi, see this chapter), Purkinje made no mention of the value of fingerprints for personal identification as evidence in a crime. (For more about fingerprints as evidence, see below and the chapter "In the Crime Lab: Patent, Latent, and Plastic Prints.")

Czech anatomist and physiologist Jan Evangelista Purkinje, who coined the term "protoplasm," also defined the nine basic geometric patterns found in most fingerprints.

When did the Scotland Yard originate?

The Scotland Yard was originally where Sir Robert Peel's new police force resided. The men were the responsibility of British colonel Sir Charles Rowan (c. 1782–1852) and British lawyer Sir Richard Mayne (1796–1868)—the first joint commissioners of the police department. They moved into a private home at 4 Whitehall Place, a residence that had a rear entrance leading to an open courtyard, or the Great Scotland Yard (it was at the site of a medieval palace that once housed visiting Scottish royalty). Both men set up a police department from scratch and managed policemen who were mainly responsible for the protection of important people and working community patrols.

Who was Sir William James Herschel?

Sir William James Herschel (1833–1917) was one of the first people to use handprints and fingerprints to prove a person's identity. In 1858, while serving in the India Civil Service in Jungipoor, India, he first used palm prints on native contracts to make them binding, then later realized that the prints of the right index and middle fingers were all he needed. Although he suggested the method as a standard for contracts to the governor of Bengal, it was not until 1877, as the then-chief magistrate of Hoogly, that he began to take pensioners' fingerprints (so the money could not be collected by impostors) and fingerprints of criminals (so an impostor could not replace the truly guilty person in jail). In 1916, he published a work called *The Origin of Fingerprinting*, and although he used fingerprints for administrative purposes, he never suggested that they could be used as evidence to find criminals.

Who was Henry Faulds?

Scottish physician Henry Faulds (1843–1930) is often called the "father of fingerprinting." While working in Japan, he recognized fingerprints on ancient clay tablets, and he began to study such prints. In a letter in the journal *Nature* in 1880, Faulds proposed using ink for fingerprint determination and to identify an individual—and also suggested that this method might be used as evidence in a criminal investigation.

How was naturalist Charles Darwin loosely connected to fingerprint identification?

After English physician Henry Faulds began to research fingerprints, he asked his cousin, naturalist Charles Darwin (1809–1882), to help with his research. After declining, Darwin suggested that another cousin, English eugenicist Francis Galton (1822–1911), could be of assistance. Although Faulds and Galton did not correspond regularly, in the next ten years, they would both develop similar fingerprint classification systems—thus, it is unclear who first invented such a system (see sidebar). Faulds was the first to publish (in Europe) the idea of using fingerprints as evidence in a criminal investigation. In 1892, Galton published his book *Finger Prints*, in which he proposed the classification system based on the three fingerprint patterns of loops, arches, and spirals (sometimes called whorls). He also suggested that fingerprints do not change during a person's lifetime.

When did forensic science truly become a scientific discipline?

Although not all historians agree, it is thought that the first known use of science for crime investigation occurred in the 1870s by French police officer and biometrics researcher Alphonse Bertillon (1853–1914). Bertillon developed the Bertillonage (also called the Bertillon System), a procedure that recorded certain body measurements, along with noting other physical characteristics. In particular, his system used the measurements of the dimensions of certain bony parts of the body, which were then reduced to a formula—the results of which could only be applied to one person. (It was thought that this measurement would not change during the person's adult life.) The information was then kept on file at the police station to help identify certain criminals. The method was generally accepted for around thirty years. Bertillon also developed the use of photography for criminal identification, or what is often referred to as "mug shots."

Who were some people thought to be responsible for inventing fingerprint classifications?

No one agrees about who truly devised the first fingerprint classification system. In 1858, Sir Richard Herschel claimed to have developed such a system for Indian criminals and to have registered fingerprints for those people signing documents in the Indian magis-

When was the first known use of fingerprints for identification purposes in the United States?

Gilbert Thompson

In 1882, geologist Gilbert Thompson (1839–1909; he was also the cofounder of the National Geographical Society) of the U.S. Geological Survey in New Mexico claimed that he used his own thumbprint on a document to help prevent forgery. The message with thumbprint stated "August 8, 1882—Mr. Jonas [or Jones] Sutler, will pay Lying Bob seventy five dollars… Gilbert Thompson, U.S.G.S." This is said to be the first known use of fingerprints for identification purposes in the United States.

Historians have their doubts, though. The document was sent to Sir Francis Galton, whose interest was in fingerprints (see above). It is thought that Thompson made up this document to show Galton how he used to do the business of pay orders for workers. The reason for doubt is that Thompson was not in New Mexico at that time but was in charge of the Pacific District in California for six weeks before, setting up headquarters and a barometric base station at Red Bluff on the Sacramento River.

trate's office in Jungipoor (where he was the head). Another is Sir Francis Galton, who wrote the popular *Finger Prints* in 1892, in which he gathered eight thousand fingerprints and classified them. Also in 1892, Juan Vucetich (1858–1925), an Argentinean policeman, created his own fingerprint identification system, and in 1896, Edward Henry created his own classification after becoming interested in Galton's work on fingerprints. (For more about fingerprints as evidence, see the chapters "At the Crime Scene: Looking for Physical Evidence" and "In the Crime Lab: Patent, Latent, and Plastic Prints.")

When were fingerprints first used to identify a criminal?

It is thought that in 1892, Argentinean police officer Juan Vucetich (1858–1925)—who had created his own fingerprint identification system—made the first criminal fingerprint identification. He identified a bloody fingerprint left on a doorpost as belonging to Francisca Rojas. Based on this, it was discovered that she had killed her two sons and cut her own throat in order to suggest that the murderer was an unknown, outside attacker. Because of his success, his fingerprint identification method was adopted by the Argentine police and eventually by many police forces around the world. In 1904, he published *Dactiloscopia Comparada* (*Comparative Dactyloscopy*).

Who was Sir Edward Richard Henry?

Sir Edward Richard Henry (1850–1931) was a London police officer who was interested in Francis Galton's work on fingerprints. He not only expanded on his own classification system, but he also used them to identify criminals. His system—called the Henry System of Fingerprint Classification—was adopted by the early forensic science movement, including the Scotland Yard, when it established the first Fingerprint Bureau in 1901. In 1902, the British judiciary recognized fingerprints as evidence in court, and in 1903, police departments in the United States began to use fingerprints as evidence.

Sir Edward Richard Henry, who was a police chief in London, devised what is now known as the Henry System of Fingerprint Classification.

Who invented the Henry System of Fingerprint Classification?

The Henry System of Fingerprint Classification (also seen as the Henry Classification System) was invented between the years 1896 and 1925 by Sir Edward Richard Henry. Along with Henry, others contributed, including police officer (in British India) Azizul Haque (1872–1935), who developed a mathematical formula to supplement Henry's idea of sorting fingerprint patterns, and Hem Chandra Bose, another of Henry's assistants who also helped refine the system.

How does the Henry System of Fingerprint Classification work?

The Henry System of Fingerprint Classification is based on an assigned value to each individual finger. Fingers numbered one and two, or the right thumb and right index finger, hold a value of sixteen. Fingers numbered three and four, or the right middle and ring fingers, hold a value of eight, and so on. If a whorl is on a finger, the corresponding value is added to the base value of one. Henry used a fraction-type primary classification that took the accumulated values of the even-numbered fingers as the numerator and the accumulated value of the odd-numbered fingers as the denominator. For example, if a person has fingerprint patterns of "Loop, Loop, Arch, Whorl, Loop" in the right hand and "Whorl, Loop, Whorl, Loop, Loop" in the left hand, they have a primary fingerprint classification of 15/1. A person with no whorl patterns would have a primary classification of 1/1. (Henry created 1,024 primary fingerprint classifications.) This classification system eventually took the place of the Bertillon System (see sidebar).

When was comparing a fired bullet first used to identify a criminal?

In 1835, a former Bow Street Runner employed by the Scotland Yard is thought to be the first person (the first documented case) to compare bullets in order to catch a criminal. British law-enforcement officer Henry Goddard (1800–1883) believed that a bullet's

Why was the Bertillon System eventually abandoned?

The Bertillon System was eventually abandoned for fingerprinting as evidence around the turn of the twentieth century for several reasons. One reason was the strong support for Sir Edward Richard Henry, who appeared before an inquiry committee to explain his own Henry Fingerprint Classification system in his book *The Classification and Use of Fingerprints*. Based on his testimony, the committee recommended the use of fingerprinting as evidence. They also wanted to replace the Bertillon System of measurement that had been used for around thirty years—and in which fingerprints for identification had only a small part.

However, it wasn't only Sir Henry's persuasiveness that caused the Bertillon system to be replaced. Bertillon's system was based on measurement, and in 1903, a major problem had developed with the method. A man named Will West was sentenced to the U.S. Penitentiary at Leavenworth, Kansas, but a prisoner at the penitentiary at that time was already there whose Bertillon measurements were nearly exactly the same—and his name, too, was William West. This confusion was based on the fact that although they were two different men (and were allegedly not related—although it was later proven that they were apparently identical twin brothers), they looked very much alike. The main problem occurred with the Bertillon measurements—they were close enough to identify them as the same man, but when both men were fingerprinted, they were definitely two different people. This misinterpretation was yet another blow to the Bertillion measurement system, and it was quickly replaced with fingerprinting—and eventually other means of identification.

original mold could cause some imperfections on the bullet (which is part of modern toolmarks and firearm analysis). In a criminal case, he compared such a flaw in a bullet removed during a victim's autopsy to the original bullet mold (at that time, most people made their own bullets by melting lead and pouring it into a two-piece mold)—and the murderer confessed. The use of toolmarks and firearm analysis was further advanced in the 1920s, when forensic specialists used a comparison microscope to compare bullets used in a crime. (For more about toolmarks and firearms, see the chapter "In the Crime Lab: Toolmarks, Firearms, and Ballistics.")

Who was Joseph Bell?

English physician Joseph Bell (1837–1911) was a pioneer in the field of forensic pathology and was known for his emphasis on observation as a key part of criminal (and medical) procedures. He was also the personal surgeon to Queen Victoria whenever she visited Scotland. Many historians state that Arthur Conan Doyle's Sherlock Holmes character was inspired by Bell. (Doyle met Bell at the University of Edinburgh Medical

School and became Bell's student; for more about Doyle, see the chapter "The Media and Forensic Science.")

Who was Edmond Locard?

French forensic scientist Edmond Locard (1877–1966)—often referred to as the "Sherlock Holmes of France"—developed the Locard Exchange Principle (or Locard's theory; for more about Locard's Exchange Principle, see the chapter "At the Crime Scene: The Crime Site and Investigation Teams"). He determined his principle throughout his career as a criminologist and in 1910 established the world's first laboratory dedicated to criminal analysis with the Lyon Police Department in Lyon, France. He was also a medical examiner during World War I, and his contributions to forensic science were influenced by the work of Alphonse Bertillon.

Forensic pathology pioneer Joseph Bell is said to have served as Arthur Conan Doyle's inspiration in creating the fictional detective Sherlock Holmes.

Why was the development of forensic toxicology necessary around the Victorian era?

Forensic toxicology was undoubtedly necessary in the late 1800s to early 1900s. This is because intentional poisoning was on the rise—it was often called the "golden age of poisoning" by historians. Some of the main reasons for an increase in poisoning were that it could be done in secrecy (with little incriminating evidence left behind if the poison was tossed away); many poisons were easily obtained by the general public (arsenic was the favorite); most poisons left few, if any, marks or physical evidence; and, as some historians point out, the idea of "life insurance" became popular, giving some people an incentive to poison others. This increased the need for more analysis and understanding behind various poisons, which eventually led to greater studies in forensic toxicology. (For more about toxicology and poisons, see the chapter "In the Crime Lab: Analyzing a Body.")

What were some suggested—and eventually abandoned—ways to keep track of criminals at the turn of the nineteenth century?

Several methods were used by the police to keep track of criminals in the 1800s and early 1900s—many of them seemingly strange by today's standards. For example, in England in 1827, the British Registry of Distinctive Marks was established in order to record the "unique" characteristics of criminals, including tattoos, birthmarks, scars, freckles, or other distinctive markings. The listing of such marks was organized based on where they were found on the criminal's body, for instance, the head and face or hands and fingers. When a suspect was arrested, and if they gave a false name, the police could use the registry to match the person to the name (if it was listed), but complications arose—especially because many people have more than one distinctive characteristic with a large number of combinations. This made the registry difficult to use, and the idea was eventually abandoned. Another way of keeping track of criminals was suggested in the early 1900s, again in France. It was thought that the only way to identify criminals was to brand them with a harmless injection of paraffin wax. This would create a bump, and, depending on the wax placement, would indicate the seriousness of the crime, such as on the upper, middle, and lower parts of a criminal's arm. This idea was also abandoned as other, less invasive methods were developed.

THE LATE 1900s TO PRESENT IN FORENSIC SCIENCE

How has technology changed the field of forensic science in the late twentieth and early twenty-first centuries?

The development of technologies in the late twentieth and early twenty-first centuries is long—and many of those technological items have been a boon to the study of forensic science. For example, some of the more well-known ones include DNA sequencers, high-speed and high-definition digital photography and video recorders, and more powerful computers to analyze and compare data. Even more recent technology is still evolving, including laser scanners, drones used to gather evidence at and around the scene of a crime, and three-dimensional optical digitizers to help gather, analyze, and process evidence.

When was DNA profiling developed?

What is called "DNA profiling" was developed by two groups working independently. In 1983 in the United States, the polymerase chain reaction (PCR) was discovered by American biochemist, Nobel Prize winner (1993), and author Kary Banks Mullis (1944–) which led to DNA profiling. At the same time in the United Kingdom, "DNA fingerprinting" was discovered by Sir Alec Jeffreys (1950–) at the University of Leicester while he was attempting to find the matching DNA in families. (For more about DNA and DNA profiling, see the chapter "In the Crime Lab: DNA Analysis.")

What is computer forensics?

Computer forensics, or often called cyberforensics, is a subfield of forensic digital analysis. It includes the processing and analyzing of data using computers and analysis of computers and digital equipment for and as evidence. For example, extracting e-mails from a victim's computer can often lead to the perpetrator of the crime, or it can include pro-

How has high-definition digital imagery helped forensic science?

High-definition digital images and videos have been a boon in recent years for forensic experts. For example, Purdue University researchers have developed a portable crime scene forensic technology that will allow crime scene investigators to produce high-resolution, three-dimensional images of shoe prints and tire tread marks in soils and snow. Modern, high-definition cameras are often installed in crime-ridden areas, and, along with special computer software, forensic experts can often digitally enhance images of potential criminals at a crime scene.

cessing images to make them clearer in order to catch a perpetrator at a crime scene. (For more about forensic digital analysis, see the chapter "Other Forensic Investigations.")

Who are some more recent, well-known U.S. experts in forensic science?

Numerous recent, well-known U.S. experts in forensic science have contributed to the field in many ways. Although this is far from being a complete list, the following mentions some of those experts:

- American William Maples (1937–1997) was involved in more than twelve hundred cases during his twenty-eight years as a forensic anthropologist. Maples assisted in several high-profile examinations of exhumed human remains, including those of President Zachary Taylor, Francisco Pizzaro, and the last Russian monarch, Czar Nicolas II, and his family.

- American physician and forensic pathologist Michael Baden (1934–) worked in the office of the chief medical examiner of the state of New York from 1961 to 1986 (he was chief medical examiner from 1978–1979). He has also helped investigate some well-known forensic cases and was once the host of the HBO series *Autopsy* (part of the *America Undercover* documentary series).

- American anthropologist and forensic anthropologist Wilton Marion Krogman (1903–1987) is thought by many to have helped bring forensic physical anthropology (he especially had an interest in dental anthropology) to the forefront in the United States. Known as the "bone detective" or "bone doctor," his career in the field spanned nearly six decades. He was also the author of the book *The Human Skeleton in Forensic Medicine* (1962).

- Clea Koff (1972–) is a British-born American forensic anthropologist who has worked on several international forensic cases. When she was twenty-three years old, Koff became a member of the first international team organized by the United Nations International Criminal Tribunals to gather evidence of war crimes and crimes against humanity in Rwanda, Africa. (Koff would later write a memoir about her experiences of the genocide that occurred there called *The Bone Woman* [2004].) In 2005, Koff founded the Missing Persons Identification Resource Center in California that helped identify bodies that were never identified in coroners' offices throughout the United States in an attempt to link families with the unidentified people; the center closed in 2012.

Dr. Henry C. Lee is the foremost forensic scientist in the United States today; he is the founder of the Henry C. Lee Institute of Forensic Science in Connecticut.

- Chinese-born American forensic scientist Henry C. Lee (1938–) has assisted in more than six thousand cases as a forensic scientist. He originally worked in the Taipei Police Department and immigrated to the United States with his family in 1965. His high-profile cases have included the JonBenét Ramsey and O. J. Simpson cases, along with the examination and study of the John F. Kennedy assassination. He is also the founder of the Henry C. Lee Institute of Forensic Science in West Haven, Connecticut.

What are the various levels of law-enforcement officers in the United States?

Law-enforcement officers in the United States are on various levels. According to the Office of Justice, these officers include the federal police, who possess full federal authority under United States Code (U.S.C., a permanent code that defines their authority), along with federal law-enforcement agencies, who enforce various laws at the federal level. The states have statewide government agencies, including investigations and state patrols—usually called state police, state troopers, or highway patrol officers under the state's Department of Public Safety—for law enforcement. County (or parish or borough) law-enforcement officers usually include sheriffs and/or county police. Finally, cities and some larger towns have municipal police, which can be either a one-person operation or similar to the New York City Police Department, with close to fifty thousand municipal law-enforcement officers. Other law-enforcement officers often have certain restrictions when enforcing the law, such as university police and park police.

What is the Federal Bureau of Investigation (FBI)?

According to the FBI site, the agency is an "intelligence-driven and threat-focused national security organization with both intelligence and law-enforcement responsibilities. It is the principal investigative arm of the U.S. Department of Justice and a full member of the U.S. Intelligence Community." Overall, the agency focuses on stopping terrorism, corruption, organized crime, cybercrime, and civil rights violations as well as investigating serious crimes such as major thefts or murders.

How do they handle a crime in Antarctica?

Because Antarctica is not a sovereign nation-state unto itself, the nation-states that claim sovereignty in certain parts of the continent often have say in criminal events. Not that Antarctica is a crime-ridden place. It has skuas, seals, walruses, penguins, and small numbers of other animals, but no permanent human population. The number of people who visit fluctuates depending on the season and the scientific studies (the people who visit the continent are either scientists or support staff), but humans are known to fight or have disagreements, and when they do, it can lead to a criminal offense.

To date, and under the terms of the fifty-three nations who signed the Antarctic Treaty, visitors to the continent who are accused of a serious crime are subject to the jurisdiction of their home country. For example, at the U.S. base at McMurdo Station, if a criminal offense takes place, it would be prosecuted under U.S. federal law under what is called the "special maritime and territorial jurisdiction of the United States." Because it is often impossible to get to and from the continent for days or weeks because of bad weather, the station manager is also a trained special deputy U.S. marshal. Complications would set in if a crime is committed by a person from outside their country's sovereign area—especially as to what country has what jurisdiction over the crime and criminal.

When was the FBI founded?

In 1908, during President Theodore Roosevelt's term, a number of special agents were organized by Attorney General Charles Bonaparte, known as the Bureau of Instigation. In early 1935, it was renamed the Federal Bureau of Investigation, or the FBI.

What is the function of today's Scotland Yard?

Today's Scotland Yard is presently located in a twenty-story building near the Houses of Parliament. It is mainly known for its investigative methods, and its officers are responsible for protecting not only citizens but the royal family and other dignitaries. Currently, about thirty thousand officers patrol the streets of London, which encompasses about 620 square miles and has about 7.2 million people.

When was the U.S. Department of Homeland Security created?

According to its website, the U.S. Department of Homeland Security is a cabinet department of the U.S. federal government with responsibilities in public security. (It is similar to the interior or home ministries in other countries.) The department was created by the Department of Homeland Security Act of 2002 (it was an outgrowth of the

The J. Edgar Hoover Building in Washington, D.C., serves as the headquarters for the FBI.

Office of Homeland Security that was established during the Bush administration after the September 11, 2001, terrorist attacks). Since then, it has been largely focused on federal preparations to deal with terrorism while trying to manage other duties, including border security, customs, and emergency management. The agency duties include working with customs, border, and immigration enforcement personnel; responding to emergencies of natural and man-made disasters; antiterrorism work; and cybersecurity. (They can be found at the website link https://www.dhs.gov/about-dhs.)

What is Interpol (or INTERPOL)?

Although it sounds like an agency in a James Bond movie, the idea of INTERPOL was to essentially pool the resources of several countries to deal with international crimes. The idea was born in 1914 at the first International Criminal Police Congress, held in Monaco. Officially created in 1923 as the International Criminal Police Commission, the organization became known as INTERPOL. (The official abbreviation is "ICPO" for the French "Organisation international de police criminelle," which is translated to "International Criminal Police Organization"; the word INTERPOL is a contraction of the phrase "international police," which was chosen in 1946.) Its main headquarters are in Lyon, France, with each member country maintaining a National Central Bureau that links to the INTERPOL's global network. For support, the intergovernmental organiza-

Who are the Shadow Wolves?

The "Shadow Wolves" are a federal law-enforcement group of Native American officers patrolling part of the border between Mexico and the United States. According to the U.S. Immigration and Customs Enforcement, the Shadow Wolves, also called a tactical patrol unit, are experts at tracking, said to be honed over generations of hunting animals. Since 1972, when the group was founded, they have patrolled the 76-mile- (122-kilometer-) stretch of the Tohono O'odham Nation territory (it covers 2,800,000 acres [11,000 square kilometers]) that runs along the border. Their main duties included tracking drug smugglers transporting contraband (mostly marijuana) on Indian reservation land. They are referred to as "shadow wolves" as it is the way they prefer to track—in packs similar to wolves. As of this writing, they have about fifteen members from nine different tribes, including the Tohono O'odham, Blackfeet, Lakota, Navajo Omaha, Sioux, and Yaqui. They are considered to be part of Immigration and Customs Enforcement (as of 2003, it became part of the U.S. Department of Homeland Security). The members of the unit have also trained other countries' border guards, including those in Tajikistan and Uzbekistan, which border Afghanistan.

tion collects dues from its around 190 member countries and relies on investments as its main means of support.

AT THE CRIME SCENE: THE CRIME SITE AND INVESTIGATION TEAMS

THE CRIME SCENE

What constitutes a crime scene?

A crime scene is an area in which a crime has potentially occurred or a crime has been committed. For example, it may be when a body washes up on a beach. It can be a car accident that claims the life of the driver and/or passengers, either with one or multiple cars involved, or it may be a suspicious fire that destroys an office building. All of these events (and more, of course) are treated as potential crime scenes (until proven otherwise) or definite crime scenes, depending on the circumstances.

Why is it important to secure a crime scene?

If certain procedures are not followed by law enforcement and others at a crime scene, they run the risk of losing or contaminating the evidence. Thus, securing a scene helps to protect the evidence that needs to be collected in order to prove whether or not it is a crime scene. This allows the pertinent evidence to remain uncontaminated until it can be recorded and collected. This manner of protecting the evidence at the scene begins with the arrival of the first responder (usually the first police officer at the scene) and ends when the scene is released from police custody.

What are some scenes that are secured, documented, and investigated?

Not every incident is a crime scene, but until it is determined whether or not a crime has been committed, it is treated as such. This includes scenes of burglaries, violent crimes, suicides (or unattended deaths), fires, auto thefts, and vehicle or other types of accidents (such as a fall that injures a person). Based on the scene, an investigator will locate and collect certain evidence. As the evidence from a scene is collected, the investigator may or may not discover a crime (or even several crimes).

What is a secondary crime scene?

Not every crime scene is at the place in which a crime was committed. Oftentimes, a primary crime scene cannot be examined because it is not known. For example, if a body is found in a field far from where the person was killed, the area where the body is discovered is called a secondary crime scene.

In general, what equipment is often needed at a crime scene investigation?

Numerous items can be used at a crime scene investigation to gather evidence. This includes blood collection and bloodstain documentation kits (to gather samples of blood at a crime scene for analysis in the lab); excavation kit (for example, using shovels and trowels to carefully exhume various items at the crime scene); fingerprint kit (for example, using lift cards, brushes, and certain powders to dust for fingerprints); an impression kit (for example, materials to take impressions in soil, dust, or even snow); and a trace evidence kit (for example, forceps and tweezers, slides, and glass vials to hold trace evidence). Other equipment is often carried by crime scene investigators, including certain instruments for testing, such as a black light to test for urine stains.

What is police or crime scene tape?

Police tape (also called crime scene, law-enforcement, caution, or warning tape) is most often used at a crime scene to isolate, preserve, and protect an area containing a possible or verified crime. It is meant to inform the public that the site is undergoing an ongoing investigation and that particular area is restricted to authorized personnel only. The plastic tape is usually bright yellow with black lettering that states "POLICE LINE DO NOT CROSS" or "Caution." It is different than barricade tape used to warn the public of a physical hazard (such as a broken sidewalk), which is a brightly colored, usually two-toned tape of alternating yellow-black or red-white stripes or the words "Caution" or "Danger."

Why are tents often erected at a crime scene?

At most major crime scenes, the police will erect crime scene tents. These special tents provide not only the privacy to work at the scene—away from the public's view—but are also used to prevent (most) contamination of the site and the destruction of evidence by weather and other environmental factors. This is definitely true

Police tape warns the public not to cross over into a crime scene. The bright yellow tape clearly indicates it is a police line.

What is spoliation?

According to *Black's Law Dictionary*, spoliation has to do with evidence at a crime or accident scene. In particular, it is the "intentional, reckless, or negligent withholding, hiding, altering, fabricating, or destroying of evidence relevant to a legal proceeding." In fact, spoliation is considered a criminal act in the United States under federal law and also in most states.

---

today, especially with the emphasis on preventing contamination by foreign human DNA at crime scenes (foreign DNA can include people who were not involved in the event and even crime scene investigation team members). The tents come in various sizes depending on the site and the evidence that needs to be protected (including even smaller "tents" to cover victims of a homicide), and some can be disposed of after use.

SEEKING CRIME SCENE EVIDENCE

What types of valuable biological and physical evidence can be collected at a scene?

A wide variety of valuable physical evidence can be collected at a scene (these items are often called probative; for more about probative evidence or facts, see the chapter "Putting It All Together"). They include the following types of evidence (all but the first on the list are physical evidence, while the first is biological; for more about biological evidence, see the chapter "At the Crime Scene: Looking for Biological Evidence"):

- Biological, such as blood, body fluids, other tissues, hair, etc.
- Patent and latent prints, such as fingerprints and palm and footprints, and plastic prints
- Trace evidence, such as fibers, vegetation, glass, plastic, and soil
- Tracks, such as from footwear or tire tracks at a scene
- Tools, such as tools used at a scene, and toolmarks, such as marks on a window frame (from being pried open with a crowbar)
- Documents, such as bank statements, etc.
- Drugs (or even alcohol)
- Firearms or explosives evidence
- Digital, such as cell phones (including contacts, texts, images, and records on the phone), Internet use, and e-mail messages

Can something as innocuous as a cigarette butt or gum wrapper provide evidence at a crime scene?

Yes, sometimes criminals are known to leave seemingly innocuous, but incriminating, evidence at a crime scene. For example, they often carelessly toss cigarettes, gum, or gum wrappers, usually interpreted as a person who is nervously waiting or committing a crime. These pieces of evidence can eventually be analyzed in a laboratory as evidence. Some brands of cigarettes may help identify the smoker, such as the plug wrap (usually used to wrap the filter) or even the adhesive used to hold the cigarette together. Plus, some brands of cigarettes have manufacturing numbers on them, allowing analysts to possibly trace where the items were sold. More extensive analysis in the lab can include more details. For instance, the saliva on a tossed cigarette often contains cells that can be extracted from the cigarette butt (or from a piece of gum). In some cases, this allows experts to run a DNA analysis and possibly obtain a DNA profile of an individual. A gum or other sticky wrapper can also be analyzed for pieces of hair and fibers that can often be matched with those found at a crime scene. Thus, these small items are oftentimes what links a suspect to a crime scene.

How easy is it to fake evidence?

Although it depends on the scene, it is possible to fake evidence, but not likely. For example, a murderer may put the gun used to kill in the victim's hand, making it look like a suicide (but in many cases, evidence to the contrary will also be present). Or, a family friend murders a victim in his or her home, then uses a tool to leave marks on an open door bolt and steals a valuable or two—making it look as if a burglar stole the valuables and killed the homeowner.

Using DNA of a person as evidence has also been thought to be planted in some cases. Perhaps the most well-known example was in the controversial 1995 trial—and subsequent acquittal—of former football player O. J. Simpson: a glove found at the scene had the DNA of not only Simpson but also of the two victims, Nicole Brown and Ron Goldman. The people who believed that O. J. did not commit the murders suggested that the DNA on the gloves was planted—but this claim has been highly refuted.

What is the Locard Exchange Principle?

The Locard Exchange Principle was developed by French forensic scientist Edmond Locard (1877–1966; for more about Locard, see the chapter "The History of Forensic Science"). Simply put, it states that every criminal leaves a trace of something behind at a crime scene, even when the person believes they have not. In 1930, Locard published three papers in the *American Journal of Police Science* about his theory. In 1934, he wrote a book titled *La police et les méthodes scientifiques* and in it expounded on his exchange principle by stating, *"Toute action de l'homme, et a fortiori, l'action violente qu'est un crime, ne peut pas se dérouler sans laisser quelque marque"* (page 8). This is translated into English as "Any action of an individual, and obviously the violent action constituting a crime, cannot occur without leaving a trace." Another translation is that every time contact is made with another person, place, or thing, it results in an exchange of physical materials. In other words, as forensic scientist Paul L. Kirk once wrote in his *Crime Investigation: Physical Evidence and the Police Laboratory* (1953), "Wherever he [the criminal] steps, whatever he touches, whatever he leaves, even unconsciously, will serve as a silent witness against him."

What are the various types of searches conducted when seeking evidence at a crime scene?

The search for evidence is the responsibility of the lead investigator. Depending on the scene, several types of search patterns are conducted in order to find important evidence. They include the following, looking in three dimensions (down, around, and up) for evidence:

- *Walk-Through Search*—This is the initial survey of the scene by the lead investigator. In this case, he or she gains an overview of the site in order to determine how to conduct the search for evidence.

- *Zone Search*—In a building or home, it is searching a small area or room within. It is most often used in homicides and rapes and explosive, drug, and bomb searches.

- *Ever-Widening Circle or Spiral Search*—This is a search in which only one official is looking for evidence. It starts at a certain point in a room or outside (depending on the scene), with the official making an ever-widening circle from that point while searching for evidence.

- *Strip or Line Search*—This is when a small number of officials are available to cover a large, outdoor area, with the searchers walking straight and then turning at right angles across the area to be covered. The sequence of search is walking down, across, up, across, down, and so on.

- *Straight Line Search*—This search is used outdoors when a large number of officials and/or assigned people are available to look for a body or to seek evidence after a mass disaster. In this case, the people stand close together ("shoulder to shoulder") and walk in a straight line across an area to look for a body or evidence, depending on the scene.

- *Grid Search*—This is used to search for evidence in a large area, usually outdoors. In this case, the area is broken down into a grid, with a search made by officials within each grid. Then, an additional search is often made perpendicular to the first.

- *Wheel or Ray Search Pattern*—This is used when several officials and/or assigned people are conducting a search. In this case, the searchers move from the bound-

Several officers perform a line search in a field, marking evidence as they go with a yellow ring.

ary of the scene straight toward the center, or they can start from the center of the scene straight to the boundary, looking for evidence.

OFFICIAL PEOPLE AT A CRIME SCENE

In general, who are the various personnel who investigate a crime scene?

After the first responder arrives and secures the scene, several other official personnel are involved in investigating a potential or actual crime scene. This includes the case or lead investigator (in charge of the investigation; in the absence of an investigator, such duties usually go to a lead uniformed officer), coroner, photographer, crime scene technicians, and others, such as detectives and other specialty investigators not associated with law enforcement (for example, a specialist in soil or firearms).

FIRST RESPONDER

Who is usually first at a potential or actual crime scene?

In many cases, law-enforcement officers (for example, local police and/or state troopers) are the first responders at a potential or actual crime scene. Other "first" responders follow, such as backup police and/or emergency medical or fire personnel. From there, crime scene personnel arrive. The people who are first at the scene have the responsibility of protecting the crime scene, preserving the evidence, and collecting any evidence that may be pertinent to further investigation of a potential or actual crime.

What are the first responder's responsibilities upon reaching the scene?

Upon reaching the scene of a potential crime or accident, the first responder has several responsibilities. This includes determining the need for medical assistance for a person or persons at the scene and confirming or pronouncing a person dead. The responder must also walk through the scene slowly and methodically—although this is not always possible in the case of arresting an uncooperative suspect or helping to save an injured victim. In such cases, the officer should make mental (or written) notes as soon as possible as to the conditions of the scene the officer saw on arrival and after the scene was stabilized.

Once the scene has been stabilized, the first responder has several duties, including taking steps to preserve and protect the area so no evidence is compromised; if possible, remove all unauthorized people from the scene; separate witnesses so they do not discuss the events among themselves; record witnesses' names; secure and isolate the crime scene (with whatever may be available, including ropes or makeshift barricades); and contact other officials for help with the scene, especially the lead investigator.

What are some of the essential items for first responding officers to have on hand?

According to the National Institute of Justice, several items are essential for first responding officers to have readily available. They include bindle paper (also called paper bindles, or folded paper used to hold evidence, such as hair, fibers, paint chips, or other small items collected as evidence); biohazard bags (for disposal of biohazard materials, such as used gloves, or to carry evidence, such as a bloody knife at a crime scene); consent/search forms; crime scene barricade tape (usually seen as yellow tape, the most common with lettering stating "POLICE LINE DO NOT CROSS"); first-aid kit; flares; flashlight and extra batteries; markers (which can be tapes, chalk, or other markers to place near possible evidence items); notebook; paper bags; and personal protection items (such as gloves, booties, overalls, mask, etc.).

What can the first responder's examination of a body tell about a crime?

In most cases, when a first responder reaches the victim of a crime scene, the deceased can be examined in several ways in order to understand the crime. For example, without moving the body, the officer can look at the body's position (how the body's various limbs and extremities are positioned). Examination of the hands, fingers, and arms can reveal defense wounds, bruises, or perhaps the wound that killed the person. He or she also looks for debris of some kind under the fingernails, hair in the hand, or even the instrument that caused the death on the victim. The officer can also—still without touching the body—look for lividity (see below), decomposition, or direction of the blood flow patterns (if any are on or near the body). They can also describe the person's clothing (or lack of clothing), including whether the person was dragged (folds or rolls under the body) and in what direction.

CASE INVESTIGATOR

In general, what are the duties of the case investigator upon arriving at a scene?

The case investigator must perform many duties and minute details upon arriving at a scene, although circumstances can cause differences (for example, arriving at a homicide versus a burglary) and/or because of state, county, or local regulations. In general, upon arriving at the scene, the inspector should identify himself or herself and determine the people essential for the safety and protection of the scene. The inspector should also determine whether anything has been introduced to contaminate the scene. They also need to make sure everything is safe for those at the scene (for example, identify whether any potential safety or health hazards are present to anyone at the scene, such as exposure to biohazards).

In addition, the case investigator is in charge of establishing and securing the physical boundaries of the scene, making sure only those people essential to the investigation are present, and communicating and coordinating with the assigned crime scene team. They should also conduct a primary survey by doing a walkthrough, identifying potentially valuable evidence, noting the location of such evidence, and documenting (with detailed notes) and recording (including initial photos) the scene and evidence. If time allows, and to make sure the scene is secure, a secondary walkthrough may be necessary. If it is a death situation, once death has been determined, all rescue efforts cease, and medicolegal jurisdiction is established (this occurs before the medical examiner or coroner assumes their responsibilities). All of this minute and detailed information is vital to not only solving the events that occurred at the scene but also, if a crime has taken place, will help fill in the blanks after the crime lab analyzes the collected evidence.

What are the four levels of certification for a crime scene investigator?

In the United States, becoming a crime scene investigator has no national requirements, but if someone wants to demonstrate their proficiency as a crime scene investigator, they can go through the International Association for Identification (IAI; for more about this group, see the chapter "Resources in Forensic Science"). Crime scene investigators in the IAI have four levels of certification: Certified Crime Scene Investigator, Certified Crime Scene Analyst, Certified Crime Scene Reconstructionist, and Certified Senior Crime Scene Analyst. Other certifications through various organizations include Evidence Photographer Certification (from the Evidence Photographers International Council, Inc.) and the Board Certified Medicolegal Death Investigator (from the American Board of Medicolegal Death Investigators).

What does "chain of custody" entail?

According to the National Institute of Justice, a way of ensuring the integrity of the evidence is by establishing and maintaining a chain of custody at the start (and throughout) an investigation. This stops subsequent allegations of theft and tampering, planting, and contamination of the evidence by others. In most instances, this is carried out by specifically assigned people who make sure that the location of the scene and time of arrival of the death investigator are documented. The investigator must further appoint custodian(s) of the various pieces of evidence and must also determine which agencies are responsible for collection and transportation of evidence to the crime lab. They must also keep extensive records of everything, including the location of the evidence, time of collection, time and location of deposition, and by whom—along with making sure that everything is properly labeled and secure. (For more about chain of custody and trials, see the chapter "Putting It All Together.")

CORONER AND/OR MEDICAL EXAMINER

In general, what are the duties of a coroner?

The coroner's role at a crime scene depends on the jurisdiction, and their usual duties often include investigative and mortuary tasks. If possible, the coroner often determines the identity of the deceased and how, when, and where the person died. If the death is thought to be suspicious, sudden (with the cause unknown), violent, or in any way unnatural, the coroner can make the decision to have an autopsy performed (also called a postmortem examination)—and, if applicable, an inquest.

A medical examiner sometimes works in autopsy rooms like this one, whereas a coroner does not have a medical degree and does not perform examinations.

What is the difference between a coroner and a medical examiner?

In most states, a coroner is an elected official and does not have to be a physician (meaning they lack the specialized medical training to do autopsies). At a crime scene, the coroner has various roles (see above), which are usually dependent on the local jurisdiction. Although it is dependent on the state, county, or district, in general, a medical examiner can be elected or not but does have to be a physician (and therefore can perform autopsies).

Do all states in the United States have medical examiners and coroners?

Not all states have the same rules and regulations when it comes to coroners and/or medical examiners at crime or accident scenes. The duties are often divided as follows: counties with medical examiners only (for example, Texas); statewide medical examiners (for example, Rhode Island); district medical examiners (for example, Florida); coroner offices only (usually by county or multicounties, such as South Carolina); and a mix of medical examiners and coroner's offices (for example, New York).

What is a deputy coroner?

A deputy coroner helps the coroner to determine the manner and cause of death in accordance with their state or local guidelines. He or she is appointed by the head coroner in most jurisdictions, and their qualification requirements vary depending on the jurisdiction. After the coroner examines a body and potentially determines the cause and manner of death—and therefore determines whether a crime has been committed or anything is questionable about the death—the deputy coroner assists the coroner in their investigations and often performs certain tasks in the coroner's place.

What is a medicolegal death investigator?

A medicolegal death investigator has the responsibility of investigating any death that falls under the jurisdiction of a coroner or medical examiner. This includes suspicious, violent, or unexplained, unexpected, or even unattended deaths. Unlike the local law enforcement who are responsible for the scene (accident or crime), the medicolegal death investigator is responsible for the deceased. They are usually trained not only in medicine but also in law.

SCENE PHOTOGRAPHER

Why is an official photographer often necessary at a scene?

An official photographer is often necessary at a scene—either of a crime or accident—as they can record the scene, victim, and/or surroundings. The photos are the permanent documentation of the crime scene and, in conjunction with sketches, gives investigators evidence from the scene. (Sketches by law enforcement are useful, as photos of a scene can often give a distorted view of the relationship of objects and/or a victim usually due to the camera angle, size of the lens, lighting, and so on.) If the investigator does not have an official photographer, he or she usually takes the photos at an accident or crime scene.

In general, what does a photographer do at a crime scene?

A crime scene photographer needs to take high-quality photos as a permanent historical record of a scene. For example, they usually take overall photos of the entire scene and surrounding areas, documenting a description of each photo so it can be used for future reference (especially if certain photos are needed as evidence). Depending on where the crime takes place, they will need to take photos of such things as walls, points of entrance and exit (in particular in an enclosed room), important physical and biological evidence in the room, and the position of the body relative to the scene. If possible, these photos should all be taken before anything at the crime scene is disturbed.

What types of photos are necessary to take at a crime scene?

In general, four types of photos are necessary to take at a crime scene, with the photographer needing to make sure each photo is recorded in a written photo log. The photos include the following:

- *Overall photos*—These photos include an overview of the entire scene. For example, if taking photos outdoors, images can include the surrounding street (approach to

It is essential to any crime investigation that the photographer take sharp, accurate photos, covering every part of the scene that may be relevant to the case.

the area, street signs, and street lights in relation to the actual crime scene) and spectators who are standing around watching (some people may be contacted as witnesses, and sometimes, perpetrators will return to observe the actions of the police or fire personnel). Inside photos could include the entire room from four corners and entryways and exits, doors, and windows. When taking a photo of a crime victim, the overall photos may include circling the body while taking the pictures in order to take in all parts of the victim. Most photographers try get as much as possible in each frame and usually with one "important item" in each photo.

- *Mid-range photos*—These photos include specific objects that may be used as evidence in a case. They may also include a scale or measuring device in the photo in order to understand sizes (many photos without a scale cannot be used as evidence in court). Mid-range photos are also taken of the victim (with or without a scale), including bruises, wounds, or other injuries that may be evident.

- *Close-up photos*—These photos include close-up views of specific objects that may be used as evidence in a case. They also include the victim and surroundings, such as the pattern of injuries on the body and/or weapons lying near or on the body. After the body is removed, close-up photos are usually taken of the area where the body was found. In addition, many of these photos are used to match evidence to the scene. For example, if a gun is found at a crime scene, the serial number on the firearm has to match the number shown in the photo (if the photographer is able to photograph the number) in order to prove that the gun was truly at the crime scene.

- *Digital and/or video photography*—These include overall shots using a digital and/or video camera. They include faraway shots and close-ups of the scene.

What are necropsy photographs?

Necropsy photographs are photographs taken both before and after a victim's clothing has been removed. They are most often taken during an autopsy. These photos include the victim's entire body, such as close-ups of scars, tattoos, wounds, teeth marks, and anything else that would help to identify the victim or to possibly learn the time of and what caused his or her death. (For more about autopsies, see the chapter "In the Crime Lab: Analyzing a Body.")

When was crime scene photography first used as a forensic tool?

By the 1840s, photos were used in prisons to keep track of inmates, and mug shots were used to identify criminals. It has been suggested that the first crime scene photo—which was used as evidence in court—was taken in 1851: a photo of a forged document. By the 1870s, crime scene photos became a boon to crime and accident cases, for example, to help in identification of a criminal and also to be used as evidence in trials.

What are some limitations of crime scene photography?

Crime scene photography has several limitations. These include the limitations of the camera or video camera itself and the lack of experience of a crime scene photographer (or even if an investigator or other person on the law-enforcement team is taking the photos). In particular, the camera cannot view what the human eye sees. For example, the lighting in the room or outdoors when photos are taken may not truly represent colors or may mask a certain view. This makes it necessary to take more than one photo of the same view, taking into account exposure and varying conditions (especially outside) when taking the image. In many ways, the use of digital cameras has helped in this capacity—the automatic exposures and instant image on the viewscreen of a camera make it "easier" to take a more accurate image of a crime scene, but even though digital cameras make the job easier, an experienced crime scene photographer still has to know how to pick the best images to use as evidence.

CRIME SCENE TECHNICIANS

Who is responsible for investigating a scene, along with searching for and collecting evidence?

The professionals responsible for investigating a scene and collecting evidence usually depend not only on the type of crime but the resources of the law-enforcement agency involved in the investigation. In many cases, smaller jurisdictions will have fewer people to work on a scene (usually the first responders and detectives who also have other duties), while larger jurisdictions will have more personnel (usually more investigators and trained crime scene specialists), but in general, a lead investigator and/or detective will investigate a case, interviewing persons of interest and victims, gathering leads, and working on interpreting the evidence collected at the scene. They will also work in tandem with the crime scene technicians who gather the evidence, including the photographer, evidence-gathering personnel, and specialists (such as those who work at the interpretations of trace evidence, latent prints, or DNA analysis in the lab).

Who are "scenes of crime officers," or SOCOs?

Scenes of crime officers, or SOCOs, are professionals who gather forensic evidence at the scene of a crime. They are employed mostly in other countries, including England and New Zealand. Occasionally, the phrase is used instead of "crime scene investigators" in the United States (see below).

Do crime scene technicians have certain specialties?

Yes, most crime scene technicians (especially those who work at larger law-enforcement agencies) have some type of specialty. For example, specialties may include an official who collects latent fingerprints, one who takes photographs of the scene, and one who collects biological samples, such as blood splatters, or physical samples, such as tire

Evidence Response Teams are manned by FBI specialists who travel to scenes to examine evidence in the field.

track impressions. In other words, the various crime scene technicians concentrate on gathering all the evidence applicable to their specialty at a crime scene—all of which is examined either on-site or in the crime lab.

What is the Evidence Response Team Unit (ERTU)?

The Federal Bureau of Investigation (FBI) has several units that were created to help investigate and gather evidence at certain crime and/or terrorism scenes, including mass grave sites, airplane disasters, and bombings. The Evidence Response Team Unit (ERTU) provides what is called traditional and hazardous evidence-collection capabilities and, along with law-enforcement partners, offers forensic training, resources, and expertise in support of the FBI's investigative tasks. The FBI's evidence-gathering teams include the following:

- *Evidence Response Teams (ERTs)*—The FBI's ERTs include field and lab specialists who collect and analyze evidence from crime scenes (including terrorism)—similar to what most forensic experts do in other laboratories. In the case of ERTs, though, the people on the team are most often special agents, mechanical engineers, forensic specialists, and forensic canine operators as well as management and program analysts that are most often involved with the FBI. They have several units, and, as of this writing, the FBI operates 141 ERTs with more than eleven hundred members through its fifty-six field offices. These teams have been—and continue to be—deployed throughout the world, investigating everything from mass graves and airplane disasters to "homegrown" and terrorist bombings.

- *Hazardous Evidence Response Teams (HERTs)*—According to the FBI, if incidences and threats involve weapons of mass destruction, their HERT program provides support to the U.S. government's response to those threats. HERTs also support investigations of terrorism and the criminal use of chemical, biological, radiological, or nuclear (often seen as the acronym CBRN) materials. They also provide training in hazardous evidence collection, crime scene management, and the processing of forensic evidence at certain CBRN crime scenes.

- *Underwater Search and Evidence Response Teams (USERTs)*—The USERT program includes trained divers who use sophisticated equipment to conduct underwater searches. In most cases, these teams locate and recover evidence from possible (or definite) crime scenes and/or search for and recover human remains. To date, the FBI maintains four USERT divisions in its Los Angeles, Miami, New York, and Washington field offices.

- *Forensic Canine Program*—Not mentioned as much, but still part of the FBI's program, is the Forensic Canine Program. In particular, the Forensic Canine Consultation program was established to provide scientifically based research methods and canine behavioral applications to forensic detection dogs. These animals often assist federal, state, and local law-enforcement agencies in their crime investigations or other scenes, such as a missing-person investigation.

What is the Technical Hazards Response Unit?

In general, the Federal Bureau of Investigation's (FBI) Technical Hazards Response Unit (THRU) protects those people who are searching for evidence at a high-crime or hazardous scene. In other words, THRU personnel are essentially responsible for protecting the FBI's evidence-gathering units from certain health and safely concerns they may encounter at crime and other scenes, which allows them to operate in a variety of hazardous environments. For example, they provide on-site expertise in health and safety matters, paramedic medical care, and help with accessing complex evidence (for instance, collecting evidence in confined spaces such as a crevice or septic tank, in high-altitude environments, or underwater situations), along with training people in on-site health and safety issues. They also manage all the safety equipment that is used by the Evidence Response Teams (ERTs) and Hazardous Evidence Response Teams (HERTs), along with those local and regional responders to a scene.

What does the acronym "CSI" represent?

CSI usually stands for crime scene investigation; it is also used to describe a crime scene investigator. A crime scene investigation focuses on using scientific and social-analysis techniques to help law enforcement ascertain all information about a certain crime. The crime scene investigator works at the scene in order to gather any relevant information and evidence that can be analyzed in the crime lab—and potentially be used as evidence in court, if necessary. (For more about crime scene investigators, see this chapter; for more about how the media portrays CSIs, see the chapter "The Media and Forensic Science.")

A crime scene investigator works at the scene to gather and analyze evidence relevant to the case.

How do crime scene technicians preserve evidence at the crime scene?

Crime scene technicians preserve the evidence they gather at a crime scene in many ways—too many to mention all of them here. For example, according to several forensic references, if the technician is collecting samples of DNA, he or she needs to avoid contamination of the sample. To do this, they wear gloves (and frequently change them); use disposable instruments and/or clean the instruments carefully and thoroughly before and after handling each sample; avoid touching the spot that may contain the DNA sample; avoid not only talking, sneezing, or coughing around the evidence, but the technician should also refrain from touching their face, nose, and mouth while collecting and packaging the sample; and put the evidence into new paper bags or envelopes (plastic bags tend to retain moisture and damage DNA samples).

Why are forensic engineers often needed at a crime scene?

Forensic engineers are often called in at a crime scene, mainly to reconstruct how the crime occurred, but overall, and although not as "dramatic" as most forensic fields (especially to those who watch crime scene television shows), forensic engineering is more of a necessity in other facets of forensics. In particular, a forensic engineer is part investigator/detective, gathering the evidence and clues that help determine the chain of events, for example, of a car crash. Forensic engineers need their engineer skills to determine such factors as the angle of the vehicle impact, how fast a car (or cars) was traveling, and even how various environmental conditions may have affected the car accident. Forensic engineers are also needed to determine certain structural failures, such as a bridge or structural collapse or, on a smaller scale, how materials fail or break. (For more about forensic engineering, see the chapter "Other Forensic Investigations.")

How is some evidence transported to the crime lab?

Transporting evidence to the lab is just as important as gathering evidence. This is to ensure that the evidence is not contaminated before it reaches the lab for examination. For example, if a crime scene technician is transporting a collected DNA sample, it is important to keep the evidence dry and at room temperature (and not in a hot police car without air conditioning, as heat can often be harmful to the DNA sample). It can be secured in paper bags or envelopes (with no staples) and should be sealed and labeled with the date, place of origin, and other pertinent information. It should also be transported in a way that allows the proper identification and information about the DNA sample when it gets to the lab.

What is a body bag?

A body bag is also known as a cadaver pouch or human remains pouch (HRP). In most cases, it is a nonporous bag designed to contain a human body or parts of a skeleton without exposing it to the elements. Depending on the conditions, it is most often used at a crime area or accident (including disaster scenes) for transporting the corpse from the scene to the morgue or a crime lab.

What is a body tag?

A body tag is often used to identify a body from a crime or accident scene, especially in the morgue or crime lab. It usually includes the person's name and case number. It is also helpful under multiple death circumstances, such as plane crashes or multiple-death crime scenes.

OTHERS AT A CRIME SCENE

What is the general procedure when interviewing witnesses at a crime scene?

According to the National Institute of Justice, interviewing witnesses at a crime scene is done according to several procedures. They include reviewing the information available (to tailor the interview to match the facts of the case so far); conduct the interview as soon as the witness is emotionally and physically capable; if possible, choose a place that minimizes distractions and increases the comfort of the witness; separate all the witnesses (so they cannot collaborate stories); be ready with notebooks, recorder, or camcorder, if required or necessary; and determine whether the witness has had any prior law-enforcement contact (in other words, whether they have a criminal record or run-ins with the law, mainly to help assess the witness's credibility and/or reliability). While interviewing,

the official should establish rapport (if possible) and never volunteer information about the case. (For more about eyewitnesses, see the chapter "Putting It All Together.")

Why are certain people who look for evidence, who are not affiliated with law enforcement, often allowed at a crime scene?

In some instances, not everyone at a crime scene looking for evidence is a member of law enforcement or the investigative team. For example, others may include firemen who are at the scene of a fire and seek clues to a suspected arson. Also, some people are not part of the forensic team but specialize in certain aspects of searching for evidence, such as a firearms or soils expert.

What is the International Veterinarian Forensic Sciences Association?

Founded in 2008, the International Veterinarian Forensic Sciences Association (IVFSA) is dedicated to the application of forensic science to veterinary medical science. In its own mission statement, the IVFSA states that it is "dedicated to promote the health, welfare and safety of animals through the fostering of current, new, and novel techniques of forensic science and crime scene processing to circumstances of animal abuse, neglect, cruelty, fighting, and death." The organization can be found at the Internet site http://www.ivfsa .org/. (For more about veterinarians' involvement with crime scenes, see the chapter "Other Forensic Investigations.")

What duties do specially trained dogs have at a crime scene?

Specially trained dogs—called "sniffer dogs" or "K9 dogs" by many law-enforcement people— are used in several ways at a crime scene. For example, dogs can be trained to find illegal drugs, a hidden body, or a missing person. The following lists some of the tasks dogs take on in criminal, accident, or missing-person investigations (of course, each K9 has different abilities, including how long it was since an event or since a person committed a crime, along with when the dog came on the scene):

- *Cadaver dogs*—As the name suggests, these dogs are trained to follow the scent of decomposing human remains. Some are trained to detect scents associated with the early decay of a body, while others detect older remains. Most cadaver dogs are trained to detect human remains on the ground, buried, or even underwater. They can also track, if applicable, other parts of a victim (such as an arm or leg) or other items associated with the cadaver. More recently, some dogs (some call them historical human remains detection dogs, not cadaver dogs) can track the scent of a historical or archaeological grave. For example, dogs were used to locate the historical burial sites at the campsite of the Donner Party—early California settlers who did not survive the winter of 1846–1847.

- *Search and rescue dogs*—Although not usually found at a crime scene, if a person has been kidnapped, these dogs are often brought in to conduct searches for the missing person, but in most cases, these dogs search for missing people, such as those lost in a forest or people trapped in collapsed buildings after an earthquake.

- *Tracking dogs*—These dogs are similar to the search and rescue dogs, but they are mainly trained to track down criminals, suspected criminals, and fugitives. This works especially well if the crime scene has any item from—or an item that has been touched by—the criminal or fugitive that the dog can smell. They then follow that same scent in pursuit of the criminal.

- *Arson detection dogs*—Again, as the name suggests, these dogs help with arson investigations. Even though smoke and other smells are associated with burned materials and structures, the dogs are able to pick out specific odors, for instance, of flammable substances that may have been used to start a fire. Not only can they detect the flammable material, but they can pinpoint where the most accelerant is found—which is often the place where the fire started.

- *Narcotic detection dogs*—These dogs are used not only at a crime scene but also in such facilities as railroad stations, airports, and governmental buildings. At a crime scene, narcotic detection dogs can pinpoint the scent of illegal narcotics—from heroin to cocaine—on a suspect or where the narcotics were potentially hidden by a suspect.

- *Explosive detection dogs*—These dogs can detect the scent of certain substances associated with explosives, such as sulfur, nitroglycerin, gunpowder, or any substances that may be used in an explosive device. They are often used at bombing scenes and are also useful in detecting explosives at airports, train stations, or government buildings. When it comes to criminals, they are also used to detect any explosive-related materials in the homes of those people suspected of making bombs or other explosive devices.

Why are dogs so helpful at crime scenes?

Besides being more trainable than other animals, dogs have a tremendous ability to smell and follow a scent because of a large number of receptor cells in their nose (although not all types of dogs have the same number of receptor cells in their noses). In addition, dogs also have a special organ in the roof of their mouth called the vomeronasal (or Jacobson's organ) that allows them to "taste" a smell, making them even better than most other domesticated animals at detecting odors. Although the numbers vary widely depending on the reference, it is thought that while humans smell the world using about twelve million olfactory receptor cells, bloodhounds, for instance, have about four billion such cells. (In fact, it is often said that the receptor patch in a human's nose is the size of a stamp, while that of a bloodhound is the size of a handkerchief.) Thus, the trace of sweat that seeps through a criminal's shoes and is left in footprints is a million times more powerful than the bloodhound needs to track someone down.

AT THE CRIME SCENE: LOOKING FOR BIOLOGICAL EVIDENCE

WHAT IS EVIDENCE?

What is evidence at a crime scene?

The term "evidence" means anything—physical (also called real or direct evidence) and/or biological—that can be used to determine what actually happened at the crime (or accident) scene. Evidence can be used to convict or identify a perpetrator, exonerate an innocent person, or allow investigators to find other evidence at the crime scene or elsewhere, but not all evidence is useful or can be used to convict or identify a criminal. For example, a bloody knife may be found at a crime scene in which someone was stabbed, but no other evidence (such as fingerprints, bloodstains, etc.) is found to connect any certain person to the crime.

What is direct versus circumstantial evidence?

Besides testimonials and documented evidence that can be used in a court proceeding, direct and circumstantial evidence are also used. Direct evidence is when a fact is actually known, with the evidence leading to a definite conclusion or direction, such as an eyewitness to a crime. For example, if a person watches as a criminal shoots another person, the observer's testimony in court is considered to be direct evidence. It can also include incriminating statements made by the criminal, victim, or others—or even photos or videos of the defendant in the act of committing the crime.

Circumstantial (or indirect) evidence is when the fact that a person has committed a crime is only inferred. It uses inductive reasoning and implies that the criminal was involved in the crime. For example, if a towel has the DNA of an alleged murderer and that person did not live with the victim, it is circumstantial evidence. Or, if a person hears a shot and sees another person running out of a room in which the shot origi-

55

nated, it is circumstantial evidence that the person with the gun shot the victim (it is usually left to a judge or jury to determine plausibility of the circumstantial evidence). Some such evidence is not always accepted or admissible in a court, especially if the judge or jury believes that the evidence is too weak to decide on a conviction or to draw a definite conclusion.

What happens if a homicide is alleged and no body can be found?

If a homicide is alleged and no body is found, a person can still be convicted. This is usually based on physical evidence (for example, finding blood with the DNA of the victim in the murderer's car) and/or circumstantial evidence (for example, a witness seeing the murderer leave the scene around the time of the murder). Numerous accounts exist of a person being convicted of a crime without a body being found, but such evidence is not foolproof—accounts also exist of people being convicted with no proof and then found not guilty when other evidence was provided at a later date.

TIME OF DEATH EVIDENCE AT THE CRIME SCENE

How is the approximate time of death of a crime scene victim determined?

Currently, when a deceased human is found, the methods for estimating the time of death at a crime scene are not precise. Therefore, such methods are only meant to be a rough estimate of the time elapsed since the person died. For example, if the body experiences rigor mortis, it has been approximately two hours or more since the person died (for more about rigor mortis, see below). In addition, some physical evidence may indicate when a person died, such as whether or not they are covered by snow (and if so, how much, based on when the snow began falling). Insects invade a dead body in a certain way and at different life cycle stages, which can also help determine the person's time of death. (For more about methods of estimating time of death using insects found on the body, see this chapter.) Or, the mystery-novel method is a favorite (but rarely realistic): the broken clock or watch on or around the victim that registers the time in which the murder was committed—but that type of evidence is usually only read in fiction mystery books or seen in the movies.

What are the three general ways in which the official time of death is categorized?

The time of death of a victim is often categorized as follows: the time when the deceased's body, specifically the vital organs, stopped functioning, called the physiological time of death; the best guess by examiners as to the death of the individual based on the available information at the

Investigators can estimate time of death based on factors such as body decomposition, rigor mortis, whether insects have invaded the body, microbe activity, and so on.

scene, called the estimated time of death; and the time at which the body was discovered or pronounced dead by the coroner or medical examiner (depending on the regulations of that jurisdiction), called the legal time of death. By law, this is also the time shown on the person's death certificate.

How have recent studies about microbes been connected to a victim's time of death?

Although such studies are relatively new, some researchers believe that microbes may be used to estimate a victim's time of death. In 2016, a study showed that certain bacteria and other microbes that live on our bodies may present clues as to the relative time of death of a victim. The researchers sampled the ear and nasal canals of twenty-one cadavers through several weeks of decomposition. From there, they analyzed the bacteria using special DNA analysis techniques, determining how the bacterial colonies changed over time on the bodies. They hope to eventually determine the time of death based on which microbes take over a dead body and how long it takes—which may help link a homicide to possible suspects or help with death investigations.

What is rigor mortis?

At first, a dead body is limp. About two hours after death, rigor mortis (also just called rigor) begins, causing the body to stiffen because of the loss of what is known as ATP, or adenosine triphosphate, from the body's muscles. (ATP is a natural substance in the body that allows the muscles to be flexible, as it allows energy to flow to the muscles; see sidebar.) Rigor starts in the smaller muscles, for example, in the face and neck, and

ATP (adenosine triphosphate) is the universal energy currency (in a way, a source) of the body's cells. The secret to creating ATP lies in its structure. ATP contains three negatively charged phosphate groups. When the bond between the outermost two phosphate groups is broken, ATP becomes ADP (adenosine diphosphate) and inorganic phosphate. This reaction creates and releases 7.3 kilocalories/mole of ATP, which is a great deal of energy by cell standards. Overall, each cell in the human body is estimated to use between one and two billion ATPs per minute. In addition, muscle cells store only enough ATP to last for about ten seconds of activity. After that is used up, the cells must produce more ATP from other sources, such as phosphate, glucose, and fatty acids. When a person dies, these sources are not produced anymore and the body eventually develops rigor mortis.

works down through the body to the larger muscles, for example, the arms and legs. In general, rigor can last from twenty to thirty hours (some references state eighteen to thirty-six or forty-eight hours—which is why it is so difficult to use rigor mortis to determine how long a person has been dead). After that time, the body will become more "flexible" again.

Why can't rigor mortis be guaranteed to determine the time a person died?

Rigor mortis is not readily used to determine the time a person died for many reasons. This is because many circumstances affect the rate of rigor mortis—most of them because of the surrounding environment. For example, temperature is important when it comes to the onset of rigor. At what would be considered average room temperature, rigor completes its process in about three to six hours. If the temperature is high surrounding the body, rigor occurs much faster, such as in tropical temperatures, when the onset of rigor can occur in around an hour. At lower temperatures, rigor onset is much slower. For instance, if a person drowns in the cold waters of a lake, rigor may not even take place until the body is removed from the water—even if the person has been submerged for days. For these reasons, it is often difficult for a medical examiner or medical personnel examining a body to determine the time of death based on rigor. Thus, it is usually used to get a very general estimate of how long a person has been dead, for instance, at a crime scene or after an unattended death.

What is lividity?

Similar to rigor mortis, lividity—or the process through which the body's blood supply stops moving when the heart stops beating—is often used to give a very general estimate of how long a person has been dead, for instance, at a crime scene or after an unattended death. In this case, the blood settles in different ways throughout the body as the blood pools in response to gravity and is most often seen as dark purple discolorations on the body. In general, lividity begins within thirty minutes after the heart stops pumping and can last up to twelve hours (although lividity in a body can be altered if the remains are moved within the first six hours after death). Depending on the person's shape, how the body lies, and what the body leans against, the blood settles in various ways. For example, blood would pool in a person's back if they are lying face-up on the ground when they died.

What is algor mortis?

Algor mortis (algor means "cooling") is the cooling of the body after death, which proceeds at a certain rate but is also influenced by the environmental temperature and where the body is located (for example, if the victim is found in a shed protected from the elements). The body does not cool at the same rate; the outer surface cools faster than the interior. Besides the surrounding environment, algor mortis can be affected by a person's build, physique, and/or clothes they are wearing when they died.

Can the body temperature of a crime victim help determine the time of death?

Although some forensic experts do not believe that body temperature is a good indicator of the time of death, a formula is often used. It equates to the body temperature of 96.8 degrees Fahrenheit (37.5 degrees Celsius—usually taken with a rectal thermometer or from the temperature of the liver), which loses around one degree Fahrenheit (1.5 degrees Celsius) per hour until the temperature of the body is similar to the surrounding environment (called ambient temperature). How low or high the surrounding temperature is determines whether the body reaches ambient temperature in minutes or hours (which is why many experts believe it is a difficult factor to use when determining the time of death). For example, if it is very cold, a body's temperature drops more slowly, including if the body is submerged in water or under icy conditions.

What can it mean if a deceased person's body temperature remains elevated for the first two hours or so after death?

Sometimes, if a person's body temperature remains elevated for the first two hours or so after death, it may be an indication of several conditions—and may be useful in determining the reason for death. For example, it may mean that the person's temperature was elevated before death, such as in the case of heat stroke. Or, it can also be indicative of intense heat production from such factors as convulsions (such as with strychnine poisoning) or excessive bacterial production, such as under conditions like cholera or other types of fever.

Why can a person die within minutes if they are deprived of oxygen?

A person can die within minutes of being deprived of oxygen because each of the trillions of cells in the human body requires oxygen to survive. In particular, after around six minutes, the brain begins to die, cutting off (by not signaling the heart to pump) oxygen to tissues, organs, and other body cells. As these cells are deprived of oxygen, they begin to die, causing the entire body to shut down. Most living organisms are aerobic; that is, they require oxygen to complete the total breakdown of glucose and other sources in the body in order to produce adenosine triphosphate (ATP; for more about ATP, see above), which gives the cells energy. Many people think that humans need oxygen to breathe—which is true—but people also need oxygen to recycle the body's spent electrons and hydrogen ions (H) in their systems.

Why is carbon monoxide deadly to breathe?

Carbon monoxide is a colorless, odorless gas that is commonly emitted by automobiles and fuel-fired space heaters. It also has the unique ability to compete with

Our cells require oxygen to survive, and when the body is deprived of this vital gas after just six minutes, the brain begins to shut down and so do the organs.

oxygen for binding sites on hemoglobin molecules found in a person's red blood cells. In particular, carbon monoxide binds to the iron in hemoglobin about two hundred times as readily as oxygen, and it tends to stay bound. As a result, the hemoglobin bound to carbon monoxide no longer transports oxygen throughout the body. It transports carbon monoxide instead. carbon monoxide. This is why prolonged exposure to carbon monoxide—such as a person who is accidentally exposed through, for example, a space heater, or who commits a crime by exposing another person to carbon monoxide—results in carbon monoxide poisoning. The initial symptoms include nausea, headache, eventually unconsciousness, and, if the exposure is not stopped, death may result.

HAIRS, BLOODSTAINS, AND OTHER BODY FLUIDS AS EVIDENCE

Why is hair as evidence used in many criminal investigations?

The characteristics of hair make it often useful as evidence in many criminal investigations. This is because hairs are readily lost from not only the perpetrator but the victim during a criminal act. They are also easily transferable (light enough to fall on both victim and criminal), are very durable, and can, in most circumstances, be readily detected and recovered. The analysis and comparisons of various types of hair often makes this part of the human body important when it comes to criminal activity—although analysis of hair as criminal evidence is often debated. (For more about the controversy of using hair for evidence, see the chapter "Controversies in Forensic Science.")

Why are hairs often important to collect at a crime scene?

Hairs—either human or another animal—can often be important to collect at a crime scene, as they may lead to the perpetrator and/or how a certain accident or crime occurred. In many cases, analysis of a human hair can reveal where on the body it originated, the color, shape, and chemical composition of the hair, occasionally the race of the individual, and whether the hair was human or another animal species.

How and what hairs are often collected from a crime scene for later analysis in the lab?

Samples of human hairs (or other animal hairs) are collected, mainly with the use of tweezers. For example, if hairs are found on a victim, they are collected and bagged, including documentation, or, if found on clothes, they can be sent by bagging the clothes and including documentation. Samples are also often collected as control samples. For instance, hairs from the victim and the suspect to be analyzed include hairs from parts of the head and/or pubic areas. In the lab, these hairs are compared to see whether any matches exist with the hairs found as evidence at the crime scene. (For more about human and animal hair analysis from a crime scene, see the chapter "In the Crime Lab: Trace Evidence.")

What tests can be performed to determine whether a fluid is human blood or a substance that just resembles blood?

Not all fluid that looks like blood from a crime scene is human blood. The first test made on the fluid is called a presumptive test, or a relatively quick test to determine whether the fluid is likely blood. This includes such tests as a Kastle-Meyer Color Test, in which compounds in the blood cause the color of a certain solution to change. This test is not always positive proof of blood, but if the fluid passes this test, then a serologist (a person who studies blood and other body fluids) often conducts a confirmatory test to confirm that it is blood. Other tests include those involving fluorescent chemicals, such as luminol, that produce a blue glow when exposed to areas thought to contain blood.

What is bloodstain analysis?

Bloodstain analysis (often called bloodstain pattern analysis) is just as the phrase sounds: it is the interpretation of bloodstains at a crime scene (or even accident site) in order to understand the actions that may have caused the bloodstain. This is because blood behaves according to several scientific principles, allowing a bloodstain expert to under-

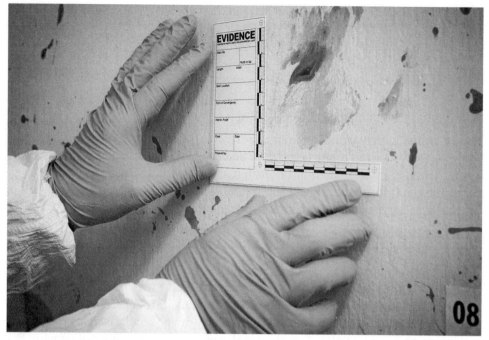

A lot can be determined about a crime by the pattern of the blood stains, including how the injury was created and environmental conditions.

stand and categorize how the blood was shed. In order to do this, the official at a crime scene must understand the behavior of blood (biology); how blood flows, along with its cohesion, and how it moves under various circumstances, such as in a warm or cold environment (physics); and how it flows in terms of distance and angles (mathematics).

Are bloodstains at a crime scene considered evidence?

Yes, in many cases, especially if the bloodstain can be connected to the crime or crime scene, bloodstains are definite evidence to understand the crime. Not all bloodstains reveal everything that happened at the crime scene. For example, if too little—or too much—blood is present, it is often difficult to interpret the cause of the stains. (For more about blood and a crime victim, see the chapter "In the Crime Lab: Analyzing a Body.")

How are bloodstain types and patterns at a crime scene categorized?

Bloodstains found at a crime scene are categorized in several ways. For example, bloodstains come in three main types: passive (or drops, flows, and pools, usually from gravity acting on the victim's body), transfer (bloodstains from objects coming in contact with existing bloodstains, such as a smear from a body being dragged), and projected or impact (stains from blood projecting through the air, usually seen as a splatter, which can also be classified as gushes, splashes, and arterial spurts; for more about blood splatter, see below). Other, lesser-occurring bloodstain patterns include a wipe pattern, which is an altered bloodstain pattern caused by an object moving through an already existing, wet bloodstain, or a transfer stain, in which the stain comes from contact between a bloody surface and another surface.

How much pressure does the human heart create on blood throughout the body—and how does it affect blood splatter evidence?

The human heart creates a great deal of pressure when it pumps blood throughout the body. Because of this, a heart is able to provide enough pressure to squirt blood from major arteries about 30 feet (10 meters). This is often associated with blood splatter evidence, which depends on the speed at which the blood leaves the body.

How are bloodstain splatters often categorized?

Bloodstain splatters are categorized in several ways. They include gunshot splatter pattern (the forward splatter [usually a fine mist] from an exit wound or back splatter [usually larger and a few drops], usually from an entrance wound, which is dependent on the gun caliber, where the victim was shot, how close the shot was made, and where the person was shot); cast-off or cessation cast-off pattern (when an object flings blood to nearby surfaces, such as if the assailant swings the bloodstained hammer back before inflicting another blow to the victim); and arterial spray pattern (when the blood is caused by the severing of a major artery, usually causing an arching pattern on nearby objects and walls). Expirated splatter is usually caused by blood from an internal injury. This mixes with the air from the lungs and tends to form a fine mist.

How are bloodstains and splatters recorded at a crime scene?

In most cases, bloodstains and splatters as evidence are recorded in various ways by bloodstain pattern analysts. For example, a stain can be cut away from a surface or ob-

What recent way of detecting bloodstains involves an antimalaria compound?

Although Luminol and other substances are used to "light up" bloodstains at a crime scene, some researchers are looking for a more accurate and quick way of detecting blood. One recent study from China combined the stable compound artemisinin—a natural peroxide and an antimalaria treatment—with Luminol. They found that fewer false positives occurred, especially when exposed to bleaches and disinfectants that are used by criminals to cover up blood (traditional methods [Luminol and peroxide] can sometimes result in false positives because certain compounds react with the Luminol/peroxide). They also found that the artemisinin/Luminol compound could discriminate between other blood-looking stains, such as coffee, tea, and brown sugar, and blood.

ject and packaged or it can be carefully sampled for DNA analysis in the lab. The most frequently used method of recording bloodstains is through photography, using a scale or ruler in the image to indicate the size of the stain. Photos can also be taken from several angles and, along with sketches and video photography, can often be used as evidence in court.

Can all bloodstains be seen with the naked eye?

No, not all bloodstains can be seen with the naked eye since some may be "cleaned up" by a criminal or others prior to the arrival of the crime scene technicians. In order to find such stains (often called latent bloodstains), investigators and crime scene technicians often use certain chemical reagents to reveal the blood. This includes Luminol, which—when combined with hydrogen peroxide—causes a bright blue luminescent glow (what is called chemiluminescence). This usually allows forensic experts to detect dried blood or blood that someone tried to clean from a surface. The mix reacts with the iron in the person's blood (hemoglobin), creating the blue glow—and therefore can be photographed and possibly used as evidence.

Why can semen be used as evidence in a sexual assault?

Semen is often collected from a victim, as it can be used as evidence in an assault case. This is because semen cells, like many tissues in the body, contain DNA. The DNA can be extracted in the crime lab, compared to a suspect's DNA, and possibly be used as evidence

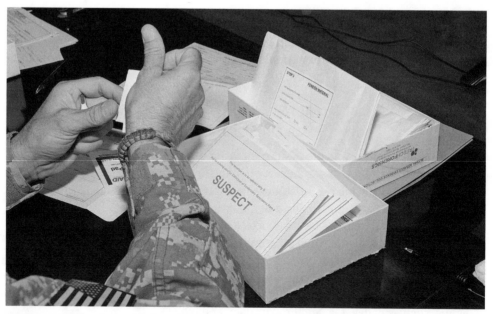

A military medical professional is shown learning how to use a sexual assault kit in Camp Phoenix, Kabul, Afghanistan.

against the perpetrator or even place someone (or not) at the scene of the assault or crime. (For more about DNA analysis, see the chapter "In the Crime Lab: DNA Analysis.")

What is a sexual assault kit?

A sexual assault kit (SAK) is just as the words imply: it is used by crime scene medical personnel (for example, a specially trained sexual assault nurse examiner, or SANE) to gather semen evidence in the case of a sexual assault. It has several other names, such as a sexual assault forensic evidence (SAFE) kit and a sexual assault evidence-collection kit (SAECK). According to the National Institute of Justice, the kits can vary based on the jurisdiction but in general usually contain swabs, test tubes, microscopic slides, and evidence-collection envelopes for hairs and fibers. (As with all evidence collection, the main purpose is to keep the evidence samples as contained and preserved as possible so they can be examined in detail in the crime lab.) Often at the crime scene, the victim is swabbed for any other evidence left by the perpetrator, such as skin, semen, or saliva—all of which may contain DNA. The SANE also takes photos of bruising, injuries, or wounds, collects the victim's clothing, and, if the victim chooses, gives them certain medications to prevent infection or pregnancy. All of this is collected and put into the SAK and, along with other possible evidence, is taken to the crime lab to be analyzed in an effort to identify (or confirm the identity of) the perpetrator.

DNA AS EVIDENCE

What types of evidence are gathered at the scene for DNA analysis?

According to the U.S. Office of Justice Programs's National Institute of Justice (NIJ), many sources of DNA can be at a crime scene. The following chart from the NIJ lists most of those ways DNA can be obtained (for more about DNA, see the chapter "In the Crime Lab: DNA Analysis"):

Possible DNA Evidence Sources

Evidence	Possible Location of DNA on the Evidence	Source of DNA
baseball bat or similar weapon	handle, end	sweat, skin, blood, tissue
hat, bandanna, or mask	inside	sweat, hair, dandruff
eyeglasses	nose or ear pieces, lens	sweat, skin
facial tissue, cotton swab	surface area	mucus, blood, sweat, semen, earwax
dirty laundry	surface area	blood, sweat, semen
toothpick	tips	saliva
used cigarette	cigarette butt	saliva
stamp or envelope	licked area	saliva
tape or ligature	inside/outside surface	skin, sweat

Possible DNA Evidence Sources

Evidence	Possible Location of DNA on the Evidence	Source of DNA
bottle, can, or glass	sides, mouthpiece	saliva, sweat
used condom	inside/outside surface	semen, vaginal or rectal cells
blanket, pillow, sheet	surface area	sweat, hair, semen, urine, saliva
"through and through" bullet	outside surface	blood, tissue
bite mark	person's skin or clothing	saliva
fingernail, partial fingernail	scrapings	blood, sweat, tissue

How can a forensic team maintain the integrity of DNA samples at a crime scene?

The forensic team can maintain the integrity (in other words, avoid contamination of) samples that may include DNA from a crime scene in many ways. In most cases, this means that the personnel at a crime scene must refrain from smoking, eating, drinking, or littering in order not to inadvertently contaminate the scene with other compounds or even their own DNA. In addition, the samples should be packed and stored in suitable cold containers—and not transported in direct sunlight or in the trunk of a police car (unless put in containers that keep the sample cool), as hot temperatures can degrade the DNA.

What samples from a crime scene are often considered unsuitable for DNA testing?

Certain samples from a crime scene are unsuitable for DNA testing in the crime lab for many reasons. For example, forensic analysts cannot extract DNA from embalmed bodies (except, in some cases, the body's bones and plucked hairs), samples that have been immersed in formaldehyde for more than a few hours, and urine stains. (Although they may contain DNA, some collected samples are not routinely accepted for testing by analysis labs, such as of feces or vomit.) Other samples that are unsuitable are usually those that have been exposed to certain conditions, such as heat, humidity, or mold—all of which cause the degradation of DNA. (For more about DNA analysis, see the chapter "In the Crime Lab: DNA Analysis.")

NATURE AS BIOLOGICAL EVIDENCE

What conditions can affect the rate of a body's decomposition?

Environmental conditions can definitely affect the rate of a body's decomposition. According to several references, including the Simon Fraser University Museum of Archaeology and Ethnology in Canada, the conditions that determine the rate of decomposition can include the following (archaeologists use some of the same techniques as forensic experts when investigating a decomposed body; for more about forensic anthropology and analyzing older remains, see the chapter "In the Crime Lab: Analyzing Older Remains"):

- *Habitat*—If the body is found in such locales as the woods, on a beach, or in a house.
- *Site*—If the body is found at a place in which it is exposed to sunlight or in a shady spot.
- *Vegetation*—If the body is found in an area that is densely populated with trees, grass, bushes, or shrubs.
- *Soil and rock type*—If the body is found in a rocky, sandy, or muddy area.
- *Weather*—What the weather is at the time that the body is gathered and transported to a morgue or crime lab, including whether it is sunny, cloudy, or rainy.
- *Environment*—What the surrounding environment is like, including the ambient temperature and humidity around the body.
- *Altitude*—Where the body was found, such as high in the mountains or along a beach at sea level.
- *Conditions*—Various conditions can also affect a body's decomposition, such as if the body was submerged in water (fresh or saltwater) or buried or on top of the ground.
- *The body itself*—If the body has wounds (loss of blood); if the body is (or was) clothed; if drugs were involved (which changes the decomposition rate); what position the body is in and what direction the body faced; and if the body was moved or disturbed. Other factors are also at play, including if a person has an infectious disease (faster decomposition), is poisoned prior to death (certain poisons inhibit decay), or if they are obese (such bodies decompose faster than emaciated people).

What is the first stage of body decomposition?

The first stage of body decomposition is called autolysis (literally "self-digestion") and starts immediately after death. When a person stops breathing and their blood stops flowing, the body cannot get oxygen or remove waste products from the blood. This causes carbon dioxide to build up, creating an acid environment. This, in turn, causes the body's cell membranes to rupture and release enzymes that begin "eating" a person's cells from the inside out.

What terms are used to describe the body as it experiences decay?

Certain terms are used as a body decays. They include fresh, putrefaction, fermen-

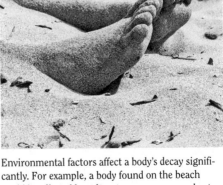

Environmental factors affect a body's decay significantly. For example, a body found on the beach could be affected by salt water, sun exposure, heat, and dessicating sand.

67

tation, dry decay, and, finally, turning into a skeleton. Each stage has its own set of organisms (mostly bacteria and, depending on the location of the body, insects) that feed off the body and essentially recycle the body's tissue (and, eventually, if the conditions are right, leave just a skeleton). The stages also have their own "time limit," taking from merely days to many years, depending on the surrounding conditions. (For more about analyzing skeletons, see the chapter "In the Crime Lab: Analyzing Older Remains.")

What is a general time sequence of body decomposition?

According to several medical and forensic references, the general time sequence of body decomposition is as follows (although the times often differ depending on the reference): In general, within twelve to twenty-four hours, the internal organs of the body begin to decompose from the bacteria in the gastrointestinal tract; two to six days after a person dies, the body begins to bloat from gases produced by the bacteria within the body, along with the body slowly turning different colors as the blood decomposes; five to eleven days after a person dies, the cadaver deflates and releases foul-smelling gases and, several days later, essentially liquefies as fluids drain from the corpse; and about ten to twenty-four days after a person dies, the smells begin to subside and almost all the flesh is stripped from the skeleton.

Why is a forensic entomologist often called to a crime scene?

Forensic entomologists are scientists who study insects in connection with medical or criminal activities. They often help to estimate the time elapsed since a person died at a crime scene or other events, such as when a body (or bodies) is found in an area or at mass grave sites. Depending on the state of decay, numerous types of insects invade a body after death, with the numbers and types often helping to determine the approximate time of death. Forensic entomologists take into account several factors, such as an indoor versus outdoor death (different insects) and the type of insects found. They also note the number of insects, which depends on how long the body has been exposed to the elements, and also where the body is found. For example, if the body is found in a dry desert or a moist and humid region, the insects will reflect such an environment. They can also often offer information about the location of death (if not where the body is found), if the body was moved or stored after death (for example, if insects found on the body do not match those of the body's location), and, if applicable, possible sites of injury on the body.

What are the first organisms to invade a decaying body?

The first organisms to invade a decaying body are microorganisms called bacteria and fungi. The presence or absence of these microorganisms depends on how fast or slow the body decomposes (usually because of weather and climate conditions), whether the body is buried, partially buried, or unburied, or whether certain conditions exist that slow the rate of decomposition, such as excess weight or thick clothing.

What insects are often associated with a decomposing body?

A decomposing body (especially if outside) attracts certain insects in somewhat of a sequence. The following is a very general list of some of the more common types of insects that invade human remains and to what stage of decomposition they are attracted:

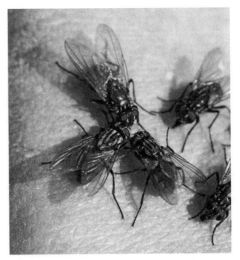

Common flies are usually the first insects to begin colonizing a dead body, followed by beetles, moths, and mites. Note that this is one way to determine the amount of time since death occurred.

- *Flies*—Flies (genus *Diptera*)—including flesh, house-, and especially blowflies—are commonly the first insects to colonize a decomposing human body. They are usually attracted to the fluids that exude from a fresh body, both in maggot (immature flies with mouth hooks that easily grasp the liquid or semiliquid dead body) and adult form. This includes such moist places as the eyes and mouth; they can also be found in areas that are commonly dry but in which the skin was damaged, such as around a gunshot wound or cuts from a person defending themselves. These insects are often used by forensic entomologists to estimate the minimum time that has elapsed since the person died. Other flies still hover around the body as it continues to decay, including dung and skipper flies. (For more about blowflies, see below.)

- *Beetles*—All types of beetles (genus *Coleoptera*) follow the blowflies, usually in the immature and adult forms of the insects' life cycle (adults, larvae, pupae, and cast skins). They show up after the body begins to dry (and the maggots cannot easily grab the drying corpse) and include hide, ham, and carcass beetles that devour the dry flesh, skin, and ligaments.

- *Moths and mites*—Moths and mites eventually find their way to the decaying body, consuming the hair. At this stage, much of the flesh and fluids of the body are gone, leaving only the bones to slowly further decay.

What are the various stages in which blowflies are found on a decaying body?

Blowflies on remains can be found as eggs, larvae or maggots, pupae (or empty pupal cases), or adults depending on how long it has been since they invaded the body. Eggs are usually small and in clumps. They can be found in a wound or natural opening, along with on clothing the person was wearing or even on objects they were holding. The larvae or maggots are found on or near a person's remains and are usually found in large masses. Experts measure the heat from the maggot masses on the body (their natural heat increases the development of the mass). In general, the larger the maggot, the older it is, but exceptions exist, as some may belong to different species that differ in size. Maggots are also collected below the body (in soil to a depth of several inches), as they leave the decaying body to pupate. The pupae (and empty pupal cases) are easy to miss as they prefer dry areas away from the wet "food source" of the body. Therefore, they are most often found in secluded areas, such as the pocket or cuff of a person's clothing. If the decaying body is indoors, they may hide in areas around the body, such as under a rug. The pupae are usually oval and dark colored; the empty pupal cases are similar but contain a hole at one end where the adult fly emerged. Finally, the adult blowflies are used only to determine the species of the insect and are therefore not as useful to the forensic entomologist in helping to determine the person's general time of death.

What else can insects reveal about a body other than time of death?

Various conditions can change the arrival of a certain type of insect to a decaying body. Therefore, when a forensic entomologist estimates a person's time of death based on insects, other factors have a bearing on decomposition. For example, the decay rate may change depending on the surroundings, such as the temperature, humidity, and vegetation around the body. Insects may reveal whether a body has been moved, such as a murder taking place in the city, but the insects that are on the body are in a country setting. Insects may also be influenced by the overall condition of the decedent. For example, some drugs can affect the lifestyle timing cycle of certain insects. For instance, if a person used cocaine, fly maggots that feed on the person may develop much more rapidly than usual (and they may also carry the drug in their system), and if a certain, unusual-for-that-area insect is found on a suspect, it may place that person at the scene of the crime.

How do insects differ at an indoor versus outdoor crime scene?

The insects indoors versus outdoors that invade a dead body are different. This is because a person inside a structure is essentially protected from various types of insects that are prolific outside. Differences in insects can also indicate different events to forensic experts. For example, because flies have a preference for cadavers in the outdoors under shade or sunny conditions, if a corpse is found indoors with the eggs or larvae of flies—ones that usually prefer a sunny location—it may indicate that the crime took place outside and the body was moved inside.

Why have pig bodies been used in the past to determine the decomposition rate of human remains?

The decomposition of pig remains has often been used to understand the decomposition of a human body. This is because pigs are similar to humans, including their relative hairlessness, torso size, and the human's and pig's omnivorous (eating meat and plant matter) diets, which affect the bacteria content of both species' guts. In fact, in one recent study conducted by Simon Fraser University in Canada, pigs were used to understand how a human body decomposes underwater. They knew that pig carcasses could remain intact for weeks or even months at the surface of the ocean, but they found that in about 1,000 feet (300 meters) of water, a pig carcass is decomposed down to the bone within three to four days depending on the season. In this study, this was mainly because of sea lice, or colonies of amphipods, that invaded and consumed the pig's body.

What is the Body Farm?

The Body Farm is a research facility where decomposition can be studied in a variety of settings. The idea originated from anthropologist William Bass after he had realized how little was known about the decomposition of the human body. He began the Body Farm in 1972 in Tennessee. The site is currently a 2.5-acre (10,000-square-meter), wooded plot of land, surrounded by a razor wire fence. In this compound, bodies are exposed to a variety of environmental conditions. This gives researchers specific insights to how a body decomposes under certain conditions for various periods of time, including what bacteria, insects, digestive enzymes, etc., affect a person after they die. This knowledge is useful, especially to a crime scene investigation, in which such details can lead to a conviction or give someone an alibi. Bodies are donated, but not just anyone can donate their body to the center's research. They have many guidelines, as to be expected; for example, a body will not be returned to the family as skeletal remains but will be placed in the program's Donated Skeletal Collection.

Where are body farms located in the United States?

As of 2017, the United States had seven body farms: Tennessee (University of Tennessee at Knoxville, the first established), North Carolina (Western Carolina University, Cullowhee), two in Texas (Texas State University, San Marcos, and Sam Houston State University, Huntsville), Florida (Florida Forensic Institute for Research, Security and Tactical Training, Tampa), Illinois (Complex for Forensic Anthropology Research, Southern Illinois University, Carbondale), and Colorado (Forensic Investigation Research Station, Colorado Mesa University, Grand Junction).

Do all countries have body farms?

No, not all countries allow body farms. For example, in the United Kingdom, it is illegal to use human remains, even for research. Thus, the United Kingdom forensic anthropologists and experts use smaller animals, such as pigs, to understand how a body decomposes at different rates under varying conditions.

AT THE CRIME SCENE: LOOKING FOR PHYSICAL EVIDENCE

PRINTS FROM FINGERS, PALMS, AND BARE FEET

What types of prints are often collected at a crime scene?

Finger-, palm (and even wrist), bare foot- (including toe, heel, and/or entire foot), and even ear or lip prints are often collected at a crime scene as evidence. Three general types of prints are used—also thought of as patent (visible), latent (mainly invisible), or plastic (roughly three-dimensional) prints. They form in distinct ways depending on how the print was transferred to the surface on which the print was found. Thus, in most cases at a crime scene, forensic experts check for prints on anything that may have been potentially touched by the criminal—including tools or objects left behind, furniture, a potential or known murder weapon, or even a person. (For more information about fingerprints, see the chapter "In the Crime Lab: Patent, Latent, and Plastic Prints"; for controversies surrounding fingerprints, see the chapter "Controversies in Forensic Science.")

How are prints classified?

In general, prints are either patent, latent, or plastic. The following lists where some of these prints are found, for example, at a crime scene (for more about print classifications, see the chapter "In the Crime Lab: Patent, Latent, and Plastic Prints"):

- *Patent or visible prints*—Patent prints are most often found when certain materials, such as dirt, ink, or blood, are transferred from the person to an object or surface. For example, if a perpetrator touched blood and then put his or her hand against a wall, it usually creates a visible print. Such prints can be found on smooth (such as a wall or table), rough, porous (such as cloth or paper), or nonporous (such as glass or plastic) surfaces (although some prints on hard surfaces can be classified as either patent or latent).

- *Plastic prints*—Molded (or plastic) prints are prints in which a person's finger, palm, or bare foot presses against a soft surface (such as wax, soap, wet paint, or soft caulking), producing three-dimensional prints. (For more about plastic prints other than prints made by the body—for instance, shoe prints—see this chapter.)

- *Latent (or mainly invisible) prints*—Latent prints (mostly invisible; some may be somewhat visible but not easy to discern) are commonly created by a person's natural skin secretions, such as an oil or perspiration. These secretions become imprinted on an object touched by the person, but it is not readily visible to the naked eye. In most cases, these types of prints—especially on hard surfaces—are what a crime scene specialist is looking for when he or she "dusts for fingerprints" or uses special lighting to reveal the prints.

What are some patterns associated with fingerprints that crime scene experts attempt to recover for evidence?

In general, a fingerprint has three types of patterns that a crime scene expert attempts to recover for evidence. Arch patterns (arches) are lines or ridges that run from one side of the finger to the other with an upward curve in the center. A loop has the ridges beginning on one side, looping around the center of the finger, and returning to the same side. Finally, a whorl has ridges that form a mostly circular pattern on the finger. (For more details about arches, loops, and whorls used in forensic science in the past, see the chapter "The History of Forensic Science"; for more details about fingerprint patterns, see the chapter "In the Crime Lab: Patent, Latent, and Plastic Prints.")

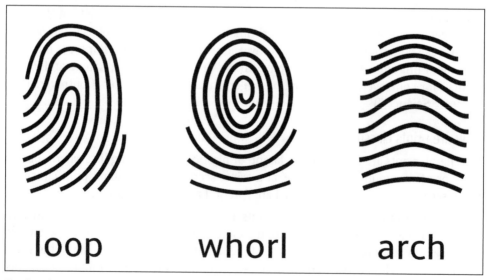

loop   whorl   arch

The three basic patterns commonly seen in human fingerprints. There are nearly infinite variations, of course.

How do crime scene technicians collect patent prints?

The most common type of patent print is the dust print. This is what most people think of when they read in a mystery novel about "fingerprints on a glass"— the dust in the person's fingerprint ridges actually transfers to the touched glass. If necessary to bring out the print, experts rely on various types of fingerprint powders normally used to find latent prints (in fact, in a pinch, any type of fine powder, such as talcum, cocoa powder, or cornstarch, can be used). These prints are collected using a method that has been in existence for decades: photography. Today's photos of patent prints are much more detailed, as they are often photographed using high-resolution cameras, with all photos including a measurement scale in the picture in order to know the size of the print.

How do crime scene technicians "dust" for latent prints?

Crime scene technicians use several powders to dust for latent prints. Many prints are brought out by "dusting" a surface with various types of fingerprint powder, including black granular, aluminum flake, or black magnetic powders, depending on the surface. In addition—and also dependent on the surface or material where a print is found or suspected—different contrasting dusting powders can be used to bring out a print (for example, white dusting powder on a dark wood makes a print easier to see and photograph). If any prints appear on an object or surface, they are photographed (similar to recording patent prints). Many of the discovered prints are also lifted from the surface with a clear adhesive tape. The print is preserved using a latent lift card in order to preserve it. This not only includes the lifted print but documentation information about the print, such as where it was found at the scene.

What are the common ingredients of fingerprint powders?

Fingerprint powders vary in their composition, all depending on the formula used. For example, some black fingerprint powders contain rosin, graphite, lampblack, and even printer toner. White fingerprint powders can be made from haddonite white, or a compound made from titanium dioxide, kaolin, and French chalk. They can also be made from such materials as titanium dioxide or purified talc. Many fingerprint powders may also contain a certain amount of other chemicals to help bring out the prints, such as lead, mercury, copper, silicon, and titanium—although many of these elements and chemicals, because of their known threat to health, are no longer in use by crime scene technicians.

What surfaces can—and can't—be "dusted" for latent prints?

Not all surfaces are good to "dust" for latent prints. In most cases, a porous surface, such as untreated wood, cardboard, or paper, can be dusted for prints. This is because the natural residues in the finger are usually absorbed into a porous surface, and the dusting material adheres to the resulting ridge and furrow impressions in the print. From there, it can be photographed and/or lifted by tape, recorded, and stored, then sent to the lab for further analysis.

Other surfaces make it much more difficult to obtain latent prints by dusting. Non-porous surfaces, such as glass or metal, are much more difficult to "dust," as the resulting prints are much more fragile. In addition, organic and highly textured surfaces, along with many types of plastics, do not take to fingerprint powders well. In these cases, and if possible, the object with the fingerprint is carefully transported to the lab for further analysis, or other methods (mainly chemical) are often used in place of dusting.

What are some problems with "dusting" for latent prints?

Some problems can occur when dusting for latent prints. For example, dusting with a powder is often good for porous surfaces, but it does not always work as well on smooth surfaces such as glass or metal. In fact, if a fingerprint is dusted on a smooth surface, it can actually destroy the prints, wiping them away. This is why (if possible) items with such surfaces are often carefully collected, packaged, and taken to the crime lab for further analysis, or they are analyzed using certain chemical techniques, such as the use of superglue fumes to bring out prints (for more about prints and superglue fumes, see the chapter "In the Crime Lab: Patent, Latent, and Plastic Prints"). Print powders themselves can also have problems, as they can contaminate the fingerprint. This, in turn, can destroy important evidence that could have been analyzed using other techniques.

Why are some chemical techniques often a problem when looking for latent prints?

Similar to fingerprint powders, using chemicals to expose a latent print can reduce the forensic expert's ability to perform other techniques that could reveal valuable information and evidence. Thus, if any question exists about destroying valuable evidence, other examinations may be conducted before the print is examined using chemical methods. For example, if a ransom note is found, it may be examined by handwriting or

What ancient pigment may eventually become a common fingerprint powder?

According to recent research, an ancient pigment known to the Egyptian pharaohs some five thousand years ago may eventually become a common fingerprint powder for use in forensic investigations. Called Egyptian blue, the material is made by heating a mix of copper, quartz sand, lime, and an alkali (such as natron, a natural salt). Unlike most fingerprint powders, the Egyptian blue can pull out latent prints on shiny or textured objects. After the surface is brushed with the mixture, it is photographed under white light (and a camera with a filter that is sensitive to near-infrared rays). If the print is partial or complete, a near-infrared luminescent impression and pattern of the print can be readily seen in the resulting image.

questioned document experts before any chemicals are used to possibly reveal prints. In this case, latent prints on paper are usually revealed using ninhydrin, which, in turn, destroys the writing by causing inks to run. (For more about ninhydrin, see the chapter "In the Crime Lab: Patent, Latent, and Plastic Prints.")

How are prints at a crime scene documented and preserved as evidence?

In many cases, after a patent or latent print has been exposed by a certain method, such as with fingerprint powders or fuming, it is photographed. The photo must include a scale (to determine the size of the print) and must be documented (for example, where it was found or its position relative to other evidence) for use as evidence.

In TV shows one often sees detectives dusting glass for fingerprints, but actually such smooth surfaces make it much harder to obtain prints.

How does a homeowner get rid of fingerprint powder on surfaces?

This is not a strange question! Many homeowners (and business owners) can be the target of a crime—from burglaries to break-ins—and, thus, their home may be searched for evidence from the crime. This includes fingerprinting in many cases, with law-enforcement or crime scene technicians using certain fingerprint powders to find evidence of the perpetrator. When the fingerprints are found (or not found), what remains is all that powder—which can truly be a mess to clean up. Although not many solutions are to be found, here are some suggestions for ridding a home from print powders: vacuuming the area, dabbing the area quickly with tape (which takes a long time if the powder is in many spots), using a damp, soapy cloth (and drying immediately) on the spots, or hiring a commercial firm that specializes in cleanup! In other words, depending on where the fingerprint powder is located—from a steering wheel and cloth car seats to a wooden cabinet and floor—patience helps, as it's often a challenge to clean up.

TIRE TRACKS AND SHOE PRINTS

What are tire tracks and shoe prints?

Tire tracks and shoe prints (from various types of footwear) are called pattern evidence, as they are the imprints of a physical object that form a unique pattern. In most cases, they can be divided into imprints (a definite print, such as one made on a concrete floor) or impressions (a print made in softer materials, such as a tire track in sand). Tire tracks can be left by numerous types of vehicles and often have a specific pattern from a certain tire brand. Footprints can be made by all footwear, including boots, slippers, shoes, and sneakers, all of which often have impressions specific to a particular brand of footwear. (For more about tire tracks and shoe print analysis in the crime lab, see the chapters "In the Crime Lab: Trace Evidence" and "In the Crime Lab: Patent, Latent, and Plastic Prints.")

How can tire tracks and shoe prints be used as evidence at a crime scene?

Tire tracks—even partial imprints or impressions—can often be used as evidence at a crime scene. If a certain tire track is found, investigators can often determine what retailers sell that type of tire or what vehicles often come with those types of tires. The tread on tires often changes over time, and the tire's wear pattern (such as the wearing down of a tire in a certain spot if the vehicle is out of alignment) can be used as evidence if a tire with the same wear is found.

Similar to tire tracks, shoe prints—even partial imprints or impressions—can often be used as evidence at a crime scene. If a certain footprint from a certain type of footwear is found, investigators can often determine the brand of shoe and what retailers sell that type of shoe. They can also base some evidence on the footprint's wear pattern (which is based on how and/or where a person walks). For example, if the perpetrator of the crime has a right shoe that is worn on the back left side, such wear on the shoe can be used as evidence or sometimes to identify the perpetrator.

What are some factors that affect imprints of footwear and tire tracks at a crime scene?

Many factors influence the overall imprint—and if it can be used as evidence—of footwear and tire tracks at a crime scene. Such prints often have to do with the surface: a shoe can leave an impression in sand but is more likely to leave an imprint on concrete, linoleum, wood floor, or other hard surfaces. In addition, the imprint or impression may be smeared, such as if a person slips while running from the scene. The weather may also have an influence on the imprints and impressions of footwear and tire tracks. For example, a tire track may be washed away during a hard rain or a footprint walked over by others at a crime scene.

A plastic print, such as from a shoe, is one that has made an imprint into something soft, such as sand or snow.

What types of tire track and shoe print impressions and imprints are taken as evidence at a crime scene?

Impressions and imprints of tire tracks and shoe prints are taken as evidence at a crime scene in several ways. For example, a visible print is one that can be seen with the naked eye and is a transfer of material from the tire or shoe to the surface. For example, it can be a bloody sneaker print or muddy tire track on a roadway at a crime scene. A plastic print is one that is visible with the naked eye but is a three-dimensional imprint in a soft surface, such as a shoe or tire track in sand or snow. A latent print is one that is not easily visible to the naked eye. It must be "treated" in order to be seen using powders, chemicals, or different light sources, such as an "unseen" boot print on a windowsill or tire track on a sidewalk.

How are tire track and shoe print impressions and imprints collected at a crime scene?

Tire track and shoe print evidence are collected in various ways at a crime scene depending on the type of impression or imprint found. For example, impressions in sand, soft soil, or snow are usually collected as casts. For imprints under certain surface conditions, experts will try to collect the entire area containing the imprint. As with all evidence, the impressions and imprints must be properly documented and preserved for further examination in the lab (for more about collecting latent prints for study in the lab, see the chapter "In the Crime Lab: Patent, Latent, and Plastic Prints").

FIREARMS IDENTIFICATION, BALLISTICS, AND TOOLMARK EVIDENCE

What is the difference between firearms identification and ballistics?

Firearms identification and ballistics are definitely different—although they have often been (incorrectly) used interchangeably. Firearms identification is the study of determining whether a bullet, cartridge case, or other ammunition component has been fired by a certain firearm, especially at the scene of a crime. Ballistics is the scientific study of projectiles in motion. Experts in firearms identification do often use ballistics in their evaluations, but it is only a part of their examination of the evidence. For instance, they may use ballistic principles when evaluating a firearm or fired bullets or need knowledge of terminal ballistics (for example, the effects of a projectile's impact on a target when the expert is recreating a shooting).

What types of firearms identification evidence are collected at a crime scene?

Several types of firearms identification evidence can be collected at a crime scene—from murders and armed robberies to burglaries and aggravated assaults. They include shotshell (or shotgun) casings, cartridge cases, bullets, and slugs. In particular, the specific characteristics of each type can often be used as evidence.

How are spent bullets used as evidence at a crime scene?

According to the Federal Bureau of Investigation (FBI) Laboratory Division, a fired bullet can be used as evidence at a crime scene. In particular, the physical characteristics of a bullet—such as its weight, caliber, and bullet design—are often used as evidence at a crime scene. The general rifling characteristics (or GRCs) are also often used to determine a connection between a fired bullet and a firearm: a microscopic examination of a fired bullet often shows the number, width, and direction of twist of the rifling grooves imparted on the bullet as it went through the firearm's barrel. (For more about how bullets from a specific firearm are examined in the crime lab, see the chapter "In the Crime Lab: Toolmarks, Firearms, and Ballistics.")

Can bullets, shell casings, wadding materials, or even bullet fragments be used as evidence at a crime scene?

Yes, firearms evidence at a crime scene often includes bullets, shell casings (or cartridge cases), wadding materials, and even bullet fragments. Each can often be collected and examined to possibly determine the type of firearm used, the gauge of the firearm, the manufacturer, and other factors involved in a crime scene (including whether the firearm was truly used in the crime).

Can the trajectory of a projectile be determined at a crime scene?

Yes, in some instances, experts at a crime scene can determine the trajectory of a projectile—but not always. Many times, the projectile trajectory evidence from the scene must be analyzed and interpreted at the crime lab. Another reason for the inability to detect the trajectory of a projectile is the contamination of the crime scene. For example, if a crime takes place in a crowd, the projectile location may

Criminal acts such as breaking and entering leave tell-tale signs of tools used during the crime. For example, a crowbar used to break down a door will leave certain characteristics that can often be used to identify the tool used.

have been walked on, knocked down, or trampled on, or the projectile may not be found or easily obtained, as it may be in an area that is not accessible. (For more about projectile trajectory examination in the crime lab, see the chapter "In the Crime Lab: Toolmarks, Firearms, and Ballistics.")

What toolmark evidence is often collected at a crime scene?

Toolmarks are the result of a criminal using certain tools in a crime, such as a forced entry to a house, store, or other structure. These types of illegal entries often leave behind marks that can often be used as evidence. In the majority of cases, no tools are alike—even if they are the same kind of tool made by the same manufacturer—as each tool carries certain characteristic markings from use or even as they were manufactured. Toolmarks at a crime scene are also often connected to firearms. In such a case, the minute impressions caused by a fired firearm on the casing and bullet inside the casing are analyzed to see if a match occurs. (For more about how toolmark evidence is examined in the lab, see the chapter "In the Crime Lab: Toolmarks, Firearms, and Ballistics.")

POWDER STIPPLING, POWDER TATTOOING, AND GUNSHOT RESIDUE (GSR)

What is a powder stippling and powder tattooing on a person or object at a crime scene?

Powder stippling is the small, hemorrhagic marks on a person's skin caused by the impact of gunpowder particles. When the particles are embedded in a person's skin with accompanying hemorrhagic marks, it is often referred to as powder tattooing (although it is rarely found on thicker-skin areas, such as the palms of the hands or soles of the feet). The particles are usually considered to be partially or unburned (or unconsumed) gunpowder. Stippling and tattooing can also be found on objects, causing small pits and defects in the item, but it is more commonly used in reference to a victim of a gunshot wound. (For more about powder stippling, powder tattooing, and crime victims, see the chapter "In the Crime Lab: Analyzing a Body.")

How does a firearm's cartridge (casing) capacity affect powder stippling?

A firearm's cartridge (or the casing that holds the bullet, primer, and gunpowder) can affect gunpowder stippling on people and objects. In particular, the greater the amount of powder in the casing (called powder load), the greater the chance of powder stippling.

Can an expert at a crime scene determine how close a firearm was to a person or object?

Under the right conditions, it is often possible to determine how close a firearm was fired at a person or object. For example, sometimes, an expert can tell how close the firearm was to the target based on the characteristics of a person's wound (for more about wounds and firearms, see the chapter "In the Crime Lab: Analyzing a Body"); it also helps if other evidence exists that can help the expert determine distances, but sometimes, it is difficult to determine just how close the muzzle of the firearm was to the target because many factors and variables are at play. For example, if the firearm type was unknown—powder stippling is often related to a firearm's barrel length or powder in the cartridge—it would be difficult to determine distance from muzzle to target.

What are gunshot residue and shot patterns on objects at a crime scene?

Gunshot residue patterns are the deposits left on evidence such as clothing, furniture, bedding, and walls (wallboard, plaster, etc.) based on the distance between a firearm's muzzle to the material or target. To interpret the marks, an expert in gunshot residue patterns must understand how certain firearms and ammunition react in order to produce known-distance patterns and compare them to the gunshot residue found as evidence at a crime scene. A shot pattern is produced by the discharge of shot pellets (and/or shotshell wads) on such items as clothing, furniture, bedding, and walls depending on the distance between the firearm's muzzle and the target. Again, like the gunshot residue pattern, specific ammunition and firearms produce certain known-distance patterns and can be used to interpret shot patterns found as physical evidence on objects at a crime scene. (For more about gunshot residue, see the chapters "In the Crime Lab: Trace Evidence" and "In the Crime Lab: Toolmarks, Firearms, and Ballistics.")

GLASS EVIDENCE

Why is glass often considered trace evidence at a crime scene?

Glass at a crime scene can come from a multitude of places. For example, it can come from windows, drinking glasses, mirrors, eyeglasses, and bottles. Not only is the type of glass or how it shatters good trace evidence at a crime scene, but this knowledge is helpful also in other physical ways. For example, evidence of fingerprints is often easily imprinted on glass. If a person commits a crime and is cut by, for instance, a broken vase used to kill a victim, it can often leave DNA evidence on the vase—based on the victim's and suspect's blood, and glass can also indicate the direction a bullet or other projectile came from by the fracture patterns in the glass. (For more about glass analysis in the lab, see the chapter "In the Crime Lab: Trace Evidence.")

What is glass?

Although glass comes in many types, in general, man-made glass is an inorganic product often made of a mix of mostly—around 70 percent—silica (silica dioxide, or what is commonly called sand or fused quartz), along with sodium carbonate (also called soda ash) and many types of impurities (for example, iron impurities in sand can impart a

Broken glass can provide clues as to weapons used, the direction from which a bullet was fired or bomb exploded, and force of impact.

greenish color to glass). It is heated to a very high temperature and cooled to form a solid piece of glass. Because glass is readily used for various purposes and in many places, it is often either damaged or destroyed at a crime scene or accident. If broken, it can also be evidence collected from an alleged perpetrator's clothes or even minute pieces from the person's hair. Thus, glass is often used as trace evidence.

How is fractured glass collected at a crime scene?

Like all pieces of physical evidence, glass must have special care taken when collecting it for evidence. Most crime scene technicians place glass fragments in paper bindles (special envelopes) and then in a sealed and labeled small box or even a film can. Larger pieces of glass can be put into larger sealed and labeled boxes with paper, cotton, or tissue to keep the glass in place and not risk further breakage.

How is common glass analyzed at a crime scene or accident in terms of fractures and breakage?

Glass found at a crime scene or accident is analyzed in several ways. In particular, depending on how a piece of glass was struck by an object—and depending on what the object is—certain types of glass will fracture in a certain way. For example, radial fractures in glass are cracks that extend outward resembling the spokes of a wheel, whereas concentric fractures connect the radial cracks in a pattern that resemble a spider's web. Another type of fracture is called conchoidal fracturing, in which the broken glass fragment

83

has an area that looks like part of a shell. These types of fractures are part of what is analyzed to determine, for example, the entry and exit of a bullet in glass from a crime scene.

How is the direction of a bullet that hit glass determined?

Some of the most well-known fractures are seen when a bullet goes through a piece of glass, creating several patterns, including radial and conchoidal fractures. A great deal of information is needed to interpret where the bullet originated. For example, when a crime scene technician looks at a radial pattern in glass, they often use the "4R rule" to determine the way the bullet struck the glass—or "Ridge lines on Radical fractures are at Right angles to the Rear." Others also use the "3R rule" or "Radial cracks form a Right angle on the Reverse side of the force." Either way, the direction that the bullet came from is revealed by where these radial lines are found in the glass. Crime scene technicians also need to check out conchoidal fractures, which are almost parallel to the side in which the projectile was fired from—or where the force was applied. The side of the glass opposite the force is called the rear of the glass and is the side in which the conchoidal fractures lie at right angles. The continued force of the bullet's impact causes tension on the front surface of the glass, resulting in concentric crack patterns, but because so many different types of glass—such as tempered glass—exist, not all glass will crack in the same way or at all.

DEALING WITH EXPLOSIVES AND HAZARDS

How are explosives investigated at a scene?

If law enforcement is called to investigate an explosion, they must first make sure the area is safe before they examine the area. This means making sure that no dangerous structural damage has occurred (if a blast is inside or near a building) and that no dangerous chemicals (flammable or toxic substances) or dangerous materials (such as glass or metal that would harm the inspecting officials) are present. If the area is deemed safe, it will be searched for possible additional explosives. In most cases, this is done by trained members of a bomb squad who wear specialized protective clothing. If no other explosives are found, investigators then seek characteristic explosive damages—to make sure an explosion has actually occurred and whether it was intentional or an accident. This includes examining such features as an explosion crater, types of melting caused by the heat of the explosion, and fragments from the explosive. (For more about explosion investigations, see the chapter "In the Crime Lab: Examining Explosives.")

What are hazardous materials?

A hazardous material is defined as a substance or material that can immediately or eventually adversely affect public safety, law officers, or handlers or carriers during transportation of such materials. In order to deal with such hazards—including at certain

> ## What is the HazMat garment worn by some crime scene technicians?
>
>  HazMat (Hazardous Material) garments or suits (sometimes called biohazard suits) are often worn by crime scene technicians, especially those involved in the removal of harmful materials. The suits cover the entire body (including boots and gloves) and are made of an impermeable material. The suit also covers the head area, and it often has a self-contained breathing apparatus, cloth mask, or gas mask, depending on the task.

crime scenes—some police and/or fire departments have special HazMat teams or units, for example, called a Hazardous Materials Unit or Hazardous Materials Response Team. These workers remove and identify such hazardous materials as asbestos, lead, radioactive waste, and other materials (such as flammable, toxic, or corrosive items) that can have an affect on public and law-enforcement health in the surrounding area (including at a crime or accident scene).

SECURING THE EVIDENCE

What is an evidence locker or room?

In order to record and store evidence, many law-enforcement agencies have an evidence locker, room (smaller agencies may even have a dedicated closet for evidence), or rooms (some larger cities often have warehouses). The room or locker is usually secured by a lock and key, with the evidence custodian having control over the locker or room. In general, when evidence is delivered by a law-enforcement person, each item is recorded and described (in terms of evidence) with the item and record placed in a locker (in law enforcement, evidence can be delivered at any hour of any day). When the evidence custodian is there, he or she opens the locker, removes the evidence to a suitable place (such as a drawer or shelf), and logs in where the item was stored.

How is evidence obtained by officials from the evidence locker or room?

The evidence can be signed out by official personnel in order to go to the crime lab or to the court as evidence in a trial, but the official must have a legitimate reason for obtaining the item or items. Not only does the person need to be involved in the case connected to the evidence, but if for court, they must have a *subpoena duces tecum*, or that the person getting the evidence must appear in court with the item or items. If the evidence was going to the crime lab, it must be officially obtained by a person from the lab who receives and transports the item or items.

85

IN THE CRIME LAB:
ANALYZING A BODY

(*Note*: The analysis/autopsy of a deceased person is broken into two chapters—a more recent death and a longer time since death—although many overlaps occur in both scenarios.)

THE CRIME LAB

Do crime labs come in various types?

Yes, different types of crime labs exist. For example, they can be divided into local, state, federal, and international crime labs, each taking on various types of tasks, especially in the analysis of criminal evidence. In general, forensic laboratories have separate and distinct laboratories within the overall lab—each with its own space, specialized equipment, and function depending on the specialization. For example, such labs often have biology, chemistry, and toxicology sections to analyze evidence.

What are the various types of microscopes used in a crime lab?

Contrary to what a person sees on television or the movies, many more types of microscopes exist than the "standard" ones used in the media or even those used by students in a high school lab. For example, when examining physical evidence in a lab—for a crime, accident, or other event—one of the standards is the use of light microscopy. This includes a stereomicroscope, compound microscope, or a comparison microscope. If more detailed analysis is needed, such as to identify certain samples and compare them to reference samples, other types of microscopy are used, such as polarized light microscopy. (For more about these types of microscopy and other instruments, see the various analyses within this chapter.)

THE AUTOPSY IN GENERAL

What is an autopsy?

An autopsy, or postmortem (after-death) examination, systematically and carefully looks at the details of a body after the person has died. The main reason for an autopsy is to determine, if possible, the cause of death. In the case of no crime, pathologists look at a body to determine how a person died, such as heart failure, complications from certain diseases, or trauma from an accident. In the case of a crime, an autopsy is carried out by several experts, including forensic pathologists, toxicologists, and, for older remains, a forensic anthropologist (for more about examining older skeletal remains, see the chapter "In the Crime Lab: Analyzing Older Remains"). Autopsies are often thought of as definite proof as to the cause of death (in the majority of cases, that is, as sometimes the cause is difficult to discern), but it does not always reveal how the death occurred. If so, an autopsy can still potentially provide information and possible evidence that may eventually lead to an understanding of how a death occurred.

When did the first recorded human autopsies take place?

The term "autopsy" comes from the Greek words *auto* and *opsis*, or, literally, "to see for oneself." In general, it is considered to be the examination—inside and out—of a deceased person to understand how and why that person died. Although the Egyptians

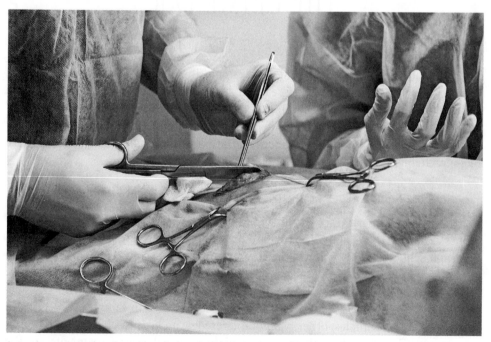

Autopsies are typically only performed when there is a question as to how the person passed away, especially if they died under suspicious circumstances.

practiced mummification (removal and examination of internal human organs) roughly five thousand years ago, it is thought that Greek physicians and anatomists Erasistratus (c. 304–250 B.C.E.) and Herophilus (c. 335–280 B.C.E.) from Alexandria were the first to conduct and record autopsies.

What were some early ways used to internally examine a deceased person?

For centuries, most physicians examined a deceased person's internal organs and tissues using invasive techniques. In addition, some would examine the deceased's prior symptoms as the basis for a diagnosis, but oftentimes, the diagnosis was flawed because the internal organ and tissue observations and/or the pre-death symptoms were misinterpreted. Some positive ways existed of examining human remains, though. For example, Dutch microcopist and scientist Anton van Leeuwenhoek (1632–1723) greatly improved the capability of the microscope (although he did not invent the instrument). His expert skill in grinding lenses achieved a magnification of 270 times, which was far greater than any other microscope of the era. Thus, he was able to observe bacteria, striations in muscles, and blood cells, which was often useful when conducting autopsies, but it took until the end of the nineteenth century before a noninvasive technique was developed to examine a body: the x-ray. By the twentieth century, significant advances had occurred in medical imaging in order to analyze internal tissues and organs, including the familiar-to-most magnetic resonance imaging (MRI) and computerized tomography (CT) scans.

What is a morgue?

In general, a morgue (often also called a mortuary) is a place where dead people's bodies are taken and kept, especially those from a crime or accident scene. The bodies are kept in essentially a refrigerated area to prevent decomposition, pending identification or claim (usually by family or friends), or awaiting an autopsy or burial.

Who is Giovanni Morgagni?

Giovanni Battista Morgagni

Italian physician and anatomist Giovanni Battista Morgagni (1682–1771) is credited as the founder of modern pathological anatomy. Unlike others before him, he emphasized the scientific study of the relationship between clinical signs and postmortem discoveries of a person in a very systematic and comprehensive way. He wrote several books on the subject, including in 1761 (translated from the Latin in 1769) *Of the Seats and Causes of Diseases Investigated through Anatomy*, which included the records of some seven hundred postmortem examinations.

What experts are most likely called in to do an autopsy?

Depending on the state or jurisdiction, experts most likely to conduct an autopsy include a forensic pathologist, coroner, or medical examiner. In fact, most of these positions are interchangeable. For example, a forensic pathologist is often the city, state, or county medical examiner, and in most cases, a forensic pathologist does autopsies in a crime lab.

In the case of homicide, can an autopsy reveal anything about the crime?

Sometimes, an autopsy can reveal something about a crime. For example, if the victim is stabbed with a knife, the forensic expert, depending on how the knife entered the body, may be able to tell if the perpetrator was left- or right-handed, short or tall, or heavy or light. If certain contusions or cuts are visible on the victim, the forensic expert may be able to tell whether the person was unaware of their attacker or if they fought to defend themself.

What specimens are looked at during an autopsy?

In most autopsies, vital organs and/or body fluids are often collected and analyzed chemically, microscopically, and with certain special instruments (if applicable). In addition, major organs such as the brain and heart may be retained after the autopsy for further diagnostic tests (although in some states, a family or next of kin who received the body after the autopsy may request the return of any collected specimens, but this is often a legal matter that varies between states and local jurisdictions).

What cases always require an autopsy?

Although some states differ, some cases generally always require an autopsy to understand the manner and cause of death. The following lists some of those reasons for an autopsy, in this case, as per the Indiana State Coroners Training Board:

- Drivers in a single car accident.
- Fire deaths, especially when the body is altered by fire or the carbon monoxide saturation is below 20 percent.
- Apparent suicides that are without clear evidence of intent, for example, a suicide without a note.
- When no one witnesses an "accident" (that may not truly be an accident) and accidents in which natural disease cannot be ruled out as a factor.
- Pilots involved in aircraft accidents.
- Homicides or any case in which another person may factor into the death of the victim.
- Deaths of persons in official custody.
- Sudden, unexpected deaths of children, especially if they are under two years of age.

What are some examples of when an autopsy is conducted that are not connected to a crime scene?

Several conditions occur in which an autopsy is conducted, including if the death resulted from disease, injury, or a combination of both—but not necessarily tied to a crime scene. For example, if the death was caused by chemical agents, an autopsy will give clues as to the effects of such agents on vital organs. Or, if the death is from physical injuries, such as a car accident, the results of the autopsy may help to reconstruct the fatal incident.

What if someone (such as a family member) objects to an autopsy?

The regulations behind autopsies vary, and it usually depends on the local or state laws and regulations. Someone might object to an autopsy being performed on someone they know for several reasons. For example, some people may have a religious objection (such as certain followers of Judaism, Christian Science, Jehovah's Witnesses, or Seventh Day Adventists). Certain objections are honored, but others, depending on the jurisdiction and/or state or local regulations, may supersede the objections. For example, if the autopsy is required by law, in some jurisdictions, the medical examiner or coroner can legally allow the autopsy without the consent of the person's next of kin, while if it is not required by law, the family must give their consent to perform the autopsy.

What is a postmortem interval?

Simply put, a postmortem interval is the amount of time that has passed since a person has died. If the time is not known, it is usually up to forensic analysts—from pathologists to entomologists—to estimate the time of death, whether it is hours, days, weeks, or months. Forensic scientists usually analyze a body at the crime scene and in the lab to determine the time of death. They use a number of analytical techniques to determine the time of death, for example, by noting the level of decomposition of the body when conducting an autopsy.

Why are forensic pathologists needed in forensics?

Pathology is the study of the nature, cause, and origin of various diseases (from the Greek *pathos* or "suffering" or "experience," and *ology* or "the study of"). In forensics, pathology is a medical specialty applied to the legal needs of society—most often determining why and how a person died in an accident or at a crime scene. Most forensic pathologists are involved in analyzing a deceased person by performing an autopsy, especially when investigating a crime or a suspicious or unusual death.

How does a forensic pathologist interpret cause, manner, and mechanism of death through an autopsy?

In most cases, forensic pathologists produce evidence that will be useful to the criminal justice system (for example, for a trial) and for public health and safety. In order to

Do forensic experts who examine human remains need to know anatomy?

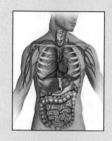

Yes, for the most part, forensic experts who examine human remains benefit greatly from the study of anatomy, or the study of a person's (or any animal's) internal structure or any of their parts (the major organs, tissues, and cells), along with how the parts are organized within the body. For example, anatomy can be generally divided into macroscopic, or gross, anatomy (not requiring a microscope) and microscopic anatomy. Gross anatomy includes the subdivisions of regional anatomy, systemic anatomy, developmental anatomy, clinical anatomy, and comparative anatomy—all of use to the forensic field, especially experts conducting an autopsy. Regional anatomy studies specific regions of the body, such as the head and neck or lower and upper limbs. Systemic anatomy studies different body systems, such as the digestive system and reproductive system. Developmental anatomy describes the changes that occur from conception through physical maturity (for example, helpful in deciding the average age of a person's remains). Clinical anatomy includes medical anatomy (anatomical features that change during illness) and radiographic anatomy (anatomical structures seen using various imaging techniques). Comparative anatomy examines the similarities and differences between structures and organizations of organisms (which can help when looking at remains that may be from another animal and not a human).

do this, they commonly want to determine a victim's (for example, from a crime scene) or person's (for example, from a car accident) cause, manner, and mechanism of death. For example, if a driver dies in a single vehicle automobile accident, the autopsy may show that the driver had a high blood alcohol level and that he or she had been pierced by a piece of metal in the chest. Thus, the cause of death would be trauma to the chest and the mechanism would be heart failure because of the metal piece piercing the heart, with the alcohol intoxication as a contributing factor. In most jurisdictions, the manner of death in this case would be considered an accident.

Do forensic pathologists work in other places besides a crime lab?

Yes, other than crime labs, forensic pathologists—who are also licensed medical doctors and usually board certified in their profession—often work in various places. These places include hospitals; commercial, private, and academic research laboratories; federal government agencies; and medical schools. (For more about forensic pathology, including careers, see the chapter "Resources in Forensic Science.")

What is the procedure while conducting an autopsy?

Although no two forensic pathologists work the same way, some commonalities exist when it comes to performing an autopsy. In general, several protocols are followed for an autopsy, including the following:

- Detailed notes of the dates, time, location, etc., before performing the autopsy.
- Known information about the deceased, such as age, race, and sex, along with descriptions of how and where the body was found.
- An external examination of the body, including the victim's clothing and valuables; body weight and length; stage of mortis; and general conditions of the body (such as hair color, scars, or injuries noted).
- Victim identification, for example, facial features, fingerprints, dental conditions, and even x-rays if necessary.
- Internal examination of the body, including a description of the body's organs and tissues, along with any wounds or injuries.
- Obtain certain samples and specimens, including blood or urine for analysis (usually by a toxicologist), fingernail scrapings, vaginal or anal swabs, and/or hair samples. It can also include the collection of nonbiological samples, such as bullet fragments, gun residue, or unexplained stains on clothing.

How long does an autopsy typically take?

According to most resources, autopsies usually take two to four hours to perform. This, of course, depends on the condition of the body or the circumstances. The first results of an autopsy are usually released within twenty-four hours, but the full results can take up to six weeks to prepare and deliver to the proper authorities, including those results

What was one of the most dangerous autopsies ever performed?

One of the most dangerous autopsies ever performed was on Russian Federal Security Service (FSB) and former KGB officer (the secret service that came before the FSB) Alexander Litvinenko (1962–2006), who was involved in organized crime investigations in Russia. He fled to England in 2000 and eventually became a British citizen. In 2006, he died of what was thought to be possible radiation poisoning. An autopsy took place, with the pathologists wearing white suits, protective gloves, and special hoods that allowed air to be filtered through a pump during the procedure. The result was acute radiation from active radionucleotide polonium-210, which was apparently slipped into his tea (and thought to be the first time this poison was used in this way) at a London restaurant. To this day, and thanks to political discourse, no one truly knows why or who poisoned him.

from a crime scene investigation. In addition, a toxicology report result can take up to two to four weeks.

Can the general public receive the result of an autopsy?

No, unlike many other public records, such as tax rolls, autopsy results cannot be readily obtained by the general public. The only people who are allowed to receive the results are those who are legally entitled to obtain the information. In terms of the family, regulations (usually from the chief medical examiner's office) state that the results are only available to the surviving spouse or next of kin—but only after certain papers are signed and procedures carried out. Of course, such rules are not always followed, as the Internet often carries the result of autopsies conducted on some famous people, such as Marilyn Monroe. (For more about who receives autopsy results, see this chapter.)

How many organs are in the human body—and have the potential to be examined during an autopsy?

About seventy-eight organs are found in the human body, each one with a different function (or sometimes the same, as with two kidneys), size, and sometimes shape. The largest organ, with respect to its size and weight, is the skin. Not everyone has organs in the same place, either, which can make a forensic pathologist's job of determining the death of an autopsied person more challenging. For example, sometimes, organs such as the kidney may be located closer to the pelvis, or only one kidney may be present. These differences can be due to genetics, differences in the organ's cell growth, or even disease.

What tools are most often used to conduct an autopsy?

Numerous tools are used when conducting an autopsy—and some, such as certain knives, saws, and cutters, have been around for over a century. For example, many forensic pathologists use rib shears to open the body's chest cavity in order to examine most of the major organs under the rib cage. Scalpels are used for deeper cuts into tissue and

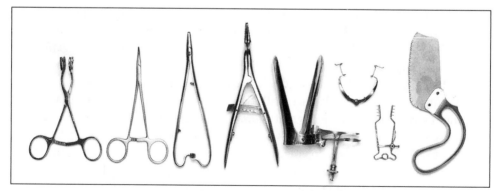

The surgical tools used in an autopsy are pretty much the same as you would see in other operations, including forceps, rib spreaders, saws, and various knives.

come in various sizes. Toothed and regular forceps can be used to grip, lift, and hold back tissue while conducting the autopsy, which also come in various sizes depending on the use. Bone saws are perhaps one of the oldest-style tools used during an autopsy and can come in various sizes and be manual or electric.

Are any photos, videos, or audio taken during an autopsy?

Yes, in many cases, a combination of photos, videos, and audio examination notes are taken during an autopsy. This usually ensures not only accuracy in terms of the examination of the body but also can be used (in some incidences) as evidence—especially if the person is a victim of a crime and the case goes to court.

What are some instruments often used to analyze a body in a crime lab?

Many instruments are used in a crime lab to analyze a body—and all depend on the evidence being investigated. For example, computerized tomography (CT) is taking x-ray images of a body from different angles, along with certain computer processing techniques that create cross-sectional images of the body. Magnetic resonance imaging (MRI) scans a person using a strong magnetic field (actually a large magnet) and radio waves to image structures, tissues, and organs of the body. Also, such instruments exist as a gas chromatograph/mass spectrometer (GC/MS), which is often used to separate and identify the chemical components of drugs in a victim's system.

Why was a virtual autopsy recently in the news?

In March 2016, Otto F. Warmbier (1994–2017), an undergraduate at the University of Virginia, was convicted of stealing a propaganda poster while on a trip to North Korea. He was sentenced to fifteen years of hard labor but in June 2017 was flown back to the United States in a vegetative state. By his parents' request, no full autopsy was done, so a virtual autopsy took place at the coroner's office in Hamilton County, Ohio, using a whole-body computerized tomography (CT, or x-ray images from different angles, along with certain computer programs that create cross-sectional images of the body) and magnetic resonance imaging (MRI) scans, along with an examination of the body. (Brain scans were taken in North Korea in April and July 2016 and sent with Warmbier when he returned to the United States.) The virtual images showed that he had extensive brain damage from interrupted blood flow—a medical diagnosis of anoxic-ischemic encephalopathy. In other words, if a person's brain is starved of oxygen for around six minutes (some say four minutes) or more, a large number of brain cells die. As of this writing, no external cause for the lack of oxygen has been determined—and only speculation remains as to how or why Warmbier was in his condition when he arrived back in the United States. Warmbier died on June 19, 2017.

What is a virtual autopsy or virtopsy?

Although not used as extensively as a "standard" practice during an autopsy, a virtual autopsy, also called virtopsy, is often used to add information about the deceased to an autopsy report. Such methods employ imaging techniques such as computer tomography (CT), magnetic resonance imaging (MRI), and so on to help uncover the cause of a person's death. Some of the reasons for the use of virtopsy include that it often helps for a better diagnosis, it can examine the entire body in a shorter period than a standard autopsy, and three-dimensional images can allow experts to sometimes see smaller details within the body's tissues. It can also be used (if applicable) when the person's family or guardian has objections to an autopsy for religious or cultural reasons.

What samples during an autopsy are recommended depending on a certain type of death?

When determining a certain type of death, some body samples could be tested to better prove how a person died. Oftentimes, the forensic pathologist will examine blood, urine, bile, fluid in the eye (vitreous humor), and/or samples of the brain, liver, or kidneys (a chemical analysis is done on these organs to look for drugs, medications, alcohol, and/or poisons) to determine the cause of death. The following lists the (possible or probable) causes of death and the general recommended samples to be taken during an autopsy that may help uncover the cause of death (based on several references; for more about such samples and testing, see throughout this chapter):

Determining Cause of Death

Cause of Death	Samples to Collect and Test
Homicides or Suspicious Deaths	blood, urine, vitreous humor, gastric contents, bile, hair, and liver tests
Drug Death	blood, urine (although for these, their interpretation requires some qualifications; see this chapter), hair, bile, liver, and vitreous humor
Poisoning (heavy metals; poisons)	blood, urine, hair, liver, vitreous humor, kidneys
Suicides (can also apply to traffic and industrial accidents)	blood, urine, vitreous humor, liver

Can a crime victim's death be masked by burning the body?

A victim's death is sometimes masked by burning the body at a crime scene, but not often. In some cases, finding evidence is difficult because the incineration heat destroys evidence on a body. It is also sometimes difficult to determine whether the burning came before or after a person's death. The true cause of death—either from burning or other reasons, such as a homicide—can usually be determined not only from an autopsy but also evidence from the scene and laboratory analysis of various other biomaterials found at the scene. For instance, burning a body at a crime scene usually does not mean it won't be identified. This is because even when a body is cremated, large pieces of bone are still left—and a burning car, house, etc., does not reach as high a temperature as a cremation. Thus, forensic pathologists may be able to determine certain information about the burned human remains to use as evidence in a crime.

Can a forensic pathologist determine whether a person has died from drowning?

Drowning is considered a form of asphyxia caused by fluid in the air passages when a person is submerged in water or other liquid. Certain characteristics help to determine whether a person has died from the drowning itself, and, most of the time, a drowning diagnosis is a matter of exclusion—or that all other causes of death have been ruled out based on an autopsy and/or toxicology tests. It is still sometimes difficult to determine, as some indications are minimal or no indication is apparent of a drowning. According to several references, some possible indicators can be used to determine whether the person died from drowning. These include a fine, white (some mention bloody, too) froth at the mouth and nose; vegetation or small stones grasped in the person's hands; fine froth in the lungs and airways; the presence of small, aquatic organisms called diatoms, a form of algae, in the person's tissues (when entering the water, only a living person can transport such organisms throughout the body); and water in the stomach and intestines. Other findings are not as conclusive or reliable, such as the shriveling of the skin when a person is submerged in water for several hours (it forms whether the person died in the water or was in the water after death).

It can be challenging to determine whether a person died of drowning or simply asphyxiation, but some clues that point to drowning include water in the digestive system, the presence of water organisms, or froth in the airways, around the mouth or nose.

DETAILS OF AN AUTOPSY–BODY FLUIDS

What is forensic serology?

Forensic serology is the study of body fluids, including blood, semen, saliva, vomit, perspiration, fecal matter, etc.—all of which may be collected as evidence at a crime scene. In addition, other aspects of the body fluids may also be of interest to the forensic serologist, such as the DNA of a body fluid or even the analysis of a bloodstain on a wall. (For more about DNA and forensics, see the chapter "In the Crime Lab: DNA Analysis.")

Who was Karl Landsteiner?

Australian biologist and physician Karl Landsteiner (1868–1943) is often called the father of hematology, or the study of blood. He was also known for his work on the immune system, polio, and allergy research. During Landsteiner's time, physicians realized that a person suffering from a loss of blood from an accident, ulcers, childbirth problems, wounds, or other trauma or disease needed their blood to be replaced, but the use of just any human blood did not work—the transfusion would often cause the blood to clot, often killing the person who needed the blood. Landsteiner discovered that people had different types of blood cells, and he devel-

Australian biologist Karl Landsteiner is considered the father of hematology.

oped the well-known idea of blood groups of A, B, AB, and O. This led to blood transfusions between people who had the same blood group. This idea also brought a new tool to forensic scientists: they could compare blood type evidence from a crime scene to the blood types of a suspect, victim, or others. (For more about blood at a crime scene, see the chapter "At the Crime Scene: Looking for Biological Evidence.")

What are the most common blood types in the United States?

Blood type is often necessary to know in the crime lab. For example, the victim may have a certain blood type, but blood found on their hands may differ in blood type—and it can possibly be the perpetrator's blood. Blood type is also often used to identify the deceased, especially if their blood type is rarer. The following table lists blood types and their rate of occurrence in the United States:

Blood Type Frequency in the United States

Blood Type	Frequency (U.S.)
O+	37.4%
O–	6.6%
A+	35.7%
A–	6.3%
B+	8.5%
B–	1.5%
AB+	2.4%
AB–	0.6%

German bacteriologist and immunologist Paul Theodor Uhlenhuth (1870–1957) helped further forensic analysis of blood. He is famous for developing the species antigen-antibody precipitin test, or the Uhlenhuth test, which allows blood analysts to distinguish between human and animal blood. The test is often important in determining events or what occurred at a crime scene, especially in terms of animals and humans.

What is the composition of blood?

Blood is classified as a connective tissue because it has both fluid and solid (cells) components. The fluid is plasma, in which various plasma proteins and cells—or red blood cells, white blood cells, and platelets—are suspended in the watery base. Each one of these components can be important to an expert analyzing blood from various crime scene locations, such as a victim, on a suspect's clothes, or blood on a floor. (For more about blood at a crime scene, see the chapter "At the Crime Scene: Looking for Biological Evidence.")

How is a blood sample from a victim taken during an autopsy?

Forensic samples of blood are usually collected from what is called femoral sites, but under certain circumstances (such as a decomposed or burned body, where it is difficult to collect from a femoral site), it can also be gathered from the heart, central veins, and the subclavian vein (the larger veins on both sides of the body under the clavicle in the shoulders, neck, and arms). Overall, blood samples are more difficult to take from a dead person than from a live person. This is because a dead person has no blood pressure pushing blood through the veins—only gravity acting on the blood. (This is why cutting into the cadaver produces little in terms of blood, too.) In addition, it is difficult to determine whether the blood has enough quality to use for analysis. This is because, depending on where the blood is collected, certain areas of the body will have different concentrations of blood—which can change the overall aspect of that blood sample.

Why may blood alcohol content (BAC) from a victim during an autopsy blood test not be reliable?

Not all blood alcohol content (BAC) readings from a victim's blood tests are reliable. Under some environmental conditions, the fluids in the body can essentially ferment, for instance, if a body is not kept cool after death. The fermentation is caused by a number of reasons, including the naturally occurring bacteria, yeast, and fungi found in postmortem blood and/or if a person has a high blood glucose (sugar) level, such as a person with diabetes, at the time of death. In some instances, this can lead to a false positive blood alcohol reading, with some erroneous results indicating two times the legal limit of alcohol in the bloodstream. Such false readings can often be misinterpreted in certain criminal or accident cases. Most references indicate that more reliable tests result if the blood sample is taken within forty-eight hours of death and the samples are collected and stored correctly.

Can a urine sample be taken from a victim during an autopsy?

Yes, in most cases, a urine sample can be obtained from the bladder of a victim during an autopsy. This is usually done using a syringe to extract the urine from the bladder.

Do urine tests from an autopsy reveal drug use?

Sometimes a urine test from an autopsy can reveal drug use, but it usually means that a drug has been used a few days before and does not mean that the drug was in the body at the time of death. This is because urine is stored in the bladder for a period of time. Thus, it takes time for drugs to travel through a person's system and be excreted.

Why do forensic pathologists often check a victim's eyes during an autopsy?

Fluids checked during an autopsy are not just the obvious blood, urine, or gastric juices. It can also mean extracting the fluid from the eye called the vitreous humor (also seen as humour), or the gel-like substance in the inner eye between the retina and lens. Forensic pathologists often chemically analyze this fluid to test for such substances as toxins, drugs, and heavy metals, as it is relatively isolated from the blood or other fluids that can be affected by pooling or other changes in the body after death. In addition, it does not decompose as fast as some other fluids in a dead body, and, contrary to fictional stories or movies about the potassium levels in vitreous humor pinpointing the

exact time of death, this element can only give an estimate of the time of death (and recently, this has been a highly debated subject). This is because potassium is subject to many factors, including changes in the levels before and after a person dies, the person's age, and/or the surrounding temperature at death.

Can semen last on a victim's clothing after washing?

In most cases, semen stains on a victim's clothing are analyzed using chemical and DNA analysis, and according to a study done in 2015, semen stains on clothing could last for up to eight months—even if the clothing has been stored for several

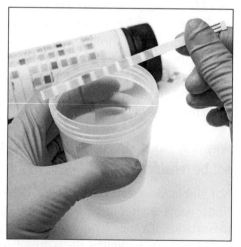

Urine tests can sometimes be used to determine if there were any drugs—legal or otherwise—in a person's system at the time of death.

months or washed multiple times—but according to other references, it is not often easy to determine semen on a victim's clothing after washing. For instance, finding semen on clothing that has been washed may depend on the type of detergent used, the temperature of the wash water, or how long the item has been immersed in water. In addition, washers are often used for multiple people, and some of the DNA samples may not be from semen but from other body fluids from different people. (For more about collecting semen as criminal evidence, see the chapter "At the Crime Scene: Looking for Biological Evidence.")

DETAILS OF AN AUTOPSY—GASTRIC JUICES AND BODY ORGANS

How and why would a pathologist obtain the stomach contents of a victim?

Similar to how forensic pathologists obtain other organs from the victim, the stomach contents are removed when the body's chest area (if possible) is cut open. In most cases, if the reason and time of the victim's death is known, little information can be gathered from the stomach contents, but if a question comes up as to whether a crime occurred (such as someone being forced to eat a toxic substance) or if the time of death is unknown, the stomach contents may (or may not) help answer some of those questions.

What can the gastrointestinal tract contents reveal about a victim before they died?

It is not only a victim's stomach the pathologist checks under certain circumstances—it is also the contents of the entire gastrointestinal tract. This includes digested and undigested material found throughout the entire tract, such as in the small and large intestines. The contents of the gastrointestinal tract can reveal several things about a victim before he or she died. For example, if they ingested a meal before death, that information may lead to the approximate time of death (if unknown) based on how much of the food was digested in the stomach and/or intestines. Or, if the person is a victim of a drug abuse, the actual drug may still be in the stomach, which may help determine the type of drug used or if the drug actually contributed to the death.

What affects the times from eating to excreting?

For a forensic pathologist, it is often necessary to know the times between eating and excreting, especially when doing an autopsy in which a victim's "time of death" is important and necessary evidence. In particular, the pathologist uses the knowledge that food moves through the digestive system at different speeds. This is dependent on many factors, such as gender, metabolism, the health of the person, if heavy or light foods (and how much) were ingested, and even the amount of water the person consumed. In addition, food is not eliminated in stools in the same order in which people ingest them. For example, vegetables are easier to digest than meat, so fibrous plants typically move through the large intestines much faster. All of these factors are taken into consideration when a pathologist is determining when a victim last ate food—and may indicate that person's approximate time of death.

Why do people debate how fast food travels through the human gastrointestinal tract?

Because so many variables exist when it comes to food traveling down the gastrointestinal tract, many researchers continue to debate just how to interpret this body's system, especially because it is often used to estimate the time of death of a crime or accident victim. Here are various views on the topic (that show how challenging an autopsy can be):

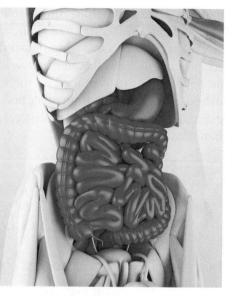

Food within the digestive tract can, surprisingly, also contribute to figuring out the time of death. Pathologists have to be knowledgable about how quickly different foods are digested.

- *Time eating to excreting*: This amount of time between eating and excreting varies depending on the study. This is mainly because of all the variables that affect digestion (see above). For example, some studies suggest that for a healthy human, the total time from eating to excreting is an average of fifty-three hours. Others suggest it can be between twenty-four and forty-four hours—and some even say twenty-four to seventy-two hours!

- *Stomach is full*: This is one analysis that almost everyone agrees on: If the forensic pathologist notes that the stomach is filled with food and the contents are hardly digested, it is usually assumed that the person died shortly after their last meal.

- *Time the stomach and small intestines take to empty*: Most studies indicate that it takes four to six hours (some say six to eight hours) for the stomach to empty its contents into the small intestines, and from there, it takes about twelve hours for food to leave the small intestine. Thus, if the victim's stomach is empty but food is in the small intestine, the person probably died four to six (or six to eight) hours after the last meal, and if the small intestine is empty, the death probably took place twelve or more hours after the person's last meal.

- *The last part of the digestive tract—the colon*: According to a study from the Mayo Clinic, the undigested remains of the digestion process stay in the large intestine (colon) an average of forty hours, though this varies significantly with gender. For women, it takes approximately forty-seven hours, while for men, it takes roughly thirty-three hours for food to pass through the colon.

> ## How does the volume of the stomach change from when it is empty to when it is full?
>
> On the average, an empty stomach has a volume of only 0.05 quarts (50 milliliters). A full stomach expands to contain 1 to 1.5 quarts (a little less than 1 to 1.5 liters) of food in the process of being digested.

How are drugs in the stomach found?

If drug abuse is thought to be involved in a crime scene or accident, the forensic pathologist can examine the deceased's stomach for possible clues. For example, the pathologist can analyze the stomach's gastric juices for trace elements that would be evident if the person had just ingested a potent drug. This can include a pill coating or cover if it has not yet been digested.

Why are the liver and kidneys of a deceased person often analyzed during an autopsy?

During an autopsy, a forensic pathologist and/or toxicologist may analyze the liver and kidneys for several reasons. This includes looking at possible poisoning (toxins can be detected in the liver), the ingestion or use of certain medications, and/or alcohol or drug abuse in connection with a crime or accident.

How else can a liver be damaged?

Not all liver damage found during an autopsy is caused by drugs, poisons, or trauma. It can also be caused by a variety of other methods. For example, excessive alcohol use damages the liver. Since the liver is the chief organ responsible for metabolizing alcohol, it is especially vulnerable to alcohol-related injury. This includes fatty liver (called steatosis; it is often associated with diabetes), alcoholic hepatitis (inflammation of the liver), and cirrhosis. When it comes to cirrhosis, it can be due not only from alcoholism but, in the United States, by hepatitis C; worldwide, hepatitis B is probably the most common cause of cirrhosis.

Why would a deceased person's brain be analyzed during an autopsy?

The human brain—with an average weight of about three pounds, or around 2 percent of a person's body weight—is very large compared to the average body size. (To compare, the human's closest relative, the chimpanzee, has relatively the same body size, but its brain is about one-third the size of a human.) In many cases, especially if drugs, toxins, or poisons are involved, the chemical analysis of a piece of a person's brain may show how much was in their system at the time of death.

What happens to an organ after a sample is extracted during an autopsy?

After a forensic pathologist extracts a small organ sample, it is put in a special container with preservative fluid until it can be further analyzed (or so it can be held as evidence). In some cases, the rest of the organ is placed in a biohazard bag that is held by a large, plastic container. If not, the organs—without the portions that have been saved for analysis or as evidence—can be put back into the body cavity. Sometimes, the organs are cremated without being returned to the body. What is done to the organs and body after the autopsy is usually governed by the jurisdiction in which the forensic lab is located and/or is based on the wishes of the deceased's family.

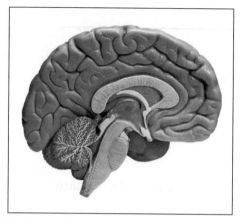

The brain can be particularly useful to find out whether any unusual chemicals were inside a body.

DETAILS OF AN AUTOPSY—TOXICOLOGY

What is forensic toxicology?

Forensic toxicologists use biological samples—especially from an autopsy—to determine the presence of such substances as toxins, poisons, alcohol, and drugs. At a crime or accident scene, these analyses are especially useful to determine whether the amount of such substances in a victim or suspect are therapeutic or at or over a harmful level. This information is often used by investigators who are attempting to put together evidence from a crime scene or accident. For example, after a fatal accident, such determinations can often suggest how the person died, whether they were ill, or whether the substance caused enough mental or physical impairment to cause the accident.

Who is called the "father of modern toxicology"?

Born in Spain and a naturalized citizen of France, toxicologist Mathieu Joseph Bonaventure Orfila (1787–1853) is often called the "father of modern toxicology." In 1813, he wrote, in two volumes, the *Traité des poisons, tirés des règnes minéral végétal et animal; ou toxicologie générale, considérée sous les rapports de la physiologie, de la pathologie et de la médécine légale,* translated into English as *A General System of Toxicology, or, a Treatise on Poisons, Drawn from the Mineral, Vegetable, and Animal Kingdoms, Considered as to their Relations with Physiology, Pathology and Medical Jurisprudence.* It was the first time anyone had published a scientific chemical analysis of poisons (in fact, some of Orfila's methods of analysis are still in use today). He became famous in his own time when, in 1840, he determined that Marie LaFarge had murdered her husband by repeatedly adding poison (arsenic) to his food.

What are some drugs and toxins that affect the ACh activity of the brain?

The human brain contains what are called synapses, or places in which certain types of cells communicate. Each synapse is associated with two cells, called the presynaptic (sends the message) and postsynaptic (receives the message) neurons—both of them involved in what is called acetylcholine (ACh) activity. However, drugs and toxins affect the ACh activity in many ways, some of which, if the drug or toxin is found in a victim in an autopsy, can indicate an overdose of the substance or that a person was given an excess of the drug or toxin. The chart below explains the various drugs and toxins and their effects on ACh activity:

Effects of Chemicals on ACh Activity

Drug or Toxin	Mechanism	Effects	Examples
Botulinus toxin (produced by *Clostridium botulinum*, a bacteria)	Inhibits and blocks ACh release	Paralyzes voluntary skeletal muscles	Used "therapeutically" such as with Botox in small doses to remove wrinkles
D-tubocurarine	Prevents ACh binding to post-synaptic receptor sites	Paralyzes voluntary muscles	Known as curare; used by certain South American tribes to paralyze their prey
Atropine	Prevents ACh binding to muscarinic postsynaptic receptor sites	Reduces heart rate and smooth muscle salivation; dilation of pupils; high doses produce skeletal muscle weakness	Used therapeutically by ophthalmologists to dilate pupils; may be used therapeutically to counteract the effects of anticholinesterase poisoning
Nicotine	Binds to nicotinic ACh receptor sites and stimulates the post-synaptic membrane	Low doses facilitate voluntary muscles; high doses can cause paralysis	Active ingredient in cigarette smoke
Black widow	Release of ACh	Produces intense muscular cramps and spasms	Spider venom
Neostigmine or phyostigmine	Prevents ACh inactivation by the enzyme cholinesterase	Extreme sustained contraction of skeletal muscles; effects on cardiac muscles, smooth muscles, and glands	Military nerve gases; an insecticide (malthion); used therapeutically to treat myasthenia gravis by inhibiting acetylcholinesterase, thereby increasing the usable amount of ACh; counteracts overdoses of tubocurarine

What is Botox?

Botox is the trade name for botulinum toxin type A, a protein produced by the bacterium *Clostridium botulinum*, the same toxin that causes botulism. In the past decade or so, Botox has been associated with anti-aging serums. This purified and sterilized botulinum toxin is converted to a form that can be injected under the skin primarily to smooth out wrinkled skin. It was first approved by the Food and Drug Administration (FDA) in 1989 to treat two eye muscle disorders (blepharospasm, or uncontrollable blinking, and strabismus, or misaligned eyes). It has only been recently that Botox has been used for cosmetic purposes. In small doses, Botox blocks nerve cells from releasing a chemical called acetylcholine, a compound that signals muscle contractions. By interfering with certain muscles' abilities to contract, a person's wrinkles appear to smooth out at the site and surrounding skin. The biggest problem with the toxin as an anti-aging serum is a possible allergic reaction. It is also one of the toxins that can be readily detected during an autopsy.

How are drugs analyzed in the crime lab?

Forensic toxicologists analyze the possible presence of drugs during an autopsy in several ways, especially in the case of a drug crime or drug overdose. For example, if powders, tablets, capsules, or other possible drug evidence is found in a person (for example, undigested in their stomach or mouth) during an autopsy, the substance can be chemically examined to determine the type of drug. This is commonly done using such instruments as a gas chromatograph/mass spectrometer (GC/MS) to separate and identify the chemical components of the drug. If a drug is suspected to have already entered a person's bloodstream, then various fluids can be collected and chemically analyzed from the body, such as blood, urine, and hair (and, less commonly, samples of the liver, kidneys, and brain).

What drugs are often routinely tested for in a postmortem autopsy?

So many drugs exist in the world and not all of them can be tested for in an autopsy, but because some are more commonly used and well-known, certain drugs are included in most routine toxicology examinations during an autopsy. For example, according to several forensic pathology references, those drugs include alcohol (chemically called ethanol); antidepressants (such as Selective Serotonin Reuptake Inhibitors [SSRIs, like Prozac®] or sertralines [like Zoloft®]); analgesics (such as tramadol or salicylates [like aspirin]); antihistamines, especially those that cause a person to become drowsy; benzodiazepines (diazepam [like Valium®], alprazolam [like Xanax®], etc.); cannabis (or marijuana); cocaine; antipsychotics (such as Haloperidol); cardiovascular drugs (propranolol [a beta blocker], diltiazem [calcium channel blockers], etc.); analgesics that are narcotics, too (codeine, fentanyl, oxycodone, morphine, etc.); and stimulants (am-

Marijuana (Cannabis) can be detected in the blood for two weeks after use, and it can be found in the urine for up to a month.

phetamine, methamphetamine, and even caffeine). Other drugs exist, of course, but they are not as readily used in an autopsy's toxicology tests unless needed as evidence, for example, designer drugs, barbiturates, or environmental toxins.

How long do traces of drugs last in the body?

Because drugs react differently in a person, no one set time period exists that a drug lasts in a person's body—living or dead. Here are a few well-known drugs and (generally) how long they can last in a *living* person's urine and/or blood:

- Cannabis—urine (seven to thirty days); blood (up to two weeks)
- Heroin—urine (three to four days); blood (up to twelve hours)
- Cocaine—urine (three to four days); blood (one to two days)

Who said "the dose makes the poison"?

Swiss physician, alchemist, and astrologer Paracelsus (born Theophrastus von Hohenheim, 1493–1541) is thought of as one of the first experts in toxicology. He also coined the phrase "the dose makes the poison," or the dose is the major reason why any substance is toxic or not—and just how harmful it can be to a living organism. (He gave himself the Latin name Paracelsus, which translated means "greater than Celsus," who was a famous early Roman physician.)

What was the Marsh Test?

British chemist James M. Marsh (1794–1846) developed the Marsh Test around the mid-1830s as a way of testing for arsenic in human tissue (arsenic at that time was readily used to poison people). The test used zinc and sulfuric acid to form arsine gas, which is highly sensitive and detects even a small amount of arsenic. This test is often considered the first time toxicology was used in a forensic capacity.

How can an autopsy reveal that a person was poisoned?

Poisoning may not be caused by another person or persons but for various other reasons. For example, the person may have

The seeds of the castor oil plant can be used to make a poison that kills people slowly over a period of two to three days.

been inhaling solvents such as butane lighter fluid, or what is often called "recreational" exposure to a poison. Or, a person can accidentally ingest a deadly plant, such as the leaves and flowers of a monkshood plant. Or, they may die from carbon monoxide poisoning because of accidental exposure to the fumes from a gas stove. Others may die of purposefully ingesting a poison, for instance, committing suicide with lethal poisons such as cyanide or arsenic. Overall, certain body fluids and parts can be analyzed during an autopsy to check for possible poisoning. For example, a forensic toxicologist can analyze the stomach contents, various fluids, and/or tissue samples from a body using various chemical tests to determine the poison—and possibly other facets of the person's death regarding the poison. (For more about poisons, see the chapter "In the Crime Lab: Analyzing Older Remains.")

What famous criminal case involved poisoning by ricin?

One of the most famous uses of ricin to poison a person was in London in 1978, during the Cold War. Bulgarian dissident and communist defector Georgi Markov (1929–1978) was killed with a poison dart filled with ricin—with the dart fired from an umbrella. While working for the BBC World Service, he was waiting at a bus stop on his way home when he felt a sharp jab in his thigh and saw a man picking up an umbrella. Four days later, after contracting a high fever, he died. The postmortem examination established that he had been killed by a small pellet containing 0.2 milligrams of ricin (they were able to discover the pellet, as it did not dissolve as expected in Markov's system). It was the third, and final, time someone had attempted to kill him—and the assassin was never found.

What is ricin?

Ricin is a naturally occurring, potent, highly toxic material from the seeds of a castor oil plant (*Ricinus communis*). It has been used for centuries to poison people with exposure by either ingesting or inhaling material containing the ricin (for example, as a powder) or using ricin itself. Less common is ricin poisoning caused by injection. According to the Centers for Disease Control and Prevention, ricin works by preventing the body's cells from making the proteins they need, causing the cells to die. It can cause death from thirty-six to seventy-two hours later, depending on how the person was exposed to the ricin.

DETAILS OF AN AUTOPSY—CONTUSIONS, BRUISES, AND GUNSHOT WOUNDS

What wounds or injuries do pathologists look for in an autopsy?

Pathologists try to interpret certain wounds or injuries when it comes to a victim of a trauma. Among these are injuries due to the following:

- Handgun or rifle
- Shotgun
- Blunt force instrument
- Fracture
- Stabbing, cutting, and penetrating instruments
- Asphyxia, hanging, strangling, or drowning
- Fire, burn, electrocution, or lightning
- Infant death, child abuse, or Sudden Infant Death Syndrome

What are bruises and contusions?

According to several medical references, a bruise (also often called a haematoma or an ecchymosis—or, more commonly, a "black-and-blue mark") is a collection of blood under the skin that is most often caused by blunt trauma, an impact, certain disease processes, or forming around certain types of wounds. Bruises are usually visible to the naked eye, as they damage or burst subsurface blood vessels with the blood collecting into the surrounding tissues (the skin is not broken). A contusion is most often used in reference to an internal trauma, but it is actually just another name for a more serious bruise. For forensic investigators, bruises (contusions) on victims or suspects can often provide information about the reconstruction of events at a crime or accident scene.

Where can bruising take place on the body?

Bruising can take place all over the body, but some places on the body bruise more (and, of course, it also depends on the intensity of the impact and the type of object impacting the body). For example, bruising occurs more often in places in which loose skin (or tissue) is, such as over the eyebrow. It also occurs where more fat tissue occurs under the skin; this is why women, who naturally have more fat than men, tend to bruise more easily than men. Age also tends to influence bruising, with the elderly and infants bruising more easily than at other ages.

How are bruises categorized?

During an autopsy, a bruise is usually categorized based on how the mark originated. For example, a tramline bruise is most often caused when a person is struck by a cylindrical object, such as a baseball bat. The mark appears as a pale, linear, central area surrounded on either side by linear bruising. Another type of bruise is the fingertip bruise. It is most often caused by a person roughly gripping another person. Such marks can be around the neck, on the arm, or almost anywhere on the body, especially in softer tissue areas. In most cases, they are either discrete marks, or they can blur into one another.

What is blunt force trauma?

One of the most common traumas encountered by forensic pathologists in an autopsy is called blunt force trauma—especially those caused by accidents and by some suicides and homicides. Such trauma may or may not be the cause of death, and it is up to the forensic pathologist to determine this, if possible, during the autopsy. For example, almost all transportation-accident deaths result from blunt force trauma. This includes motor vehicle collisions (with another car or a single-car accident, such as hitting a tree); airplane crashes; boating accidents (boat collisions or a person being hit by a boat); and pedestrians being struck by a vehicle (such as a hit-and-run). Other blunt force traumas are also evident if a person falls to their death from a great height (or not a great height because it is also dependent on the person and how they fell); being hit by a hard, solid object, such as a bat or even a fist; or injuries from a blast of almost any kind (the extent of the injury is dependent on how close the person was to the blast).

How do pathologists interpret a body's injuries caused by "pointed objects," such as a knife?

When a body has injuries caused by pointed objects (or even objects with sharp edges), they are referred to as sharp force injuries. Such injuries are not as common as blunt force traumas—nor are they as common as gunshot wounds, smothering or strangulation (asphyxial) methods, or drug toxicity (overdose). Sharp force injuries have certain characteristics, including a well-de-

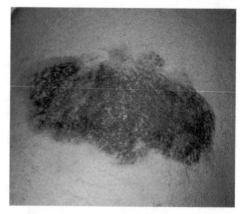

This is an example of a bruise caused by a blunt object striking a person's leg. Such bruises are quite commonly found in autopsies but are often the result of accidents.

> ## What is range shot or range of fire?
>
> **A**t a crime scene, the range shot or range of fire is the distance a shot is fired from muzzle to target. This often means between a victim and the person who shoots the victim.

fined separation of skin at the site on the body—in other words, a cut that separates skin tissue. Sharp force injuries are categorized into three common types: stab, incised, and chop wounds. Stab wounds are caused by sharp, pointed objects. In this case, the stabbing motion is more perpendicular to the skin (not parallel), with such wounds deep with a small opening. Incised injuries are also called cut wounds. They are caused by sharp-edged objects with the motion more parallel to the skin, causing a cut that is longer as opposed to deeper. A chop wound is thought of as a combination of sharp and blunt force injuries. It is caused mainly by a somewhat bulky object with an edge, causing a wound that is a cut and blunt force (usually forming a bruise) on the skin.

How are entrance wounds interpreted in an autopsy?

Entrance wounds are usually divided into four classes, depending on the range of fire. This includes distant or indeterminate range; intermediate or medium range; close range; and in contact with the person. Each one of these conditions results in a certain type of wound depending not only on distance but also on the type of firearm used.

Can stippling patterns of a gunshot wound on a person be used to determine the range of fire?

The stippling patterns of a gunshot wound can give forensic pathologists a general picture of how close the victim was to a fired firearm. Stippling usually occurs if the distance between the victim and muzzle is not at a close or far range, but overall, the actual distance varies according to the gun, and in most cases, the distance can be from a few inches to several feet. (For more about stippling, see the chapter "At the Crime Scene: Looking for Biological Evidence"; for more about firearms, see the chapter "In the Crime Lab: Toolmarks, Firearms, and Ballistics.")

How do shotgun wounds look depending on the range of fire?

Because shotgun ammunition contains numerous pellets, the wounds on a person would differ from other firearms, such as a pistol. If a victim was shot at close range or up to a few feet, the entrance wound would be round; if the victim was shot at a range between about 3 to 4 feet (1 to 1.3 meters), it would result in a large, central wound surrounded by smaller wounds (from the pellets), and as the range of fire increased, the central wound would be smaller, with many more pellet wounds surrounding the central wound as the pellets spread out before reaching the body.

111

Because shotguns use pellets as ammunition, a wound from such a weapon will look very different compared to a pistol, which shoots a bullet, or an AR-15, which shoots ammunition designed to completely destroy internal organs.

What does an exit wound look like on a victim?

In most cases, an exit wound would be more irregular in shape than an entry wound. In addition, the wound would not show any signs of stippling, soot or blackening of the edges, or a muzzle imprint. The characteristics of the wound would change if the skin was in contact with an object (such as against a wall) when the bullet exited.

What does a wound look like if a gun is fired against a victim's skin?

A wound can be interpreted in several ways during an autopsy, especially if a gun is fired against a victim's skin (this does not include rifles or shotguns). In general, if the muzzle is pressed against the skin when fired on a chest or abdomen (or areas that have relatively "loose" skin), a circular wound may occur, with the edges of the wound blackened and seared. If the muzzle is pressed against "tighter" skin, such as the top of the head, the entry wound may appear in several different ways. The wound may be circular, with the edges blackened and seared. It may be a star-shaped wound because of the tearing of the skin from the bullet's expanding gases (from the barrel). Or, it may be a round wound with a muzzle imprint (the gases cause the skin to press back against the gun, causing the imprint).

DETAILS OF AN AUTOPSY—BONES

What characteristics of bones do forensic pathologists use in an autopsy?

A forensic pathologist uses several characteristics of bones when conducting an autopsy. In particular, he or she needs to know the four major types of bones: long, short, flat, and irregular bones. The name of each type of bone reflects the shape of the bone, with the shape of the bone indicative of its mechanical function. Bones that do not fall into any of these categories are sesamoid bones and accessory bones. Knowing the characteristics of each bone type can help in several ways. For example, if the victim was shot, how and at what angle the bullet hit a certain bone may help to "reconstruct" the details of the crime, such as the distance from the firearm and in what direction the shot was fired.

How are the impacts of bullets in bone interpreted?

Various bones respond differently to the impact of bullets from firearms. For example, in the flat bones of the skull, an entrance wound will be round with sharp edges, with the path of the bullet producing a cone shape. Such wounds also cause numerous fractures in the skull because of the pressures of the bullet traveling through the bone.

How many pairs of ribs does an individual have?

Most individuals have twelve pairs of ribs that form the sides of the thoracic (upper) cavity. Approximately 5 percent of the population is born with at least one extra rib, or about 1 in 200 people. This extra rib, also known as a cervical rib, is considered a congenital condition. The upper seven pairs of ribs are true ribs and are attached directly to the sternum by cartilage. The lower five pairs of ribs are known as false ribs because they either attach indirectly to the sternum or do not attach to the sternum at all. The eighth, ninth, and tenth pairs of ribs attach to each other and then to the cartilage of the seventh pair of ribs. The eleventh and twelfth pairs of ribs are floating ribs because they only attach to the vertebral column and do not attach to the sternum at all.

How strong is bone?

Bone is one of the strongest materials found in nature. One cubic inch of bone can withstand loads of at least 19,000 pounds (8,626 kilograms), which is approximately the weight of five standard-size pickup trucks. This is roughly four times the strength of concrete. Bone's resistance to load is equal to that of aluminum and light steel. Ounce for ounce, bone is actually stronger than steel and reinforced concrete since steel bars of comparable size would weigh four or five times as much as bone.

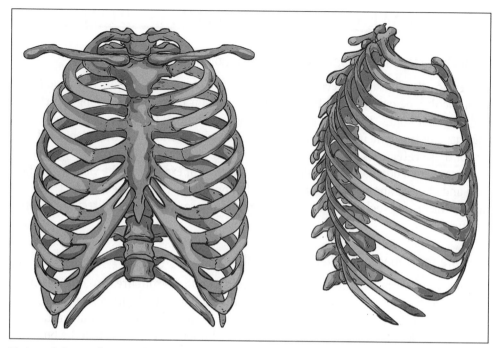

Most people have twelve pairs of ribs, but about one in every two hundred people have an extra set.

What are the most frequently fractured bones in the body?

Because of their vulnerable position and their relative thinness, the clavicles (also called collarbones) are the most frequently fractured bones in the body. The two bones run almost along the top of a person's shoulders on both sides and connect the arms with the rest of the body. Fractured clavicles are caused by either a direct blow (for example, during a fight) or a transmitted force resulting from a fall on the person's outstretched arm.

What does trauma to a person's spinal cord possibly indicate?

Injury to the spinal cord produces a period of sensory and motor paralysis termed spinal shock. The severity of the injury will determine how long the paralysis will last and whether permanent damage will occur. Many times, such traumas can be found by a forensic pathologist during an autopsy, and based on the type of injury, the expert may be able to determine how the person died (or didn't die) from the injury. The following lists some of the types of spinal injuries:

- *Spinal concussion* results in no visible damage to the spinal cord. The resulting spinal shock is temporary and may last for as short as a couple of hours and, thus, may not be known to the pathologists since little evidence exists of the trauma.

- *Spinal contusion* involves the white matter of the spinal cord being injured (bruised).

- *Spinal laceration* is caused by vertebral fragments or other foreign bodies penetrating the spinal cord.
- *Spinal compression* occurs when the spinal cord is squeezed or distorted within the vertebral canal.
- *Spinal transection* is the complete severing of the spinal cord.

DETAILS OF AN AUTOPSY—TEETH AND DENTAL RECORDS

What is forensic dentistry?

Forensic dentistry is also called forensic odontology (or the study of the structure and diseases of teeth). According to a recent article in the *Journal of Forensic Dental Sciences*, forensic odontology has traditionally been practiced mainly for human identification (for example, to identify victims of homicides or suspicious deaths, or accident victims) and/or injury analysis (for example, bite marks or broken teeth from an accident). Today, forensic odontology can also be used to contribute information for such issues as child abuse, domestic violence, human rights protection, insurance claims, and professional ethics, and in the case of an unidentified victim of a crime or accident victim, experts can compare human remains with dental records to determine a person's approximate age based on dentition and possibly identify that person. (For more about using teeth to identify skeletal remains, see the chapter "In the Crime Lab: Analyzing Older Remains.")

Why are physical and digital records important to forensic odontology?

Digital records and physical evidence from a person's dental examination can be of great use to a forensic odontologist in their investigation of a known or unknown victim of a crime or accident. A person's dental records may have various elements, including written notes, study models (casts and molds), referral letters, consultant reports (such as from an orthodontist), drug prescriptions, identification information, and medical history. More modern ways of keeping records also can contribute to an investigation, such as digital photographs, radiology, and digital x-rays. Such digital data takes up less space, is easier to preserve and document, and can be better disseminated to the authorities in a forensic investigation.

What is a human dental record comparison?

Human dental record comparison is just as the phrase sounds: available dental records compared to, for example, an unknown victim's teeth at a crime scene. In most cases, people have gone to the dentist and have dental x-rays. In addition, dentists also often have a person's record of which teeth have been filled or pulled, or other tooth-related factors, such as tooth implants or dental caries.

How are teeth analyzed by forensic odontologists—especially during an autopsy?

Three major types of teeth are analyzed by forensic odontologists when gathering information about a person—especially an unknown victim: incisors, cuspids (canines), and molars, with each type performing different functions. The incisors, located at the front of the mouth, are blade shaped and suited for clipping or cutting and are important to bite off pieces of food. Located next to the incisors are the cuspids or canines. Their characteristic pointed tips make them suitable for tearing, shearing, and shredding food. Both premolars (also called bicuspids) and molars have flattened crowns with prominent ridges and are essential for crushing and grinding food.

Each type of tooth is carefully analyzed by comparing them to dental records and/or by certain aspects of the person's teeth being autopsied. Dental records will have a report of the bridges, dentures (full or partial), or implants a person may have received in the past. The records will also indicate what teeth are still in the person's mouth or even which teeth have been filled, capped, or crowned. In addition, x-ray records will also indicate a certain aspect of a person's teeth and may tell something about their identity. For example, impacted wisdom teeth or bone loss are two dental problems that would show up in an x-ray and may help to identify a victim.

How do teeth indicate trauma experienced by a crime or accident victim?

Teeth can show trauma in a crime or accident victim in several different ways. For example, a person's front teeth in a car accident can be knocked out, or a tooth may be chipped during a crime scene fight. Tooth trauma can also be used to determine an unknown deceased victim at a crime or accident scene. For example, fragments of a single tooth can often be used to identify the victim as long as dental x-rays or digital records are available for comparison.

Can a person tamper with dental records?

As with many cases in this digital and computer-hacking world, dental records have been illegally altered at times. For example, it is often easy for people who know how to work with digital images or files to modify or adjust a dental record. They may make additions, remove various pieces of information, blend multiple images into a single one—or perform a combination of each. In some cases, a skilled forensic computer technician can determine that changes were made to the dental records (and if such alterations are done with malicious intent, it is usually called digital fraud).

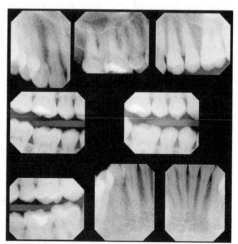

Like a set of fingerprints, everyone has a unique set of teeth, so dental records can be a great way of identifying a body, even one that has been subject to decay or fire.

What are antemortem and postmortem dental casts?

An antemortem (before-death) dental cast is a plasterlike cast of a living person's teeth. The casts are often made at a dentist's office if a person needs dental work, such as teeth straightened or a partial denture. A postmortem (after-death) dental cast is made from a deceased person's teeth or tooth fragments in order to help identify an unknown victim. The cast is often compared with existing dental records, such as x-rays (bite wing or panoramic) or records of fillings.

Are human and nonhuman teeth different?

Yes, human teeth and most nonhuman teeth are different—something that a forensic odontologist often has to determine when certain teeth (or even bite marks) are found at a crime or accident scene. Most differences depend on the animal's main diet and whether they need to chew, cut, grind, slice, or crush their foods. For example, animals that eat only plants have sharp incisors to bite off grass, reeds, leaves, and other plant material; they also have flat molars for grinding and crushing plant material so it is better digested in their specific digestive tract. Animals that eat meat usually have pointed incisors and very large canine teeth (dogs and cats come to mind), while their molars are rough and jagged to help them chew the flesh of other animals. For animals that eat plants and meat (omnivores such as bears and pigs), the teeth include modified versions of the canines and molars so they can eat both meat and plants—which is similar to human teeth, but differences still exist that help to identify human versus animal teeth. For example, human teeth are usually more rounded than other omnivores, and both have a different number and combination of tooth types.

Do some animals swallow food whole?

Yes, some animals swallow food whole out of necessity. For example, birds do not have teeth in the same sense as human teeth but have beaks that can pound, rip, or shred food before it is swallowed, and crocodiles, alligators, and most sharks don't chew but rip and tear, then swallow the big chunks whole. Overall, how an animal eats its food can be thought of as forensic evidence. For example, if a victim is found washed up on a beach, a forensic expert in sharks may be able to tell if a person died from a shark bite.

DETAILS OF AN AUTOPSY—BITE MARKS

What are bite marks?

Bite marks are just as the word implies—marks made by the bite of an animal or human. When forensic scientists analyze bites to a victim's skin during an autopsy, the expert interprets whether the marks are made by the teeth of humans or other animals.

What forensic experts study bite marks?

Scientists in the field of odontology (forensic dentistry) are most often experts in bite mark analysis. Overall, they compare known dental characteristics—often from available dental records—of an alleged perpetrator with the bite mark left on a victim (living or deceased).

In general, how do forensic odontologists interpret bite marks?

Overall, forensic odontologists interpret a victim's bite mark in several ways. Initially, they record the shape of the bite marks, such as oval or circular in shape. Then they classify the mark from seven categories. This includes a contusion (bite mark that causes a bruise), artifact (when a bite causes a piece of the body to be removed, such as a finger or earlobe), abrasion (a scrape from a bite), avulsion (skin removed from a bite), hemorrhage (profuse bleeding from a bite), incision (a clean wound from a bite), and laceration (a puncture wound from a bite). Degrees of a bite depend on how hard the perpetrator bites the victim—from a clear to vague impression. They may also collect samples, if applicable, of the perpetrator's saliva left at the bite mark (for possible DNA analysis).

Why do forensic experts look at bite marks?

When it comes to crime, bite marks found on victims are most often associated with murders, rape, torture, or abuse (of adult and children). For instance, a bite mark on a victim may be compared to a suspect who has dental injuries or tooth shapes that can be eventually matched to the bite. Animal bites may also be interpreted in the case of a crime. For example, certain bite marks may indicate that a person was bitten by a certain dog and, thus, the person may want to use the bite mark evidence to take legal action against the owner. However, not all bite marks are thought to be useful in terms of evidence, and many controversies have occurred surrounding the use of human bite marks in court. In response to these controversies (especially the accuracy of matching bite marks to a suspect), many organizations no longer support bite marks as evidence in court. (For more about the debates surrounding bite mark evidence, see the chapter "Controversies in Forensic Science.")

What instruments are used to evaluate bite marks on a victim?

Bite marks on a victim can be evaluated in many different ways using various technologies, including regular photography, digital imagery, and other types of light to

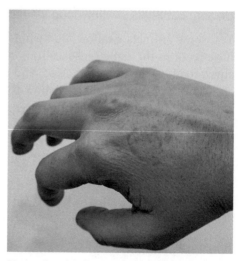

Bite marks might be on a victim or, perhaps, on a perpetrator who was bitten by their victim. Either way, bite impressions can also be used to identify people in a case.

> ## Can bite marks change over time?
>
> Yes, bite marks can change over time. For example, if a victim of a bite is deceased, their skin can literally droop after death as the body decays, making it difficult to interpret a bite mark. This is why, if the inspector at a crime scene suspects a bite mark on a recently deceased victim, a forensic dentist and crime photographer are immediately called in to examine and record the mark. This change, too, is another reason for the controversy surrounding using bite marks as evidence. (For more about the bite mark controversy, see the chapter "Controversies in Forensic Science.")

examine the bite mark(s). For example, they can be analyzed using a regular color photograph of the bite mark on a person's skin with an ultraviolet photograph, a transilluminated image, or using alternate light photograph (ALI). Each one of these types of images can reveal certain physical aspects of the person or animal that caused the bite.

DETAILS OF AN AUTOPSY—NAILS AND HAIR

How can experts use fingernails and toenails to help identify a crime victim?

Fingernails and toenails may help to identify an unknown crime or accident victim in several ways. For example, when comparing fingernails and toenails, toenails are approximately twice as thick as fingernails. Thus, if a nail is found near the body or if the victim fought off a suspect and a finger- or toenail is found on the alleged perpetrator, it could be used as evidence. Bumps or ridges on a finger- or toenail often indicate a previous injury to the nail, such as a blow (such as accidentally hitting the fingernail with a hammer). Or, an injury can occur due to the normal aging process, if a person has a certain disease (such as diabetes), or even if a person is malnourished. Some of these nail characteristics may have been recorded in a medical and/or criminal record and may aid in identifying a person.

What are fingernail scrapings?

Fingernail scrapings are just as the phrase sounds—scraping under a victim's fingernails (and sometimes toenails) for evidence, especially of a crime such as an assault. This is commonly done if the victim has abrasions or scratches on the body—most often the face, neck, arms, thighs, and, for females, the genital region—which usually means that they tried to fight off their attacker. Minute particles of skin, blood, hair, cosmetics, and/or even other body fluids can often be found under the fingernails, all of which can be used as evidence, for example, in a sexual assault or homicide case.

What can an analysis of a fingernail reveal about drugs?

A fingernail can often be used when determining if a person has used narcotics or marijuana, usually within the past three to six months. Drugs get into a person's bloodstream, which means it ends up in various places, including a person's fingernails (and hair, which is why hair is often used in drug testing). Thus, because it takes months (usually over six months) for a fingernail to grow out, if a sample of a person's fingernail tip is taken for a nail drug test, it will often reveal drug use during that time.

What is the best way to obtain fingernail scrapings as evidence?

Certain precautions are taken when collecting fingernail scrapings as evidence. At a crime scene, crime scene technicians taking under-the-fingernail evidence from a victim or suspect use scraping, clipping, or swabbing, with scraping being the most common. The person collecting the scraping never uses a knife, file, or anything hard or sharp, as it may cut the person, and blood would contaminate the evidence. The best collection method is often a wooden toothpick, using a different one for each finger. The evidence is then commonly put in a clean paper bindle, folded, and packaged in a suitable marked (indicating what finger the scraping came from) container or containers. From there, it is sent to the crime lab for analysis. Fingernail (and toenail) scrapings can also be taken during an autopsy. Such evidence is not only looked at in terms of com-

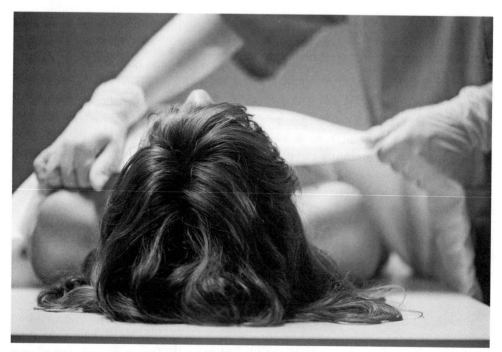

If illicit drugs or other chemicals have been ingested, strands of hair can preserve this evidence for about three months. The hair on a victim can also be compared with any hair found at the crime or accident scene.

Do a person's hair and nails continue to grow after death?

No. Between twelve and eighteen hours after death, the body begins to dry out. That causes the tips of the fingers and the skin of the face to shrink, creating the illusion that the nails and hair continue to grow after death.

---

position (blood, skin, etc.) but also may be checked using DNA analysis. (For more about DNA and forensics, see the chapter "In the Crime Lab: DNA Analysis.")

Why are hairs important in an autopsy?

The hair on a victim of a crime or accident can often be used for identification or comparison purposes (for example, if a hair is found on a victim, it may match a suspect's hair). In addition, if a victim's hair is torn out in any way, it may indicate that a struggle took place (which can be used as evidence against or for a suspect of the crime). Hairs can also be used to determine the presence of some drugs in a person's system. This is because hair takes a long time to grow and can hold evidence of drug abuse going back about three months. (For more about identifying hairs from the crime scene—human and otherwise—as evidence, see the chapter "In the Crime Lab: Trace Evidence," and for controversies surrounding hair as evidence, see the chapter "Controversies in Forensic Science.")

What are some differences between human and animal hair/fur?

Forensic pathologists often have knowledge of the major differences between human and animal hair in order to identify certain hairs that may be found on a victim. ("Fur" and "hair" are actually synonymous, but it is more common to refer to other animals' hairs as "fur.") Animal fur can have a banded appearance; untreated human hair never does. The diameter of an animal fur's inner core (medulla) is larger than half of the entire hair shaft, and they have different root shapes (animals look brushlike, whereas humans have a bulbous root). Animal fur also includes longer hairs in spots such as the tail, and most have whiskers (also thought of as "hair"). All these attributes can often distinguish a human hair from an animal fur, but it is often difficult to determine just what type of animal, as so many different variations occur among species.

AFTER THE AUTOPSY

Can a reason for death always be determined from an autopsy?

No, not every reason for death can be determined by an autopsy. Oftentimes, the body is too decomposed or burned to determine anything about the person or no records

121

(such as dental or fingerprints) are available to compare to the victim's particular physical characteristics. The results of such an autopsy are said to be "inconclusive."

Why is it important to identify an unidentified victim of a crime, suspicious death, or accident?

It is important to identify a victim of a crime, suspicious death, or accident for several reasons. Most importantly, it is vital to have an accurate identification for relatives and law enforcement, especially at a crime scene. In the case of relations, it is often a matter of needing to go through the grieving process for the individual, and especially, for many, knowing what happened to cause the death of their relative. On the legal side, until a person is identified, their estate cannot be settled, death benefits and insurance policies cannot be paid, and/or a spouse cannot remarry.

What happens to a crime scene victim's body after an autopsy?

No set "rules" are in place for after a crime scene victim's body has been autopsied, as it depends on the person, family, conditions, and legal jurisdiction rules. Some general things can happen to the body after an autopsy. For example, in some jurisdictions, after the autopsy, the pathologists put the organs in separate bags and place them in the body's chest cavity. Small pieces of organs are also collected for possible further examination, if needed. The incisions in the body are then closed. In some jurisdictions, the body is then embalmed (in case a second autopsy is needed, especially in a criminal case), or the body is eventually released to the deceased's family.

How long after death can an autopsy be performed?

An autopsy can be performed at any time that a body exists, which is why forensic pathologists are often involved in performing autopsies of older human remains (such as mass graves or decades-old remains). However, more information about a person can be obtained if their death is recent, especially within a few days. (Hospital autopsies mainly for medical reasons are usually performed within twenty-four hours.) This is because decomposition has not interfered as much with the body's tissues. In most instances, a body that has gone through embalming at a funeral home can still be autopsied, although the embalming process can interfere with most of the toxicology tests.

Who receives the data and conclusions from an autopsy?

In most states, autopsy results are held in the chief medical examiner's offices. Also in many states, the autopsy results are not supposed to be for the public to view but are available only to those who are legally entitled to receive the records. This is not always true, though, as some states make certain autopsy results available to the public after a time (usually a few months). This was evident recently, as autopsy reports have shown up on the Internet for such celebrities as Michael Jackson and Marilyn Monroe.

In general, if the autopsy is performed because it was an unattended death and no criminal activity is determined, the conclusions from the autopsy usually go to the deceased person's family—the surviving spouse, next of kin, or guardian. If a crime has been committed, the data and conclusions from the autopsy usually go to the coroner or medical examiner's office, where it is available for the criminal investigation (and possible use as evidence in a future trial). Of course, this all depends on the jurisdiction.

What is a death certificate?

A death certificate is the official and legal document that details the deceased person's death details. It includes the person's last known residence, their attending physician (if any), diseases they may have had, and how they died (if possible, including approximate time and location). It is signed by the coroner or medical examiner and usually the person's last attending physician. As usual, death certificate details all depend on the jurisdiction and therefore may vary between states or counties.

IN THE CRIME LAB: ANALYZING OLDER REMAINS

FORENSIC ANTHROPOLOGY AND ARCHEOLOGY

What is forensic anthropology?

Forensic anthropology uses certain anthropological techniques to analyze and understand skeletal remains. It also includes its own subfields, including osteology (study of bones) and the interpretation of the human skeleton to help at a crime or accident scene. Experts in this field can also have a background in excavating and mapping, which is useful at a crime or accident scene.

What are the differences between forensic anthropology and forensic archaeology?

Although it often seems confusing, subtle differences exist between forensic anthropology and forensic archaeology. Forensic anthropology is a subfield of physical anthropology and most often is used to make sense of an individual's remains or a collection of remains. (Physical anthropology studies human remains to determine details about past human societies and cultures.) It entails using the types of techniques, analysis, and often tools used in archaeology. Forensic archaeology (also seen as archeology) is the use of archaeological methods for medicolegal issues, including obtaining information about a specific ancient or historical person. In fact, forensic archaeology and anthropology both are intertwined—and, overall, use meticulous methods of recovering human remains. (Another field also exists called bioarchaeology, in which experts work with individual skeletal remains to understand that person's relationship to others within a certain population.)

How have the tasks of forensic archaeologists changed over the years?

Although forensic archaeology has not been around for long, it has changed in focus over time. For instance, according to several forensic references, in the 1970s and 1980s, forensic archaeologists were asked by crime scene investigators to help with certain crime scenes. Many aided in the location and excavation (along with keeping careful documentation of the excavation that archaeologists are trained to do) of missing persons and/or clandestine burials of murder victims. Over the next couple of decades, they became more actively involved in different types of investigations, especially the excavation of mass burial sites (such as victims of modern warfare) and the recovery of bodies from large-scale fatality events (such as airplane crashes, fire scenes, or even mass shootings). Today, they also assist in the same types of activities, helping with evidence search and recover, recording the scene of the event, and interpretation of the scene.

What is osteology?

Osteology is a branch of anatomy—and often is also considered a subset of anthropology and archaeology—that deals with the study of the skeleton (or bones). This includes bone structure (including features of the body's bones and problems with bones from disease or injury), resistance and hardness of bones, and the interpretation of bones in terms of age, gender, and death—all of which are often important to a forensic investigation of older remains.

ANCIENT BONES

What is paleoanthropology?

Paleoanthropology is similar to forensic anthropology, albeit examining more fossilized skeletal remains and ancient settlements to better understand certain cultures and early humans. Many paleoanthropologists study the origins of modern-day humans, constructing the human "family tree" based on ancient bones found in various places around the world, including possible DNA found in those bones. Such studies also include determining how certain early humans died (although it is not common to find a complete enough skeleton to determine an ancient human's manner of demise). For example, recently, experts in ancient human remains conducted a CT scan on the bones of "Lucy," an early ancient human ancestor whose fossilized skeleton was found in the Hadar area of central Ethiopia. (Her species may be a link between modern humans and tree-living human ancestors.) Based on the bone analysis—which found a compression fracture in her shoulder bones and several other broken bones—the researchers believe Lucy died 3.2 million years ago as a result of a catastrophic fall from a great height, probably from a tree.

Can the cause of death be determined for bodies buried over a hundred years ago?

Yes, in some cases, the cause of death can be determined for ancient human remains that have been buried for over a hundred years—or even millions of years. For example, a portion of a fossilized skull was recovered in Swartkrans, South Africa, and was determined to be around 1.5 million years old. The piece, probably from an adolescent of the

What did forensic anthropological analysis of Roman gladiator bones reveal about their diet?

According to a recent forensic anthropological analysis from the Medical University of Vienna, Roman gladiators ate a mostly vegetarian diet and also drank ashes as a tonic after they trained. Along with the Department of Anthropology at the Institute of Forensic Medicine at the University of Bern, forensic experts examined certain bones from a gladiator cemetery that dates back to the second or third century B.C.E. Once called Ephesos and now in modern Turkey, the site held both the bones of gladiators and residents of the Roman city. The differences were evident in the amount of strontium measured in both groups' bones, which is thought to show that the gladiators took in a higher amount of minerals from a strontium-rich source of calcium. Thus, the experts believe the stories of an ash-rich tonic are now true—a drink given to the gladiators to help after physical exertion and to aid bone healing.

Paranthropus robustus species, had two wounds caused by a pointed object. At first, it was thought that the wounds were the result of an attack by another humanoid, but upon further analysis, they were found to match the distance between the lower canine teeth of an African leopard.

Why are some bodies disinterred (dug up) for an autopsy?

Although not common, a body may be disinterred for an autopsy for several reasons (sometimes even if a preliminary autopsy occurred). For example, if an incorrect identification of the deceased occurred; more toxicology—or even DNA—information needs to be gathered; if some trace evidence was overlooked or missing; if something was thought to be misinterpreted during the autopsy; or if more information was needed in terms of wounds or fractures and breaks of bones. (For more about DNA and forensics, see the chapter "In the Crime Lab: DNA Analysis.")

EXAMINING HUMAN REMAINS

How fast do bodies decay if they are buried versus aboveground?

Overall, how fast a body decays depends on the surrounding conditions, including the weather, soil, pH and oxygen levels, and temperature, or if the person is buried or exposed to a certain climate. The following lists some of the overall factors that affect a decaying body above- and below ground:

- *Body is buried*—If the body is buried around six feet underground in ordinary soil (for example, in sand or hardpan), the body of an adult normally takes eight to twelve years to decompose to a skeleton. If it is buried in soil with a low pH—or is highly acidic—the body will decompose very rapidly and, over a long period of time, will not retain even the skeleton.

- *Body is aboveground*—If a dead person is on top of the ground and exposed to the elements, many factors control how fast a body decays. In general, it depends on how the body was left after death (for example, if the body was clothed or if air was lacking); the exposure to the surrounding environment (for example, if the body is exposed to sun, rain, or blowing sands, the remains can quickly wear away); the temperature (high, low, and ambient temperatures all cause the body to decay at different rates; for instance, a desert can cause the body to mummify); if any predators are in the area in which the body is located (for example, scavengers and predatory animals can greatly damage a body, including those animals that crush large bones [mainly for marrow] and scatter the bones, leaving them to the elements, which often means the body is unrecognizable in a short period, depending on how much damage is done); and insects (for example, insects vary depending on where a body is located, such as in the desert versus mountains). Plant growth can also affect how fast a body decays. For example, if it is in a location containing rapid and/or heavy vegetation growth, the body can not only be covered by the plants but also become part of the growth, hiding the victim from view. Thus, if the body is on top of the ground under optimal conditions (exposed to all of the above), in general, in one to three years, the victim will be reduced to smaller components or disap-

What is the National Missing and Unidentified Persons System?

The National Missing and Unidentified Persons System (NamUs) is a national, centralized repository and resource center under the Department of Justice that supports the tools to investigate and solve cases of missing persons and unidentified deceased people. Along with the missing and unidentified persons database, the unclaimed persons database contains information about deceased persons who have been identified by name but for whom no next of kin or family member has been identified or located to claim the body for burial or other disposition (the database is searchable by the public using a missing person's name and year of birth). NamUs is a free, online system open for searches by medical examiners, coroners, law-enforcement officials, and the general public in hopes of resolving such cases. (It can be found online at https://namus.gov/about.htm; for more about NamUs, see the chapter "Resources in Forensic Science.")

pear altogether. After five years, it would mainly be up to specialists in forensic anthropology to understand what truly happened to the victim.

What do some insects indicate about human skeletal remains?

Although not as likely as finding relatively recent human remains, oftentimes the types of insects may indicate certain aspects of the person's death. Forensic entomologists, or those who look for certain insects in specific life cycles around a body, are usually called in to examine older human remains. They can often uncover certain aspects of the death based on the insects on the skeleton and around the body.

What are some human remains that give information about a victim?

Depending on how long the human remains have been in a certain place—and depending on the conditions surrounding the remains—experts may be able to discover some information. Most of these items are harder body parts that have not decayed too much over time. This includes the skeleton (bones can reveal much information about the victim), teeth (teeth can be compared with dental records), and even nails and hairs.

What can interfere with the collection of human remains?

Several things can happen to human remains, making it difficult to ascertain any information about the victim. For example, the bones of the deceased may be spread out,

Some parts of the body last longer than others during the process of decaying, including bones, fingernails, and hair.

buried, or eaten by predators. If the climate is humid, hairs, clothing, and other "soft" items may disintegrate over a short period.

What can head and body hair still on or near human skeletal remains indicate?

If head and/or body hair is still on or near skeletal remains and they have not disintegrated, hairs may be used to help identify the unknown body. In particular, if the hair sample is complete enough, DNA may be taken—possibly identifying a person's race, sex, and other characteristics that may lead to their identity. (For more about DNA and hair samples, see the chapter "In the Crime Lab: DNA Analysis.")

EXAMINING OLDER
HUMAN SKELETAL REMAINS

What are some factors an expert in forensic anthropology examines at a crime or accident scene?

An expert in forensic anthropology examines several items at a crime or accident scene or even at an area in which human remains are found. For example, they look at the skeleton to determine how many people are represented by the bones; if the remains are ancient or modern; and the characteristics of the human (depending on the condition of the bones, they can sometimes determine sex, age, ancestry, stature, and possible timing of the person's demise). They are also often able to reconstruct the incident in which the person died or even potentially identify the person based on where the bones are located.

How can certain bones indicate the general age of a young crime victim?

Different bones vary as to when certain ones (called the epiphyseal plates) ossify (harden) and the bones fuse that can often help identify the general age of a young crime victim. The following table indicates the average age of ossification for different bones that may be used by forensic anthropologists to determine the relative age of human remains:

Age of Bone Ossification

Bone	Chronological Age of Fusion (years)
Scapula	18–20
Clavicle	23–31
Bones of upper extremity	17–20
Os coxae	18–23
Bones of lower extremity	18–22
Vertebrae	25
Sacrum	23–25
Sternum (body)	23
Sternum (manubrium, xiphoid)	After 30

How many bones are in the human body?

A forensic anthropologist needs to know about bones in the body, especially when it comes to determining the age of human remains. For example, babies are born with about three hundred to 350 bones; from birth to maturity, bones fuse together to produce an average adult total of 206. (*Note*: In some references, bone counts vary according to the method used to count them. This is because a structure may be treated as either multiple bones or as a single bone with multiple parts. In addition, some bones often "fuse" as a person gets older.) The following lists the location and number of bones in the human body that are commonly cited in the literature—and the number of bones that may have to be "put together" by a forensic anthropologist in order to determine more about skeletal remains:

Bones in the Human Body

Location of Bones	Number
Skull	22
Ears (pair)	6
Vertebrae	26
Sternum	3
Ribs	24
Throat	1
Pectoral girdle	4
Arms (pair)	60
Hip bones	2
Legs (pair)	58
TOTAL	206

Can a forensic anthropologist determine whether the victim is older by their skeletal remains?

Yes, some skeletal remains may help the forensic anthropologist to determine the victim's approximate age and sometimes even gender (for more about gender and bones, see below). For example, the sternum can often indicate approximate age, as it is not a weight-bearing bone (and is thus not changed over time as much). A joint located in the pelvis (the pubic symphysis) can also be used to determine approximate age. Older people will have a more pitted pubic symphysis; in addition, if a female has borne children, the joint will have marks on nearby cartilage left by childbirth. Another example is the wrist, in which bony ridges form in the area in which attached muscles pulled over the years. A forensic anthropologist may even be able to tell what the victim often did, such as if they were a chef or seamstress, based on the ridge wear.

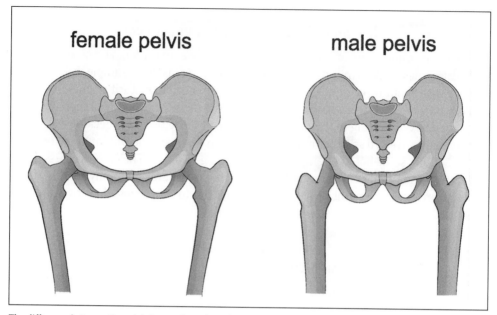

The difference between the pelvic bone of a male and that of a female is pronounced and easy to spot, which makes the identification of sex, at least, a simple matter.

How are bones used to determine the gender of a decomposed body at a crime scene?

Several general differences exist between the male and female skeletons, some of which can be used to determine the gender of a decomposed body found at a crime scene. The male skeleton is generally larger and heavier than the female skeleton. The bones of the skull are generally more graceful and less angular in the female skeleton. A female also has a wider, shorter breastbone and slimmer wrists. The pelvis of a female and a male are significantly different, which in a female is related to pregnancy and childbirth. The female pelvis is more circular, wider, and shallower than the male pelvis. Men have a narrow, deep pelvis by comparison. (In fact, in the field, a forensic anthropologist can often determine gender by putting their thumb into the notch in the pelvis's fan-shaped bone; if they have room to move their thumb, it is most often a female, and if it is too tight to wiggle, it is usually the skeleton of a male.) The angle between the pubic bones is much sharper in males, resulting in a more circular, almost heart-shaped pelvis. Not all these characteristics will be obvious at a crime scene, but it often helps the investigators determine gender before the body is sent to the crime lab. (For more about bones and crime victims, see the chapter "In the Crime Lab: Analyzing a Body.")

What details can a human skeleton reveal about a person's life?

The bones of a skeleton can reveal several details about a body. For example, certain differences in bones can reveal congenital conditions, nutritional habits, diseases, and

> ## Can a forensic expert look at skeletal remains and tell if the person was obese?
>
> Although it may seem like a magic trick, even if only a skeleton—teeth and bones with no soft tissues—are found in a shallow grave, a forensic expert may be able to tell whether that person was overweight. This is because if a person has a greater body mass, it can change the weight-bearing bones of the legs and spine. In a recent study, it was shown that even bones that do not bear body weight, such as the arms, can still have a greater bone mass (and are even stronger) in obese people. Therefore, the forensic expert may sometimes (but not always, as other conditions exist that affect bones) be able to tell if that person was obese based on the greater bone mass.

signs if a person has been beaten or murdered. By looking at other textural characteristics, a forensic expert may be able to tell whether a person did heavy or light work based on the muscle attachment to the bones that can indicate a person's occupation or even habits, such as running or weight lifting. Certain bones can also be indicative of a certain family relationship, especially within facial bone characteristics, and race and even gender, such as whether a woman has had a child, can often be determined by detailed analysis of skeletal remains.

How are human skeletal remains often used as evidence at a crime scene?

Human skeletal remains are used as evidence at a crime scene in numerous ways. Most remains are usually bones, teeth, and hair, which are collected and sent to the crime lab. If they are in good enough condition (so that DNA can be extracted), they can undergo DNA analysis, especially to try to identify the body or to verify the person's identity. (For more about DNA analysis, see the chapter "In the Crime Lab: DNA Analysis.") Teeth can also be compared to dental records to see if a match occurs with a known person. The skeletal bones can also hold many clues to the crime. For example, the skull may show cracks or fractures indicating a blow to the head that caused death. Other types of holes may indicate a heavy, blunt force trauma or that a person has been shot in the head. Cracks and fractures in the legs and arms may indicate that the person was beaten before they died or may have died from those injuries. (For more information about analyzing recent human remains from a crime scene, see the chapter "In the Crime Lab: Analyzing a Body.")

How old can a human skeleton be and still be used as evidence?

The human body can take a short or long time to become merely a skeleton. For example, at a crime scene, by the time a skeleton has been uncovered by investigators, it may have been buried for weeks, months, or even years. The overall condition of the body to use as evidence depends on the surrounding environment in which the body sits, including the climate (such as hot or humid), insects, and/or animals that feed on the body.

How are human skeletons—especially at a crime scene—excavated and mapped?

Human skeletal remains—whether buried or on the surface at a crime scene—need to be carefully excavated and mapped. This is done in order to preserve evidence of the possible murder victim, or in other cases, such as determining whether the death was by accident. The process is similar to an archaeological excavation (which is why forensic archaeologists exist; for more, see this chapter). Such experts usually use a grid method of mapping the site for collection, recording everything around the skeleton, including the soil, items and fragments of items, indentations, etc., during the processing of the site. They must have written notes and documentation, photos, and digital data as evidence, and they must maintain the integrity of the scene so nothing is contaminated that could have been used as evidence.

Who was Clyde Snow?

Clyde Snow (1928–2014) was a forensic anthropologist who worked on the analysis and confirmation of skeletal remains. For example, he confirmed the remains of President John Kennedy (at the bequest of Congress, Snow confirmed that the x-rays from the assassinated president's autopsy were truly those of Kennedy); the victims of serial killer

A lab technician places a row of PCR tubes into a thermal cycler, which will amplify samples of mitochondrial DNA for identification.

John Wayne Gacy; Egyptian pharaoh King Tutankhamen (also seen as Tutankhamun; Snow helped another scientist reconstruct "King Tut's" face); and the victims of the Oklahoma City bombings.

How are older skeletal remains examined in the crime lab?

Older skeletal remains are examined in several ways in a crime lab. For example, bones are usually photographed and documented, x-rayed, examined under high-power microscopes, and even CT scanned to determine detailed information about the skeleton's condition. In this way, too, the analysis does not alter the remains. If necessary, chemical analysis can be done, including those involving isotopes that can provide information about the age of a person's bones (and even what the person ate, in some cases).

What are some ways experts obtain DNA from ancient bones?

In many cases, bones are analyzed by DNA methods in order to either establish identity or determine certain characteristics of the person. If the nuclear DNA is degraded, forensic DNA experts use the mitochondrial DNA in bones and teeth to determine the possible identity of ancient bones or even the lineage of the person (when compared to their possible living descendants). This process, called a PCR (polymerase chain reaction) assay, is a test to see if any usable DNA is inside ancient bones and/or teeth. Using a certain process (which includes some heating and certain primers), PCR allows small amounts of DNA in a bone or tooth to be copied or "amplified" for better analysis of the sample. Another example of extracting DNA from ancient bones uses a technique called the silica extraction method. Simply put, in this technique, the DNA binds to silica (a fine glass powder) that allows unwanted chemicals to be washed and isolated from desired bone materials. This is because ancient bones have been exposed to many environmental organic contaminants, such as bacteria or fungi (and even the DNA of the people doing the lab work). This technique allows the older DNA to be examined—and less of the DNA that may have contaminated the bone. (For more about DNA analysis, see the chapter "In the Crime Lab: DNA Analysis.")

What is radiocarbon dating of ancient bones?

Also referred to as carbon or carbon-14 dating, radiocarbon dating is a way to determine the age of an organic item, such as wooden artifacts, and in the case of ancient unidentified remains—including bones, teeth, nails, cloth, wood, and plant fibers associated with the remains—to potentially determine the person's age and possibly the year of death. Radioactive carbon forms from cosmic ray bombardment of nitrogen in the Earth's upper atmosphere. From there, carbon is taken up by plant tissues and incorporated by means of the food chain into all living organisms. After an organism dies, their carbon-14 declines at a predictable rate and has a half-life of around 5,730 years. By knowing the level of the isotope and half-life, the time that has passed since the levels were identical to a living organism can be calculated. Thus, it can be used to determine organic remains between five hundred and fifty thousand years old (some references say as old as about sixty-two thousand years).

> ## Why is carbon dating linked to the Shroud of Turin?
>
>
>
> Shroud of Turin
>
> **A**merican chemist Walter McCrone (1916–2002) was an expert in chemical/forensic microscopy and is often referred to as the "father of modern microscopy." In 1978, he worked on the Shroud of Turin Research Project. He contended that the shroud—a linen cloth bearing the image of a person and thought to be the burial cloth of Jesus of Nazareth—was actually a medieval painting. Not everyone agreed, but in 1988, thanks to carbon-14 dating, his suggestion was vindicated, as the cloth was found to be from the Middle Ages (although, as with many such relics, the date result—and the true origin of the image on the cloth—continues to be a highly debated subject). The Shroud of Turin is currently in a secured vault in the Cathedral of St. John the Baptist in Turin, Italy.

What is referred to as the "bomb pulse"?

The "bomb pulse" is often used to define a period in the 1950s and 1960s in which a great increase in atmospheric carbon-14 occurred. This was due to hundreds of above-ground nuclear weapons testing sites in the United States and several other countries. The Nuclear Test Ban Treaty of 1963 ended the testing for most nuclear powers, and since then, carbon-14 levels have declined as radiocarbon is soaked up by oceans and the biosphere. This also means that people born within the "bomb pulse" period usually have artificially high levels of carbon-14 in their system—because of the ingestion of dietary components (plants absorb the carbon-14, animals eat the plants, humans eat the animals and plants) that also absorbed the carbon-14 during those years. Forensic experts can use this information to help determine the age of an unknown victim, as they can compare how much carbon-14 was in the atmosphere in a certain year with the human's tissue (blood, tissue, hair, bone, cartilage, teeth, bacteria, etc.) levels. The use of the "bomb pulse" will not last forever, however, as carbon-14 levels will continue to drop in the next few decades to normal, or what is called "baseline" level.

INTERPRETING MORE REMAINS

Why are teeth used for identification of human remains?

Teeth are used for identification of human remains for several reasons. For instance, in the case of a crime victim, no fingerprints may be on file, or the person's prints are destroyed by decomposition, fragmentation, mutilation, or fire. In addition, at a terrorist or accident scene (such as an air disaster), fingerprints and other identifiers may be destroyed. For example, remains of teeth were used in many of the identifications from the 2001 World Trade Tower attack in New York. Even after a major natural disaster, once buried bodies may need to be identified if caskets are washed out of the ground after a flood, hurricane, tornado, avalanche, or tsunami. This is when teeth also may help in the identification of victims.

Can forensic experts analyze teeth to tell the general age of a young crime victim?

In some ways, it may be possible to tell the general age of a young crime victim by analyzing their teeth. For example, the "baby" teeth (also referred to as milk or deciduous teeth) start to erupt from the baby's gums at about six months, with the first being the lower jaw's central incisors. From there, each tooth type erupts in a predictable way (babies usually have a total of twenty baby teeth). At about six years old, the child's permanent teeth begin to replace the baby teeth. Teeth stop erupting at about age twenty-one, as all thirty-two permanent teeth have usually come in by then. In addition, odontologists can estimate age based on x-rays of how a young person's teeth (and teeth into the upper and lower jaw bones) are growing. For instance, a tooth's crown forms first, followed by the root.

How can an antemortem (before-death) dental cast help to identify an accident or crime victim?

If available, an antemortem dental cast can be used to identify a person from an accident scene (for example, from a house fire) or an unidentified victim of a crime. Because the cast is made from the teeth before death, it may then be used to identify the person based on certain characteristics of the teeth. For example, if a photograph or image is available of the suspected person smiling, the casts (mainly front teeth) can often be used for comparison—and possibly identify the victim. (For more about teeth and identification of a crime victim or accident, see the chapter "In the Crime Lab: Analyzing a Body.")

What is WinID, and how can it be used with postmortem dental data?

WinID (found at www.winid.com) is a database used by odontologists to potentially identify an unidentified body using postmortem dental data. The information from a victim's postmortem dental analysis is rapidly compared to this database that—along with other data—contains antemortem dental data. This produces a list of the best comparison matches for an odontologist to use in order to potentially identify an unknown victim. (For more about WinID, see the chapter "Resources in Forensic Science.")

Can experts find various drugs in older human remains?

Yes, it is possible to find drug evidence in older human remains but only under certain conditions. If the remains are not too old, forensic toxicologists may be able to determine whether a controlled substance was given to or ingested by a victim of a crime (or accident). For older decomposed or skeletal remains, fewer tissues and fluids come from the body that can be used to determine the presence of drugs, but it is still possible in several ways to determine drugs in a person's system, usually by analyzing—chemically, DNA, and otherwise—hair, teeth, nails, and bones (depending on their condition). However, it may still be difficult to determine the presence of drugs if a great deal of deterioration of the body has occurred (especially of the bones). Because of this, the analysis may not tell what drug was in a person's system but only (possibly) that the person was exposed to drugs.

FACIAL RECOGNITION AND RECONSTRUCTION

What is facial recognition?

Facial recognition is a way of identifying a suspect, with the most commonly known method being the identification by an eyewitness or by a photograph taken by a witness. Determining the identity of a suspect is also carried out by facial-recognition software, which uses certain points on an image and compares them to the same points in an image database. The software systems work with certain numeric codes called faceprints, such as one that compares around eighty points on a human face.

Why is facial recognition often questioned?

Facial recognition is often questioned, as certain facial expressions, the angle of a photo, and even the photo quality can affect the outcome of the facial-recognition analysis. This includes identification by a witness from a photograph and images that are put into a computer to compare to other images in a database.

What is facial reconstruction?

Facial reconstruction is commonly used to possibly identify an unknown victim. It is either done using two-dimensional reconstruction or photography and sketches to reconstruct the victim's face. It is also the use of three-dimensional reconstructions—the art of using special markers on a mold of a skull that is overlain with clay to give an approximation of the person's face. (In general, the link between facial recognition and reconstruction is that both are a way of trying to identify a person—to identify a suspect and to identify a victim, respectively.)

Why are facial reconstructions made?

Facial reconstruction is done for several reasons. First, it is used to make a positive identification of the unknown victim. Second, if the person is still not identified, the facial reconstruction can be used to ask the public for help—in other words, someone may know the person or may have witnessed something around the deceased's disappearance or death.

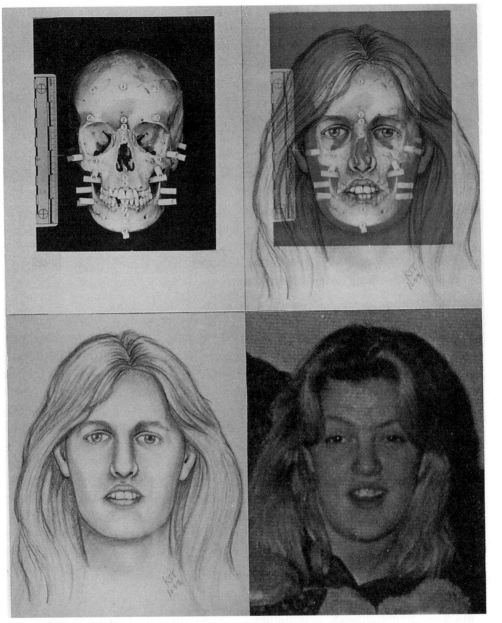

Using a considerable knowledge of anatomy, a facial reconstruction expert was able to use a skull to recreate what the victim looked like when she was alive. The photo at the bottom right matched the end result well enough for a positive ID.

What are the two sets of bones of the skull?

The skull consists of two sets of bones: the cranial and the facial bones. The cranial cavity that encloses and protects the brain consists of the eight cranial bones, and fourteen facial bones form the framework of the face.

In general, how do experts three-dimensionally reconstruct a victim's face?

Several steps are used to reconstruct a victim's face based on their skull. First, the artist makes a plaster cast model of the skull. Then, features based on the skull, such as the size of the eye sockets, the shape of the nose, the width of the mouth (using the jaw), and the height of the cheekbones are examined and measured to eventually recreate the entire face in clay. Such a reconstruction of a victim's face can take weeks or months to accomplish. Another way is to pinpoint certain spots on the skull and map them into a computer. The resulting image can then be sent to a missing person's database to see if a match occurs.

Why are three-dimensional facial reconstructions often questioned?

Although many victims have been identified using the three-dimensional clay technique over the years, such reconstructions are not an exact science. Thus, the results are often questioned as to their use, as they are actually the interpretation of the artist doing the reconstruction. In fact, some experts believe that the results are inherently inaccurate, as various artists reconstructing a face with the same skull will come out with different interpretations of what the person truly looked like.

Is it possible to tell the age of an unidentified person based on their skull?

No, it is not possible to tell the exact age of an unidentified person based merely on their skull, but the person's age can be estimated. Forensic experts check to see if the sagittal suture is fused or not (the squiggly line that runs along the entire length of the skull). If it is fused, the remains are probably from a person older than age thirty-five. If the coronal suture at the front of the skull is completely fused, the person is usually more than forty years old.

Can certain skull traits help determine the ancestry of unidentified remains?

In some instances, it may be possible to tell a person's ancestry, for instance, if the person is of Asian, African, European, etc., descent by looking at their skull traits, especially form and structure, but because of the blending of ethnic groups over time, these skull traits are not as reliable as they have been in the past, as the morphology of people's skulls is now quite similar. This is why forensic experts must rely on other types of analyses to determine the ancestry of unidentified skeletal remains.

IN THE CRIME LAB: TRACE EVIDENCE

DEFINING TRACE EVIDENCE

What is trace evidence?

Trace evidence in the crime lab is the analysis of traces of physical evidence collected at a crime or accident scene. This includes evidence from homicides, assaults, rapes, burglaries, and transportation accidents, such as from cars, buses, trains, and planes. (For more about the collection of trace evidence at a crime scene, see the chapter "At the Crime Scene: Looking for Physical Evidence.")

What are some examples of trace evidence?

Numerous examples exist of trace evidence—either microscopic or macroscopic—that can be collected from a crime or accident scene. They include human and animal hairs, fibers, soil, plastic bags, glass, cordage, paint, building materials, and even feathers. Trace evidence can also include impressions, such as tire or shoe print impressions, especially if they are found in different types of materials, such as soil, paint, or blood. It can also include other physical evidence, such as gunshot residue on a piece of clothing or object or explosive residue. (*Note*: For this text, some biologically related trace evidence such as gunshot residue on a body can be found in the chapter "In the Crime Lab: Analyzing a Body"; fingerprints, which are often included as trace evidence in some references, are detailed in the chapter "In the Crime Lab: Patent, Latent, and Plastic Prints"; and information about explosive residue as evidence can be found in the chapter "In the Crime Lab: Examining Explosives.")

Can forensic experts determine the usefulness of certain trace evidence?

Forensic experts have used several ways to determine the usefulness of certain trace evidence. For example, a scale developed in 2009 (but not official in its use) was called the

"Trace Evidence Conclusion Scale" and has eight defining outcomes when it comes to evidence. For instance, at one end of the scale are the terms "identified," or when a positive identification occurs (when items have characteristics that are definitely proven to be from the same source) and "very strong support" (or after analysis, the association between items share unusual characteristics that are associated with each other) to "inconclusive" (no conclusion can be reached regarding the connection between the items) and "elimination" (no physical or chemical characteristics prove that the items came from the same source).

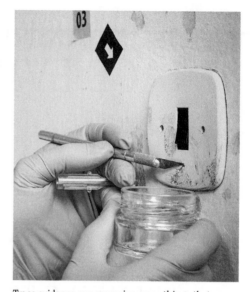

Trace evidence can comprise many things that are tiny or even microscopic, such as dried blood samples, dirt particles, pieces of fiber, or samples of bodily secretions (sweat, urine, semen, etc.).

What is a trace sample?

A trace sample is when the amount of some evidence collected is so small it cannot be weighed. This type of sample is usually analyzed by means of quantitative chemical analysis using special instruments in the lab.

What is a Trace Evidence Unit?

According to the Federal Bureau of Investigation (FBI), the people who deal with trace evidence in a crime lab are usually members of a Trace Evidence Unit. In particular, they look at, identify, and compare certain trace materials that may be involved in—or used as evidence from—a crime or accident scene.

What is physical matching?

Physical matching (or sometimes referred to as fracture match analysis) is as the words imply: matching two items to determine whether they once formed a single item. This is often listed under trace evidence, in which the two items are analyzed to determine whether they fit together like a jigsaw puzzle. Items for physical matching from a crime scene often include glass, metals, wood, tape, paint, broken clothing notions (such as buttons) or torn clothing, or plastics.

Why is trace evidence important to forensic science?

Trace evidence interpretation is important to forensic science in several ways. For example, trace evidence can link suspects to a crime scene victim. It can help prove a person's innocence or guilt, and it can help the reconstruction team understand what occurred at a crime scene based on what and where trace evidence was found at the scene.

Do databases exist for the various types of trace evidence?

Yes, as of this writing, many different databases exist for the various types of trace evidence. For example, several agencies, such as the FBI and some state police, have a Trace Evidence Unit that collects various trace evidence samples, such as automotive paint pigments, human hair, animal hair, fibers, black spray paint, rope, soil, silicone adhesive, electrical tape, and duct tape to use to compare such items found at a crime scene. As of this writing, no one single database exists for trace evidence, but several agencies and organizations are working to find ways to "centralize" such data and make it more accessible to the entire forensic trace evidence community.

HAIRS AS TRACE EVIDENCE FROM A CRIME SCENE

What types of human hairs can be distinguished in the crime lab—and possibly be used as evidence?

Hairs found at a crime scene (for instance, on a piece of clothing) are often examined in the crime lab to attempt to determine their characteristics and thus are often used as evidence in a crime. Several distinct human hairs can be analyzed, depending on where they are found on the body. The most common are as follows:

- Vellus hairs: These are the "peach fuzz" hairs found over much of a person's body.
- Terminal hairs: These are the thick, more deeply pigmented, and sometimes curly hairs that include hair on a person's head, along with their eyelashes, eyebrows, and pubic hair.
- Intermediate hairs: These are the hairs that include the hair on a person's arms and legs.

How do human male and female body hairs differ?

On the average, the human body has approximately five million hairs. In fact, humans are born with as many hair follicles as they will ever have, and hairs are among the fastest-growing tissues of the body. Each hair follicle on the scalp grows almost 30 feet (9 meters) during an average lifetime, making humans the mammals with the longest hairs (the musk ox is second) on Earth. Males and females have differences, too. For example, males have a few hundred thousand more hairs than women. In both males and females, hormones are responsible for the development of such hairy regions as the scalp, armpits, and pubic areas, and, in addition in men, on the chest. Overall, the various types of hair grow all over the human body except for the soles of the feet, palms of the hand, eyelids, and lips.

143

What can a forensic expert determine based on the size and shape of hairs?

Several conditions can help a forensic expert determine the area in which a certain hair came from on the human body. For example, hairs are short and stiff in the eyebrows and long and flexible on the head. When the hair shaft is oval, an individual more often has wavy hair; when it is flat and ribbonlike, the hair is curly or kinky; if the hair shaft is perfectly round, the hair is most often straight. Of all the hairs on the body, those from the head and pubic areas are most often used in forensic analysis.

What can hair analysis in the crime lab reveal?

An analyzed hair can reveal several characteristics in the crime lab but with limitations as to how much information can truly be determined. For example, certain

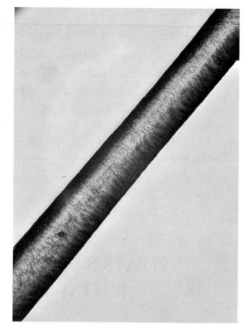

Under the microscope, the image of a strand of hair can be identified as human or otherwise by the trained eye.

analyses will reveal whether the hair is truly from a human or animal, and if it is found to be human, further analysis may show whether the hair has been altered in any way (for example, by bleaching or dyeing), whether the hair is damaged or decomposed, or whether a hair has been forcibly removed (for instance, pulled out during a struggle) or naturally shed.

How are human hairs analyzed in the crime lab?

Human hairs—composed of the cuticle (outside), cortex (surrounding the core), and medulla (inside core)—are analyzed in several ways in the crime lab. For example, most hair examinations start with a high-powered microscope, which can often reveal such information as the origin of the hairs (for instance, hairs from the head or face), whether the hairs are damaged or treated (for instance, dyed or chemically treated hair), and possibly ethnic characteristics. Further DNA analyses of the hair (especially if the hair follicle is still attached) can potentially identify the person who had the hair along with other characteristics, such as the gender of the person.

Can human hairs found at a crime scene be used against a suspect in a crime?

Microscopic analyses of human hairs from a crime scene are not always dependable as evidence of a crime. Powerful microscopes are often used to decipher characteristics of hairs, including treating it with certain chemicals or substances that will make the hairs easier

> ## How does human hair compare to the hair of other primates?
>
> In general, humans have as many hair follicles as gorillas, but the type of hair differs. Gorillas are covered with terminal hairs, while humans are mostly covered with vellus hairs.

to see. They can use these microscopic characteristics of certain hairs for comparison but won't truly be able to identify the person who owned the hair. In fact, it is often thought that microscopic examination of a person's hairs *alone* cannot conclusively prove that a certain hair came from a specific individual, which is why using hairs to identify a criminal is often questioned, but if known hairs are analyzed from the victim and/or suspect, comparing certain hairs—especially from the head and pubic hairs—can sometimes (but not always) be *part* of the evidence used to make a connection between the victim and the suspect of a crime. (For more about how hairs are questionable as evidence in a crime, see this chapter and the chapter "Controversies in Forensic Science.")

Can a human hair be used to determine race?

Determining if a certain human hair came from a person of a specific race is often questioned, especially in terms of criminal evidence. Essentially, part of the reason has to do with the inbreeding of humans—few people are racially pure. Thus, an expert in hair analysis can only suggest a person's race based on a human hair. In addition, some people may also have certain hair characteristics that may *suggest* a certain race, but the other features they have may or may not indicate that race.

What can hairs of a victim or perpetrator indicate about drug use?

Hair evaluation in the crime lab can also be used to determine the drugs and narcotics the individual has used (up to ninety days previously). In this way, especially at accident scenes, the hairs may indicate that a person was under the influence of drugs or that they had a past history of drug use.

How is hair color determined?

Overall, hair color is determined by the amount of pigment produced. For example, if the hair cells have an abundance of melanin, the hair is dark. If an intermediate quantity of pigment is produced, the hair is blonde. If no pigment is produced, the hair appears white. A mixture of pigmented and unpigmented hair is usually gray. Another pigment called trichosiderin is found only in people with red hair. However, a suspect or victim may have no hair, or their hair may be damaged or treated with chemicals, making it difficult to determine color. (For example, a suspect may change their hair color so they cannot be identified.) In such cases—and because a person's genes determine hair color—DNA analysis of body-fluid samples gathered at a crime scene as evidence can often reveal the true color of the person's hair. Such tests for genetic hair markers are not perfect, but in recent studies, red and black hair were identified with around 70 to 90 percent accuracy, while brown and blonde hair with 60 to 80 percent (it may be more difficult to tell if an older person is a true blonde, as some people's hair color changes from light to dark as they get older).

How is DNA determined in a hair sample?

In many cases, an expert may suggest that certain hairs (or a hair) are possible evidence from a crime scene. A human hair may be tested using DNA analysis—most commonly, nuclear DNA (nDNA, which exists inside a cell's nucleus), but only if the hair has a hair follicle (also called a hair root or root sheath). If the nDNA evaluation and a hair sample comparisons are both made, the information can often lead to the age and/or sex of the owner (and, in some cases, the DNA will help lead to the identity of the owner of the hair). Although not as useful as nDNA, another type of test is the mitochondrial DNA analysis (mtDNA; mitochondria are located outside a person's cell nucleus). This test is often conducted if no follicle is attached or if the hair is in its "resting stage" of growth. In this case, the results of the analysis are usually used only for comparison's sake and to possibly exclude one person versus another. (For more about DNA analysis, see the chapter "In the Crime Lab: DNA Analysis.")

Can analysis of a hair tell if the person was male or female?

Maybe, but it depends on whether the root sheath is still attached to the end of a hair. In many cases, a forensic nuclear DNA (nDNA) analysis of a hair can be used to determine whether the person was male or female if the entire or a major portion of the root sheath is found. (For more about DNA analysis, see the chapter "In the Crime Lab: DNA Analysis.")

Why are the hairs of an animal often useful as evidence in a criminal situation?

Pet hair can definitely be used as evidence in a criminal situation. This is because it is easily transferred from the pet to victim, a suspect, or on objects (such as upholstery) at a crime scene—no matter who is the pet owner: perpetrator or victim. It can also be transferred to a person's clothing (or even skin) when a crime is committed in a place in which animals are kept, such as an animal shelter or zoo, a barn or stable, or in a person's car or animal-transport vehicles.

FIBERS AND CLOTHES

Can fibers be considered trace evidence?

Yes, fibers—the small, threadlike material that comes from various types of fabric—are often used as trace evidence at a crime scene. They are usually divided into three types:

natural (such as animal [various wools, alpaca, etc.] and plant [cotton, flax, etc.] fibers), manufactured (fibers that contain reprocessed natural materials, such as rayon), and synthetic (completely manufactured, such as nylon and polyester).

Where are fibers gathered at a crime scene for analysis in the lab?

At a crime scene, fibers from a victim's clothing or found on other parts of an exposed body (such as in the hair or on an arm) can be collected for analysis in the crime lab. Other places include the area surrounding the victim's body, such as the carpet, bedsheets, or in an upholstered chair. Fibers are also often gathered from weapons found at the crime scene or the

Fibers—even tiny ones—can tell investigators things such as what a victim or perpetrator was wearing, whether the body was moved from another location, or even if there was a struggle during the crime.

area surrounding the weapon, but such fibers should be collected quickly from a crime scene before they become contaminated or even fly away from movement of people at the crime scene.

How are fibers collected from the crime scene?

Individual fibers are most often collected using tweezers. Larger amounts of fiber at a crime scene often call for carefully vacuuming an area to collect the fibers and separating them in the crime lab. Unlike what people see on television or in the movies, fibers can be collected by lifting them with tape, but it's not a good idea—the fiber is often destroyed by the nature of most adhesives.

How are fibers analyzed in the crime lab?

In most cases, experts in the crime lab use high-powered comparison microscopes in order to match texture and type of fiber. They may also determine the chemical composition of fibers using chemical analysis. In this way, fibers can often be traced back to the manufacturer using several available standards databases.

Do any databases include fibers for comparison or matching in the lab?

Yes, several fiber databases are used for comparison or matching in the crime lab—both commercial and government owned. For example, the Federal Bureau of Investigation (FBI) has a fiber library. As of this writing, the database of eighty-six records includes certain special characteristics of textile fibers used to identify fiber types, and it also has physical samples of certain fibers.

SOILS AND GEOLOGY

What can soil reveal about a crime scene?

Soil type can often be used as evidence at a crime scene, especially if it can link the victims, suspects, and/or crime scenes. Soils have the advantage of revealing not only the types of soil at a crime or accident scene but also possibly the surrounding environment. In particular, soils contain minerals, vegetation, animal matter, and other materials (many man-made, such as glass, paint, or building materials). Also, the contents of soils vary between states and locally and range from such rocks and soils as the limestone rock of Florida to the volcanic ash beaches in Hawaii.

What do forensic experts in geology look for when it comes to soil?

Most forensic soil experts are geologists or have knowledge of the field. In terms of a crime scene, the soil itself can be analyzed by color, pH (if the soil is acidic or basic), mineral content, thickness, and consistency (for instance, if it is sandy versus rocky soil). Elements within the soil can also be compared using color, size, distribution within a soil, and composition—all of which can be compared from a crime scene and used as possible trace evidence. For example, mud on a suspect's shoes could be matched with the type of soil found at the crime scene. Or, if a certain glass is found embedded in a suspect's sneakers and that type of glass is found in the soil at the crime scene, it could be used as evidence.

PLASTIC BAGS

Why are plastic bags often considered to be evidence at a crime scene?

Plastic bags, or polyethylene film products, are often used in a number of crimes, such as homicides, bank robberies, kidnappings, and drug dealings. These plastic bags can be analyzed in a number of ways. This includes checking the plastic bags for evidence inside (for instance, for drugs or fibers from a crime scene), on the bag itself (such as fingerprints or shoe prints if someone stepped on the bag), or the bag itself (for instance, if a piece of plastic is found as evidence at a crime scene, it can be compared to other plastic bags at the scene or elsewhere).

Not all soils are alike, and for that reason soil evidence can sometimes betray a person's movements when dirt gets on their clothes, for example.

More detailed analysis of a plastic bag includes the color, capacity, number of perforations, and type of closure.

Can the manufacturer of a plastic bag be determined?

In many cases, the manufacturer of a plastic bag from a crime scene may be determined. Most plastic bags have various telltale characteristics. For example, the type, size, color, and even type of closure (for instance, a drawstring closure) on the plastic bag can be analyzed. The construction of the bag (for instance, if it has certain known bag perforations made at certain intervals when the bag was made) or manufacturing impressions (such as impressions created during the manufacturing's heat-sealing process) can also be analyzed. When a plastic bag is made, the molten plastic passes through a die, forming die and pigment bands, some of which can help identify a specific type of plastic bag. Individual characteristics can also help experts in plastic bag identification, including fisheyes and arrowheads (the result of undissolved pigment that gets trapped in the polyethylene film) and tiger stripes (caused by the vibration and stretching of the plastic during the manufacturing process). All of these characteristics are used to help identify a possible crime scene connection, such as comparing a questioned plastic bag with a bag taken from a known source.

Does a plastic bag database exist?

Yes, the Federal Bureau of Investigation (FBI) maintains a polymer database called the Polyethylene Repository and Information Database for Evidence (PRIDE) that provides information on the origin and characteristics of most plastic bags for comparative and other forensic purposes. In 2004, the FBI laboratory's Questioned Documents Unit, along with the Center for Innovative Technology (Virginia) and the Virginia Institute of Forensic Science and Medicine, developed the PRIDE system in answer to numerous requests from law-enforcement personnel who needed to know the origin of plastic bags collected as evidence. The database is updated frequently, as many manufacturers change methods and/or introduce new products—most of them on an annual basis.

What was the first known case that used forensic geology?

It is thought that the first known case that used forensic geology was in 1904 (although in 1891, Hans Gross suggested that such materials could be used as evidence; for more about Gross, see the chapter "The History of Forensic Science"). German scientist Georg Popp (1861–1943) determined that of the two samples of soil collected from the pants of a murder suspect, one was similar to the crime scene's soil mineral composition. The second sample was from the pathway that connected the crime scene to the suspect's home. Presented with the soil evidence, the suspect confessed to the murder.

Does a plastics database also exist?

Yes, several commercial companies have databases that include all types of plastics from plastic wrap to containers. For example, Scientific Polymer Products, Inc. has a catalog of over a thousand monomers, polymer (polymer means many monomers), and plasticizers (or a substance that, when added to another material [most often a plastic], causes it to become more flexible and easy to handle) and offers analysis, identification, and molecular weight of those types of plastics.

GLASS

Is it possible to tell the difference between types of glass in the crime lab?

Yes, one can tell the difference between types of glass in the crime lab in many ways—all based on the material's composition and manufacturing. Each type of glass is made a certain way, has certain chemicals associated with it, and breaks in a certain way. Thus, various types of glass are often found as trace evidence at a crime or accident scene and brought back to the crime lab to analyze. The following lists some of the more common forms of glass that can be analyzed in the crime lab:

- *Soda-lime-silica*—The most common type of glass is often referred to as soda-lime-silica glass, which is used for windowpanes and glass containers (including food- and beverage-safe bottles and jars).

- *Borosilicate glass*—This is often referred to by the commercial name Pyrex, which is made to withstand high temperatures and used in cookware.

- *Alumino-silicate glass*—This glass is made mostly of aluminum, oxygen, and silicon and is used for such items as cell phone cover glass.

- *Light-sensitive (or photosensitive or photochromatic) glass*—Although most light-sensitive materials are made of plastic, those made of glass contain special internal materials that help to darken the lens when exposed to ultraviolet light from the sun. Without the light, the lenses fade back to what is considered to be clear.

- *Leaded glass*—This glass, also called crystal, contains lead as opposed to the calcium found in most potash glass and is most often used for glassware and stained glass.

- *Wire glass*—Wire glass is often considered a safety glass and is often used as a fire retardant (although fire-retardant glass has been suggested as a better substitute in the past few years, as a hot fire may expose dangerous wires). A wire mesh is laid inside the glass to prevent pieces from shattering, which also makes it less likely to pose a problem if broken. It also strengthens the glass, making it more difficult to break or shatter when hit or under physical stress. It is commonly used in hospitals, schools, and businesses.

- *Tempered glass*—This type of safety glass is also often called tempered glass. It is much stronger than regular glass because of the heating and cooling process (controlled thermal processes) when manufactured and/or the chemical treatments during processing. When tempered glass breaks, it falls into small cubes with no sharp edges, which is why it is most often found in places where human safety is priority, such as in the windows of a car.

- *Laminated glass*—Another type of safety glass—and more often stronger than tempered glass—is called laminated glass, which includes two layers of glass with a layer of plastic in between. It is also used in vehicle windows.

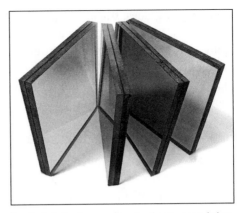

Laminated glass is even stronger than tempered glass. Investigators can distinguish between types of glass based on thickness, color, how they break, and so on.

How is glass analyzed in the lab?

Along with fractures, glass can also be analyzed in several other ways. The "simplest" method is to check the glass's color, diameter, and thickness and compare it to glass at the crime scene. The shape of the glass can also be important. For instance, if it is curved or flat, it could be an indication of a drinking glass or windowpane, respectively. Another method to look at glass uses the refractive index of the glass. This test looks at the reflectivity of the glass found as evidence. The test measures how much light is reflected and/or absorbed in the glass, which can be compared to other glass. For example, it can be compared to glass from a car or house window or a glass item found at the scene of the crime (or accident).

Another method of analyzing glass is to test the piece chemically and includes using certain instruments such as a scanning electron microscope, or SEM (this instrument can examine a piece of glass at a high resolution to determine the chemical composition). This, too, is a way to compare a sample collected as evidence and compare it to other glass at the crime scene (or accident). Yet another method is looking at the physical characteristics, such as grooves, dents, and other features (such as whether the glass contains wire or is made of stained glass) under a high-powered microscope. This is often used to compare a sample of glass collected as evidence with glass at the crime scene (or accident) to see if a match exists.

PAINT AND BUILDING MATERIALS

Why is paint often collected as trace evidence?

Paint is composed of a mix of numerous components that allows it to come in a variety of colors. Because most manufacturers use different components in their paint to create different grades, thicknesses, luster, types, and colors, paint is often used as traceable evidence from a crime scene. In some cases, paints from a crime scene can be chemically analyzed and its manufacturer determined based on certain characteristics and composition of the paint. Overall, the main objective of looking at paint from a forensics point of view is to differentiate between samples and eliminate the possibility that they came from different sources.

In what forms are paints found at a crime scene?

Paint at a crime scene is often found in the form of a paint chip (or paint pieces that have dry, multiple intact layers), often as fragments or torn into chunks, for example, from a wall or object. Wet paint can also be found on various surfaces, such as a painted wall, with imprints of fingerprints or palm prints within the wet paint. Or, obvious prints may be visible on a dry wall from when a person accidentally touched the wet paint and then the wall.

How is paint analyzed in a crime lab?

Paint is often analyzed in a crime lab using a comparison microscope. For example, such a microscope can examine two paint samples, revealing such features as the paint, primer, additional coating, and damage that may be common to both. Paint can also be analyzed in more detail using chemical testing. For example, pyrolysis gas chromatography (PYGC) is often used to help determine certain paint's chemical composition, color, pigments, and other factors.

Do any paint databases exist?

Yes, as of this writing, several paint databases exist. For example, an automotive paint database is run by the Federal Bureau of Investigation called the National Automotive Paint File (NAPF). According to the National Institute of Standards and Technology, the database is a physical collection of automotive paint panels put together and maintained by the FBI's Chemistry Unit. The collection has paint color standards, and the agency currently maintains about fourteen thousand full automotive paint panels (as a vehicle would be painted, not just the top coats). These panels are used in an investigation to make a physical comparison of paint chips collected as automotive make and model evidence in order to identify a possible vehicle, for instance, in a hit-and-run investigation.

What are some ways in which building materials can be used as evidence of a crime?

Depending on the criminal activity, of course, building materials can be used as evidence at a crime scene. In particular, these materials can undergo a microanalysis in the crime lab, possibly revealing fibers, glass, or even fingerprints that can be used as evidence at the accident or crime scene, especially how they break or are damaged

Building materials have become much more diverse over the years. There are many types of bricks, drywall, engineered woods, and so on, and this has made it easier for forensic scientists to narrow down the circumstances behind certain crimes.

under certain criminal activities. For instance, determining how a projectile from a firearm at the crime scene reacts after striking a certain building material, such as engineered wood materials (for example, particle board, wood-plastic, hardboard, and plywood) can possibly determine a bullet's path. In addition, certain types of building materials—such as fibrous insulation, gypsum wallboard, concrete, paint chips, glass, wood dust, or particle board dust—can disperse in various ways at a crime scene. These small particles can transfer to a suspect's clothing and hair, for instance, during a burglary. They can even fall on a suspect's tools that they use to break into an establishment or even on the weapons used during a homicide, and if the building material is a certain type, such as an asbestos-containing material, it can sometimes be traced to the manufacturer.

What types of building materials are often analyzed as trace evidence?

Numerous types of building materials can be analyzed to reveal evidence of a crime. They include such materials as brick, special types of concrete, engineered woods and plastics, insulation board, wallboard, and manufactured stone. Each material has certain characteristics that often make it possible to use as evidence at a crime scene and to be analyzed as trace evidence in the crime lab.

GUNSHOT RESIDUE ON OBJECTS

What is gunshot residue?

Gunshot residues (GSR) are particles most often from the discharging cartridge primer compound or found in bullets and their casings of a gun or shotgun. They are composed of burned and unburned particles and several chemicals, including lead, barium, and antimony—all of which vaporize when the primer ignites and then condenses into GSR particles. Gunshot residue tests are often done in cases in which a shooting has taken place. This depends, of course, if contamination has occurred at the crime scene, which can cause false positive or negative results when analyzing GSRs. (For more about GSR at a crime scene, see the chapter "At the Crime Scene: Looking for Physical Evidence.")

Why do experts in the lab analyze gunshot residue (GSR) on objects?

Experts in the lab often analyze GSR on objects or clothing from a crime scene to understand how and if a firearm was used. Most of the residues produced are burned and partially burned gunpowder and the vaporous lead from the ejection of the bullet from the barrel. The experts may examine GSR or other materials, for example, if a certain gun or shotgun is found at a crime scene in order to verify that the firearm was fired.

How do experts in the lab analyze nonvisible gunshot residue (GSR) on objects?

In some cases, the gunshot residue (GSR) on objects may not be visible to the naked eye. In those cases, experts in the lab use several types of chemical techniques to extract more details from collected evidence. For example, the Sodium Rhodizonate Test (SRT) is used to detect the presence of lead in any form. This is especially useful to determine the vaporous lead (often seen as smoke coming out of a barrel of a gun or shotgun), particles of lead, a lead bullet, or a shot pellet wipe (also called a bullet wipe).

Why is nonvisible gunshot residue (GSR) often challenged as evidence?

Looking for nonvisible gunshot residue (GSR) isn't always the best way to determine guilt or innocence of a person at a crime scene. For example, GSR lasts a very long time. It doesn't degrade but is easily transferred from one surface to another. Thus, it can land on anything, staying there indefinitely. This makes possible contamination an issue: if a person practices on a range (including police, military personnel, or people who practice at a fir-

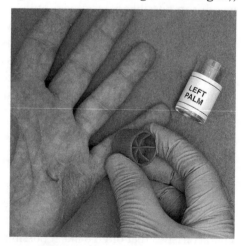

A gunshot residue test is performed on a suspect's hand. When someone fires a gun, it can leave traces of GSR on their skin and clothes.

ing range or at their own personal range in a rural area), the GSR will stay on that person. When he or she comes into contact with others, the GSR can "rub off" (in other words, the person who is touched or touches someone who has fired a firearm can test positive for GSR). In fact, a source of contamination may even be an arresting officer. The only time such evidence may be valuable is if the GSR can definitely be traced back to a piece of clothing or other person or object at a crime scene. Because of this problem, the FBI stopped using GSR analysis in 2006, claiming it wanted to use more of its resources to fight terrorism, but in general, most forensic groups agree that agencies like the FBI determined that GSR has its limitations when it comes to using it as a definite proof in a crime.

SHOES AND TIRE PRINTS

Why are shoe prints and tire impressions considered trace evidence?

Shoe prints and vehicle tire impressions are often considered trace evidence, especially if a possible connection exists between the prints found at a crime scene, a victim, and/or a suspect. For example, a shoe print can be used to determine such crime scene aspects as the number of people involved or where the perpetrators walked at the crime scene. A vehicle's tire impression may reveal how many vehicles were involved or the direction a vehicle was traveling. (For more about shoe and tire prints as patent and latent print evidence, see the chapter "In the Crime Lab: Patent, Latent, and Plastic Prints.")

Do databases exist for shoes and/or shoe imprints?

Yes, according to the National Institute of Justice, several databases are used by forensic experts to determine details of shoe imprints. For example, one is called TreadMark™ that uses pattern, size, damage, and wear to identify a person's outsole impressions. This is then compared to other shoe print data from the suspects in custody and the crime scene trace evidence of shoe imprints. Another footwear database sold on DVD and updated every three months is SoleMate™. The database from this commercial company presents specific information about shoes, including the manufacturer, date of market release, an image or offset print of the sole, and images of the uppers for more than twelve thousand sports, work, and casual shoes. One caveat to identifying a shoe based on this database is that various manufacturers sometimes use the same sole on their shoe, often making it difficult to definitely identify a certain shoe print.

Do databases exist for tires that are useful to forensic experts?

As with several of the other trace evidence databases, the database available for tire treads is maintained by a commercial concern. For example, TreadMate™ is owned by the same United Kingdom company that markets SoleMate™ (see above). This database offers information on more than five thousand vehicle tires and tire tread patterns (for instance, waves, lines, diamonds, or zigzags in the tread), including the tire manufacturer, the date the tire was released to the market, images of the tire, and features of the tread patterns. Such identification has one caveat: sometimes, manufacturers use the same tread, so the match will not be completely reliable. In such cases, records are linked so that all tires that might match a crime scene tire mark may be considered.

OTHER PHYSICAL TRACE EVIDENCE

What is cordage?

In terms of evidence at a crime or accident scene, cordage is considered to be such items as rope, string, or twine. Cordage is often referred to in the crime lab as textile fiber analysis. Such materials differ based on such factors as being natural or synthetically made, the ply (for example, a two-ply yarn, in general, means two yarns twisted together), or the origins of the cordage's composition (for instance, if it is made from wool, cotton, or nylon).

How can a simple knot analyzed in the crime lab be used as evidence?

Yes, how a rope is tied in a knot—or even other trace evidence caught in the knot—can often be analyzed in the crime lab and used as evidence. In particular, if a knot that is thought to be involved in a crime (such as a suspicious death) is found, photographs are taken of the knot(s) *in situ* (or right where it was found) from several different angles. In addition, knot evidence may not tell who tied the knot, but it may determine whether the knot was self-tied (as in a suicide) or externally tied (as in a homicide). Data must also be collected as to the length of the cord or rope segment(s), the circumference of each loop in the knot, the knot structure (type of knot tied, such as half knots, granny knots, overhand knots and loops, and half hitches), the color and composition of the rope, and the quality of the rope ends (cut, melted, or frayed). The knots can also be analyzed in the lab to see whether any biological elements are caught in the rope, such as blood, semen, or saliva, that can be used for DNA analysis, and/or other physical evidence, such as paint, glass, or fibers.

How are different types of tapes analyzed in the crime lab?

Physical examinations of tapes found at a crime scene include assessment and documentation of such features as the backing, adhesive, tape width, and the fabric reinforcement, such as that found in duct tape. Once physical examinations are completed, a chemical analysis is often conducted on the adhesive and backing layers. Most of the time, this analysis of the adhesive composition is done using such instruments as a Fourier-transform infrared spectroscope (FTIR) and/or scanning electron microscope with energy dispersive x-ray spectroscopy (SEM/EDS).

Do any databases exist for adhesive tapes?

Yes, several databases have extensive files on the characteristics of tape. For example, the Federal Bureau of Investigation's (FBI) National Forensic Tape File is used for determining the manufacturer and/or product for duct tape. At this writing, between four hundred and five hundred tape samples are in the repository, most of them from local retailers and others from the actual manufacturing plant or from requests for samples from specific companies. In some cases, the physical properties and chemical composition of a tape can be searched in the Spectra Library for Identification and Classification Engine (SLICE) computer program to determine a possible manufacturer or to uncover the actual product. From there, the SLICE results can be used with the NFTF for a direct comparison.

What is forensic palynology?

Forensic palynology is the study of pollen and spores (some references add other minute plant particles, such as single-celled dinoflagellates, which are mostly marine plankton). These small microorganisms can be used as crime scene trace evidence. Although their use as evidence has been known for over five decades, they are often ignored. Based on where and when certain pollen and spores are produced in a certain area, forensic palynologists can use these microorganisms as evidence to determine whether a victim of a crime (or a suspect) was in a specific area at a certain time.

What are pollen and spores?

Pollen and spores are measured in micrometers. For instance, some of the largest are around 250 micrometers (0.0098 inches) to less than 2 micrometers (0.000079 inches) in size. Pollen comes from pollen-producing plants, with the pollen most often carried by winds and occasionally by animals, people, or insects. They are divided into two classes: angiosperms (vascular seed-bearing or flowering plants that reproduce by enclosed seeds, such as sunflowers and roses, and oak and maple trees); they make up 80 percent of all living plant species on Earth) and gymnosperms (vascular plants in which the seeds are exposed, such as ginkgos and conifers). Spores come from spore-producing plants such as algae, fungi, liverworts, mosses, ferns, and so on. They reproduce with tiny spores, which are usually carried by winds and less often by animals, people, and vehicles.

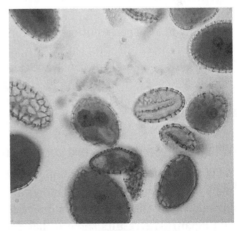

Pollen granules such as these, as well as spores from plants, are studied by forensic palynologists to help determine where people have been or even where crimes have been committed.

How can pollen and spores be useful as trace evidence?

Pollen and spores are of use to forensic experts for many reasons. For example, the distribution of pollen and spores carried by the wind is considered a somewhat inefficient system. This is because many of the tiny particles do not travel far, with most falling to the ground. This forms a record of the vegetation in the area, which can be used as a way of determining a certain area. In addition, because the majority of pollen and spores are microscopic, they can become trapped or carried away by a person's clothing, vehicle, or virtually any type of surface. This can enable the particles to be used as clues to link a suspect with a victim, crime scene, or even geographic region. Another reason is that each plant releases certain types of pollen and/or spores that can be identified to the genus and species, making them useful as trace evidence. Finally, because these particles are so small and needed for reproduction of the plant, they are highly resistant to decay or destruction, and if the pollen or spores—for example, on clothing or an object—are collected and stored correctly, they can often be analyzed not only for recent crimes but for crimes or accidents that took place years ago.

Can feathers be used as trace evidence?

Yes, feathers have been used as trace evidence, but it is uncommon. In particular, certain feather characteristics, such as size, color, pattern, and where the feather came from on the bird, can often be used to identify certain bird species. Thus, if a feather is found in association with a crime scene, it may be identified in order to determine whether it is instrumental to a crime. For example, if a victim was killed in a room that had a parrot, a feather on a suspect may be used as evidence.

Can money be examined for trace evidence?

Yes, money is often examined for trace evidence, especially in association with criminal activities. For example, money is often analyzed to determine trace amounts of drugs, especially in a suspected drug bust. Money can also be examined for traces of blood or other fluids in connection with a burglary and subsequent murder. However, money is not always a good indication of trace evidence. For example, according to the American Chemical Society, money is contaminated with traces of cocaine and other drugs in various countries and can be found—in minute amounts—in most people's wallets, purses, or pockets.

What recent study examined cocaine contamination of money?

A 2009 study using gas chromatography/mass spectrometry was carried out to determine the contamination of banknotes of several different denominations. The sampling included more than thirty cities in five countries (United States, Canada, China, Brazil, and Japan). The results showed that cocaine is present in up to 90 percent of paper money (they sampled 234 banknotes) in the United States, especially in larger cities such as Boston, Detroit, and Baltimore. They also found that 95 percent of the banknotes from Washington, D.C., had traces of cocaine. This was quite a contrast to a study con-

What happened to an English bus driver and banknotes contaminated with cocaine?

For law-enforcement officers and experts in forensics, banknotes contaminated with cocaine can lead to an arrest of a criminal—or it may backfire. For example, in 2015, a bus driver in Bristol, England, was fired from his job because he tested positive for drugs, and even though another test proved he had not taken any drugs for ninety days (by a hair follicle test; plus, he claimed he had never taken any drugs), they still did not give him his job back. The driver proved that on the day of his test, he had handled several hundred pounds of banknotes from riders and suggested that drugs on the notes were transferred from the money to his hands and into his body. (He also claimed he had not washed his hands before the test.) A tribunal agreed, and the driver won a substantial payout from the company.

ducted two years before, in which it was determined that 67 percent of paper bills in the United States were contaminated with cocaine—or about a 20 percent rise in contamination. Canada also had a high contamination rate of around 85 percent; Brazil had fewer notes analyzed, but those that were checked showed an 80 percent amount of contamination; China and Japan had between 12 and 20 percent contamination. (The amounts of cocaine ranged from 0.006 micrograms to over 1,240 micrograms of cocaine per U.S. bill; to compare, a grain of sand weighs about twenty-three micrograms, and a gram contains one million micrograms.) The researchers did add an important caveat: these amounts of cocaine are not any concern to the general public, and the notes should not have any legal or health ramifications.

IN THE CRIME LAB:
PATENT, LATENT, AND PLASTIC PRINTS

DEFINING PRINTS

What are the general types of prints that can be analyzed from a crime scene?

Prints are categorized into three general types: patent (visible), latent (invisible or rarely visible), or plastic (roughly three-dimensional) prints. Each one forms and is collected as evidence at a crime or accident scene in a certain way (see below). The patent and latent prints in forensics include such evidence as fingerprints, while plastic prints are mainly evidence such as shoe and tire impressions. (For more about prints collected at a crime scene, see the chapter "At the Crime Scene: Looking for Physical Evidence.")

What is the earliest use of certain types of prints in terms of forensics?

It is thought that several Chinese records from the Qin Dynasty (221 to 206 B.C.E.) indicate the first use of handprints as evidence. In particular, the records include details about using such prints as evidence from burglary investigations.

Can fingerprints be recovered from an underwater crime scene?

In some cases, yes, fingerprints can be recovered from an underwater crime scene, but it depends on several conditions, including the type of surface, the amount of time the item was submerged under the water, and whether the recovery technique preserves the print. According to some underwater criminal investigation agencies, submersion of an item does not mean that prints will be found, but in some instances, fingerprints on such surfaces as metal, glass, and plastics have been recovered after being underwater for several days (several references mention at least five days). In addition, if some prints are out of the flow of water (for example, away from a river's currents, such as inside a submerged vehicle), the better the chance of finding a print after a few days, but overall, the longer the item is submerged, the less chance that exists of finding prints of any kind.

Why can prints be hard to collect or see at a crime scene?

Prints of any kind—from palm and fingerprints to lip and footprints—can be found on almost any surface at a crime scene, but with some challenges. This includes prints on rough, uneven, or heavily textured surfaces (the ridges of the print do not readily adhere to such surfaces); prints on materials that rapidly decay (such as fruits); or prints that have been contaminated by other sources (such as people or animals at the crime scene).

In what form are prints taken from the crime scene to the lab for analysis?

In general, patent (visible) prints are mainly collected by photography, as are plastic prints. Latent (mostly invisible) prints take more time and effort to collect as evidence, as they have to be gathered using other means, such as being exposed to certain special chemicals. From there, a latent print can be photographed and documented to use as evidence. (For more about such prints, see this chapter.)

DEFINING PATENT, LATENT, AND PLASTIC PRINTS

How do patent, latent, and plastic prints form?

Patent prints most often form in two ways. When a person's fingers (or foot, lip, etc.) come in contact with an object, the natural oils and other residue in the fingers make a print on a surface, for example, fingerprints on a knife. The other way is when a person's fingers come in contact with a foreign material, for example, blood or paint, and leave a visible fingerprint. Latent prints are those that are invisible, or partially visible, and are formed when the body's natural oils and sweat are found on certain surfaces through various techniques. (Sweat may be 99 percent water, but other contaminants, such as amino acids, fatty acids, and salt, are left behind.) For example, if the print is not readily visible, such techniques as using fingerprint powders can be used to see the ridges more easily. Plastic prints are three-dimensional impressions left in a soft surface, such as sand, mud, or snow, collected for the crime lab in various ways depending on conditions. (For more information about prints, see the chapter "At the Crime Scene: Looking for Physical Evidence.")

How are crime scene patent prints examined in the lab?

Patent prints from a crime scene are usually analyzed by comparing the unknown prints to known prints on file. Before this can be done, the crime lab experts need to conduct an examination of the print. For example, patent fingerprint examiners use a small magnifier called a loupe to view the small details of a print, which also has a pointer called a ridge counter. The process is often referred to by forensic references as the ACE-V method—or the analysis, comparison, evaluation, and verification method. The "analysis" involves looking at a print to see if it is suitable for comparison study, and if so, further analysis of the print's physical features (for example, creases and various standard fingerprint patterns; for more about fingerprint features, see this chapter). The "comparison" involves a side-by-side look at a known print with a suspect's print. For fingerprints, this is usually done using a computer fingerprint database system, for instance, the Integrated Automated Fingerprint Identification System (IAFIS; for more about the IAFIS, see this chapter). The "evaluation" is when the examiner de-

A loupe is a small magnifier that is easily held in between your fingers to take a close look at small items of evidence.

termines whether the prints are from the same source, different sources, or the examination was inconclusive. Finally, "verification" is when other experts examine the same known and unknown prints thought to be identical, and they support or don't support the conclusions of the original examiner.

Why are some patent print—and some latent print—examinations determined to be inconclusive?

Not all studies of patent prints—and some latent prints—in the lab result in matching a suspect with a known print. This is due to several reasons, such as a poor sample quality (often from contamination or only partial prints), not enough features in the print to verify identification, or no (or few, and they are questionable) areas of the found print compare to a known print.

What are some conditions that affect a latent print?

Collecting latent prints as evidence at a crime scene can often be a challenge. This is because many factors influence the overall condition of the print. For example, the environment surrounding the print may be too hot, cold, wet, etc. (for instance, since a latent print is mostly in the form of natural sweat and oils, if the print is made outdoors in an arid climate, it may not survive). Or, the surface conditions of the object containing the print may also be too hot, cold, textured, snowy, etc., for a print to survive or even form. The print may not even be found—especially if other evidence may supersede the crime scene technicians' attention or "enough" evidence exists. Even the perpetrator's biology (for example, they are sweating too much—or too little—meaning that no sweat or oils are on their fingertips) can influence the resulting latent print.

What are some ways to reveal latent prints in the lab?

Latent prints can be revealed in the lab in numerous ways. In fact, several methods and more than two dozen types of chemicals are used to process the prints (but only a few are mentioned here), depending on the print's condition or where it was discovered. The following lists some of those methods:

- *Alternate light source*—If a forensic examiner determines that fingerprint powders will contaminate possible latent print evidence, they may examine the object with an alternate light source. This is also done at the crime scene to any likely surface that a suspect may have touched, such as doorknobs, windowsills or glass, desks, chairs, stairway railings, etc.

- *Laser or LEDs*—Some "subdivisions" of the alternate light source are laser or LED devices that emit certain wavelengths of light. They are often used in the lab to examine latent prints, especially using certain powders or dye stains. For instance, a fluorescent dye stain and an orange alternate light source are often used to make the latent print easier to appear and document.

- *Superglue*—Another method is known as cyanoacrylate (superglue is made up of 98 percent cyanoacrylate), which is used to reveal latent prints, especially from nonporous surfaces such as metal, glass, or plastic. The glue is heated to a vapor (fumes) and exposed to the latent print. The vapor literally clings to the residue of the fingerprint, which can be viewed with an oblique ambient light or white light source. It can then be photographed and/or further examined using different types of powders.

- *Chemical developers*—If latent fingerprints are suspected on porous surfaces, especially paper, they are usually processed in the crime lab using various chemicals to reveal the print details. For instance, ninhydrin and a physical developer react with certain components of a person's finger residues, such as salts and amino acids. In particular, once heated, the ninhydrin causes the print to turn purple and thus be easily photographed and documented. (Many of these chemical treatments are performed *after* the evidence is examined using nondestructive techniques, such as an expert in handwriting checking a questioned document; for more about examining questioned documents, see the chapter "In the Crime Lab: Questioned Documents and Cryptanalysis.")

How are latent prints collected for the lab?

Latent prints—especially fingerprints—are collected for the crime lab in several ways. For example, the most common method is using fingerprint "dust," or dusting smooth surfaces with certain types of powder, such as black granular, aluminum flake, or black magnetic powders. When revealed by the powder, the print is photographed and/or lifted from the surface with clear adhesive tape. The tape is then added to a specially designed latent lift card to document, record, and preserve the print for further analysis in the lab. Once in the lab, the details of the prints (or the patterns of the print) are examined for potential matches using various computer fingerprint databases and other comparisons.

Can fingerprints be found on the human body—especially a murder victim?

Yes, fingerprints—or other types of prints—can be found on almost every type of solid surface, including the human body. That being said, obtaining prints from a murder victim's skin can be very challenging. For example, the print may be smudged due to a struggle between the victim and perpetrator. The victim may also have a great deal of hair on their body, so the perpetrator's finger ridges don't make enough contact to produce a good print. The victim may be covered in some type of residue (such as dirt), so no prints were formed. Or, if a long period of time has passed since the victim was murdered and the body decomposes in days, the prints can be lost.

THE DETAILS OF FINGERPRINTS

Are fingerprints considered to be patent, latent, or plastic prints?

Prints from a person's fingers can either be patent, latent, or plastic prints. Fingerprints that are patent prints usually show up readily as impressions on objects, walls, and other items. Fingerprints that are latent prints usually show up after experts at a crime scene "expose" the print using chemical or physical means. Plastic fingerprints are often found in soft substances, such as in wax or caulking.

What is dermatoglyphics?

Dermatoglyphics, or the study of fingerprints (roughly translated as "skin" [*derma*] and "curves" or "carving" [*glyph*]), recognizes the basic patterns of fingerprints called arches, loops, and whorls. Dermatoglyphics is of interest in such diverse fields as medicine, anthropology—and, for over a century, as evidence in criminology cases. (For more about the history behind fingerprints and crime, see the chapter "The History of Forensic Science.")

What is dactyloscopy?

Dactyloscopy is the analysis and classification of patterns observed on a finger—or fingerprints. It is translated from the Greek words (with many different spellings): *daktylos* (or *dactylo*, "finger") and *skopein* (or *skopeo*, "to examine").

Who was the first to recognize that fingerprints were unique to each individual?

German anatomist Johann Christoph Andreas Mayer (1747–1801) was the first person to realize that fingerprints were unique to each individual. In his *Anatomical Copperplates with Appropriate Explanations*, he wrote that "the arrangement of skin ridges is never duplicated in two persons." It would take many more years before the idea would be applied to using fingerprints as evidence at a crime scene. (For more about early work with fingerprints, see the chapter "The History of Forensic Science.")

According to some historical records, when were fingerprints first used for identification?

According to some historical records, it is thought that fingerprints were first used for identification around 600 B.C.E., but instead of using it for criminal actions, it was used by merchants. In particular, Arabic merchants would obtain a debtor's fingerprint and attach it to a bill for identification.

Can fingerprints be permanently changed or destroyed?

An individual's fingerprints remain the same throughout his or her entire life. Minor cuts or abrasions, and some skin diseases such as eczema or psoriasis, may

There's a scene in the science fiction film *Men in Black* in which an agent has his fingerprints permanently removed for the sake of anonymity. In the real world, this is not possible to do. Even if you burn them off with acid, the prints will return.

cause temporary changes to the fingerprints, but when they heal, the fingerprints will return to their original ridge patterns. More serious injuries to the skin that damage the skin might leave scars that change or disrupt the ridge pattern of the fingerprints, but examining the skin outside the area of damage can often reveal the same fingerprint pattern.

At what stage of development do fingerprints form?

For humans, at about thirteen weeks of gestation, the fetus has developed outer ridges that will eventually develop into fingerprints. These become more and more defined, and at about twenty-one to twenty-four weeks, the ridges resemble their adult form.

What is the evolutionary reason for fingerprints?

No one truly agrees why humans have fingerprints, but several theories exist. For example, it is thought that fingerprint friction ridges developed to give humans a better grip on things (although one recent study suggested that the ridges did not improve human ancestors' grips as well as previously thought). Another suggestion is that the ridges caused water to wick from the hands, allowing a better grip on wet surfaces. Still another suggestion is that the ridges improved human hands' tactile sensitivity.

What are friction ridges and furrows?

Friction ridges and furrows form a person's fingerprint pattern found on the pads of their fingers and thumbs. The friction ridges are the raised part of the pattern, while the furrows are the recessed parts. When a person is "fingerprinted"—or the print left when

---

What is the name of the protein that holds the body's skin together?

The protein that holds the skin together is called collagen. It makes up between 25 and 35 percent of the body's proteins, making it the most abundant protein in the entire human body. Humans are not the only ones, as collagen makes up most of the proteins found in all mammals.

---

a person's inked finger is pressed on a special paper—it is actually revealing the friction ridges and furrows of that particular finger.

Who first wrote about ridges and furrows on a person's hands and feet?

English plant anatomist and physiologist Nehemiah Grew (1641–1712; he was also known as "the father of plant anatomy" and was a contemporary of Marcello Malpighi [for more about Malpighi, see the chapter "The History of Forensic Science"]) was the first to publish information about ridges, furrows, and pores on the hands and feet. Although no connection was mentioned about using these structures as evidence in criminal investigations, he is considered one of the pioneers in the field of dactyloscopy. In 1684, he published a paper on finger ridge patterns, or fingerprints, titled "The description and use of the pores in the skin of the hands and feet" in the *Philosophical Transactions of the Royal Society of London*. (For more about fingerprints as evidence in a crime, see this chapter and the chapter "At the Crime Scene: Looking for Physical Evidence.")

What are often called "Galton's details"?

Galton's details are named after Francis Galton (1822–1911), who was the first person to classify fingerprints. They are often thought of as characteristics of a person's fingerprint—sometimes called minutiae—including identifying points such as ridge endings, ridges that seem to divide (called bifurcations), short ridges, spots (also called dots), and even enclosures that resemble an island.

Who first used fingerprints as a means of identification in terms of forensics?

It is generally acknowledged that Francis Galton was the first to classify fingerprints. However, his basic ideas were further developed by Sir Edward Henry (1850–1931), who devised a system based on the pattern of the thumbprint. In 1901 in England, Henry established the first fingerprint bureau with the Scotland Yard called the Fingerprint Branch. Today, the Federal Bureau of Investigation (FBI) files house the fingerprints and criminal histories of more than 75 million subjects in a criminal master file, along with more than 34 million civil prints. (For more about Galton, Henry, and fingerprinting, see the chapter "The History of Forensic Science.")

Are footprints and palm prints unique to each person?

It is thought that bare footprints and palm prints are unique to each person—and such evidence has been used to catch criminals. For example, in 1968, a burglar took off his shoes and used his socks to cover his hands so he would not leave any fingerprints. He was later caught—the evidence based on the imprint of his bare feet.

What are groups of patterns often used to identify a person's fingerprint?

Four distinct groups of friction ridge and furrow patterns were developed by Sir Edward Richard Henry in the late 1800s. Today's groupings usually only include three of the four—loops, whorls, and arches. Each pattern has a certain variation depending on how the friction ridges and furrows formed. Loops curve back on themselves, creating a loop shape; around 60 to 70 percent of the fingerprint patterns contain loops. Whorls create a circular pattern (or spiral whirlpool pattern); they constitute about 25 to 35 percent of the fingerprint patterns. Arches have a wave (some say hill- or dunelike, too) pattern; they represent about 5 percent of the fingerprint patterns encountered.

What are some terms associated with fingerprint patterns?

Friction ridge patterns have several terms associated with their patterns. For example, certain classes (or levels) are associated with a fingerprint. The class one/level one is the general ridge flow of a fingerprint; class two/level two is the details of the friction ridge path, such as ending, division, or bifurcations (it is also referred to as "Galton's details"; see above); and class three/level three are the smallest, finer details of the individual ridges, such as the width and shape of the ridge edge, and whether pores exist within the individual ridges (called poreoscopy; see below).

What are poreoscopy and edgeoscopy?

Poreoscopy is the study of the minute pores that appear in fingerprint ridges. Edgeoscopy is the study of the shape or contours of the edges of fingerprint ridges. Experts often use poreoscopy and edgeoscopy to identify possible perpetrators, mainly using latent fingerprints collected from a crime scene. Both of these concepts were first presented by French forensic scientist Edmond Locard (1877–1966; often referred to as the "Sherlock Holmes of France"), who also developed the Locard Exchange Principle. (For more about Locard, see the chapter "The History of Forensic Science.")

What are the common types of friction ridge/furrow patterns?

The three overall types of friction ridge/furrow patterns of loops, whorls, and arches have several more divisions. The following lists the general types of each that are most commonly used today:

- *Radial loop*—This loop points toward the radius bone of the hand, or the thumb. In other words, the downslope of the loop is from the direction of the little finger toward the thumb.

- *Ulnar loop*—This loop points from the thumb toward the little (pinky) finger, or just the opposite direction from the radial loop.

- *Plain whorl*—A plain whorl looks like concentric circles, or complete circles within circles.

- *Central pocket whorl*—This pattern has one or more simple recurves of the plain whorl.

- *Double loop whorl*—This pattern has two separate loop formations.

- *Accidental whorl*—This pattern comes from two distinct patterns with at least two deltas.

- *Plain arch*—This type of pattern has a more subtle pattern, similar to a wave. The pattern usually starts on one side of the finger and rises in the middle like a wave to the other side of the finger.

- *Tented arch*—This type of pattern—which is often said to resemble a pitched tent, thus the name—rises to a sharper point than the plain arch. Like the plain arch, it starts on one side of the finger, rises more sharply in the middle, then goes down to the other side of the finger.

What are some further descriptions of friction ridge/furrow patterns?

In order to better identify fingerprints, experts include certain other shapes in the common types of friction ridge/furrow patterns. For example, "delta" is a point in a loop and whorl that lies within an often triangular, three-pronged, or funnel-shaped structure.

What were some additional types of friction ridge/furrow patterns suggested by Sir Edward Richard Henry?

Several other types of friction ridge patterns were suggested by Sir Edward Richard Henry toward the end of the nineteenth century called composites— or combinations of arches, loops, and whorls. They are still used today but not as much as the other patterns (see above). They include the central pocket loop (a recurving of the loop that forms a pocket within the loop), lateral pocket loop (with ridges that bend sharply down on one side before recurving, forming a pocket), double or twin loop (or one that has two separate loop formations that create an S-like pattern), and accidental loop (irregular-shaped or a combination of two types of patterns [except that it does not include the plain arch because it has no true pattern]).

Loop patterns have one delta, while whorls have two or more. Another feature is called a "shoulder" and is the point of a loop's recurving ridge, which curves back around.

Do identical twins have the same fingerprints?

No. It was once thought that identical twins had the same fingerprints, as they have the same DNA and look the same, but their fingerprints are different. Some of the ridges and patterns may be very similar but can be discerned by fingerprint experts. In fact, research indicates that fingerprints would not be the same even if an individual were to be cloned.

Are fingerprints always well defined at a crime scene?

No, not all fingerprints are well defined—especially at a crime scene. Some prints may be smeared due to movement of the person's hand, while other prints may be contaminated by the people who were at the crime scene. In addition, certain types of surfaces, such as plastics, can break up the imprint of the finger's friction ridges and furrows, causing the print to lose details necessary when using a fingerprint as evidence. (For controversies surrounding fingerprints, see the chapter "Controversies in Forensic Science.")

How did John Dillinger and Roscoe Pitts attempt to change their fingerprints?

American criminal John Dillinger (1903–1934) used acid to burn his fingerprints in an attempt to permanently change them by removing the ridge patterns. He failed, and the fingerprints that reappeared were identical to the ones he had tried to change. Another American criminal named Roscoe Pitts (real name Robert Phillips) asked a New Jersey physician (and ex-con) to perform a more dramatic way to permanently alter fingertips. The physician taped Pitts's cut right-hand fingers to the criminal's chest. After three weeks, when the chest skin had grown into the fingertips, Pitts's hand was separated from his chest, resulting in smooth fingertips. Pitts's endured the procedure on his left hand for

What animal has almost humanlike fingerprints?

Humans are not the only mammals with fingerprints. Most primates, not including humans, have a type of "fingerprint" that resembles ridges—mainly to give the animal a better grip on the ground or in bushes or trees. This includes primates such as the ape, chimpanzee, and gorilla, and one animal has fingerprints that are almost humanlike: the cuddly koala bear. The fingerprints of these Australian creatures are sometimes difficult to distinguish from a human's, as they are similar in size, shape, and type of patterns. No other mammals have such distinct ridges or "fingerprints," but many animals do have other types of "prints." For example, animals such as pigs and dogs have hairless snouts and unique noseprints.

three more weeks. In the end, though, his girlfriend told authorities about his fingerprint procedure—and enough of the old prints were still at the edge of his fingertips to allow him to be identified.

Do fingerprints survive bomb blasts?

In some cases, yes, fingerprints can survive many types of bomb blasts, but it depends on the size of the bomb that causes the explosion and/or the surface material on which the fingerprint was imprinted. In addition, it also depends on a bit of luck, especially if investigators are fortunate enough to find a fingerprint(s) on a piece that has not been blown apart by the explosion. (For more about fingerprints and bombs, see the chapter "In the Crime Lab: Examining Explosives.")

Can fingerprints reveal gender?

Although it is currently still being debated by the scientific community, studies have shown that latent fingerprints—especially those that have been smudged so badly

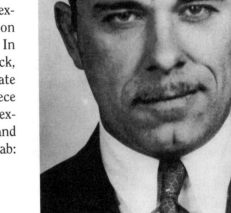

The famous American gangster John Dillinger tried to burn off his fingerprints—unsuccessfully.

that it is difficult to make a positive identification—may reveal a person's gender. In particular, one study from the University of Albany (New York) in 2015 showed that the biochemical content of a latent fingerprint (formed when a person's sweat and oils in the finger leave a mostly invisible print) may reveal the person's gender. By heating the latent fingerprint sample to a specific temperature, then analyzing it using a chemical dye, the sample oxidized to a certain color, indicating the amount of amino acids, and since the level of amino acids in sweat is about twice as high in women as in men, they believe that this method can be used to determine gender from a latent fingerprint.

What are some recent fingerprint and palm print databases?

Several newer fingerprint and palm print databases are being used for comparison and identification. For example, the Federal Bureau of Investigation (FBI) implemented the NGI, or Next Generation Identification. A subgroup of the NGI is called the Advanced Fingerprint Identification Technology (AFIT), which contained a new fingerprint-matching algorithm that improved matching accuracy from approximately 92 percent to over 99 percent. In 2013, a NGI called the National Palm Prints System (NPPS) was expanded and contains millions of palm prints that are now searchable on a nationwide basis. The

FBI also maintains the Integrated Automated Fingerprint Identification System, which, by 2012, had 72 million print records from civilian and government employees, military personnel, and criminals—and continues to expand as more fingerprints are added.

Why are the fingerprints of a person taken at a police station?

Many people need to "get their fingerprints taken" at a police station for various reasons: criminals, of course, who must be fingerprinted after being arrested, whether they are eventually convicted or not; people who want a pistol or other firearm permit; immigrants who are filing for a visa; federal employees (especially if they need a security clearance to do their job); and people entering the military.

How are fingerprints used for personal computer security?

Certain devices often have optical scanners and solid-state readers linked to software that analyzes the geometric patterns found in a person's fingerprint. These special devices then compare that person's fingerprint with those of registered, legitimate users of a network system, and if it is a match, they allow access to the system. Although such technology does not work all the time (false readings can occur), it is becoming more sophisticated and readily used. For example, in 2015 (and still in use as of this writing), the Apple computer company presented Touch ID, in which a user's fingerprint can be used as a passcode to unlock a personal computer system, such as the iPhone, iPad Air 2, or iPad Mini 3. Using a person's fingerprint instead of passwords is also starting to be used to link to individual bank accounts and automated teller machines and for credit cards and Internet transactions.

What is one new way of looking at fingerprints?

Currently, several companies are researching how to obtain more information from fingerprints. For example, the ArroGen Group (with offices in North Carolina and the United Kingdom) has developed a powder that contains submicron particles that stick to natural

What was SWGTREAD?

The Scientific Working Group for Shoeprint and Tire Tread Evidence (SWGTREAD) was created in 2004 by the FBI Laboratory to standardize and advance the forensic analysis of footwear and tire impression evidence. The first meeting took place in September 2004 and the last in March 2013. From 2004 to 2013, the working group was cofunded by the FBI and the National Institute of Justice (NIJ). However, in October 2014, the Footwear and Tire Subcommittee of the National Institute for Standards and Technology (NIST) Organization of Scientific Area Committees (OSAC) was created. At that point, SWGTREAD decided to discontinue its operations and focus.

amino and fatty acids that are found in the skin (often called biomolecules) and, thus, are found in that person's fingerprint imprint. The company's Finger Molecular Identification (FMID) process takes fingerprint samples collected from a scene; the powder is sprinkled on the print at the scene, removed using special lift tape, sealed, and transported to the lab. The print is then scanned with a mass spectrometer's laser, ionizing and vaporizing the particles in the powder and the human residue in the fingerprint. Those molecules are then examined. Depending on the quality of the print and the quantity of the biomolecules in the person's print, the results can indicate the person's gender, whether the person had contact with a gun or explosive, whether the person is a smoker, or even whether the person had recently used drugs (such as cocaine, marijuana, or heroin).

DETAILS OF SHOE AND TIRE PRINTS

Why are shoe prints important in crime scene analysis?

Shoe imprints are often important to a crime scene, as they may reveal a suspect. This includes such crimes as breaking and entering, assault, armed robbery, hit and run, rape, and homicide. For example, a shoe print found on a windowsill at a house that was burglarized may reveal suspects or even the perpetrator. Such prints will also reveal whether more than one person was involved and the direction a person may have walked or run before, during, and after the crime, and if the same shoe print is found at two crime scenes, it may reveal information about both scenes—or a suspect or victim at those scenes.

What are the differences between patent, latent, and plastic shoe or tire prints?

When it comes to examining various types of shoe or tire prints, each type of print has differences. Patent prints of shoes or tires are transfers of material from a shoe or tire to the surface. This is usually seen visually without additional aids, such as a bloody shoe print on a wood floor of a crime scene or the tracks of a vehicle's tires in a driveway covered with snow. Latent prints of shoes or tires are caused by static charges between the sole of a shoe or the tread of a tire and the surface. They are not readily seen, such as a shoe print on a windowsill or tire tracks on a driveway—all seen only after investigators use powders, chemicals, or special lighting to detect the prints. Plastic prints of shoes or tires are three-dimensional impressions that are left on a soft surface, such as a shoe imprint in the sand or tire track in mud.

How are shoe imprints taken at a crime scene?

Depending on the type of print impression—or whether it is considered a patent, latent, or plastic print—a shoe imprint will be examined in various ways. For example, for shoe impressions in soft surfaces (patent print), taking a cast of the impression is the most common way of collecting the evidence. A cast is made using powdered stone material (which looks like a fine cement) that can be mixed with water and poured into an impression. This creates a three-dimensional look at the shoe imprint for study. (For more about shoe and tire imprints from a crime scene, see the chapters "At the Crime Scene: Looking for Physical Evidence.")

If a shoe or tire print cannot be sent to the crime lab, what are some techniques to recover the evidence?

Examiners try to collect the entire object containing an imprint of a shoe or tire if possible; if not, such as a shoe print on a windowsill, a lifting technique can be used to transfer the imprint to a medium that would allow for transfer to the crime lab. These lifting techniques include an adhesive lifter, in which a heavy coating of adhesive lifts the imprint from a smooth surface, such as a metal container. A gelatin lifter is a sheet of rubber with a low-adhesive gelatin layer that can lift prints from almost any surface, such as rough, textured, or curved surfaces. It is less sticky and more flexible, allowing the imprint to be obtained from more fragile surfaces. Electrostatic dust-print lifting devices are tools that electrostatically charge the particles within a print impression under such conditions as dust or light soil. The particles are then attracted and bonded to a lifting film—a method that is good for collecting dry or dusty impressions.

IN THE CRIME LAB:
DNA ANALYSIS

DEFINING DNA

What is DNA, or deoxyribonucleic acid?

DNA, or deoxyribonucleic acid, is a nucleic acid formed from the repetition of what are commonly called "simple building blocks of life" (the scientific name is nucleotide). A nucleotide consists of a phosphate (chemical formula of PO_4), sugar, and a nitrogen base. Bases come in five types, called adenine (A), thymine (T), guanine (G), cytosine (C), and uracil (U). DNA is associated with adenine, thymine, guanine, and cytosine, whereas uracil is associated with RNA (or ribonucleic acid, a single-chain nucleic acid).

What does DNA resemble?

In a deoxyribonucleic acid, or DNA molecule, a basic unit is repeated in a double-helix structure made from two chains of nucleotides linked between the bases. This structure is often said to resemble a twisted ladder, with the steps, or links, either between adenine (A) and thymine (T) or between guanine (G) and cytosine (C). These are the only links, as the structures of the bases do not allow other kinds of connections.

How much DNA is in a typical human cell?

If the DNA (deoxyribonucleic acid) molecules in a single human cell were stretched out and laid end to end, they would measure approximately 6.5 feet (2 meters). The average human body contains 10 to 20 billion miles (16 to 32 billion kilometers) of DNA distributed among trillions of cells. If the total DNA in all the cells from one human were unraveled, it would stretch to the sun and back more than five hundred times.

What is a genome?

A genome is thought of as a living being's genetic material, whether it is an animal, plant, or bacteria, and so on. Genomes contain the hereditary instructions that allow an organism to function and maintain life. Each species on Earth has its own distinctive genome, which is why the media presents discoveries in certain genomes, including those of a dog, cow, virus, pepper, or even bacteria. In the majority of organisms—simply put and in sequence—the genome is divided into chromosomes, chromosomes contain the organism's genes, and genes are composed of DNA. In other words, people are unique mainly because their genomes are unique, and although a person is "unique," their genome is still recognized as a human genome, as the genome differences between two humans are much smaller than the genome differences between humans and, for example, the chimpanzee.

What is a chromosome?

A chromosome is the threadlike part of a cell that contains the hereditary material DNA. This single, tightly coiled strand of DNA's main function is to carry the genetic material of the body's many types of cells (what is often referred to as a membrane-bound unit). The human body consists of fifty trillion to one hundred trillion cells (the varia-

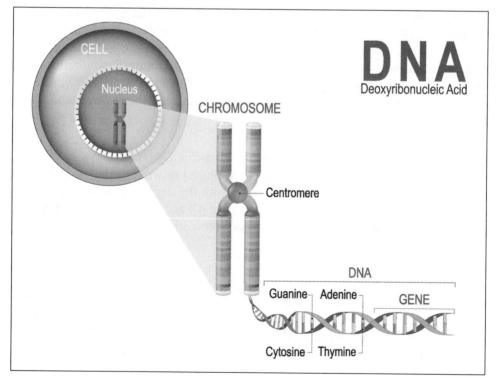

An illustration showing how a gene is a segment of a DNA molecule, which, in turn, is found as part of a chromosome.

tion in amount depends on the research). Each cell has forty-six chromosomes (also referred to as twenty-three pairs), which are structures in the nucleus containing the DNA. Each chromosome has a certain number of genes (see below). The largest chromosome (referred to as chromosome 1) has about eight thousand genes; the smallest chromosome (referred to as chromosome 21) contains less than three hundred.

What is a gene?

A gene is one of the complex protein molecules that are associated with chromosomes. They are responsible for—either as a unit or in certain biochemical combinations—the transmission of certain inherited characteristics from the parent to the offspring in humans and other animals. The term "gene" (from the Greek term *genos*, meaning "to give birth to") was first used in 1909 by Danish botanist Wilhelm Johannsen (1857–1927), who is considered to be one of the founders of modern genetics.

Can a person see a gene or a chromosome?

A gene cannot be seen because it is so small (what scientists call submicroscopic), whereas a chromosome that contains genes can be seen with an ordinary microscope. In fact, scientists can pinpoint the location of a gene on a chromosome, but the actual gene cannot be seen.

Is DNA unique to each person?

No, DNA is not unique to each person—but almost. It is known that more than three million differences exist between one person's genome versus anyone else's genome, but when you examine humans, their DNA is 99 percent the same. It is only "99.9 per-

Do humans share any DNA with other animals?

Yes, humans do share a certain percentage of their DNA with other animals—from large to small. For example, humans are members of the family Hominidae, of which the closest relatives are the great apes, orangutans, chimpanzees, gorillas, and bonobos (formerly called the pygmy chimpanzee and, less often, the dwarf or gracile chimpanzee, considered an endangered great ape). Of the great apes in particular, the great apes and humans share 98.4 percent of their DNA, and of the bonobos and chimpanzees, humans share 98.8 percent (although these numbers differ by ±0.3 percent depending on the reference) of their DNA. Other animals share a great deal of DNA with humans: Mice share about 90 percent of their DNA (this is why mice have been used in laboratories and experiments to understand human disease processes for decades); dogs share 84 percent of their DNA (which is why dogs, too, have been studied to understand certain human diseases). Even birds share a certain amount of DNA with humans—a decent 65 percent.

cent" because some humans do have the "same" DNA: identical twins. (This is also known as having the "same" genome; see above.)

What percentage of human DNA gives a person their physical characteristics?

Certain characteristics of a person are determined by their genes. In fact, such features as hair and eye color, height, and some other characteristics are all determined by genes that are found in only 2 percent of human DNA (called the coding region, as it provides the instructions to the human proteins to form these features). The other 98 percent is considered to be the noncoding region, and in the past few years, scientists have only begun to realize this region's functions. In terms of forensics and DNA analysis, this noncoding DNA is definitely used, as the area contains unique repeating patterns that may be used to distinguish one person from another.

What are the various types of DNA?

DNA can be found in the center of a cell (the nucleus) or the mitochodria outside of the cell nucleus. The inside of the nucleus (which is often seen as nuclear DNA, or nDNA) can house two types of DNA—the autosomal chromosomes or the sex-determining chromosomes. In criminal investigations, the autosomal DNA is most used, as no two people (except identical twins) have the same autosomal DNA. If certain criminal cases are in question, such as a sexual assault, then the DNA in the sex-determining chromosomes may be useful to determine the assailant. Mitochondrial DNA (mtDNA) is found in the cell's mitochondria, or the part of the cell that supplies it with energy. It is the DNA inherited from a person's biological mother. Thus, in the majority of cases (and it is rare if not), all people who are related to a certain mother have the same mtDNA. (For more about using the various types of DNA in the crime lab, see this chapter.)

What are some good body sources of human DNA?

Many good sources of human DNA associated with a person's body can be analyzed in a crime lab. The best one is blood (it is found in the white blood cells, but not the red, as the red blood cells have no nucleus). DNA from sperm heads are also a good source of DNA and are most often used for identification in sexual assault cases. Saliva contains DNA and is often found in association with bite victims and on such items as cigarette butts and envelope flaps. Hair—as long as a hair follicle is attached—is a good source of human DNA. Bones and teeth are also often good sources of DNA and are commonly used to help identify decomposed bodies or skeletal remains. (For more about DNA and recent remains, see the chapter "In the Crime Lab: Analyzing a Body," and for DNA and ancient remains, see the chapter "In the Crime Lab: Analyzing Older Remains.")

Can two people have identical DNA?

Yes, two people can have identical DNA, but they have to be identical twins. No case, to date, has existed in which two people who are not identical twins have had the same DNA.

How long does DNA last?

The amount of time it takes before DNA disappears from any animal—including humans—is a matter of debate. Some scientists believe that DNA has a half-life (under the best conditions) of about 521 years, but it also depends on the type of sample in which the DNA is found. This means that after this time, DNA would break down and be useless for analysis. (This is also why most scientists believe we cannot extract DNA from dinosaur remains, as the creatures died out roughly sixty-five million years ago.) In terms of human remains, DNA longevity is mostly connected to the nature of the sample and where the DNA originated. For example, in a crime lab, DNA in saliva (if collected and stored under the best conditions) can last from about four to fourteen days. More solid evidence, such as DNA and skeletal remains, has a better chance of lasting for a much longer time.

OBTAINING DNA

What kinds of human substances found at a crime scene can contain DNA?

Many body fluids and biological tissues, if found at a crime scene, can often contain DNA—and, thus, be used as evidence. For example, body fluids include blood, urine, feces, semen, saliva, and sweat. Biological tissues include skin tissues and cells, hair, teeth, and bone.

What crime scene items have the potential to contain DNA?

Several types of items may be collected at a crime scene, all of which have the potential to contain DNA. Possible biological materials include those found on hats (with hair or sweat), masks (with saliva, hair, sweat, or skin tissues and cells), gloves (with sweat and skin tissues and cells), and clothing (a multitude of human biological material on clothes, underclothes, and even dirty laundry). Other items include tools and weapons, stamps and envelopes, various tapes, cups, bottles, glassware, bedding, and more personal items, such as a toothbrush, toothpick, facial tissues, handkerchief, hairbrush, eyeglasses, condoms, and jewelry (earrings, piercings, necklaces, bracelets, etc.). In other words, those items that have been touched or worn by a person have potential biological material that contains DNA that can be analyzed and used as evidence.

What are the types of samples used to make comparisons between a victim's or suspect's DNA?

In order to compare DNA between a victim, suspect, or other "person of interest," forensic experts collect various types of biological samples. Reference samples are the known biological samples that are on file already. In most jurisdictions, DNA samples are routinely obtained when a person is arrested, along with fingerprints (if anyone refuses to give a DNA sample, a court order is often required). Elimination samples are collected from con-

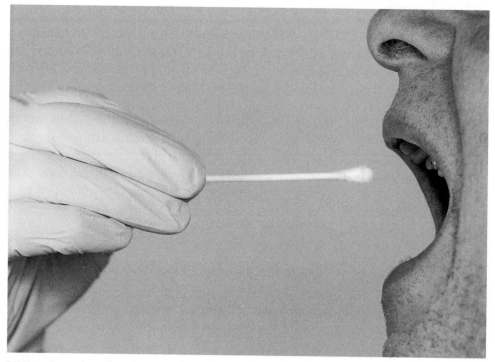

DNA samples can be easily gathered from skin cells or bodily fluids such as saliva. You may have even had a DNA test done by a doctor yourself; all that is needed is a cotton swab to collect the samples.

sensual sex partners and others, including first responders, analysts, and crime scene personnel who are working on a case, so they can be excluded from the investigation.

What is a buccal (cheek) swab?

A buccal (from the Latin *bucca*, or "near, around, etc., the cheek" or "mouth") swab or smear (or cheek swab) is one common way DNA cells are collected from the inside of a person's cheek. The reason for such a test is threefold—it is simple, can produce a larger sample size, and is noninvasive, as the cells from the cheek are collected using what resembles a small spatula. The cells are then evaluated in the lab for certain structures. For example, if a mass of what are called Barr bodies—structures seen in a normal female sex chromosome—are present, the test can confirm whether a person is male or female. If buccal cells are collected from various suspects and undergo a DNA analysis, the results can often link a person to a crime scene.

Do hair samples have any DNA?

Yes, hair samples from a crime scene often have DNA that may be useful to analyze in a forensic lab. Two types of DNA are usually analyzed: mitochondrial DNA (mtDNA), if no hair root (follicle) is attached, and nuclear DNA (nDNA), if a hair follicle is attached to the end of the hair. The following lists their characteristics and uses as evidence:

- *Mitochondrial DNA*—Mitochondrial DNA is more abundant than nuclear DNA, with thousands in a typical human cell, while a cell may have only one single copy of nDNA, but mtDNA is not as useful as nDNA, as mtDNA analysis of a hair cannot easily be used to discriminate between people and therefore is used only for comparison's sake and to *possibly* exclude one person versus another.

- *Nuclear DNA*—Nuclear DNA is the most useful as evidence in a crime. A human hair itself does not contain any nDNA, but it can be attached to the hair root, as they contain keratinocytes, or cells that are ideal for the extraction of nDNA. (A follicle can often be seen with the naked eye as a small, gray-white ball at the tip of the hair shaft.) However, according to several agencies involved in nDNA analysis, it is often estimated that extraction of a complete nDNA profile is only successful 60 to 70 percent of the time. (For more information about using human hairs as evidence, see the chapter "In the Crime Lab: Trace Evidence.")

Can chemical treatment to hair cause problems with DNA extraction?

Yes, chemical treatment to hair, such as using hair dye, can contribute to the degradation of DNA. In particular, peroxides—one of many chemicals found in most hair dyes—break down certain bonds in the DNA.

Is hair analyses in paternity tests similar to those used in forensics?

Yes, in most cases, companies and laboratories that offer consumer paternity or other types of family/relationship tests offer DNA testing that is similar to those used in forensics, but they will not offer DNA testing unless the hairs have the follicle attached.

What can affect DNA samples from a crime scene?

Several conditions can affect DNA samples from a crime scene, making the DNA worthless as evidence. For example, the age of the sample (older samples may not be as useful) or the surrounding environment of the sample collected (such as very high temperatures or chemical agents that may damage the DNA) can affect DNA samples. In addition, how the sample was collected before reaching the crime lab and how it was stored at the crime lab may have a bearing on how useful the DNA sample is to experts in hair analysis.

DNA TESTING

How is a DNA sample from a crime scene prepared for analysis?

A DNA sample from a crime scene is prepared in several steps. The first part of the process involves determining whether the sample is valid, useful, and truly a biological specimen. The next step is the process of extracting the DNA from the cell(s). This includes lysing (or breaking open) the cell; from there, certain chemical solutions are used to isolate the DNA from other components of the cell and to extract the DNA to use for analysis. The next steps include quantifying (determining) the amount of DNA extracted, called quantitation, and amplification (or the process of making multiple copies of the DNA to understand its characteristics). From there, separation (or separating the amplified DNA to allow subsequent identification), detection (or being able to "read" the various strands of DNA), and finally, analysis, interpretation, and quality assurance (or comparing the extracted DNA with known DNA sample profiles and verifying results).

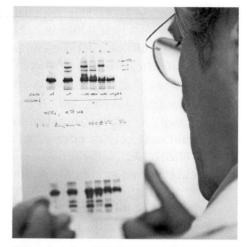

DNA analysis for criminal cases can take up to six months because of backlogs and the need to compare the results to more than one database on many occasions.

Do different types of DNA tests exist?

Yes, when discussing DNA in terms of analysis—including for forensic science—several different types of DNA tests exist. In general, the following lists the three types of DNA testing that are often used by forensic experts in the analysis of evidence:

- *Y-DNA*—This test involving nuclear DNA (or DNA from chromosomes inside the nucleus of the cell) reveals the male-gender-linked Y chromosome, which is passed from father to son, and so on. This is often used to eliminate cells that may have been from a female (who has X chromosomes). In addition, it can be used in identification purposes. This is because the Y chromosomes are passed through the father, and the males in line (brother, father, and male children) will have the same Y chromosome.
- *Mitochondrial DNA (mtDNA)*—This tests the mitochondrial DNA that is passed in the female line. It is passed from a mother to her children but can only be passed on by a daughter. Again, it can be used to eliminate cells that may be from a male (who has Y chromosomes) and used for possible identification in terms of the females in a family.
- *Autosomal DNA (atDNA)*—This test involves nuclear DNA from all of the chromosomes except the gender-linked X and Y chromosomes. It is often used for identification and can link cousins across genders.

How long does it take to analyze a DNA sample?

The time it takes to analyze a DNA sample varies considerably. Forensic references state that DNA samples from a crime scene can take two weeks to six months to analyze. To compare, a personal genetic test using DNA usually takes between twenty-four to seventy-two hours to complete. Although this longer time span for the forensic test often means the suspect or other person of interest is released from jail or custody, the wait is understandable. The sample has to be collected properly at the crime scene, trans-

> ## Why is mitochondrial DNA so important to forensic analysis?
>
> Mitochondrial DNA (mtDNA) involves the mitochondria, or small "organelles" that exist outside of a cell nucleus. One reason for using the mtDNA in forensic science is because of this frequency—it is present in much higher quantities than nuclear DNA (nDNA) and does not decay (degrade) as quickly. Forensic experts typically analyze for mtDNA in evidence containing naturally shed hairs (especially if the hair does not have any root or follicle attached), hair fragments, bones, and teeth. Because the mtDNA analysis is so sensitive, it is also used not only on recent evidence but can be used with evidence from cold cases, samples from mass disasters, or evidence that has only a small amount of biological residue attached.

ported to the lab, and analyzed using many databases in order to correctly identify the DNA of a specific person (if possible). In addition, as not every jurisdiction has its own DNA analysis lab, backlogs and reviews take place, slowing the results.

What is low-level DNA?

Low-level DNA (often called "touch DNA") is the DNA obtained from very small samples. For example, if a person touched a certain weapon at a crime scene, a small sample of their skin cells may be left behind (some references state that it only requires seven or eight cells from the outermost layer of a person's skin). From that touch, forensic experts may be able to extract DNA—even obtaining it from a victim's skin where they were roughly handled—in order to determine the identity of that person or to compare it to DNA obtained from a suspect.

What is low template and low copy number DNA analysis?

Although some references differ as to the actual definitions, in general, low template and low copy number DNA are connected. The low template DNA (seen as LT DNA or LTDNA) analysis is used when a small amount of DNA is present in a collected sample or evidence, the sample may contain mixed DNA profiles (in other words, be from two or more people), or the quality of the DNA is low. In some references, LTDNA is also often referred to as low copy number (seen as LCN DNA or LCNDNA), but even though they are connected, they do differ: LCNDNA is the process of using extra amplification of samples that have a small amount of DNA. In the overall interpretation of the DNA sample, these types of analyses use sophisticated algorithms to determine the statistical probabilities that a specific sample belongs to a certain person.

What are some problems with low template (low copy number) DNA analysis?

The use of low template (and low copy number) DNA (LTDNA) analysis has several problems. For example, in 2007 in the United Kingdom, a trial based on the 1998 Omagh bombing in Northern Ireland—a bomb that killed twenty-nine people—was terminated early and the defendant acquitted. The main reason was criticism of the LTDNA evidence from the judge. This was the impetus to review LTDNA evidence by the UK Forensic Science Regulator. According to its report, the underlying science was "sound" and the LTDNA profiling "fit for purpose," but the report also questioned the technique, stating that a lack of agreement existed "on how LTDNA profiles are to be interpreted." Since that time, other concerns have surfaced about LTDNA, including differences in interpretation of the resulting LTDNA profile and contamination of the samples obtained for analysis using LTDNA.

What is rapid-result DNA testing?

Rapid-result DNA testing is the function of a device called IntegenX RapidHIT ID. The device allows law enforcement to quickly analyze (a turnaround of less than ninety minutes) DNA collected from a suspect's buccal (cheek) swab to see whether it matches DNA from the DNA database in the local area. The pilot program began in 2017, with the first police department in the United States to use the device in Bensalem, Pennsylvania. If it succeeds, the unit may eventually be able to access the national CODIS database run by the FBI (such legislation is pending as of this writing; for more about CODIS, see this chapter).

What is the Next Generation Sequencing?

The Next Generation Sequencing (NGS, or Current Generation Sequencing) is a way that analysts reveal DNA sequences of the thousands of individual molecules found in a forensic sample. It uses mitochondrial DNA, with the specialized instruments carrying out massively parallel sequencing on thousands of DNA sequence clusters from samples. Through the process, experts can link an association between the various fragments— from a high- to low-quality and recent- and older-remains sample—that allows a deeper view of the sample's individual characteristics. From there, experts can make use of the DNA databases available to them to determine a possible match.

DNA PROFILING
AND PHENOTYPING

What is the difference between DNA profiling and forensic DNA phenotyping?

DNA profiling and forensic DNA phenotyping are two different things. The traditional DNA profiling—once and still often called DNA fingerprinting and oftentimes DNA testing, or genetic testing—uses DNA as a biometric (statistical analysis that is applied to biological data) identifier. (An identifier is a way of determining uniqueness and includes such things as fingerprints, hand geometry, a signature, the eye's retina and iris patterns, DNA, etc.) A person's DNA profile is unique (with the exception of identical twins), and if forensic experts can match a DNA profile with another individual in a DNA database, it can help eliminate (or not) certain suspects at, for example, a crime scene. On the other hand, forensic DNA phenotyping is used to narrow a group of possible individuals based on the person's traits found in their DNA. It is also used to help identify unknown human remains, as the phenotyping can reveal (to a point) a person's ancestry and possible appearance. Simply put, DNA profiling helps confirm a suspect's identity, while forensic DNA phenotyping helps to predict the suspect's (or unknown victim's) appearance and possible ancestry. (*Note*: DNA profiling differs from psychological profiling; for more about psychological criminal profiling and forensics, see the chapter "The Criminal Mind.")

A professor of genetics at Leicester University, Alec Jeffreys created the highly valuable technique of DNA fingerprinting.

Who is Alec Jeffreys?

British geneticist Alec Jeffreys (1950–) of Leicester University developed a technique he called "DNA fingerprinting" in the mid-1980s (references vary from 1984 to 1986, with the majority noting that his discovery was in the autumn of 1984). This technology— which is now more commonly known as DNA profiling—is often used to help identify individuals based on quality DNA samples collected as evidence at a crime or accident scene. In 1986, DNA profiling was first used by Jeffreys to aid in a criminal investigation in England.

What is polymorphism?

Polymorphism—or something that takes on several different forms—is often applied to the human DNA molecule. British geneticist Alec Jeffreys and his team discovered that these long DNA "threads" exhibit polymorphism, meaning that they are unique to everyone, which allows DNA experts to distinguish between individuals. This is particularly helpful when it comes to crime scene DNA analysis.

What are short tandem repeats (STR)?

The human genome, or a person's hereditary instructions, contains many repeated DNA sequences that come in various sizes. They are classified according to several properties, especially those found in what are classified under various repeat units. DNA regions with short repeat units (usually 2 to 6 bp, or base pairs) are referred to as short tandem repeats (STR), found at the structural center of the chromosomes. These short tandem repeats have become part of the DNA analysis in forensic science—especially as DNA biomarkers (or sometimes called biometric identifiers). One of the main reasons for their "popularity" in forensic DNA analysis is that they are easily amplified by a polymerase chain reaction (PCR; it allows small amounts of DNA in a sample, such as bone, to be copied or "amplified" for better analysis of the sample; see sidebar), which means better analysis of the DNA. In humans, a person inherits one copy of an STR from each parent (they may or may not have similar repeat sizes), but the STR markers are highly variable between individual people. Because of this uniqueness, the STRs are often used in forensics for human identification purposes, especially in DNA profiling (also called STR analysis).

What is polymerase chain reaction (PCR)?

A polymerase chain reaction (PCR) is a modern technique that can help create millions of precise DNA replications from a single sample of a person's DNA. For a forensic DNA analyst, depending on the methods used, this means that it is feasible to obtain even a few skin cells from a crime scene to create a duplicate of a person's DNA, but some controversies exist about this supersensitive method of analyzing a person's DNA. In particular, a possibility exists of contamination from another person's DNA, including those at the scene collecting evidence—or even if a person who was not involved in the crime was near the victim before the crime.

Why was DNA profiling not always possible in the 1980s and early 1990s?

DNA profiling was in its infancy in the 1980s and early 1990s, which meant that the collection of DNA at a crime scene was not as thorough or understood as it is today. Early DNA profiling also meant—even though it was considered accurate in most cases—the use of large quantities of high-quality DNA from the crime scene. This was not always possible during a forensic investigation, and certain procedures would often contaminate samples, but during this time, several breakthroughs occurred in DNA analysis, including the short tandem repeat (STR or microsatellite) marker and another way of visually seeing DNA called polymerase chain reaction (PCR) amplification (along with

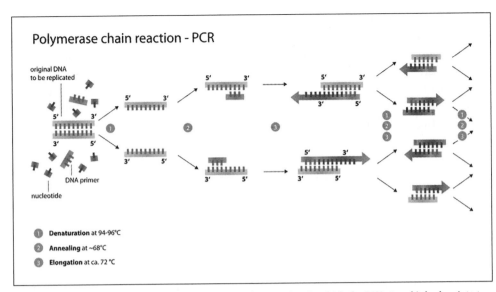

There are several steps in a polymerase chain reaction: denaturation, in which the DNA strand is broken into two single strands: annealing, in which primers—short, single-stranded sequences—attach to the broken DNA; and elongation, in which new, complementary DNA strands are created. The entire process is repeated multiple times to create enough DNA to analyze.

fluorescent labeling). Both of these processes meant an increase in "seeing" DNA—and interpreting the DNA's use in profiling for a criminal investigation.

How does forensic DNA profiling work?

Forensic DNA profiling has two main uses: it is used to confirm whether people are related to each other (such as a paternity test) or for helping to solve criminal cases. It is a sensitive technique and uses only a small amount of carefully collected material from a person or crime scene, such as skin cells, a hair root, or a drop of blood or saliva. The collected material's DNA STR profile can be compared to another DNA STR profile from a suspect (or victim) to determine whether a match exists. If one does, a one-in-a-billion chance exists that the profiles are from two different people (unless they are identical twins)—and the suspect will most likely be called the perpetrator.

How does forensic DNA phenotyping work?

Forensic DNA phenotyping is somewhat still in its infancy. It is determining the traits of unknown deceased people based on biological materials usually found at a crime or accident scene. This type of DNA analysis is used to match the appearance characteristics of a perpetrator from crime scene biomaterials (such as the DNA analysis of a stain [such as blood or other body fluids] or from a deceased person's remains) to a group of suspects. These characteristics include hair and eye color, possible ancestry, and other traits. Such traits are often referred to as an individual's phenotype, or the expression of his or her genes—thus, the name forensic DNA phenotyping. Traditional DNA profiling does not reveal any personal information about a person but is used to determine whether two collected samples—one from a suspect and one from the crime scene—are from the same person. If they are, they have their perpetrator—but if no suspects are found, this type of DNA typing is of little use. Thus, as technology improves, forensic DNA phenotyping will help to determine more about the possible perpetrator based on their genetics—allowing law enforcement to narrow its search for suspects.

DNA DATABASES

What was the world's first national DNA database?

The world's first national DNA database was founded in 1995 in the United Kingdom. Called the National DNA Database, the information is stored in the form of a digital code. As of 2015, more than 5.7 million DNA profiles were in the database, mostly from suspects in investigations or those convicted of a crime. (The second country to set up a DNA database was New Zealand.)

When did the United States establish a DNA database?

In 1994, the DNA Databank legislation was enacted, authorizing the FBI to create a national DNA database. DNA samples were submitted, and by 1998, a national level of the DNA database was implemented (called CODIS; see below). Currently, all states have their own DNA databases that are interconnected to the central databases. Depending on the state requirements within their respective database, DNA sample information can include various criminals, including sex offenders and certain violent offenders. For example, in New York in 2012, the DNA database was expanded to include anyone convicted of a felony or penal law misdemeanor (it only included penal law crime before).

What is CODIS?

If no suspects are found in a crime, DNA experts who analyze certain crime scene evidence in which DNA may be extracted can potentially develop a profile of the person by searching what is called the Combined DNA Indexing System (CODIS). This program is maintained by the Federal Bureau of Investigation (FBI) and contains the criminal justice DNA databases, along with the software to run the databases.

What are the various levels of CODIS?

The Combined DNA Indexing System (CODIS) has three levels of operation:

- LDIS—The Local DNA Index System (LDIS) is the local part of CODIS and includes local laboratories. These facilities are responsible for the entry and search of DNA profiles at the LDIS levels and usually set their own policies and procedures.

- SDIS—The State DNA Index System (SDIS) is another part of CODIS, in which state laboratories are also responsible for their own entry and search of DNA profiles. For example, New York State has its own DNA database (New York State DNA Databank) and has, at this writing, eight DNA laboratories that process forensic evidence.
- NDIS—The National DNA Index System (NDIS) is one part of CODIS (the national level) that contains the DNA profiles contributed by federal, state, and local participating forensic laboratories. Implemented in late 1998 by the FBI, all fifty states participate in the NDIS, including the District of Columbia, the federal government, the U.S. Army Criminal Investigation Laboratory, and Puerto Rico.

From whom does the National DNA Index System (NDIS) obtain DNA samples to create DNA profiles?

The NDIS contains several profiles from various individuals. They include the DNA records of arrested people (this is only if the state law permits such a collection of DNA from arrested people), convicted offenders, missing persons (DNA reference profiles from missing persons), forensic "unknowns" (profiles of unknown people; it is most often collected at crime scenes as evidence, such as blood or semen), biological relatives of missing persons (samples that were collected from relatives of missing people who voluntarily offered their DNA), and unidentified humans (DNA from human remains that were never identified).

SOME CASES IN DNA ANALYSIS

Can DNA show what a person's ancestors looked like?

Although such research is still in its infancy, some studies have determined that DNA can show certain characteristics of a person's ancestors. In particular, they have determined eye and hair color for ancestors who have been dead for about eight hundred years. The researchers compared genomes for thousands of people, uncovering genetic variations at twenty-four points in the human genome, all linked to eye and hair color. This may one day be a way of determining what a person's ancestors looked like, but for now, it may help solve some decades-long controversies about the looks of certain historical figures.

How did DNA help "discover" King Richard III?

The question "Where was the body of King Richard III buried?" has long been a curiosity in England. Historians knew that Richard rode out from Leicester to meet his death on the Bosworth battlefield in August of 1485, ending the Plantagenet reign—but no one knew where his body ended up. Legends told of tossing the body in the river or bringing the body back to town. Still others say the body was claimed by Franciscans and buried hastily near the high altar of their church—and it was at that church where the alleged remains of King Richard were found. In 2013, several tests were carried out—

including radio carbon dating of bone samples—with several forensic pathologists determining the cause of death based on the bones, but one clue was the key: comparing the DNA from the leg bone of Canadian Michael Ibsen, believed to be a direct descendant of Richard's sister Anne. When all the tests came in, the researchers concluded that the bones found at the church site were truly those of King Richard. Alas, King Richard's lineage apparently stops here—as neither Ibsen nor his sister (mitochondrial DNA is passed on through the women) have any children.

King Richard III was killed in the 1485 Battle of Bosworth Field, leading to the ascension of the Tudor family. His body was lost until 2013, when DNA tests verified the bones found at the church site belonged to King Richard.

How did DNA analysis lead to the discovery of the Romanov (Russian tsar) family remains?

During the Bolshevik Revolution in 1917, Russian Tsar Nicholas II (Romanov family) gave up his crown. Nicholas, along with his wife, five children, and four servants were exiled to Yekaterinburg, Russia. The next year, the entire family was executed—including the servants—with no survivors. They were allegedly buried in an unmarked grave nearby. With no evidence of their deaths, rumors began that the family (or certain members) had escaped, and in the late 1970s, a grave was found with nine bodies thought to be the tsar's family and servants. DNA testing indicated that indeed, the bodies were his family, with two missing. By 2007, two more bodies were found in a grave about seventy-five yards away—their DNA indicating that they were also from the Romanov family. In this case, the DNA extracted from the bone remains included not only mitochondrial DNA but Y chromosome and autosomal DNA. Then the results were compared to the living Romanov relatives (including Prince Philip of England), with a 99 percent probability that the remains were from the Romanov family.

What was the Jesse James identification project?

The Jesse Woodson James (1847–1882) identification project was performed to determine whether certain human remains truly belonged to the famous American gunfighter and outlaw. Preliminary analysis of the bones (and materials with the bones) showed that they fit James's height, age, sex, and racial profiles. A fired bullet near the skeleton's right ribs added to the confirmation, as James had once been hit by a bullet and never had it removed. A bullet wound was also found in the reconstructed skull just above the right ear. To make sure it was truly James, a mitochondrial DNA test was done on the skeleton's teeth—and the results were a match with blood samples from two of

Tsar Nicholas II of the Romanov dynasty is shown here with his family (and Cossack guards behind them) a year before the Bolsheviks slaughtered them in the Russian Revolution of 1917. Their bodies were tossed in unmarked graves but later identified with DNA testing.

James's known descendants (from his sister's family). The bones in a marked grave were truly from Jesse James.

Was DNA used to identify victims of the 9/11 World Trade Center tragedy?

Yes, some of the victims of the 9/11 World Trade Center disaster—killed when hijackers crashed two airplanes into the Twin Towers on September 11, 2001—have been identified using DNA analysis. Analysts use the DNA (and other means) to match bone fragments of the 2,753 people killed, but not all victims have been identified, as the conditions were such that the DNA was not recoverable, and for some, it may have been impossible to compare the DNA found with a known DNA profile. As of this writing, the remains of 1,641 victims have been identified, but around 40 percent of those who died remain unidentified.

How was DNA evidence recently used to find certain details about a murderer?

Many murders have recently been uncovered thanks to DNA evidence. For example, in 2016, New York City Google marketing account manager Vanessa Marcotte, 27, was visiting her mother in Princeton, Massachusetts. She left her mother's house for a run on a country road, and after she was missing for two hours, the police were called in. A canine unit found her body about a half-mile from the house in a wooded area. Two leads were reported: the first reports were of a dark-colored sports vehicle and witness accounts of a Hispanic man around thirty years old around the area where Marcotte died.

The second was DNA evidence: Marcotte apparently struggled during the encounter, and the DNA collected from her hands during the autopsy helped to create a description of the killer—an athletic, light-skinned Hispanic or Latino male with short hair and about thirty years old. A state trooper in Worcester, Massachusetts, noted a man matching such a description and driving the same type of sports vehicle. Running the plates led the trooper to Angelo Colon-Ortiz's apartment, who voluntarily provided a DNA sample. The DNA samples matched and Colon-Ortiz was arrested, charged first with aggravated assault and battery and assault with attempt to rape, with a $10 million bail set. As of late 2017, he was arraigned for the murder of Marcotte.

IN THE CRIME LAB: TOOLMARKS, FIREARMS, AND BALLISTICS

DEFINING TOOLMARKS

What are toolmarks (also seen as tool marks)?

Toolmarks are striations or impressions made by the forceful contact between two objects that differ in hardness. For example, in terms of tools and toolmarks, a hard crowbar will mark the softer wood of a door that is pried open. In terms of firearms, the barrel of a firearm is hard and leaves minute impressions on the softer bullet as it passes through the muzzle after firing.

What are two common classes of toolmark characteristics?

Experts often divide toolmark characteristics into two classes. The first class of characteristics are those that are common to a group of objects, such as a hammer with its distinctive shape and typical size. The other class is the individual characteristics, or those that are unique to a certain object, such as gouges or scratches from use or the manufacturer. These tools can also be identified based on such things as paint on a handle, which may match paint at the crime scene.

What are two general ways of looking at toolmarks in forensics?

Forensic experts look at toolmarks in two general ways. The first way concerns the imperfections, patterns, and marks on physical tools used at a crime scene, such as from a burglary, theft, or vandalism. The tools' unique marks are formed naturally during the manufacturing process of the tool and can change as the owner uses the piece, further making the marks unique to that tool. In a situation such as the forcing open of a window, forensic experts can analyze the unique marks made by a tool to possibly determine what type of tool was used, and if the tool is found at a scene, they can match the markings of the tool itself to the toolmarks found, such as in a doorframe. The second way of looking at toolmarks is in association with firearms. Such marks as striations are usually found on a bullet or casing made as the projectile travels from the breech through the barrel of a firearm. For example, a toolmark forms when a weapon's firing pin hits the softer primer material of a cartridge. This forms a pin impression on the cartridge. (For more about toolmarks and firearms, see this chapter.)

How are toolmarks in tools analyzed?

Toolmarks from tools are usually found as negative impressions (almost like stamping by the tool) or as an abrasion mark (as it slides by where the tool was used). Some of these patterns, striations, and other marks are visible to the naked eye, while others are only seen under a microscope, with most patterns and marks made by the tool's cutting surface.

What are some of the causes of a tool's toolmark impressions?

Toolmark impressions are made in several ways. For example, static marks are made when a tool is pressed into a softer material, such as a crowbar used to open a window that has a wooden sill. Cutting marks are made when pressure is applied on both sides of an object, such as cutting a screen with scissors. Dynamic marks are made when the tool slides or scratches a surface leaving a pattern of lines or striations, such as when a person uses a key to scratch along the side of a car. Multistroke marks are caused when something is moved back and forth in a repetitive motion, such as a saw on metal.

How are tools and toolmarks from a crime scene examined?

Tools and toolmarks at a crime scene are often examined and photographed *in situ*, or where the tool and toolmarks are found. If appropriate, the tool can be removed for analysis in the lab and, if applicable, along with an object with toolmarks to see if they are a match. If it is impossible to move the object with the toolmark, a cast of the marks, usually using silicon rubber, is made.

What are some of the most common tools used that create toolmarks at a crime scene?

So many "tools" are used at various crime scenes—too many to mention here. For instance, tools used in property crimes include bolt cutters (for example, to cut locks), knives (to stab tires or tear screens in windows), chisels and crowbars (for prying open windows or doors), hammers (to

A damaged car bumper can be an example of "toolmarks" left behind in a crime scene such as a hit-and-run.

shatter breakable materials), vice grips (to hold something in place), or wire cutters (to cut copper piping). Tools used in homicides usually include knives (seen as marks on bone or cartilage) or objects to bludgeon a person (pipes or large pieces of wood). Also, some "toolmarks" a person might not think about—for example, when a car's bumper hits the frame of a cyclist's bicycle in a hit-and-run incident, the impression made by the car's bumper is considered evidence—and a toolmark.

Can a bomb have toolmarks?

Yes, in some cases, pieces of an exploded bomb may carry toolmarks, such as those made by certain tools used to make the original explosive. Toolmarks on an unexploded bomb—for example, found in a bombing suspect's home—can also be used as evidence if they match certain tools found in the home or elsewhere (such as the scene of a previous explosion).

Why can it be difficult to analyze certain toolmarks?

Not all toolmarks are created equal—and many are found in certain soft materials that do not readily hold their shape. For example, toolmarks are usually found in soft metals, such as lead, but toolmarks in plastic can be more difficult to decipher, as the plastic can deform, causing the mark to become misshapen.

Can toolmarks on human bones help in the analysis of a crime victim?

Yes, toolmarks on human bones have often been used in a crime scene victim analysis. In fact, toolmarks on bones are often investigated during an autopsy but are most useful if all that is left of a victim is a skeleton. Found human bones from a crime scene often have the imprint from a sharp implement. They include such cutting tools as a knife (leaves a V-shaped trough in the bone), a saw (leaves a wide, square-bottomed cut in the bone and often striations from the cutting action), and an axe (leaves a wide, V-shaped trough that is more truncated than a cut from a knife). Such toolmarks on human bones may also reveal the physical event that took place, such as the position of the victim and their attacker or the motion(s) of the blade or other implement.

DEFINING FIREARMS

Why is firearm identification often erroneously called ballistics?

Although several references refer to ballistics as a field of forensic science that concentrates on firearm identification, most people agree that ballistics is the scientific study of projectiles—especially bullets—in motion. Ballistics evidence at a crime scene is often used to determine how the bullet or other projectile made its way over, under, around, or through to its target, while firearm identification is used to determine whether a certain bullet or cartridge case was fired from a specific firearm. Thus, while firearm examiners benefit from the study of ballistics when evaluating a firearm or fired bullets in their investigation, it is only a portion of their focus.

What is a firearm?

According to several federal government agencies, a firearm is defined as "a shot gun or rifle having a barrel of less than eighteen inches in length, or any other weapon, except a pistol or revolver, from which a shot is discharged by an explosive if such weapon is capable of being concealed on the person, or a machine gun, and includes a muffler or silencer for any firearm whether or not such firearm is included within the foregoing definition." Unofficially and simply put, a firearm is usually considered a rifle, pistol, handgun—or, in other words, the majority of "simple," portable guns.

What is a "gun"?

The term "gun" is usually used by most people to define a smaller weapon, such as a revolver or semi-automatic handgun. In most cases, a gun has several specific characteristics: a relatively short, metal barrel from which ammunition (bullet or other projectile) is propelled outward by an explosive force (mostly from gunpowder) and that makes a loud, sharp, cracking noise when discharged.

What is the difference between a revolver, pistol, and rifle?

According to the U.S. government's ATF (Bureau of Alcohol, Tobacco, Firearms, and Explosives) agency, the following are the "official" definitions of rifle, pistol, and revolver:

There is a difference between a pistol and a revolver. A revolver (top) has several bullet chambers in a revolving cylinder; a pistol (bottom) has one or more stationary chambers.

- *Rifle*—"A weapon designed or redesigned, made or remade, and intended to be fired from the shoulder and designed or redesigned and made or remade to use the energy of the explosive in a fixed metallic cartridge to fire only a single projectile through a rifled bore for each single pull of the trigger." They include semi-automatic rifles, along with lever, bolt, and slide-pump action rifles.

- *Pistol*—A weapon "originally designed, made, and intended to fire a projectile [most commonly a bullet] from one or more barrels when held in one hand, and having a chamber(s) as an integral part(s) of, or permanently aligned with, the bore(s); and a short stock designed to be gripped by one hand at an angle to and extending below the line of the bore(s)." They include semi-automatic, single-shot, and multibarreled pistols.

- *Revolver*—"A projectile weapon of the pistol type, having a breechloading [loaded at the rear rather than where the projectile exits] chambered cylinder so arranged that the cocking of the hammer or movement of the trigger rotates it and brings the next cartridge in line with the barrel for firing." They include single-action, double-action, and top-break revolvers. (This is the typical type of weapon most people think of when someone mentions a shootout in an old western movie—although rifles were also popular in the real West.)

In general, how is a bullet fired from a firearm?

Simply put, a bullet or slug is found in the cartridge casing. At the end of the casing, a primer is pressed in. When a weapon is fired, the firing pin hits the end of the casing that holds the primer, creating a high-pressure reaction in the chamber. Typically, the primer is a mix of lead styphnate (the initiator), antimony sulfide (or the fuel), and barium nitrate (called the oxidizer). This combination essentially causes a chemical chain reaction, helping the gunpowder to ignite. Like a tiny pressure cooker, the burning gunpowder creates a buildup of pressure and high temperatures, with the expanding gases forcing the projectile to eject from the weapon's muzzle. In most cases, the cartridge casing that contained the powder stays in the chamber (for example, a revolver) or the weapon ejects the spent casing (for example, a semi-automatic). This also results in a discharge of certain gases and particulates, which form what is called gunshot residue (GSR; for more about GSR, see this chapter.)

What is the caliber of a firearm?

The caliber of a firearm refers to the weapon's internal barrel measurement and, thus, the bullet size (bullet diameter, or actually the measurement of the slug within the bullet's casing) must also be close to the same caliber. It is often expressed in metric or standard form (U.S. standard measurements). For example, a "9mm-caliber gun" means that the gun must use 9-millimeter ammunition to travel through the 9-millimeter barrel; a "22-caliber gun" means that the ammunition is 0.22 inches wide, as is the barrel (most people when discussing a 22-caliber gun drop the decimal point).

What is a suppressor on a firearm?

Many people erroneously use the term "silencer" for a suppressor, or a device added to the end of a muzzle to moderate the expanding gas that makes the popping noise when a firearm is fired. ("Silencer" is considered a slang term by many gun enthusiasts, and most never use the term.) The noise when a firearm is discharged is caused for two reasons: the high-pressure gases escaping from the muzzle of the firearm and the "sonic boom" of the bullet as it passes through the air (it is faster than the speed of sound).

EXAMINING AMMUNITION
IN THE CRIME LAB

What is a cartridge?

A firearm cartridge is the complete, unfired round of ammunition. It is composed of a cartridge case, the projectile (bullet, also often called a slug), the primer (at the end; it is the igniter), and smokeless powder (or gunpowder, or the propellant).

What is a "spent casing"?

A "spent casing" (or spent cartridge) is a term often used by law enforcement (and others, such as the military) to describe an individual round or cartridge that has been fired by a firearm. (Many people use the term "spent bullets" [or "spent rounds"] instead of "spent casings"; "spent bullets" actually defines the fired slug inside the casing, but both "spent bullets" and "spent casings" are often used interchangeably.) Spent casings are often found at a crime scene if certain types of firearms are used that eject the casing after firing, such as some semi-automatic handguns, while other types of firearms, such as a revolver, do not drop the casings after the bullet is fired.

How can a spent casing from a crime scene possibly be used as evidence?

Often investigators and crime scene experts discover spent casing, especially at a crime scene involving a shooting. If the casings are whole or fragmented, several features may be used in a forensic analysis to possibly determine the make or model of the weapon. For instance, on the softer material of the spent casing, usually, minute impressions are made by the firing pin, from around the breech, and—in the case of automatic and semi-automatic weapons—the marks made when the cartridge was ejected from the gun. If the casing is fragmented, whole or parts of manufacturing marks (such as logos, trademarks, or bullet caliber) may also be traced.

What is a detonator cap?

A detonator is a device that triggers an explosive device, such as a handgun's bullet. They are commonly mechanically or electrically started but can also be chemically started. A detonator is not only used in terms of firearms but also in other types of explosives, in which the term "blasting cap" is used. (A blasting cap is a small, sensitive primary explosive device generally used to detonate a larger, more powerful, and less sensitive secondary explosive such as TNT, dynamite, or a plastic explosive. For more about explosives, see the chapter "In the Crime Lab: Examining Explosives.")

What is a bullet?

In general, a bullet is a projectile that is fired from a firearm, such as a rifle, small handgun, revolver, or assault weapon. Typically, they are made of metal, are cylindrical, rounded, or even pointed, and sometimes contain an explosive.

What are some types of bullets?

Forensic firearms experts need to know about many types of bullets when analyzing projectiles in the lab—especially from a crime scene. In general, bullets are categorized as nonjacketed and jacketed (although some categorize them as semijacketed and fully jacketed bullets). In the majority of cases, the nonjacketed bullets are made of lead (mainly for low-velocity weapons, such as a 22-caliber handgun), or an alloy of lead and antimony (lead is very soft, while antimony gives the bullet added hardness). Jacketed bullets are laminated, including a harder covering (or jacket) over a core of lead, and, less commonly, steel, small, lead pellets, plastic, or other materials, such as

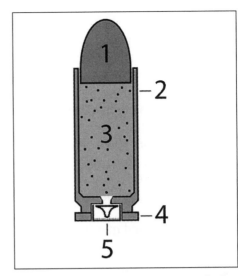

A bullet includes several parts: 1) the projectile; 2) the case; 3) the propellant (gunpowder or cordite); 4) the rim, which provides a grip for the casing to be removed from the chamber; and 5) the primer to ignite the propellant.

silicone rubber. The most common covering is copper, or they can be plated with nickel, steel (these are further coated so they will not rust), or aluminum. Most jacketed bullets are used for high-velocity weapons, such as a .44 Magnum handgun. Many have an opening at the base or nose of the cartridge, while some have no opening. They also include some different types of bullets, such as the armor piercing bullets, which have a steel covering over a thick layer of lead—all surrounding a steel core.

How fast does a bullet travel?

On the average—and according to most references—the average bullet travels (also called muzzle velocity) around 2,500 feet per second, or around 1,700 miles per hour, from the average handgun. (To see how fast such a bullet flies, if a person reacted to the firing of a gun, and, for instance, it takes 0.2 seconds to respond, they would need to be at least five hundred feet away from the weapon to successfully dodge the bullet—if they could truly move that fast!) Some of the fastest bullets from smaller firearms travel more than 2,600 feet per second, which is about twice the speed of sound. This, of course, is dependent on the caliber, condition, and even the type of bullet used in the weapon. Bullets move at a range of speeds when a rifle is fired, too, and this depends on the type of rifle. For example, black powder muskets have muzzle velocities that range from about 390 to 1,200 feet per second. Some modern rifles produce muzzle velocities around 2,600 to 3,900 feet per second. But their speed changes. This is because rifles are usually used for long-distance shooting, with the bullet slowing down over a distance because of atmospheric friction and the Earth's gravitational pull.

Why are bullet markings analyzed in the crime lab?

Although firearms have certain general characteristics (such as caliber, make, or model), they also have certain physical features that often make them unique (although some researchers argue that some firearm features are not unique but are so similar that it is difficult to tell them apart). In particular, the various surfaces of a firearm—such as the barrel, breech, or firing pin (or striker)—that come in contact with the softer cartridge casings and bullets usually cause certain distinctive, mostly microscopic, irregularities. Thus, one of the major examinations of bullets (or any other similar type of projectile) in the crime lab is to identify those minute cuts and striations to possibly help identify a firearm used in criminal activity. (For more about firearms and bullets as evidence from a crime scene, see this chapter.)

Are gunpowder and gunshot residue (GSR) different?

Yes, gunpowder and gunshot residue are different. In terms of the firearm, the gunpowder is the propellant in a cartridge before the gun is fired. Gunshot residue is what results when the gun is fired, leaving a residue on the hands and clothes of the person who dis-

Why do many people want to see changes in bullet composition?

To forensic firearm analysts, having a softer lead bullet to examine as evidence at a crime scene is a positive aspect that may lead to a criminal being sent to jail, but to people who shoot, especially those who practice on ranges around the country, lead in ammunition is a major concern, as it is a potentially toxic metal (it is a neurotoxin when ingested in sufficient quantities). This poses environmental hazards at outdoor firing ranges used by the public, law enforcement, the military, and even hunters. This is because lead in spent bullets and even bullet fragments can leach into the local groundwater and soil and/or can contaminate a person's clothes and skin. Thus, many ammunition manufacturers offer alternatives to lead bullets, such as copper, copper/tin, and other such materials.

However, even though a great deal of evidence exists linking lead ammunition to several environmental and public health problems, according to the National Shooting Sports Foundation and the National Rifle Association (referenced in 2013; the numbers have probably gone up in recent years), about 90 percent of the ten billion or so rounds purchased each year in the United States still contain lead. Until recently, the only federal regulation regarding lead ammunition requires that lead-free shotgun pellets be used for the hunting of waterfowl. Another piece of legislation came at the end of President Barack Obama's term in 2017. The U.S. Fish and Wildlife Service issued a decree that would phase out the use of lead ammunition (and some lead-containing fishing tackle) on federal lands, but in March 17, new president Donald Trump's interior secretary, Ryan Zinke, rescinded Obama's order.

charges the firearms and also on the target, either victim or object. Both are examined in a crime lab in different ways; for example, gunpowder particles (and often primer) are analyzed with instruments, while GSR is examined using visual and chemical methods. (For more about gunshot residue, see the chapters "At the Crime Scene: Looking for Physical Evidence" and "In the Crime Lab: Trace Evidence.")

How does gunshot residue form?

When a bullet is fired from a weapon, at the same time, a discharge of gases—usually observed as a "smoky haze" or plume—around the firearm is often seen immediately after a weapon is fired. The gases include burnt and unburnt gunpow-

Lead in bullets has caused problems for wildlife such as bald eagles. The lead poisoning gets into fish, which the eagles eat, and this can sicken and kill them.

der particulates, metallic particles from the ammunition used and even the firearm itself, and parts of the primer mix, including lead, antimony, and barium. Because these particles are "heavy" and the plume so saturated with the particles, the individual particles begin to fuse together. These elements help to create the gunshot residue (GSR) used at some shooting and/or crime scenes as evidence, usually found on the person firing the gun, a victim's clothing, and objects nearby.

How is GSR analyzed in the crime lab?

In order to interpret the marks and patterns made by gunshot residue, the forensic expert must understand how certain firearms and ammunition react to produce known-distance patterns. These patterns are then compared to the GSR patterns found as evidence at the crime scene. The common method of analyzing GSR is with a scanning electron microscope-energy dispersive x-ray spectroscopy (SEM-EDS), allowing for a high magnification of particles (around five thousand times or greater) and to interpret the various elements found in the sample. This creates a profile of a certain particle collected as evidence—often including the particle's composition and shape. All this can be used to compare various GSR sites (objects, clothing, a victim) and possibly connect them to a victim or suspect.

What is changing in terms of analyzing gunshot residue?

Because of the major concern for lead in bullets, a push for lead-free ammunition has been happening and, thus, a change in gunshot residue. This has also changed the way forensic firearms experts examine the components of GSR from a crime scene. Because of this, researchers have been (and are) developing additional tests to identify some of the different residue that is often found in more modern cartridges and their internal components, such as stabilizers and plasticizers.

Can gunshot residue be misinterpreted as evidence?

Yes, like any evidence, gunshot residue can be misinterpreted. This is because some other sources have various materials that are similar in shape and chemistry as GSR. For example, other sources that are similar to the particles found in GSR include fireworks, brake dust (some researchers found that certain brake pad linings have the same types of particles), primer-actuated nail guns, and even exhaust from a vehicle's deployed airbag!

BALLISTICS AND THE CRIME SCENE

What is the study of ballistics?

Simply put, ballistics is the scientific study of projectiles in motion. In terms of forensics, ballistic examiners try to reconstruct a crime scene involving firearms based on certain evidence associated with the shooting. For example, ballistic studies at a scene may include measuring angles (for instance, the angle in which a bullet would bounce off a metal door rather than go through it), looking at entry and exit paths (such as in a victim or object like a door), noting how a bullet impacted and/or penetrated a person or object, and determining from which possible direction and range the shooter fired the shot.

What affects the trajectory of a projectile?

The trajectory of a projectile is the path it follows after being fired from a firearm (the study of projectiles' motions is called ballistics). In general, a bullet follows a parabolic trajectory (also called a bullet path). The bullet starts below the line of sight, rises above the line of sight, then crosses this line again as the bullet falls to its target. (It is most noticeable when a bullet is fired from weapon to target for a long distance.) The reasons for such a parabolic trajectory have to do with gravity (pulling the projectile down), air resistance (slowing the projectile as it travels to the target), muzzle velocity (how fast the projectile leaves the firearm's muzzle), and, often, other surrounding environmental factors. Other components should

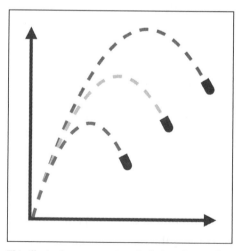

This illustration exaggerates a bullet's trajectory, but they do follow a parabolic path as shown here, one influenced by gravity, air resistence, and other environmental factors.

Who is often called the "father of ballistics"?

Forensic scientist, Army officer, and researcher Colonel Calvin Hooker Goddard (1891–1955) is often referred to as the "father of ballistics." In the 1920s, he was the inventor of the comparison microscope, in which two microscopes are attached with a "bridge" allowing two items to be compared side by side under the one device. The instrument can be used for many types of evidence such as hair and fiber, but because of his intense interest in firearms, Goddard used his invention mostly for bullets and cartridge casing analysis.

be considered when determining the trajectory of a projectile. For example, the bullet coefficient (or BC) refers to the aerodynamics of the projectile itself. For instance, a long, sleek bullet with a pointed tip will slip through the air much more easily than a blunt-nosed bullet.

What is the Federal Premium® Ballistics Calculator?

The commercial company Federal Premium® Ammunition offers a "Ballistics Calculator" that allows the user to quickly determine the trajectory of any handgun or rifle load (bullet). It includes input parameters such as load type, caliber, setup height, temperature, and wind speed. It can be found at https://www.federalpremium.com/ballistics_calculator/.

Why is it sometimes difficult to trace the track of a bullet?

The path of a bullet is not always predictable, and, under certain circumstances, it is difficult for a forensic ballistic expert—or, in the case of a body, a forensic pathologist doing an autopsy—to trace the track of a bullet. For example, the projectile may strike a victim's skull or rib, causing the bullet to ricochet to a different part of the body that is distant from the original entry wound. The bullet can also be deflected by other objects in a room, for example, from a metal windowsill and into a sofa. These changes in direction are not always readily noticeable, often making conclusions about what actually happened at a shooting scene difficult.

What methods are often used to visualize the flight path of bullets at a shooting scene?

Ballistic investigators try to visualize the flight path of bullet(s) at a crime scene in several ways. For example, they often use rods, probes, or strings to understand the pathway of the bullet based on the location of the victim, possible suspects, and other objects that may have been hit by a bullet. Most of these methods are used under certain conditions, such as using string during light hours, which makes it easy to see and photograph pathways. Lasers are also used to reconstruct a shooting scene, as they allow a much straighter line depicting the pathway, they can be used in areas in which a string is difficult to use, and they can be projected for longer distances. Lasers have disadvantages, too, including difficulty in seeing the laser line in bright daylight or other conditions (depending on the color of the laser line), which also makes it difficult to photograph.

FIREARMS AND THE CRIME LAB

What evidence from a crime scene can be used for firearm analysis in the lab?

If a weapon has been fired at a crime scene, firearm analysts can examine several pieces of evidence in the crime lab. They include examination of shotshell casings, shot pellets, spent bullets and slugs, cartridge casings, gunshot residue (on a person or object, such as a wall; see below), powder burns, and bullet fragments, and, of course, if the firearm used during the crime is found, it is one of the best pieces of evidence to take back to the crime lab. In such a case, the examiners may be able to determine whether the weapon is truly functional (and thus was used), whether any alterations were made to the firearm, and whether it is safe to discharge—mainly by making a series of test fires in the lab. If no firearm is recovered, the fired (and unfired, if found) ammunition can still be examined to possibly determine the manufacturer, how many weapons were involved in the crime, and possibly even the type(s) of weapon(s) used. Because each firearm is thought to have unique characteristics, the forensic investigator examines the microscopic markings on the bullets and cartridge cases, noting whether they match the markings on the firearm.

What does a firearm investigator look for in a weapon from a crime scene?

If investigators need to tie a certain weapon to a crime scene—or if no weapon is found—the firearm investigator can use certain examinations to help with either scenario. In particular, they look for several types of features and markings. Two of the more common ones include the following:

- *Caliber*—The caliber is also called the bore diameter of the weapon. Each firearm has a certain caliber. In many cases, a firearm investigator can match the diameters of spent bullets or casings (if any are found) to determine the caliber of the crime scene firearm.

- *Rifling grooves (toolmarks)*—The manufacturer of firearms (pistols, revolvers, rifles, and some shotguns) cut spiral grooves lengthwise into a barrel in order to stabilize the flight path of a bullet and give it a spinning motion. Because bullets are oblong, they must spin to stabilize their flight, like how a person throws a football to be accurate. (The metal rise between each of the grooves is called the land.) Investigators can compare the surface of the spent bullet to the direction of the rifling grooves twist—clockwise or counterclockwise—to see if it matches a certain weapon (if one is found at the crime scene or on a suspect). If no weapon is found, they can match the twists on the spent bullet to narrow the possible weapons in a particular class of firearms that may have been used at the crime scene. This is because each barrel has a certain number and dimensions of grooved impressions depending on the make and model of a firearm, so they can often be used to narrow down the specific type of firearm.

How are toolmarks made during the manufacturing process of a firearm?

The twists and turns of the rifling grooves (see above) are all part of the manufacturing process of most firearms. During this process, random, microscopic imperfections form naturally on the breech (or breechface), in the barrel, and on other parts of the weapon. This is because the process is constantly changing—minutely, but still enough so that when the piece is ground, cut, or shaped, it leaves certain impressions (also referred to as imprints). In addition, after a piece is used by a person, it goes through other changes from use, corrosion, rusting, cleaning, and even abuse—all creating the firearm's uniqueness and individuality. In most cases, these toolmarks and imperfections are imparted on the bullet and/or cartridge casing. Those microscopic markings are then often used by a forensic examiner, for example, to determine whether the markings on evidence are the same as the markings on a found firearm from a crime scene.

What are the possible conclusions from a firearm bullet and casing analysis?

In general, four conclusions can be drawn from a firearm bullet and casing analysis: the bullet or cartridge casing is proven to be fired by the firearm; the bullet or cartridge

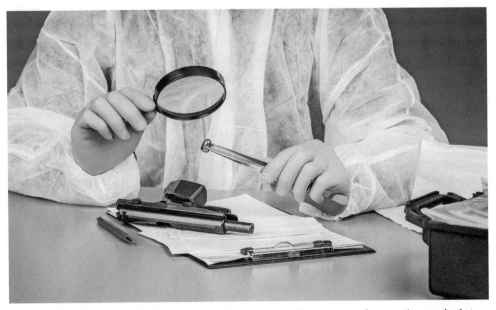

Working in the lab, firearms specialists examine bullets and toolmarks on weapons for any unique marks that can help identify or trace them to their source.

casing was not fired by the firearm; the bullet or cartridge casing does not have enough markings and characteristics to come to a definite conclusion that it was the firearm that was fired; or the bullet or cartridge casing was not good enough to use for a comparison (for example, they were too damaged or mutilated).

How are distances between a firearm muzzle and target determined at a crime scene?

In many cases, the distance between a firearm and target (a victim or object) can be determined by understanding the residues that form after a weapon is fired. In particular, when a firearm is discharged, the projectile (bullet or slug or pellet) leaves the barrel along with other residues. These include certain gases and primer components, along with burnt, partially burnt, and unburnt gunpowder particles. The results of the firing of the gun on people and objects is called gunshot residue (GSR, also called cartridge discharge residue; for more about GSR, see the chapter "At the Crime Scene: Looking for Physical Evidence"). The distance between a firearm's muzzle and the target is often based on the GSR's density, size, and how it formed certain patterns, either on a person, wall, vehicle, or other object. (Gunpowder found at a scene is also sometimes examined but uses different types of analyses.) Some analysis of the GSR can be made visually at the scene of the crime, while more detailed analysis of GSR is carried out in the crime lab.

How are distances between a firearm muzzle and target determined in the crime lab?

In the lab, several types of examinations determine the distance between a victim and shooter. Examining an object or person's clothes with gunshot residue (GSR) can be done microscopically and chemically tested (usually as patterns left behind by lead and nitrates) in order to reveal certain patterns from that firearm. In addition, if a firearm is gathered as evidence at a crime scene, the suspect weapon can be fired at certain distances in the lab under controlled circumstances and compared with the GSR evidence. In most cases, the resulting distances are only estimates, such as "the firearm was at a range greater than ten inches but less than twenty inches." (In addition, most references agree that the best distance estimates are made if the weapon is thirty-six inches or less from the target.) The reason for an estimate is understandable, as other factors control how close the muzzle is thought to be to a target. This includes the type of ammunition load (for example, factory or homemade loads), the surface in which the residue is found, temperature and humidity (including various weather conditions), or even objects (such as doors) that were between the firearm and the target.

How are firearms compared to known weapons?

In the crime lab, firearms are compared to known weapons in several ways. For example, weapons that are submitted from a crime scene are test fired. In this way, the forensic analysts know how they compare to other fired bullets (and cartridge cases) collected at crime scenes. To do this, forensic experts use such databases as the National Integrated Ballistic Information Network (NIBIN; for more, see below), which holds images of markings created by a gun when a cartridge is fired. This database contains a large number of images and has several systems that allow digital photographs of fired cartridge cases (from criminal and noncriminal activities) to be stored and electronically compared to others in the database. A technician then visually compares the images that display similarities (often with a comparison microscope) for possible identification purposes—and that can sometimes connect the firearms to other shooting occurrences.

Can a scratched-out serial number on a firearm be restored?

The Gun Control Act of 1968 requires that all imported and newly manufactured firearms have a certain identifier in the frame or receiver of the weapon. (Other items, such as all types of motor vehicles, industrial machinery, electronic equipment, etc., also have serial numbers.) This usually is in the form of a serial number, which can include letters, numbers, and even special characters. Criminals often attempt to obliterate, overstamp, or change the serial number on a firearm by grinding, filing, or sanding, usually in an attempt to conceal ownership of a stolen weapon or using the firearm illegally. No matter how or why, obliterating a firearm's serial number is considered a federal (and often state) crime. If such a firearm is connected to a crime scene, forensic analysts have several ways to recapture the number. This includes thermal, chemical, polishing, and chemical etching to bring out the scratched-out numbers or letters. For example, an analyst will pol-

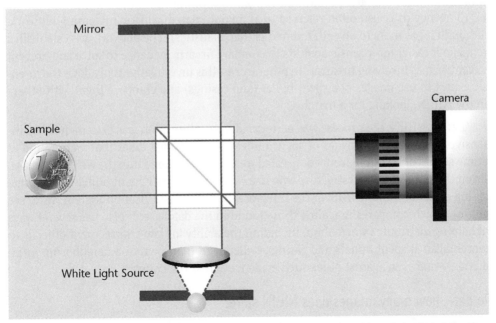

One tool used in forensics these days is white-light interferometry, a technique that records details in 3-D without having to touch the actual object.

ish the metal with a sandpaperlike material to get rid of the scratched metal from around the obliterated serial numbers (usually on the barrel or near the trigger). By applying certain chemical reactants—most often various acids that etch the specific metal where the serial number is located—the number will often be discernable.

How has forensic firearm analysis changed with new technology?

The field of forensic firearm analysis has changed over the past decade or so as it integrates more modern computer and imaging technology. For example, instruments are available such as the three-dimensional (3D) optical microscope white-light interferometers and certain types of laser scanning microscopes. These instruments allow the forensic analyst to measure and compare in scientific and mathematical terms the three-dimensional toolmarks and other surface features of interest on a firearm and/or ammunition in an investigation.

KEEPING TRACK OF FIREARMS AND AMMUNITION

What is the National Integrated Ballistic Information Network (NIBIN)?

The National Integrated Ballistic Information Network (NIBIN) is a national (United States) network maintained by the Bureau of Alcohol, Tobacco, Firearms, and Explosives (ATF) agency (it is also often referred to as an automated ballistic imagining network, although it has more to do with toolmarks than ballistics). The network was established to make it easier for forensic analysts to compare firearm evidence to solve and prevent violent crimes involving firearms. In other words, this investigative tool allows the forensic expert to use images of a spent bullet (and casings) and compare them with others in the NIBIN, looking for a match.

Before NIBIN, the process was performed manually, which was extremely labor intensive. Today, digital images of spent bullets and cartridge cases that were found at crime scenes or test-fired from confiscated weapons are entered into the NIBIN database. From there, forensic investigators who use NIBIN enter their spent bullet or cartridge casing evidence into the IBIS, or the Integrated Ballistic Identification System (IBIS; see above), which compares it against those found in the database. It also has several ways of helping distribute information, including the ability for law-enforcement officials to search against spent bullets and casings evidence in their own or a neighboring jurisdiction—and even against other such evidence across the country.

To date, how many images does NIBIN store?

Since the program's inception in 1999, to date (the last reference was 2016), NIBIN has established approximately 2.8 million images of ballistic evidence and confirmed more

What is the Reference Firearms Collection?

The Reference Firearms Collection—which contains over seven thousand firearms—is maintained by the Federal Bureau of Investigation's (FBI) Laboratory. The collection was started in 1933 and includes some of the more "notorious" firearms from certain eras, such as the "1930s gangster" era; for example, firearms that belonged to Kate "Ma" Barker (1875–1935; the matriarch of the Barker-Karpis Gang—she had four sons involved—who were guilty of kidnappings, murderers, and bank robberies, all of which led to her and the gang members' violent deaths) and John Dillinger's (1903–1934; American gangster and bank robber) revolver. The collection is used for several reasons in forensics, too, including for training purposes (for example, to train new firearms examiners), allowing the trainee to see how certain firearms function, operate, or to understand certain background information about a firearm model.

The collection is also used for forensic purposes. For example, when a forensic investigator submits certain characteristics of a firearm or components of a firearm, the RFC can often provide a list of manufacturers, models, or calibers from the collection that may indicate where the forearm and/or component(s) originated. The weapons are also used to compare surveillance videos and images, bank robbery photos or videos, or an image of a criminal holding what looks like a firearm. Comparisons are made with the collection to determine the type of weapon and, in some instances, even the make and model.

than seventy-four thousand NIBIN hits, but according to the ATF, the true consequence of the NIBIN is the number of successful arrests and prosecutions of shooters that have occurred because of the use of the database.

What is firearms tracing?

Firearms tracing is just as the phrase implies: the systematic tracking of the movement of firearms. This is accomplished by certain law-enforcement (and government) agencies that track the movement from the first sale by the manufacturer or importer through the distribution chain (where the public and others buy wholesale or through retail) to the first person who purchases the firearm. Also, what is officially called a comprehensive firearms tracing is the routine tracing of each crime gun recovered in a certain geographic area or specific law-enforcement jurisdiction (state or local).

What is the ATF's National Tracing Center?

The Bureau of Alcohol, Tobacco, Firearms, and Explosives (ATF) agency maintains the National Tracing Center (NTC). It is the only authorized organization in the United States that is allowed to trace U.S.- and foreign-manufactured firearms for international, federal, state, and local law-enforcement agencies. According to the ATF, the purpose is to provide investigative leads in the fight against violent crime and terrorism—and, of course, to enhance public safety.

What is the Brady Handgun Violence Prevention Act of 1993?

The Brady Handgun Violence Prevention Act of 1993 amended the Gun Control Act of 1968. In particular, it required all federally licensed firearms dealers (but not private sellers) to perform background checks on all their prospective handgun buyers. This was done to ensure that firearm purchases and/or transfers would not violate any state or federal laws. Before this act, all sales of firearms were conducted with a handshake and "honor system." This also meant that the gun dealer

The Brady Handgun Violence Prevention Act of 1993 was the result of the work of James Brady, the White House press secretary who suffered a severe head wound when John Hinckley Jr. tried to assassinate President Ronald Reagan in 1981.

relied solely on a person's word when it came to whether or not it was "legal" for the purchaser to own a firearm, creating a loophole for those criminals who wanted to purchase a firearm (although, according to many, it is still a broken system that often allows people—and especially criminals—to purchase weapons illegally).

IN THE CRIME LAB: EXAMINING EXPLOSIVES

BOMBS AND EXPLOSIVES DEFINED

What is the general definition of an explosion?

In general, an explosion is caused by a certain chemical reaction dependent on the composition of the explosive. This results in the release of a great amount of chemical or physical energy in a short span of time. At the time of detonation, the explosive more often than not emits a blast (sound), light, and heat. An explosive can range from an exploded gas can in a person's garage to a massive blast from a terrorist incident. (For more about explosive evidence at a crime scene, see the chapter "At the Crime Scene: Looking for Physical Evidence.") Not all explosions are associated with criminals or terrorists. They can also be used for a number of legitimate reasons, such as in mining (to extract valuable minerals or rock) or military operations.

Are a bomb and an explosive different?

Although the words "bomb" and "explosive" are often used interchangeably, they are slightly different. A bomb is referred to as a form of high explosive, but an explosive does not mean a bomb, as it can be, for example, a pyrotechnic device, which is a form of low explosive.

How are bombs often classified?

In general, bombs can be classified as either explosive or incendiary devices or a combination of both. An explosive device contains a liquid, powder, or solid explosive material. An incendiary device usually contains a flammable material that is meant to start a fire. According to another classification, bombs are divided into ordnance (those built in factories) and improvised explosive devices (those built by individuals; see below).

How are explosives classified?

Explosives are often classified into two categories depending on the velocity of detonation—or the speed in which they react to the internal materials. The high explosives detonate at a rate much greater than the speed of sound (which causes the loud detonation associated with such explosives). They do not need to be in a confined area and include such high explosives as RDX (a solid, white, organic compound), TNT (the yellowish compound trinitrotoluene), HMX (some disagree as to what HMX stands for, but it is chemically related to RDX), and HMDT (hexamethylene triperoxide diamine). The low explosives deflagrate (not detonate), which is a reaction that occurs particle to particle at subsonic speeds. This explosive also needs to be confined (for example, in a container) in order to function properly. They include such materials as black, smokeless, or flash powders, or some black powder substitutes, such as Hodgdon®.

How much destruction do bombs cause?

The strength of a bomb can vary greatly, some yielding little power and others causing mass destruction, depending on the chemical reactants used and the construction of the device itself. They can include destruction with a small, homemade device (for example, a crude pipe bomb) to a weapon of mass destruction (for example, a dirty bomb, which releases harmful materials, such as a bomb that releases a toxic chemical or a nuclear bomb that releases varying levels of radioactivity).

What are some typical components of an explosive and a bomb?

Not all bombs or explosives are alike, but overall, they do have some similarities in their construction. Simply put, explosives/bombs have a mechanism that creates an initial spark (such as a timer or remote control device). The spark then ignites the explosive material and detonates the explosive bomb, causing the blast.

What are some bomb blast effects?

A bomb's detonation causes several effects. For example, the initial blast wave (also called shock wave) is the most damaging part of an explosion. In this phase, a wave of highly compressed air rapidly radiates outward from the detonation point, causing the first (and often the most) damage to people and/or structures. This also sends fragments of the bomb's container (called casing) outward as well as any materials that may have been added to the interior of the bomb, such as shrapnel or nails. If large enough, the initial blast may also cause a fireball with high heat, possibly starting fires or secondary explosions depending on where the bomb is detonated.

What does the "seat of the explosion" mean?

The origin of the blast of a bomb—or the point of detonation—is frequently referred to as the seat of the explosion, or blast seat. It is not necessarily obvious in some cases because whether a crater is there or not is dependent on the device and where it is placed.

Forensic experts look for the seat of the blast not only to find possible pieces of the explosive device but also to find residue on surfaces (objects, grass, soil, roadways, etc.) to collect as evidence for further analysis in the lab.

What is dynamite?

Dynamite is considered a high explosive and is *not* nitroglycerine or TNT alone, as many people believe. Dynamite consists of nitroglycerine mixed with absorbent materials (such as powdered shells or clay) and stabilizers. It was first invented by Swedish chemist, engineer, and inventor Alfred Bernhard Nobel (1833–1896) in response to the unsafe manufacturing and use of nitroglycerine, a highly unstable explosive (his brother had been killed in such an explosion). Thus, he incorporated nitroglycerine into the inert substance silica,

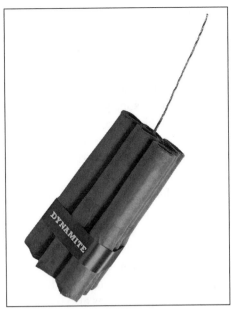

Dynamite is a mix of nitroglycerine with stabilizers such as silica to prevent the volatile nitro from exploding before it is supposed to.

making it safer—and patented it under the name "dynamite." Today, it is used in heavy groundwork, such as building roads or extracting commercial stonework (such as marble or granite). Dynamite is most typically molded into sticks, which, thanks to television and movies, is the form most people think of when they hear the word "dynamite."

What is trinitrotoluene (TNT)?

TNT, as it is commonly known, is actually trinitrotoluene, which is considered a high explosive. Molecularly, it is created from toluene (also called toluol)—a colorless, water-insoluble liquid—by the substitution of nitro groups for three hydrogen atoms. Toluene is relatively insensitive to shock and can be conveniently melted, and it is a pale yellow, solid, organic nitrogen compound. (It is also considered a toxic chemical and can be found in nail products, hair dyes, glues, inks, stain removers, paints, lacquers, and paint thinners.)

What is C-4?

C-4, or Composition C-4, is a white, pliable, plastic explosive; it is also considered a plastic bonded explosive, or PBX. It is most associated with the military but also has been used for commercial industrial purposes, too. The British form is called PE4 (for "Plastic Explosive"). According to several references, the constituents of C-4 are the high explosive RDX (91 percent), along with 1.6 percent processing oils, 5.3 percent plasticizer, and 2.1 percent polyisobutylene (PIB).

What is an improvised explosive device (IED)?

An improvised explosive device (IED; often erroneously called *incendiary* explosive device) is a homemade device that can come in a multitude of forms, including letter and roadside bombs (the term has been used in the media many times, too, especially since the U.S. involvement in the Iraq and Afghanistan wars). The devices have certain commonalities, including a power supply, initiator (causes the bomb to explode), explosive material, and a switch. It can also be connected to certain components from various types of technology, including a cell phone or an automatic garage door opener. If triggered from longer distances, the perpetrators often use radios or cell phones to remotely control the detonation.

What are incendiary devices?

Incendiary devices (also called incendiary weapons or bombs [they are considered to be high explosives], or firebombs) are devices that are made to quickly start fires or destroy areas with extensive weaponry or equipment. They include smaller devices to start fires, such as "Molotov cocktails" (flammable liquid in a bottle, in which a rag or fuse is attached, lit, and tossed, with the liquid igniting on impact) often used by rioters to start fires. Larger devices also use incendiary (materials designed to start fires) components, such as thermite, magnesium powder, or white phosphorus, all of which are quick to ignite and spread a fire. Incendiary devices can also contain napalm, a flammable liquid—a mix of plastic polystyrene, hydrocarbon benzene, and gasoline that, when ignited, sticks to anything it touches. It has been used at times for warfare, including its controversial use in the Vietnam War (1965–1972).

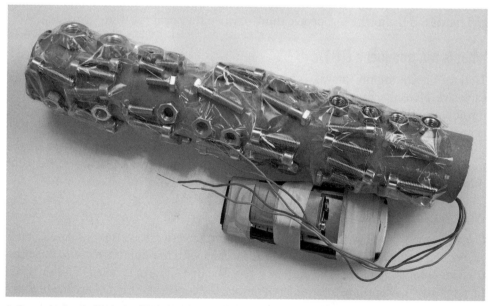

An improvised explosive device (IED) can take a number of shapes. Here is one consisting of a pipe bomb, a cell phone to set it off, and nuts and bolts as fragmentation metal to cause more damage.

What are pyrotechnic devices?

Pyrotechnic devices are considered to be low explosives. They are often used in various crimes but also for nuisance and vandalism crimes. In fact, pyrotechnics are what keep people entertained during many concerts, or theatrical special effects (including the Super Bowl), all of which provide a combination of explosions, smoke, flames, colored lights, or other effects for the audience. Overall, these devices include a confined explosive powder and a wick for ignition. In the crime lab, they are examined for debris, usually with a stereomicroscope. The containers—usually of plastic or paper—often have identifiable markings, and any unexploded powder can be analyzed to determine the actual powder used. This often involves the scanning electron microscope with energy dispersive x-ray spectroscopy (SEM/EDS) for the inorganic composition of objects and Fourier-transform infrared spectroscopy (FTIR) for the organic composition of the internal chemical mixture.

Why do fireworks come in various colors?

One of the most well-known pyrotechnics is fireworks—and the reason for their explosions is complex. In general, these devices include a container, main fuse, time-delay fuse, and bursting and lifting (usually black powder) charges. Certain chemicals added to the mix create the color seen in the displays. For instance, barium produces green, calcium salts orange, blue is from copper, reds are from strontium and lithium, white is from magnesium, and gold from sodium. To make the fireworks sparkle and crackle, magnalium (an aluminum alloy with magnesium and a small amount of nickel and tin) is used.

What materials are often collected for analysis after an explosion?

Several materials can be collected for analysis after an explosion. Investigators can collect residue from the explosion (on objects, clothing, etc.); some investigators use a

---

Why does NASA study pyrotechnic devices?

Pyrotechnic devices are not only for vandalism or entertainment. They can be useful in a variety of fields, including the National Aeronautics and Space Administration's (NASA) space program. In particular, NASA states that the devices are used "in launch vehicles, tactical missiles, cargo and parachute deployment, and payload release mechanisms." Most of these devices are used only once. For instance, when activated, a small explosive charge fires to create a high-speed, shearing effect that can do several actions, depending on the task. For instance, it can cut off electrical circuits at a specific time; open or close a certain valve; ignite solid rocket boosters; release and/or separate a bolted connection to separate or jettison hardware; or move a joint or junction to deploy a robotic arm, but NASA is currently trying to develop alternatives, as the devices often release debris that can damage a spacecraft or cause such vibrations that it damages the hardware on the vehicle.

handheld device called an ion mobility spectrometer (IMS), which can help identify chemical residues around the blast site. Investigators can also seek fragments of the explosive device for examination in the lab, along with pieces of the device (such as wires, switches, or timers). They can also collect any evidence that may (or may not) be connected to the perpetrator(s) of the explosion, such as a discarded backpack, weapon, or cell phone. They can also document and video-record the condition surrounding the blast site, including structural damage, and they can interview eyewitnesses and note casualties and/or fatalities. All this information will allow investigators to possibly understand the kind and nature of the explosive device.

EXAMINING EXPLOSIVES
IN THE LAB

What do experts seek when analyzing a bomb in the lab?

Experts look at several characteristics when analyzing a bomb. For instance, they want to identify the type of explosive(s) used in the device and/or the actual bomb materials (bulk explosives)—if one or both can be collected as evidence. Several other components are involved in the analysis of a device, especially the construction and manufacturing of the explosive, especially examining not only the container but shrapnel or other materials from inside the container. Other aspects of the explosive can be checked, such as the type of explosive material or any materials that were used to start the explosion, such as diesel fuel or ammonium nitrate.

What else is examined besides the main device?

Other pieces also make up the device. For example, experts will also want to examine and identify such items as fuses, detonators, batteries, switches, timing mechanisms, wraps (such as types of adhesives that hold some explosives together), coated or uncoated wires, and even paints or oils on the device. Each one of these pieces may provide evidence as to who was responsible for the manufacturing of the explosive device.

What types of instruments are used to analyze explosives in the lab?

Many instruments are used to analyze explosives in the lab. For example, when analyzing explosive evidence, experts often start (after a first-look, visual examination) with stereomicroscopy to determine the physical characteristics of the material. Further examination of the evidence most often means testing chemically and depends on whether the explosive is intact or post-blast. For instance, the explosives and their residues may be examined using such instruments as Fourier-transform infrared spectroscopy (FTIR), x-ray fluorescence (XRF), and polarized light microscopy (PLM). Each instrument's use is dependent on what materials are being analyzed in connection with the explosive.

What are explosive (or post-blast) residues?

According to the Federal Bureau of Investigation (FBI), two sources of residue are found after an explosion: residue attached to or associated with the device, container, or nearby object's fragments, and the residue from the surfaces or items that are not associated with the explosion. (Some references also include the residue of the device's fragments.) These fragments and particles that make up a residue are often analyzed in the lab with high-powered microscopes and, if necessary, with sensitive chemical analysis on various instruments. In terms of collecting the residue at a crime scene, it is of primary concern to the investigator to gather as many samples of the residues as possible, as some particles can wash away under such conditions as rain or fog or even contamination by those on the scene.

Can clothing contain explosive residue?

Yes, oftentimes, if a person is exposed to an explosion site, analysts may examine the person's clothing to obtain explosive residue. For example, when Oklahoma bombing suspect Timothy McVeigh was on trial, the FBI crime lab alleged that the clothing he was wearing when arrested had explosive residue, but such connections can be difficult. Some references state that not all explosive residues on a person's clothing come from a criminal explosion. For example, if a police officer (or even a public citizen) who has been practicing on a shooting range had their clothes examined, gunpowder residue is usually found—and may be misinterpreted as explosive residue. In addition, people who work for laboratories specializing in commercial or military explosives will also test positive for explosive residue.

Who looks at explosive evidence in the crime lab?

Several experts look at explosive evidence in the crime lab. For example, specialists in chemistry are usually involved in examining explosive residues in the lab. They also work with specialists in explosive devices, or those who are experts in electrical components, how such devices are constructed, and what type of damage comes from a certain type of explosion. If fragments of an explosive are found, they may also be analyzed by fingerprint and/or DNA experts to see whether a match occurs in fingerprint and/or DNA databases. If the type of explosive device is determined, this can be used to search against national databases that deal with trends in the manufacture of explosives and track trends of

American terrorist Timothy McVeigh (in background, center) perpetrated the 1995 Oklahoma City bombing that killed 168 people. His clothes were examined for explosives residue.

bombs and other explosives used by terrorist groups or serial bombers, for example, the FBI's Terrorist Explosive Device Analytical Center or the ATF's Arson and Explosives National Repository.

MORE ABOUT BOMBS AND EXPLOSIVES

Who was the first known person to use a bomb?

It is difficult to determine the first known person who used a bomb, but the first use of one is thought to have occurred in China in 1221 by a Jin Dynasty army to attack a Song Dynasty city. Cast iron shells packed with gunpowder are thought to have been invented in China around the thirteenth century—the bomb's name translated to "thunder-crash bomb"—with a record of use during a naval battle (1231) by the Jin Dynasty against the Mongols.

What was once called a "bomb squad"?

In general, a bomb squad—now more commonly called a hazardous devices team—is a group of specially trained personnel primarily from local, state, and/or federal law enforcement who investigate all kinds of explosives discovered under various conditions (such as a suspicious package at an airport or to defuse an explosive device planted by criminals and/or terrorists) or investigate where explosions have occurred. Less common are hazardous devices teams that are part of a fire department or emergency management agency.

Are any bombs left over from World War II?

Yes, many unexploded and leftover "duds" from World War II are still in existence. It is estimated that between 1940 and 1945, United States and British aircraft dropped close to 2.7 million tons of bombs on Europe, half of them on Germany—with around 10 percent of the devices failing to detonate. As of this writing, each year, around two thousand tons of unexploded munitions are uncovered in Germany, with evacuations necessary in many places. (In fact, officials are becoming even more concerned because after more than seventy years, some of the casings are breaking down.) For example, in late 2013, twenty thousand people in the city of Dortmund were evacuated when a four-thousand-pound "blockbuster" bomb was uncovered—a bomb that could easily destroy a city block—and in May 2017, fifty thousand people in Hanover were evacuated after five suspected World War II bombs were uncovered—two turned out to be harmless, and three were defused.

When was the first U.S. "bomb squad" created?

The first "bomb squad" created in the United States was in late 1908 through the New York City Police Department (NYPD). It was headed by detective Lt. Joseph (Giuseppe) Petrosino (1860–1909), who was investigating Mafia activity in New York. He and his "Italian Squad," as the team was called, worked to uncover bomb plots and perpetrators, as many Italian immigrants were being extorted by the Mafia, often by using what are now called improvised explosive devices (IEDs). On a secret visit to Sicily to identify criminals, news of his mission was leaked to the press. Petrosino went to meet an informant, but it was a trap, and he was shot to death by Mafia assassins.

What are some duties of various hazardous devices teams?

Hazardous devices teams have several specific tasks. For example, UnExploded Ordnance (UXO) technicians systematically search for and eliminate ordnance that was (and is) left behind on former and current government bomb ranges. Military Explosive Ordnance Disposal (EOD) teams most often handle improvised explosive devices (IED; for more about IEDs, see this chapter) and ordnance on the U.S. Department of Defense (DOD) property as well as any ordnance found on public or non-DOD lands. Outside of the government, public safety bomb technicians, most from local or state law enforcement, handle IEDs that are found on non-DOD property. Besides other administrative duties, such as investigating and reporting explosions, these specialists are also in charge of destroying commercial explosives and fireworks and old or unused ammunition.

In this photo, a bomb disposal robot retrieves and disarms an explosive device from a suspected terrorist's car during a police exercise.

What is a bomb disposal robot?

Unlike television or the movies, a hazardous devices team does not always "suit up and head out" to check out a suspicious item. The preferred method is to do an investigation remotely if possible, and in the past several decades, advancements in technology and robotics have allowed humans to limit their exposure to the extremely hazardous task of getting rid of a bomb by using remote sensing devices. Usually termed "bomb disposal robot," these unmanned devices (some people argue that they are not truly robots) act similar to a drone. They are controlled by a human operator who is at a safe distance from a possible explosion, whether it be from a bomb, unidentified package, land mine, or unexploded munitions. These machines are outfitted with cameras, giving the human operator a close look at the explosive device on a computer monitor (the majority of bomb disposal robots are controlled through wireless communications) and possibly allow the bomb to be rendered inert. Since most bombs need a power supply to detonate and water can break the circuit, a typical way of defusing a bomb with a robot entails firing a high-pressure jet of water at the bomb's wires, but if the bomb has a secondary system that causes it to go off if tampered with or if the water jet does not break the circuit, the bomb can detonate, with the robot being sacrificed—and not a human.

What is the Bomb Data Center?

The United States Bomb Data Center (USBDC) is a national repository for explosive- and arson-related occurrence data. According to the ATF (Bureau of Alcohol, Tobacco, Firearms, and Explosives), its purpose is to "collect data and to provide those federal, state, and local agencies having jurisdiction with information and intelligence to assist in the investigation of bombings, arson, and the criminal misuse of explosives." In 2004, all of the data and information about such arson and explosive incidents were consolidated into one database called the Bomb Arson Tracking System (BATS). As of this writing, BATS contains information on more than four hundred thousand explosive- and arson-related incidents—all of which have been investigated by many government agencies, including the ATF, FBI, and local law-enforcement and public safety agencies. Along with BATS, the USBDC maintains the National Explosives Tracing Center (NETC), which keeps track of and identifies domestic, foreign, commercial, and military explosives and artillery, along with other munitions (military ammunitions, weapons, and equipment).

Where do many explosive events occur?

In terms of criminal explosive events, the more well-known explosive events are extensively covered in the media, such as the Oklahoma City or Atlanta Olympic bombings, but certain explosive incidents commonly occur elsewhere. According to the National Institute of Justice, this includes residential properties, mailboxes, and vehicles. Most of these are carried out by smaller groups or by individuals, in which vandalism and revenge are the most common motives.

What are some types of explosives that are often encountered by law-enforcement and/or government agencies, such as the FBI?

Not all explosives are created equally, but some are commonly encountered by law-enforcement and/or government agencies. The following lists some of those explosives and how they may be analyzed by forensic experts:

- *Pipe bombs*—These explosives usually have a short length of pipe capped off at both ends. Inside is either a high- or low-explosive powder mixture, with a detonator (fuse) inserted into a drilled hole in one end. When it explodes, it rapidly sends out shards of the pipe; if it is a hard casing, large pieces may be found, but if it is a soft casing, smaller fragments will be left behind. In most cases, fingerprints or pieces of the bomb are often recovered for forensic analysis. These are the most common explosives encountered by hazardous explosive device teams ("bomb squads").

- *Mines (or land mine or sea mine)*—These explosives are commonly used by the military (by both sides in a war, such as in World War II or the Vietnam wars). They contain a high explosive and are buried slightly underground or hidden in higher, grassy terrain. When a person or vehicle puts pressure (or falls over a tripping wire) by stepping on such a mine, it will detonate. This is unlike in the movies or television, in which the mine will not explode unless a person steps off the mine, releasing their weight. In this case, pieces of the mine will often help forensic experts determine where the device originated.

- *Letter bomb (and many other names, such as parcel bomb, mail bomb, etc.)*—These explosives—which some claim may have been used as far back as the 1700s—contain a small amount of a high explosive inside a letter (or package), which is triggered by the opening of the mail. Forensic examination of the package pieces may help identify some information about the perpetrator, including the paper used, the handwriting or typing on the package, and perhaps even fingerprints. (This is because, in most cases, the explosion rarely causes a fire, so evidence can be collected.)

- *Suicide bombers*—This type of explosive is unfortunately pervasive in modern times, especially in terms of terrorism, although the tactic has been used for centuries. In this case, the person(s) wears a vest or belt of explosives (commonly high explosives), walking into a target location and detonating their bomb. After such a bombing, forensic experts look for pieces of the bomb itself and evidence of the bomber to identify not only the type of explosives used but the bomber or bombers as well. In addition, many times, the person responsible for the bombing can be viewed via surveillance cameras and eyewitness reports from or around the the bomb site, and many times, too, a terrorist organization will claim responsibility, along with identifying the bomber.

Are canines used in the detection of explosives?

Yes, dogs are often used in the detection of explosives. Special training allows a dog to use their exceptional smelling ability to detect certain aspects of an explosive, such as the materials used in the production of the device or the explosive materials, for example, nitroglycerin or the sulfur in gunpowder. Oftentimes, dogs are able to detect more explosive devices, pieces of a device that have not been put together, or even the explosive residues in a suspect's home or on the person's clothes.

IN THE CRIME LAB: QUESTIONED DOCUMENTS AND CRYPTANALYSIS

DEFINING QUESTIONED DOCUMENTS

What are questioned documents?

In forensic science, questioned documents, simply put, means the discipline of forensic document examination. It is often associated with what are referred to as "white-collar crimes," such as check fraud, or criminal financial activities, such as embezzlement (which is often referred to as forensic accounting; see this chapter). Questioned documents can also include cases that range from malpractice suits in medicine and art forgeries to a civil suit or a certain aspect of a homicide case. In each case, the investigators need to examine or verify the authenticity of a document—to determine whether it is original, forged, or altered—which could be used as possible evidence in court or aid in a criminal investigation.

What are some examples of questioned documents often collected as evidence in an investigation?

Questioned documents (or materials) often collected as evidence in an investigation can include contracts, wills, currency, identification cards, seals, titles, deeds, checks, bank and financial organization statements, and even the examination of machine-generated documents (such as from typewriters, printers, photocopiers, and fax machines). It can also mean the collection of such evidence as writing instruments (pens, pencils, crayons, markers, etc.), envelopes, and stamps (postal and rubber stamps).

What does the investigation of questioned documents involve?

In general, forensic questioned document investigations concentrate on the question of document(s) authenticity. In order to prove whether a document is genuine, a forensic expert takes on such tasks as confirming who actually wrote or created the document (for example, the interpretation of any handwriting on the document), identifying materials used in the document (such as inks, paper, stamps, etc.), determining when the document was created, and/or finding out whether any modifications, substitutions, or eliminations were made within the original text (such as in check fraud or financial corruption cases).

What are some situations in which a document's authenticity is investigated?

Numerous situations need the investigation of document authenticity. According to several sources, this includes a long list of cases. For example, they include such cases as forgeries, counterfeit documents, identity theft, fraud (check and other), wrongly cancelled checks, personal notes, debated leases, extortion, poison-pen letters, questioned wills, contested contracts, larceny, death threats, medical malpractice, title or deed lawsuits, suicides, homicides, bank robberies, kidnappings, or stalking. At a crime scene, any documents or written material may be the clue to solve the overall case—whether it was found written on paper, a wall, or a mirror or written in ink, lipstick, or blood.

How has digital analysis of questioned documents changed over the past few decades?

The analysis of questioned documents by forensic experts has changed over the past few decades because of the advancement of digital technology, but such changes have been both good and bad. While technology has improved the techniques used to analyze a questioned document, some believe that the improved technology of printers, copiers, and computers has made forging and counterfeiting that much easier for criminals. (For more about digital crime, see the chapter "Other Forensic Investigations.")

What are some tools used to examine questioned documents?

A multitude of tools and equipment are often used to examine questioned documents. For example, microscopes and digital imaging can be used, as can infrared and ultraviolet light sources. Also, specialized equipment is used, including electrostatic detection devices (EDD; see below) and analysis using certain specialized chemicals. In many cases, the equipment used depends on the questioned document. For example, in order not to damage a document, nondestructive techniques such as the use of light or electrostatics are often used to examine a document, but if, for example, ink on a questioned document needs to be analyzed, destructive means, such as liquid chromatography, are used to examine small samples removed from the document.

How are questioned documents often damaged?

Questioned documents as evidence can often be damaged through various means that may make it difficult to analyze. For example, a document may be torn up by someone with pieces missing, shredded with a cross-shredding device, making it difficult to reconstruct. It may be damaged by fire or an explosion. The document may be damaged by various environmental conditions, such as being water-soaked from rain, or exposed to damp conditions, forming mold or mildew on the surface or permeating the paper. Or, it can be buried outside for a long period, with damage not only from dirt, humidity (or excessive heat), and vegetation but by various animals, such as mice that chew or even birds that use it for nesting material. In addition, some chemical analyses may destroy a document, which is why forensic experts often have the questioned document (for example, a ransom note) examined by an expert in the lab before being treated with chemicals to possibly reveal fingerprints.

How do experts in questioned documents help investigators involved in trace evidence?

Questioned documents and trace evidence often cross over. For example, if a shoe impression is collected as trace evidence, the information is often sent to experts in questioned documents. From there, those experts identify the manufacturer, make, and model of the shoe—and possibly help identify the victim or criminal who owned the shoes. (For more about deciphering trace evidence, see the chapter "In the Crime Lab: Trace Evidence.")

Do any limitations exist in questioned document analysis?

No matter how careful investigators are in collecting evidence, limitations exist when it comes to questioned document analysis. For instance, an insufficient amount of the questioned material may be available to analyze or to compare to a known sample. It may be of poor quality, so no conclusive results can be determined, such as documents that have been burned to ashes or cross-cut shredded. The actual handwriting may be distorted or disguised, such as oversized words written in lipstick on a mirror at a crime scene. Or, the actual evidence may have been copied over and over, making it difficult to determine the defects or flaws within the original document.

Does a database for printers exist?

Yes, because questioned documents are often printed out on printers, the U.S. Secret Service maintains a database for printers—and it's considered to be the largest known collection in the world. The database includes the brands of printers used

Cross-cut shredders destroy documents so thoroughly that it is usually impossible to reconstruct the documents for evidence.

based on the physical and chemical characteristics of collected questioned documents. It is most often used to investigate events involving anonymous letters, counterfeit IDs, and other types of documents.

Does a database for faxes exist?

Yes, because faxes are often used in collection with criminal evidence, the Fax Font Database IV is maintained by the American Society of Questioned Document Examiners (ASQDE). The 950 samples in this database include images of faxed TTIs (transmitting terminal identifiers) that can be used to match a questioned TTI to a reference standard. This can allow the expert to determine the possible make and model of the fax machine used in a crime or legal dispute.

FORENSIC ACCOUNTING

What is forensic accounting in terms of crime?

Forensic accountants use their knowledge and skills of finances, financial law, and accounting principles to reveal such crimes as embezzlement, fraudulent financial information, or corruption committed by an individual, business, government agency, and others. They often work directly with law-enforcement agencies on accounting concerns connected to a crime, and the results are commonly used in legal proceedings in court or as evidence at a criminal trial. Forensic accounting and questioned documents share a connection—especially in terms of working to determine the legality (or criminality) of financial documents and records.

Where do forensic accountants work?

Forensic accountants work for a multitude of groups, agencies, and institutions. For example, according to the FBI, forensic accountants' tasks include the investigation of "complex financial crimes involving corporate fraud, financial institution fraud, health-care fraud, mortgage fraud, and securities and commodities fraud. Their expertise is also applied to counterintelligence, counterterrorism, cybercrime, organized crime, public corruption and violent crime investigations." Forensic accountants are also employed by public accounting firms' forensic accounting divisions, by consulting firms that do risk consulting and forensic accounting services, and by lawyers, law-enforcement agencies, insurance companies, financial institutions, and other organizations that need accounting expertise, especially in terms of criminal acts.

Can a person be certified in finances and forensics?

Yes, one can become certified in both finances and forensics in several different ways. For example, according to the American Institute of Certified Public Accountants, CPAs can obtain a certification called Certified in Financial Forensic (CFF). This entails such things as financial fraud, misstatements on financial documents, and the misappropriation of funds; if the person is familiar with computers, it can also entail cybercrime and data integrity of financial information. The National Association of Certified Valuators and Analysts also has a "Masters Analyst" certification, which entails financial litigation and other topics in financial forensics. (*Note*: Some groups call this field certified financial forensics, while others call it certified forensic financial analysis—both of which are, in general, almost identical.)

What are some crimes in which forensic accountants are needed to help solve?

A forensic accountant is needed for many crimes, including following a "paper trail" to determine the legalities of an organization's financial information. Some forensic accountants deal with what is often called a "new" type of crime—mainly the more recent ease in using digital media and computer hacking to commit certain accounting and financial crimes. The list of crimes analyzed by forensic accountants is long and includes white-collar crime; money laundering; fraudulent insurance claims; telemarketing, check, credit card, bankruptcy, securities, and financial statement fraud; embezzlement; financial data analysis of incorrect information; financial evidence integrity; and the tracing of illicit funds.

It might not seem as glamorous as other types of forensics, but forensic accounting is a critical part of crime investigations as well, involving such activities as fraud, theft, cybercrime, and insider trading.

ANALYZING PAPER AND INK

How do forensic experts analyze paper products from a crime scene?

Paper and paper products are often analyzed by forensic experts, especially with respect to products based on composition, which can provide information such as the age of the paper and ink (for more about ink, see below). In order to analyze paper, forensic experts use several tools, such as standard magnification with a microscope, to molecular spectroscopy to analyze the elements within the papers—alone or in combination. The various types of analysis show the different properties of the paper. For example, a qualitative analysis shows what materials are in and on the paper, such as ink, fibers, the paper itself, especially such characteristics as strength, fiber content, direction of grain, finish, watermarks, opacity, weight, thickness, size, and/or color. A quantitative analysis would show how much and the composition of these materials in the paper, including the composition of the ink, pigments, and fibers (many times from plants) in the paper. Not only can such analyses lead to the age of the paper but also to the possible origin.

Where can questioned document analysts find information about paper products?

Several places have information about paper products, many of which can be used by questioned document analysts to interpret document characteristics and properties. For example, public centers that house information about paper and paper products include the Robert C. Williams Museum of Papermaking—an international resource about the history of paper and paper technology. (The museum has more than two thousand books about paper and a collection of over ten thousand watermarks, along with papers, tools, machines, and manuscripts.)

How do forensic experts interpret the information gathered from paper analysis?

A forensic expert can interpret several things from the analysis of a questioned paper document. For example, if the paper is a common, low-grade type of product, it is difficult to find clues as to the originator of the document, except just to determine the general area or place in which such paper is sold. If the paper is less common—and usually more expensive and sometimes exclusive—it may be possible to trace the originator of the document. This is because such paper is usually only purchased by a limited number of people.

Why is paper often analyzed to determine its age?

Sometimes it is possible to estimate the age of certain paper (although it is not thought of as an exact science). For example, the relative age of a document is often needed in forgery cases, in which the paper may not be as old as the alleged date it was signed. Other such papers that may need an age estimate include documents, photographs, books, artwork, and any other objects made of paper. In some cases, the estimate of a paper's age is done by examining its composition (type of fiber, color, etc.) or watermark (see below). Also, chemical reagents can be used to determine certain composition, or even an instrument called a tintometer, which can gauge the shade of paper colors. The

---

What is a legal document?

According to the U.S. Central Intelligence Agency (CIA), a legal document is defined as being of any material on which marks may be inscribed. This includes gravestones and even certain engravings of a famous person's signature found on certain materials, but in the majority of cases, a legal document is written on paper.

results of such examinations are often compared to known types of paper in hopes of obtaining a match that will give a better age estimate of that paper.

What are watermarks on paper?

Watermarks on paper were once used to identify types of paper or even a name brand of paper. It was a semitransparent image or text—sometimes made thicker, lighter, or darker than the original paper—that was specially applied to a piece of paper and gave the information about that paper. In terms of monetary or stamp paper, watermarks were also semitransparent images or text, with some colored images, that made it more difficult to make counterfeit money or stamps. More recently, watermarks have become more intricate, using an identifying image or pattern in paper that, when viewed, would reflect light or display a holographic image.

How do experts often reveal indented impressions on a document?

In some cases, a document may have indented impressions—or depressed areas on the surface of a document that are made by the pressure of a person writing or printing—that are not visible to the naked eye. One way experts often use to determine what is written is with an electrostatic detection device (EDD), for example, the electrostatic detection apparatus (ESDA). For instance, if the top page of a pad of paper has been removed and impressions of the writing are visible on the next sheet of paper, an ESDA can show the writing on those pages. Simply put, to see the indentations, the document is put into a high-humidity device and transferred onto a bronze vacuum plate. It is then covered with Mylar film and electrically charged. This allows special toner particles to be applied and stick to the impressions, revealing the "hidden" writing. In fact, this technique can reveal impressions even if around seven layers of paper are beneath the original writing—and even impressions in documents around sixty years old.

How do experts reveal alterations, deletions, erasures, and page substitutions on a questioned document?

A questioned document can be examined in several ways, especially to determine whether any alterations, deletions, and erasures are there that should not be on the document—and even page substitutions. In order to determine whether the documents have changes that are not visible to the naked eye, they can be examined using such techniques as photography or imaging devices that use ultraviolet and/or infrared wavelengths. For example, experts use such instruments as video spectral comparators or forensic imaging spectrometers. These instruments use ultraviolet and infrared wavelengths to "see" writing that has been changed in various ways, including blacked-out, erased, faded, physically or chemically altered, or scribbled out, or if the person added writing with different ink.

What is "invisible ink," and who invented it?

Invisible ink is just as the phrase sounds: "ink" that is invisible to the naked eye but, when treated in a certain way, reveals writing, drawings, etc. Many stories of "invisible ink" are being used throughout history—going back tens of centuries. Thus, no one claims to have invented invisible ink, but plenty of "formulations" were used over time. For example, Roman philosopher and naturalist Pliny the Elder (23 [or 24]–79 C.E.) found that by using the milk from what was once called goat or sea lettuce (or tithymalus; it is now reclassified as modern-day spurge of the genus Euphorbia), when put on an object and dried, would reveal writing when sprinkled with ashes. The Revolutionary War in the United States also had its fair share of invisible ink stories. For example, George Washington and his agents would send and receive "hidden" messages using a chemical solution containing tannic acid.

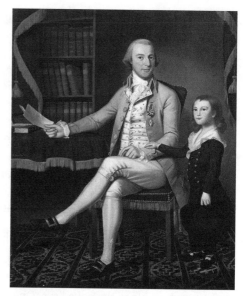

Major Benjamin Talmade (pictured here with his son) organized a spy ring under orders from George Washington during the Revolutionary Wary. After the execution of the spy Nathan Hale, the Americans tried using invisible ink to send messages covertly.

How are inks on a questioned document analyzed?

An ink's chemical composition can be determined using certain methods, such as high-performance liquid chromatography (HPLC). For example, according to the Central Intelligence Agency (CIA), modern inks come in three general types: gallotannic (the most common), chromic, and aniline. Other types exist, such as those made for stamp pads—each with enough chemical differences to allow for their identification in the lab.

How is the age of ink determined?

According to the Central Intelligence Agency (CIA), the age of ink can often be determined if certain data is on file, such as the different manufacturers' formulas for various inks over the years. For example, if a company changes its ink formulas four times in ten years, a sample of that ink can be linked to a certain manufacturing period. Age can also often be determined based on the ink's color. For instance, permanent inks often contain a temporary dye (which soon fades), iron and sulfur compounds, and a weak acid. Because of this, after a certain time, the acid, oxygen, and humidity that helped create the dark color works on the ink; the sample will then eventually fade into a faint mark. Even though it is faded, it can still be analyzed using chemical reagents (taking into consideration the color of the paper with the ink) and the color compared with standardized color charts.

What is the International Ink Library?

The International Ink Library is a collection of more than 9,500 inks dating from the 1920s. The database—maintained jointly by the U.S. Secret Service and the Internal

How was a chemical analysis of ink important in the conviction of Martha Stewart?

In 2004, American businesswoman, author, and television personality Martha Stewart (1941–) was convicted of four counts of obstruction of justice, including conspiracy (a felony), obstruction of an agency proceeding, and making false statements to federal investigators. She was sentenced to five months in a federal correctional facility. She allegedly lied about why she sold a stock called ImClone in 2001—right before the stock price plunged. A part of the evidence in the conviction of Martha Stewart was based on ink. In this instance, ink on a certain document was analyzed, indicating that the entry was made at a different time than the original document. This was then interpreted as a possible attempt to cover up insider trading.

Martha Stewart

Revenue Service (IRS)—requires pen and ink manufacturers to submit their new formulations each year. In terms of ink, they are chemically tested, compared with library specimens, and added to the reference database collection. Writing instruments are identified by type and brand. Both the ink and writing instrument help investigators of questioned documents to possibly determine, for example, the earliest possible date that a document could have been written or produced.

EXAMINING HANDWRITTEN DOCUMENTS

What is handwriting in association with forensics?

In forensics, handwriting analysis—also called graphology—includes the examination and comparison of mainly hand-printed and written signatures. It is based on several ideas, including when comparing a sufficient amount of handwriting between two writers, they will not have identical features in their handwriting, as everyone has a natural variation within their handwriting or hand printing. In fact, comparisons of individuals' handwriting samples have never, so far, had the same combination of handwriting characteristics, which is why a handwriting sample in some crimes or other fraudulent activities is often considered good evidence. These include differences in cursive and print writing, along with numerals and signatures in documents.

What does a handwriting expert look for in a questioned document?

A handwriting expert looks for various things in a document to determine whether it is forged or to determine the identity of the writer. For instance, they look at the letter

231

forms, including the curves, slants, links between letters, proportional sizes of the letters, and the placement of each letter within the words. They also look at the line form, or how light or dark the lines are that indicate the pressure the writer used on the writing instrument as they were writing. They also check for formatting, or the use of space in the document, such as the margins and spacing between letters, words, and lines. It is not only the physical aspects of the writing but also the writing itself, such as the grammar, punctuation, phrases, and spelling. From there, experts evaluate the similarities in known and unknown samples of writing, such as comparing them to other writing samples in available handwriting databases.

Do any handwriting databases exist?

Yes, many handwriting databases exist that are often used by forensic experts. For example, the U.S. Secret Service, the German Federal Police, and the Federal Bureau of Investigation (FBI) all maintain databases that contain hundreds of thousands of handwriting samples. Another example is the Forensic Information System for Handwriting (FISH), which is maintained by the U.S. Secret Service (see below).

What is the Forensic Information System for Handwriting (FISH)?

The Forensic Information System for Handwriting (FISH) is maintained by the U.S. Secret Service Forensic Laboratory (it is customized specifically for its Forensic Services Division). This database contains handwriting samples from tens of thousands of writers and includes all threatening correspondence received by federal and other governmental agencies, along with threats to governors, senators, and members of Congress. The database allows a forensic document expert to scan and digitize text writing, such as on threatening correspondence, which is then plotted using certain mathematical parameters. A search is then made in the database, allowing the expert to receive a list of probable similarities. The questioned writings, along with the possible similarities, are then sent to the Secret Service's Document Examination Section for confirmation. FISH also has a database that contains letters submitted by the National Center for Missing and Exploited Children (NCMEC). Over twelve thousand samples are in the FISH database, with the NCMEC containing around four hundred samples.

What are the FBI's Anonymous Letter File and the Bank Robbery Note File?

The Federal Bureau of Investigation's (FBI) Laboratory has a database called the Anonymous Letter File that holds anonymous letters submitted from their cases. This is used to determine whether the writer has written any previous letters and is based on text, not handwriting characteristics. This includes such features as the postmark, postal code, addressee, and phrases used in the text. As of this writing, it contains over eight thousand samples—which will continue to grow as future anonymous letters from various cases are added to the database.

The FBI's Bank Robbery Note File (BRNF) is also based on the note and not necessarily the handwriting. In this case, the note is compared to others in the database to determine whether the writer has written previous demand notes. The search is based on such factors as wording (single key words or words in combination), underlined, italicized, etc., words, the placement of words on the paper (including margins or certain types of formats), and grammar, misspellings, punctuation, and/or overwriting or certain cross-outs. This database of over 9,600 samples (to date) relies on submitted evidence from various robbery cases.

Can handwriting be perfectly forged?

According to most forensic handwriting experts, usually, some font or quality of a person's handwriting versus what they are trying to forge gives the document away as a forgery. That being said, in 2016, researchers at the University College of London developed software based on special algorithms that can simulate the way a person creates their handwriting—some say perfectly. It was developed for good, such as for stroke victims who wanted to personalize their writing again, but others believe that such forging abilities may extend to criminal activities.

CRYPTOGRAPHY AND CRYPTANALYSIS

What do the terms cryptology, cryptography, and cryptanalysis mean?

Although the terms cryptology, cryptography, and cryptanalysis are often used interchangeably—and all deal with deciphering that which is undecipherable to anyone other than the intended recipient—differences exist. Cryptology is the scientific study of reading hidden messages using a linguistic (language) or code-breaking approach (cryptography is from the Greek *kryptos* or "hidden" and *graphein* or "writing"). Cryptography is the study of writing hidden messages using codes or ciphers, and cryptographers often provide security for information by developing certain cryptosystems (or ways of coding communications). Cryptanalysis (also seen as cryptanalytics) is analyzing hidden or undecipherable messages, often using a statistical or analytical approach. Cryptanalysts decipher coded messages, evaluate flaws or weaknesses in cryptosystems, and help to break into the security provided by such systems. In fact, most cryptosystems are only considered secure if they go through the scrutiny of an extensive cryptanalysis.

When was cryptography first used?

No one really knows when the first use of cryptography actually began, but many historians point to the Egyptians: evidence exists that around 1900 B.C.E., a scribe used unusual hieroglyphs in an inscription carved into the wall of a tomb. The use of cryptography in association with writing came much later, and many historians believe that secret writings may have been developed not long after writing was invented. Since then, and throughout history, disguising messages has been used for a multitude of reasons, such as sending secret, diplomatic notes between warring countries or even encrypted battle plans from a military base to troops in the field. Today, cryptography has taken on the task of interpreting technology and computer communications—including interpreting "secret messages" that may be found in any network, such as the Internet. (For more about forensic digital analysis and the Internet, see the chapter "Other Forensic Investigations.")

What are the two major categories of cryptographic systems?

The two major categories of cryptographic systems are ciphers and codes. According to the FBI, ciphers are the replacement of true letters or numbers (plain text) with different characters, which is called cipher text. Ciphers are also the systematic rearrangement of the true letters without changing their identities. Both conditions create what is called an enciphered message. Coded communications take information, such as in a letter or note, and turn it into another form that represents numbers, letters, words, or phrases. Both ciphers and codes were—and still are—often used extensively for communication and other reasons by the military, government agencies, and certain commercial concerns. Unfortunately, and often to the chagrin of experts who try to break ciphers and codes, they are also used by criminals to conceal certain records, conversations, and writings. For example, criminals may use a substitution cipher, or when two alphabets are one above the other, which are shifted to the left of right to create words. Or, drug traffickers often use code words to disguise their activities, such as certain color codes meaning the sale of certain drugs to users, or number codes a "customer" might use to clandestinely ask the price of an ounce of a certain drug.

What was an Enigma machine?

An Enigma machine (also often referred to as the Enigma Cipher Machine) was patented by German inventor and electrical engineer Arthur Scherbius (1878–1929) in early 1918, mainly for commercial use and in order to transcribe coded information for safety reasons. By the late 1920s, the military had produced its own version, and over the next several years, it became a much more complex machine. Simply put, the Enigma would allow a person to type in a message and scramble it by using three to five rotors, which displayed different letters of the alphabet. Understandably, Poland was concerned about

One of the Enigma machines used by the German army to create coded messages. The machines worked so well that it took math genius Alan Turing and his team in England to finally break the code in 1941.

an invasion by the Germans in the late 1930s and worked to break the code. They did so in 1938, but by that time, the Germans had changed the physical machine (adding two more rotors), making the Polish deciphering ineffective.

One of the most famous uses of Enigmas was by the Germans during World War II, who believed the codes from the Enigmas could not be broken and therefore used the codes to communicate plans of many land, sea, and air battles. After the war began, the British sought to break the code of the Enigmas and used as their headquarters an estate north of London at Bletchley Park under British mathematician Alan Turing. After building a deciphering machine of their own, along with the help of captured German codebooks and Enigma machines, British codebreakers were able to decipher signal traffic sent back and forth between the German military units throughout the war. According to many historians, this probably helped to end the war much earlier.

What are some famous ciphers and codes used for criminal activities?

Numerous famous ciphers and codes have been used in criminal activities over time—too many to mention them all here. Some of the more well-known ones include the Unabomber (sought from 1978 to 1996), in which American mathematician and domestic terrorist Theodore Kaczynski (1942–) kept notebooks filled with a numeric code to disguise his writings of crimes (and future ones he wished to commit). The Teapot Dome Scandal of 1924 included coded telegrams exchanged by the then secretary of the Interior, Albert Fall, which involved the secret leasing of U.S. government-owned lands to private developers in exchange for bribes. Still another use of ciphers included John

Wilkes Booth (1838–1865), an American actor and the assassin of President Abraham Lincoln. He used ciphers to contact his fellow conspirators and the Confederate government in Richmond, Virginia (a specialized cipher called the Vigènere cipher table was found among Booth's possessions after his death).

Are "gang signs" a form of code?

Yes, law-enforcement experts in codes realize that many gangs in various places have their own form of code, either verbal or nonverbal. Nonverbal codes are usually signs, symbols, and/or colors to differentiate each gang or groups within gangs, and many of these "codes" are displayed in the gang's graffiti, tattoos, and in their selected clothes and jewelry.

OTHER FORENSIC INVESTIGATIONS

DIGITAL/COMPUTER FORENSIC INVESTIGATIONS

What are digital crimes and computer forensics?

As the term implies, digital crime is usually one that involves the use of digital technology. For example, crimes such as forged passports, driver's licenses, computer-generated documents, and digital images fraudulently inserted in official documents are all considered digital crimes. These are usually investigated by digital forensic experts that specialize in computer forensics, including those familiar with digital manipulation of data and questioned documents. (For more about questioned document analysis, see the chapter "In the Crime Lab: Questioned Documents and Cryptanalysis.")

What is digital evidence?

Digital evidence is the coded (or software) information that is stored or transmitted in binary computer code (binary units of ones [1] and zeros [0]) and that is in unaltered condition so it can be used as evidence in a court. The binary codes can be created to form various types of information, including photographs, words, and spreadsheets, all of which can be used as evidence. Such evidence is often found in a number of technological devices, including cell phones, computer hard drives, personal digital assistants (PADs), compact discs (CDs), flash drives, SD cards in a digital camera, and computer tablets. Digital evidence in a crime is commonly associated with e-crimes (electronic crimes), such as credit card fraud or child pornography, but it has gone even further than e-crimes and includes digital evidence gathered from all types of crimes. For example, an examination of a person's cell phone that also has a GPS locator can often be used as evidence, especially to see if a person was or was not at the scene of a crime.

Why are Internet crimes so prevalent?

After the Internet (World Wide Web) was introduced to the public in the 1990s (it used to be for academics and used mostly for information exchange), individuals could access information from all over the world. With the further development of the technology, it became easier (and with smaller devices) to contact others faster, from greater distances away, and with more information, such as words, photographs, and instant messages, WWW browsing, and videos, but along with the positive aspects of the Internet—and its "offshoots" that use the WWW, such as cell phones and tablets—came the use of the technology to traffic illegal information, images, and contacts in the criminal world. In addition, digital crimes also include hacking into financial, communication, and government computer networks in order to disrupt and/or steal (mostly money or stocks) and sabotage various systems.

Where did the first computer crime law originate in the United States?

The first computer crime law originated in the state of Florida called the Florida Computer Crimes Act. It was enacted in 1978, with the impetus being the highly publicized Flagler Dog Track incident in Miami. In this scam, several employees, including some who knew how to work computers, created and printed out fraudulent winning tickets— essentially taking not from the track but from the people who were making the bets. The resulting law made unauthorized access to a computer a crime, even if no malicious intent was in the action. It further caused enough of a stir to have Congress enact a stronger federal law in 1986, called the Computer Fraud and Abuse Act (CFAA), making it a crime to access a computer without authorization or in excess of authorization. The CFAA was an amendment to the existing computer fraud law that was a part of the Comprehensive Crime Control Act of 1984. For the entire written law in detail, see the Cornell University Law School site at https://www.law.cornell.edu/uscode/text/18/1030.

What types of data are often retrieved from a crime scene cell phone?

Several types of data can be retrieved from a crime scene cell phone and used as possible evidence. For example, many cell phones have "location" capabilities, allowing forensic computer experts to extract information about the owner's whereabouts that can often be used as evidence in many cases. (Location data can also be obtained from newer cars that have satellite navigation systems or satellite radio.) Messages (text and instant) can also be extracted from a cell phone, as can phone numbers called, answered, and in a suspect's contact list. If a suspect uses an online backup system for their cell phone— called "the cloud" by most companies that offer the service—forensic investigators can often access sent and received text messages and images (the cloud can hold an average of one thousand to fifteen hundred of the last text messages from a person's phone).

How are cell phone devices treated at a crime scene?

Although they often hold a great deal of evidence at a crime scene, not all digital cell phone devices can be retrieved for evidence. One reason is familiar to many people who own a cell phone—the devices can be damaged and data lost if dropped on a hard surface, in a river, lake, ocean, or bathtub, or even if left out in a thunderstorm. When investigators and crime scene technicians discover a cell phone at a crime scene that has not been compromised (or thought not to be damaged), they usually immediately turn off the device and remove the batteries. For most devices, this preserves the cell tower location information and call logs, does not allow anyone else to use the phone (and possibly destroy or alter evidence from the phone), and stops anyone from possibly making alterations in the phone from another computer device. If it cannot be turned off, the crime scene personnel can isolate the phone from the cell

Retrieving information from cell phones found at crime scenes can be problematic. Encrypted data, laws that vary from jurisdiction to jurisdiction, and restrictions on such things as wiretapping complicate matters.

tower by enclosing it in a bag made of blocking material (some say even to set it to airplane mode) and put it in an antistatic bag, box, or envelope—but not plastic, as it can cause damage from static buildup or humidity. (For more about collecting evidence at a crime scene, see the chapter "At the Crime Scene: Looking for Physical Evidence.")

What are some concerns regarding the use of cell phones as evidence?

Because digital devices are relatively new to forensic analysis, questions have come up about what types of information gathered from a cell phone can truly be used as evidence. Although the rules change constantly—and often depend on the jurisdiction of the crime—evidence gained from such digital devices has some limitations. For example, contrary to most television programs, it is often very difficult (and a long process) to decipher encryption and proprietary systems before data from certain devices can even be accessed. Also, obtaining certain data has legal ramifications. For example, data ownership is often questioned, such as a 2012 ruling in Colorado where a question came up regarding passwords: the holder of a password had to divulge the device's password but did not have to admit knowledge or ownership of the data protected by the password. Questions even arise about intercepting a call on a device: if a cell phone is confiscated in a crime, wiretapping laws state that any calls or messages received by that phone cannot be used by the holder of the phone—or, in this case, law enforcement—if they are not the intended recipient.

What are some qualifications to become a digital analyst?

As of this writing, only a few standard qualifications and certifications exist for a person to become a digital evidence expert or certified digital media examiner (although out of necessity, this is rapidly changing). In many cases, the person examining digital evi-

> ## What is a recent connection between digital evidence and the Xbox?
>
> Although most people use an Xbox (XFT) for gaming, the device often has certain forensic connections. For example, some criminals use the device to hide illicit data. Thus, in recent years, digital forensic specialists have developed certain "toolbox" computer technologies in order to allow investigators to visually access hidden illicit files on the Xbox hard drive.

dence may have certain digital media specialties, such as understanding cell phones, while others may have knowledge about cell phone technology but not know much about social media.

Do any groups deal with the exchange of forensic digital evidence?

Yes, several working groups cooperate by exchanging information and helping educate those who deal with digital evidence in forensic science. For example, founded in 1998, the Scientific Working Group on Digital Evidence (SWGDE) task is—according to its website—to bring together "organizations actively engaged in the field of digital and multimedia evidence to foster communication and cooperation as well as to ensure quality and consistency within the forensic community."

BIOMETRICS AND FORENSIC INVESTIGATIONS

What is the study of biometrics?

The measurement and resulting statistical analysis of an individual's physical characteristics and behavioral traits is called the study of biometrics. (Biometrics is from Greek *bio*, or "life," and *metric*, meaning "to measure.") Although it is not a foolproof system, it is based on the idea that everyone is unique and that a person can often be identified by those certain intrinsic traits. It can include several biometric identification methods, including fingerprinting, handwriting, signature recognition, and even characteristics such as the eye's iris or a person's voice. It is most commonly used in conjunction with identification for secure access or to identify people who may be under surveillance. For example, it can be used to help identify certain criminals based on their traits. Certain traits, such as retinal scans, are often used for security reasons, helping to stop unauthorized access to certain facilities, secure rooms, or information systems and computing devices. (For more about fingerprinting, see the chapter "In the Crime Lab: Trace Evidence"; for more about handwriting or signature analysis, see the chapter "In the Crime Lab: Questioned Documents and Cryptanalysis.")

What are some examples of physiological characteristics used in biometrics?

Physiological characteristics in biometrics—especially to determine authenticity—include many personal physical and behavioral traits. Physical traits include fingerprints (and other prints, such as palm and footprints), a person's DNA, certain features of the face (including eye and ear traits), and, in some cases, even odor. Behavioral traits include such actions as a person's gait or method of walking, gestures they use over and over, their voice, and even such less common characteristics as the "rhythm" of their finger strokes as they type.

What is one of the oldest known uses of biometrics?

It is thought that fingerprinting is one of the oldest known uses of biometrics, although not in the capacity of forensics. In ancient China (references mention during both the Qin and Han dynasties from 221 B.C.E. to 220 C.E.), a person would put their thumbprint on a clay seal for identification. (For more about fingerprints, see the chapter "In the Crime Lab: Patent, Latent, and Plastic Prints.")

What are some ways in which biometrics is used to identify a person?

Certain personal characteristics (biometrics) are used in numerous ways to help with the identity of a person, especially for such things as access to secure areas or even computing devices. The following are only a few such characteristics:

- *Retinal scans*—The eye's retina is located inside a person's eye. These scans produce an image of the blood vessels located in the light-sensitive surface lining of the inner eye, or the retina.

- *Iris-recognition scan*—The iris is the ring-shaped region around a person's pupil. It is the area that contains what is commonly referred to as a person's "eye color. Each iris is unique, with several features, marks, and colors that can be used for recognition.

- *Finger scanning*—Almost everyone is aware of fingerprinting, and this is the digital version of that process. In this case, the details of a fingerprint pattern in a human finger are scanned digitally, making what is hoped to be an accurate image of a person's unique print. (For more about fingerprinting, see the chapter "In the Crime Lab: Patent, Latent, and Plastic Prints.")

- *Finger-vein identification*—Each person also has veins, capillaries, and arteries (parts of the human vascular

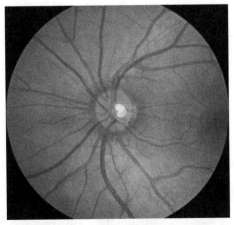

Retinal scans take advantage of the fact that the pattern of blood vessels inside each person's eyes is unique to them.

system) throughout their body that carry unique characteristics. Finger-vein identification takes the unique vascular configuration in a person's finger and scans it for identification purposes. (Veins in the palm are often used, but not as often.)

What was voiceprint identification?

The term voiceprint identification is not commonly used by forensic speech experts. When first developed in World War II, it meant comparing the listening and instrumental part of a known voice with an unknown voice as a means to identify an individual. Today, forensic experts talk about speaker recognition and verification. (For more about voice and forensics, see sidebar.)

What is speaker recognition versus speaker verification?

In general, speaker recognition automatically recognizes the person speaking on the basis of certain unique information included in speech signals. It uses speech recognition technology to allow a person's voice to control access to certain restricted services and/or facilities, for example, access to phones, banking services, databases, or even

When was "voiceprint identification" developed?

The first "voiceprint identification" was developed at Bell Laboratories in New York in the early 1940s. It was first developed to help with the war effort—in particular to be used by the American military during World War II. The Bell researchers invented what was called an electromechanical acoustic spectrograph in 1941, which is said to have led to a sound spectrograph, or a device that would display speech visually, but the research slowed dramatically after the war. It was picked up again in the late 1950s when the New York City Police Department was receiving numerous telephone bomb threats to the airlines. The department asked Bell Laboratories to help, and the task of identifying the voices went to physicist Lawrence Kersta (1907–1994). By 1962, he made improvements to the sound spectrograph, producing what he called a "voiceprint," and by 1966, the Michigan State Police began to apply the voice-identification method as an investigative aid to solve certain criminal cases and also developed a voice identification unit.

By the 1970s, the word "voiceprint" was discarded (it was too close to the word "fingerprint," which has a different scientific validation in forensics) and the methods were improved. The spectrographic technique gained even more notoriety during the examination of President Richard M. Nixon's White House tapes (an analysis that led to the Watergate conspiracy and Nixon's eventual resignation). Today, modern voice and speech forensic experts rely on more sophisticated methods and instruments to analyze voices potentially involved in criminal acts or events.

voice mail. Speaker recognition, in turn, can further be divided into speaker identification (determines a certain speaker from a set of known speakers) and speaker verification (or the acceptance or rejection of the identity of a speaker).

How can a voice be identified?

Determining a person's identity by their voice is not always a foolproof method in biometrics, but it sometimes will help with the identity. For example, a person's voice is based on the physical characteristic shape of their mouth and throat and even if they have certain mouthpieces, such as dentures. Using voice recognition (also called speaker recognition), analysts may

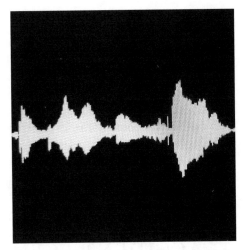

People have unique voice patterns. Even a master voice impersonator cannot duplicate these patterns, though they might sound the same to the human ear.

be able to identify or confirm an individual based on their voice. This is based on a physiological component of their speech, such as the physical shape of the person's voice tract, and the behavioral component, such as the physical movement of their jaws, tongue, and larynx, which can move in various ways based on the person's behavior.

What is the difference between speaker recognition and speech recognition?

Speaker recognition and speech recognition are definitely different. In particular, speaker recognition is the means of recognizing who is speaking. Speech recognition is the means of recognizing what is being said by that person.

What are forensic phonetics and acoustics?

According to the International Association for Forensic Phonetics and Acoustics (IAFPA), forensic scientists and researchers in both phonetics and acoustics analyze voices, speech, and audio recordings. They are involved in such activities as speaker identification and elimination, speaker profiling, voice lineups, transcription, authentication, signal enhancement, and sound propagation at crime scenes. For example, speaker identification uses certain analyses to determine that a certain person's voice is truly their voice, such as verifying a person on a tape made during a telephone conversation that led to a crime. It also includes audio enhancement and transcript verification by analyzing an audiotape (for example, a video with sound when a criminal's face is not easily seen on the tape) or comparing the speaking voice of the person in question with audio material (such as a cell phone recording). A forensic expert in audio may also analyze sounds that are not made by a person, such as possibly determining the type of weapon heard discharging during a 911 call or even interpreting the sound of a certain dog barking in the background of a 911 or other message associated with a crime.

What is forensic linguistics?

Forensic linguistics is connected to forensic phonetics and acoustics. According to the International Association of Forensic Linguists (IAFL), forensic linguists' work involves them in the law, or the use of linguistic evidence in court (authorship attribution, disputed confessions, etc.). For example, forensic linguistics is used to help determine certain aspects of a person's speech, voice, and even writings, including those associated with criminal actions. Some forensic linguists also determine authorship attribution and plagiarism in certain cases, analyze certain writings such as statements, confessions, suicide notes for language used, and language as evidence in civil cases (for instance, trademark, contract disputes, defamation, product liability, deceptive trade practices, and copyright infringement).

ACCIDENT SCENE INVESTIGATIONS

What is an accident scene?

As the terms imply, an accident scene is any place in which an accident has occurred, especially in terms of transportation, such as cars, trains, and planes. For example, an accident can occur when a vehicle hits another vehicle, a person, or an object (tree, guardrail, etc.) that causes injury or death to a person or damage to an object or another vehicle. It may also mean a personal accident that causes injury or even death, such as a fall down a flight of stairs.

What types of accidents need investigation?

According to many references, numerous types of accidents commonly need investigation. For instance, some references state that accidents come in thirty-six types, all of which can be grouped into seven categories: falls (persons and objects); vehicles (all transportation); hazardous atmosphere (presence of toxic substances or lack of oxygen); aggression and extreme muscular exertion (for example, fights); machines and handheld tools; contact with certain objects; and hazardous substances (along with fire, explosions, etc.).

How are accidents investigated?

In order to determine the root cause of accidents, injuries, property damages, and so on, investigations need to be made so the incident can possibly be avoided in the future. The process of an accident investigation, of course, depends on the event and the people (or objects) involved. In general, several questions should be addressed after an accident. They include the following:

- Determine what happened.
- Determine why the accident (or incident) occurred.
- Describe the accident (or incident) and why the need to investigate.
- Investigate the who, what, when, where, why, and how of the accident.

Who is usually the first to investigate an accident scene?

Depending on the accident scene, numerous people can investigate the incident. For example, in the case of a motor vehicle accident that causes injury or death, the police are usually the first to investigate the accident to determine whether any criminal action was involved. In such a case, they may look for evidence of speeding, mechanical violation (such as driving with a burned-out headlight), alcohol or drug use, and so on. For instance, if someone falls asleep while driving a commercial truck and law enforcement discovers that the person exceeded their hours of service on the road, he or she will likely be criminally charged. If the accident has any fatalities, depending on the jurisdiction, the truck driver will likely be charged with homicide.

What is an independent accident investigator?

In many cases, insurance companies and/or attorneys (mainly of the people involved in the accident) will hire an independent accident investigator. These investigators analyze the information from the accident (and possible witnesses, etc.) to determine the liability or financial responsibility of the person or persons involved. They come from various backgrounds but more commonly are off-duty or retired police officers, vehicle technicians, and engineers.

What are some aspects of investigating a motor vehicle accident site?

Investigating a motor vehicle accident site has several aspects to it. For instance, at the accident site, certain measurements (using instruments similar to those used in surveying) must be taken to determine such factors as the angle of impact (of another vehicle or object), the exact point (or points) of impact, marks left in the road at the site (such as skid or gouge marks), and the final position that the vehicle or vehicles came to rest at after the accident. This allows people who reconstruct the accident to produce accurate, scale diagrams of the incident, which, if necessary, can be used in a court as evidence. (For more about reconstruction of accidents, see below.) Another aspect to such an in-

---

What are several ways in which car accidents differ from truck accidents?

A car accident differs from a truck accident in several ways (mainly because of the physics behind a big versus little vehicle), of which accident inspectors and reconstruction analysts must be aware. For example, if an average-sized truck has good brakes, it can take 25 to 65 percent longer to stop than a car. The larger percentage would be for a fully loaded truck, whereas the lower percentage would be for an unloaded truck. Plus, the hard rubber truck tires cause an increase in stopping distances for a truck because a car's softer-compound tires would allow more road grip to stop faster.

vestigation is inspecting the vehicle or vehicles involved. This is done by measuring damage to the mechanical components of the vehicle, including the condition of the post-accident brakes, steering, lights, tires, and so on. In this way, the inspectors can determine whether any of the components were the actual cause of the accident or contributed to the accident.

A thorough investigation of all aspects of a car accident help police and legal teams reconstruct the incident in detail.

What is accident reconstruction?

The information gathered by the accident investigation teams is often used for accident reconstruction, or the process that uses physics to determine the details of what occurred to cause the accident. For example, in the case of a motor vehicle, such parameters as the speed of the vehicle or vehicles before and after the accident are important, along with the distance the vehicle traveled because of the accident and/or the vehicle's direction of travel. They also take into consideration such factors as the length of the skid, whether the car was hit on the side, head-on, or back-ended, whether it rolled over or slid off the road, and even the weights of the vehicle or vehicles involved. This information is gathered to reconstruct what occurred before, during, and after the accident.

What types of accidents do reconstruction experts analyze?

Reconstruction experts deal with many types of accidents, especially those involving criminal activities. For instance, they reconstruct such events as airplane, railroad, subway, vehicular, and maritime accidents, along with industrial and commercial accidents—events with or without criminal intent. They can also help with crime or personal accident scene reconstruction that may eventually be used as evidence in court.

What is forensic animation?

Forensic animation—often called full-motion computer graphics—is often used to re-create an accident or crime scene activity, such as an automobile accident, explosion, or assault of a victim, or to explain the breakdown of a mechanical instrument that may have caused an injury. The input includes the conditions, witness accounts, and experts in various fields that are needed to complete the animation. For example, in a car accident, evidence from witnesses and experts from various disciplines can be incorporated into the input data, such as meteorologists (who would explain the weather conditions at the time), a car mechanic (especially if the car is thought to have caused the accident), and/or a witness (their interpretation of how the accident occurred). Those certain measurements and aspects of an accident or crime scene are entered into a computer, which then generates an animation of what most likely happened at that event.

What are the various types of forensic animation?

In general, animations are split into two different types. The first type is called substantive animation and uses simulation software that (mostly mathematically) indicates the movement of objects based on data inputs. For example, in an automobile accident, data from the surrounding scene (terrain, road conditions, impact speed, etc.) are entered into the simulation software, resulting in an animation of the movement of objects. This data is also used in many three-dimensional animation programs, which can show a more detailed and realistic view of the event. The second type of animation, and the most common, is called demonstrative animation. In this case, the computer program is used to re-create accidents or crime scene activity, but it is based on evidence collected at the scene. In particular, it is not based on mathematical equations and physical input but on the data supplied to and interpreted by the animator, often confirmed by an expert if necessary.

Why are forensic animations sometimes questioned, especially in a court situation?

Similar to any other computer result, forensic animations are not perfect. This is because they can sometimes be based on interpretations of what a person saw or an expert witness's opinion. Thus, some forensic animations may be questioned in a criminal or lawsuit situation, as the computer input data is only as "good" as the interpretation—and some people may question those interpretations.

What is mechanical failure analysis?

Vehicle accidents happen for several reasons, including mechanical failure. In this case, forensic analysts who are experts in failure analysis are often asked to examine the parts and equipment that may have been faulty in a vehicle or other machine. For example, the failure analysis of a bolt in the engine could indicate that it caused the engine to seize, causing the car to stop—and thus cause an accident. Mechanical failure analysis is also used in other accident cases. For example, it is used to determine how airplane crashes occurred, such as tears in the wings, or even terrorist bombings.

GOVERNMENT INVESTIGATIONS OF TRANSPORTATION AND SAFETY ISSUES

What U.S. government agencies are often involved in transportation accident investigations?

Several U.S. government agencies are often involved in certain accident investigations. For example, for transportation accidents caused by criminal activity, the Federal Bureau of Investigation (FBI) is often called in to help with or carry out an investigation. The National Transportation Safety Board is another one, which conducts independent investigations of all civilian aviation accidents in the United States and also major accidents in other means of transportation, such as train derailments. It is not part of other government transportation groups, such as the Department of Transportation, and has no regulatory or enforcement powers, but it is one of the first groups at a scene and puts together the technical experts to determine what caused the accident.

What is the Federal Aviation Administration?

The Federal Aviation Administration (FAA) is an agency of the U.S. Department of Transportation that ensures the safety of civil aviation. In particular, it is responsible for the regulation and oversight of civil aviation within the United States. It is also

The FBI is sometimes called upon to investigate transportation accidents that are suspected of being linked to criminal activities.

in charge of the operation and development of the National Airspace System. Under the FAA is the Office of Accident Investigation and Prevention that provides investigations of aircraft accidents and all activities related to the National Transportation Safety Board (NTSB; see above).

What is the U.S. Chemical Safety Board?

The U.S. Chemical Safety Board (CSB) is an independent government (federal) agency that investigates industrial chemical accidents, including those caused by human or mechanical error. It does not issue fines or citations but makes recommendations to industry and labor groups and to certain agencies, such as the Occupational Safety and Health Administration (OSHA) and the Environmental Protection Agency (EPA).

FORENSICS AND PERSONAL INJURY INVESTIGATIONS

What is a personal injury investigation?

A personal injury investigation is just as the phrase indicates: an investigation into an accident/incident in which a person was physically injured, such as falling on the slippery floor of a store or being injured in an auto accident that was the fault of another party. It can also include injury due to product failure or even a medical device failure. (Although not common, some references also indicate that personal injury can not only be physical but also, for instance, financial, such as the stealing of a person's credit card number.)

> ## What is an "incident" versus "accident" in the workplace?
>
> According to the Occupational Safety and Health Administration (OSHA), the term "accident" was formerly used to define an unplanned and unwanted event, but this definition, which often implied that the event was random and could not be prevented, was changed. Now for workplace accidents, OSHA suggests the term "incident" investigation, as it believes that nearly all workplace fatalities, injuries, and illnesses could have been prevented.

How is the field of digital forensics often used in personal injury investigations?

Digital forensics can often be used in personal injury investigations—and it is a recent way of gathering evidence. In particular, digital evidence is almost everywhere, including texts, pictures, videos, or other documentation about an accident. Most cell phones can track where a person travels, and if a person has the correct "app," companies can market certain products to a person when they are in a specific store. Along with other evidence, such as witnesses or physical evidence, digital tracking and image information (often called leaving a digital trace) is often used and interpreted by digital forensic experts as evidence in personal injury investigations.

How can the field of forensic odontology be of use to a personal investigation?

Odontology, or the study of forensic dentistry, is often used for various personal investigative circumstances. For example, it can include the evaluation of a person's dental or oral injuries from an assault in order to resolve a civil dispute. Or, data from a forensic dentistry analysis can be used as evidence in a personal injury, malpractice, or negligence case. (For more about odontology, see the chapter "In the Crime Lab: Trace Evidence.")

What are design versus manufacturing defects in terms of personal injury?

In terms of personal injury (and possible litigation about the injury), a design defect is when an inherent flaw or error is in the original design that makes it dangerous to the person using the product. A manufacturing defect is when a flaw or error is in the product that is caused when the product is manufactured.

FORENSICS AND ARSON INVESTIGATIONS

What is arson?

Arson is the deliberate setting of a fire (which can also be started by an explosion). It is started by a person in order to, for instance, cause harm to another person, cover up a crime, or damage a structure. Several references define it as "Any willful or malicious burning or attempt to burn, with or without intent to defraud, a dwelling, house, public building, motor vehicle or aircraft, person or property of another." (For more about the motives behind arson, see the chapter "The Criminal Mind.") Also by definition, a fire is called an arson fire when all other accidental causes have been ruled out. If arson is suspected, a fire investigation (often called a cause and origin investigation) is conducted. This occurs after firefighters extinguish the fire, with the fire investigators gathering evidence to determine the origin and cause of the fire or explosion. (For more about explosion investigations, see the chapter "In the Crime Lab: Examining Explosives.")

Arsonists are criminals who deliberately start fires to hurt people or cover up crimes.

What are the three conditions that create a fire?

Three conditions help to create a fire (often called the fire triangle). They include oxygen, a fuel source, and heat. The oxygen is from the surrounding air, with the fire following the highest concentration of oxygen to its source. A fuel source is any flammable substance that can cause and spread the fire, such as gasoline. The heat source matches the ignition temperature of the fuel and can range from a match lighting a paper to chemicals that ignite at very low temperatures.

What are some ways firefighters help investigators determine arson?

Firefighters can help investigators determine arson in several ways. Foremost, the investigators rely on the observations of the first firefighters who respond to and fight the fire at the scene (and they also often interview eyewitnesses at the scene, especially those who may have reported the fire). These early observations are important to an investigator, as fire often destroys evidence of arson, along with water and certain chemicals used to extinguish the flames. Arson evidence firefighters may mention includes the discovery of certain accelerants (or even an empty gas can), an open door (or even if a door looked forced open), what the structure contained (if it was a house, were the furniture and household items "normal" for a house), or even certain smells from a specific accelerant. Often, no true signs of arson may be present, but the firefighters may notice that the fire or fires are not responding normally. They may also note the colors of the fire and smoke at the scene, as different substances produce various colors. For example, gasoline produces a yellow or white flame with black smoke, while wood produces a red or yellow flame and brown or gray smoke. Thus, a mostly wooden house that produces black smoke when burning may indicate the presence of gasoline—which would be suspicious, since people do not normally keep gasoline in their home.

What happened to arsonists in nineteenth-century Britain?

In the early nineteenth century, Britain did not tolerate arsonists, especially if someone set fire to any domestic or commercial area or "any stack of corn, grain, pulse, straw, hay, or wood." In fact, it was, under British law, punishable by death. The stack burning was removed from the capital crimes list by 1837, but arson under the other conditions was (and still is) a serious offense—and was usually punishable with a life sentence. By the late 1800s, arson was not as much an issue about destroying property but became a crime against people—especially in terms of arson to cause murder.

How do investigators look for possible arson?

Investigators look for possible arson in several ways. After the fire is extinguished and the firefighters are interviewed, the investigator looks for some telltale signs of arson at the fire scene. For example, if it is known that the structure's windows were open or if holes are punched in a wall or ceiling, it may indicate that the arsonist was trying to increase the oxygen inside to help spread the fire. In addition, physical evidence is gathered and taken back to the crime lab, where it is analyzed by several instruments, including gas chromatography to check for possible accelerants (and what type of accelerant, if applicable). Details of the surrounding conditions at the fire scene are also documented, which are often looked at using digital analysis to understand where the fire started, how it grew—and possibly whether it indicates arson.

What is the Fire Research Laboratory Center?

The Bureau of Alcohol, Tobacco, Firearms, and Explosives' (ATF) Fire Research Laboratory (FRL) is the world's largest research lab dedicated to forensic fire scene investigations. It is located in Beltsville, Maryland, and uses special instruments to understand fire scene phenomena, conducts fire science and engineering tests on actual structures built in the lab, and investigates the science of fire, in particular, fire's dynamics and growth under various conditions. The researchers also investigate fire scene reconstruction, including the impacts of accelerants on the growth of a fire, how certain materials ignite, and how electrical fires occur.

What is an ATF Certified Fire Investigator?

The Bureau of Alcohol, Tobacco, Firearms, and Explosives (ATF) certified fire investigators (CFIs) investigate violent crimes and arson-for-profit cases, conduct fire scene examinations, make origin and cause determinations, and act as a resource for local and state fire investigations in possible arson cases. They are also the only investigators trained by a federal law-enforcement agency to qualify as expert witnesses in fire origin and cause determinations. According to the ATF, CFIs' duties include fire origin and cause determination, fire dynamics, fire modeling, building construction, electricity and fire causa-

251

tion, health and safety, scene reconstruction, and evidence collection. For example, they often use computer programs to describe the chemical and physical behavior of a fire—depending on the structure and the growth of the flames within that structure—as evidence. To become an ATF CFI, people who are considered ATF special agents go through a two-year training program that includes such forensic-oriented training as scene reconstruction and evidence collection. In addition, they must help investigate at least one hundred fire scenes under the guidance of an experienced ATF CFI.

What is the International Association of Arson Investigators, Inc.?

Started in 1949, the International Association of Arson Investigators' (IAAI) mission is to provide support to fire, arson, and explosion investigation professionals through "education, training, professional development, certification, networking, advocacy, and the provision of resources." The majority of the around nine thousand international members (to date) work with fire, arson, and explosion investigations, especially in terms of criminal activity and/or insurance and other fire loss claims and litigation.

What is the NCETR?

According to the Bureau of Alcohol, Tobacco, Firearms, and Explosives (ATF), the National Center for Explosives Training and Research (NCETR) is a consolidation of the ATF explosives, fire, canine, and response operations. The NCETR has several divisions that deal with fire, explosives, and response, including the Explosives Enforcement and Training Division, the Explosives Research and Development Division, and the Fire Investigation and Arson Enforcement Division (all at Redstone Arsenal, Alabama), along with the National Canine Division (Front Royal, Virginia) and the National Explosives Task Force (Washington, D.C.).

What is the National Fire Research Laboratory?

The National Fire Research Laboratory (NFRL) is located on the National Institute of Standards and Technology's (NIST) Gaithersburg, Maryland, campus. It is a unique experimental facility dedicated to understanding fire behavior and structural response to fire. Scientists and engineers from industry, academia, and government agencies collaborate with NIST researchers to not only understand the dynamics of fires but also to help localities improve fire and building codes for all structures.

FOOD FORENSIC INVESTIGATIONS

What is food forensics?

Food forensic investigations are conducted in order to determine the what, how, and when of food safety and quality issues. It is done for several reasons, including consumer safety, industry liability (and reputation), and especially in terms of food safety perception of a product. Food forensics does not include just one field in forensic science but many, including microbiology, analytical chemistry, microscopy, entomology, knowledge of physical items, such as hair, glass, etc., and many other fields of expertise. Many of these fields are necessary to uncover and understand how certain types of nonfood materials (often allegedly) end up in food products.

What do forensic food experts look for in terms of food contaminants?

Forensic food experts examine food in several ways, especially in terms of contaminants. For instance, experts want to identify where and when the contamination has occurred, identify the contaminant, and possibly determine its source. Not only do they examine the biological aspect, such as microbes (for example, fungi and bacteria), plant materials, insects, human and animal hairs, and blood, but also nonbiological contaminants, such as glass, plastics, metals (regular and heavy), synthetic fibers, minerals (toxic and nontoxic), pharmaceuticals (drugs and medications), dirt and deposits, and certain unknown (and sometimes unidentifiable) items are examined. In addition, forensic analysis can help protect certain food companies when accidents allow foreign matter to enter a food product; it can also provide scientific analysis that helps fight fraudulent claims against a company's food product.

What are two U.S. government agencies that deal with food safety?

Several U.S. government agencies deal with food safety. One of the main agencies is the Food and Drug Administration (FDA; also seen as USFDA), a federal agency of the U.S. De-

Food forensics deals with the examination of foods for signs of contamination—both organic and inorganic. Inspectors work to determine the source of contaminants, or, sometimes, the source of the foods themselves.

partment of Health and Human Services. This agency is responsible for protecting and promoting public health, mainly through the control and supervision of food safety, but according to the FDA, it is also a watchdog for the public concerning "tobacco products, dietary supplements, prescription and over-the-counter pharmaceutical drugs, vaccines, biopharmaceuticals, blood transfusions, medical devices, electromagnetic radiation-emitting devices (ERED), cosmetics, animal foods and feed, and veterinary products." Under the FDA is the Office of Criminal Investigations (OCI). The OCI was established to provide the FDA with an office to conduct and coordinate criminal investigations, especially those that entail possible violations of the law that regulate food and drug products. The OCI is also a liaison and often helps with investigative efforts with various federal, state, local, and international law-enforcement agencies. OCI special agents (to date, about 180) use federal law-enforcement methods and techniques (including forensic) in order to investigate suspected criminal activities and violations of the Federal Food, Drug, and Cosmetic Act, the Federal Anti-Tampering Act, and other related federal statutes.

How are suspicious foods analyzed by the various forensic experts?

Forensic experts analyze suspicious foods in many ways. For example, forensic DNA experts often determine food fraud and wrong representations of food (or when the description of a certain food or food composition is not true). They can also test food for possible genetic modification, especially if the modification has not been claimed. Chemical and physical forensic experts can examine foreign matter contamination with certain specialized instruments, such as microscopy, x-ray diffraction, and chemical spectroscopy. Even analyzing types of insects (and fragments) allegedly found in foods can be performed by forensic entomologists.

FORENSICS AND ATHLETIC INVESTIGATIONS

Why are drug tests for athletes needed?

Athletic investigations are usually conducted if a suspicion arises of certain drugs being taken to enhance an athlete's performance. In the case of such events as the Olympics, drug testing is necessary in order to make the competition "even"—or that everyone has the chance to compete without any drugs to enhance their performance. Such drug investigations have been performed in national and international (and some local) athletic activities, such as professional baseball, bicycle races, and football.

What is blood doping?

Blood doping refers to the use of artificial means to increase the number of red blood cells. For example, erythropoietin, a hormone produced by both the kidney and liver, increases the maturity rate of certain structures (called erythrocytes) in the body's bone marrow. A genetically engineered form of erythropoietin (EPO) can be injected into athletes before an event with a resulting increase of red blood cell count of 45 to 65 percent. With more red blood cells, more oxygen is available for heavily exercising muscles—an artificial enhancement. (Blood doping is often dangerous, too, as in some cases, if an athlete taking the EPO becomes dehydrated, the blood can become too thick, causing clotting, stroke, or serious heart problems.)

What is the World Anti-Doping Agency?

The World Anti-Doping Agency (WADA) was established in 1999 in Canada and acts as an international independent agency that performs scientific research, education, and development of antidoping capacities. It is supported and funded equally

Some athletes use doping to improve performance. By adding red blood cells through doping, the body has more oxygen available for the muscles.

by the sports movement and several governments of the world. WADA also monitors the WADA Code, the document that suggests antidoping policies in all sports for all countries. (According to the code, doping is defined as "possession, administration or attempted administration of prohibited substances or methods, trafficking or attempted trafficking in any prohibited substance or methods.") WADA also presents an annual list of the substances and methods that are prohibited to athletes to use in and out of competitions.

Can analyses similar to those used in forensics be used to uncover doping in athletics?

Yes, analyses similar to those used in forensic science have been used to uncover doping in some athletic events. For instance, DNA analysis similar to that used at a crime scene has been used to uncover doping. For example, in 2016, the World Anti-Doping Agency released information about alleged Russian doping in certain athletic events. For instance, a DNA analysis of urine supplied by two female Russian ice hockey players revealed male DNA.

Digital forensics has also helped to uncover doping activities in certain professional athletics. Similar to an investigation of terrorist or criminal activities, certain athletes often leave a digital trace. This includes phone calls, text messages, photos, and other incriminating items that reveal who the person talked to, when they talked, and what was said or written. These data are analyzed by digital experts—especially digital traces of athletes who may use drugs to enhance their performance in professional and nonprofessional games.

Why is urine used to test for drug use?

Urine drug testing is commonly used for opioids and illicit drugs. The liver is where drug detoxification occurs, but the byproducts of this process are excreted by the kidneys. The two types of tests are a screening test and a confirmatory test. Depending on the athletic event, a urine drug screening for athletes can include marijuana, cocaine, opiates, and amphetamines, along with tests for drugs that can enhance athletic performance.

What are anabolic steroids?

Properly called anabolic-androgenic steroids, anabolic steroids are hormones that work to increase certain reactions in the body, particularly in the muscles. They are synthetic versions of the primary male sex hormone called testosterone. Overall, they promote the growth of skeletal muscle (anabolic effects) and the development of male sexual characteristics (androgenic effects).

How are anabolic steroids abused?

Anabolic steroids are often abused by teenagers, adults, and athletes, both professional and amateur, for bodybuilding and to enhance athletic performance. Although they have clinical applications for certain medical conditions, the doses prescribed legally to treat these medical conditions are ten to one hundred times lower than the doses that are abused for performance enhancement.

BIOFORENSICS AND BIOTERRORISM

What is forensic microbiology?

Forensic microbiology is the study of microorganisms; a subset of forensic microbiology is called microbial forensics. Forensic microbiology and microbial forensics are often used to determine how an outbreak occurred of a certain microorganism, to identify a criminal, or to trace the origin of a certain strain of biological weapon or contagion that may present a danger to public health. In fact, microbial forensics is needed in today's world more than ever, as it involves the characterization of microbial agents used as weapons—and hopefully to identify and eventually convict those responsible. For example, in terms of bioterrorism and biocrimes, it may become necessary to quickly determine the agents of a certain infection or other biological contagion. In such cases, analysis called microbial genetic analysis is the most valuable technique to determine the microbial genome—and hopefully identify the organisms responsible for the infection (for example, to identify bacteria [such as *Bacillus anthracis*, or anthrax] or toxins [such as *Clostridium botulinum*, or botulism]).

What is bioterrorism?

According to the Centers for Disease Control and Prevention (CDC), bioterrorism is "the deliberate release of viruses, bacteria, or other germs (agents) used to cause illness or death in people, animals, or plants." Most of these agents are found naturally, but in bioterrorism, they are enhanced or modified to cause harm. Terrorists may spread such agents through the air, water, or food, or even person to person (such as with small-pox). Most of the viruses or other harmful bioagents may be extremely difficult to detect or can take hours or days to cause illness—thus making them difficult to trace.

What are some examples of bioterrorism agents?

Several types of biological agents can cause disease—and can be used as bioterrorism agents. The following lists some of those agents that are of concern to most countries and government agencies (and the public, of course):

Bioterrorism Agents

Biologic agent	Disease caused by the agent
Bacillus anthracis	Anthrax
Clostridium botulinum toxin	Botulism
Yersinia pestis	Plague
Variola major	Smallpox
Francisella tularensis	Tularemia
Filoviruses (for example, Ebola, Marburg) and arenaviruses (for example, Lassa, Machupo)	Viral hemorrhagic fevers
Brucella species	Brucellosis
Epsilon toxin of *Clostridium perfringens*	Food poisoning
Salmonella species, *Escherichia coli* O157:H7, Shigella	Food poisoning
Burkholderia mallei	Glanders
Burkholderia pseudomallei	Melioidosis
Chlamydia psittaci	Psittacosis
Coxiella burnetii	Q fever
Ricinus communis (castor beans)	Ricin poisoning
Staphylococcal enterotoxin B	Food poisoning
Rickettsia prowazekii	Epidemic typhus
Vibrio cholerae	Cholera
Cryptosporidium parvum	Cryptosporidiosis
Alphaviruses (for example, Venezuelan equine encephalitis, eastern equine encephalitis, western equine encephalitis) and flaviviruses (for example, West Nile encephalitis, Saint Louis encephalitis, dengue fever)	Viral encephalitis
Influenza virus	Influenza
Mycobacterium tuberculosis	MDR TB and XDR TB

What is anthrax?

Anthrax is actually the spore form of a bacterium called *Bacillus anthracis*. It can be made into a powder by drying; once it is inhaled, the spores can become active and reproduce in the body. This can result in disease, but anthrax spores don't always become active immediately. A person can take at least a day, several days, or even weeks to become ill. If someone is exposed to anthrax, the usual way of counteracting the spores is to take antibiotics for around two months, although this depends on the exposure.

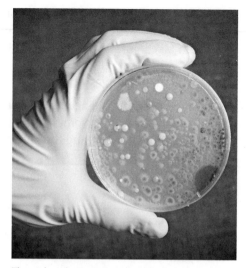

The anthrax bacterium is shown here being grown in a petri dish. Anthrax is spread as a dry spore inhaled into the lungs.

How does the Centers for Disease Control and Prevention classify bioterrorism agents?

According to the Centers for Disease Control and Prevention (CDC), bioterrorism agents can be classified into three categories based on how easily the agent spreads and the severity of illness or death the agent causes. The following gives the three categories:

- Category A—This includes organisms or toxins that pose the highest risk to the public because the agents are easily spread and transmitted from person to person, have the highest public health impact and often death rates, can cause public and social disruption, and need special action for public health awareness.

- Category B—These agents are moderately easy to spread and result in "moderate" illness and death rates.

- Category C—This category is one of the "newest," as it includes emerging pathogens that could be developed and eventually spread *en masse* in the future. No one knows what these organisms will be, but they could be engineered to spread rapidly and have a major health impact on many areas.

What is the National Biodefense Analysis and Countermeasures Center?

The National Biodefense Analysis and Countermeasures Center (NBACC) in Maryland, under the U.S. Department of Homeland Security, is the foremost U.S. biodefense research institution involved with bioforensics. It was created as a federal response to the anthrax letter attacks of 2001 as the first national laboratory operating under the Department of Homeland Security. Its primary task is to provide a continuously available national security biocontainment laboratory capability for newly identified biological threats.

LESSER-KNOWN
FORENSIC INVESTIGATIONS

What is forensic meteorology?

Forensic meteorology is using weather and weather events to determine certain aspects of a crime or accident—in particular, the timing and location. This includes gathering information about the type of weather the day of (and sometimes days before or after) a crime or accident, or if any extreme weather events happened that could have affected the scene. In the past decade, more data has been available to forensic meteorologists, including Doppler radar, satellite imagery, and detailed surface information from various local and remote weather station locations. The experts can use this information to verify eyewitness accounts of what the weather conditions were like before, during, or after a crime or accident. For example, they may testify as to whether it was raining or snowing during a crime or accident—evidence that may be important to the case. The forensic meteorologist is also often asked to be an expert witness in a court of law (for more about meteorology evidence in court, see the chapter "Putting It All Together").

What is forensic nursing?

Forensic nursing combines nursing with aspects of the legal system, including a knowledge of medical evidence collection and the criminal justice system. They often treat sexual and physical assault victims, help at a crime scene investigation, or work in health care at a correctional facility and are often called upon to testify as an expert witness. They also may use special equipment to help with certain aspects of their job. For example, in order to clearly show bruises under the skin of an assault victim before the marks are visible, they may use a special camera. For example, a forensic nurse may use an Omnichrome, an instrument that uses blue light and orange filters to see the not-yet-visible bruises from an accident or assault.

How was forensic meteorology used in the Mosley murder trial?

In 2002, Michael Mosley was accused of bludgeoning two people to death in Troy, New York. He had a cut on his hand but said he hurt himself while snowboarding with his son. The district attorney's office in Rensselaer County called meteorologist Howard Altschule to testify. The reason was obvious—the prosecutors were going to rely on weather reports to dispute Mosley's claim but thought the meteorologist could give so much more detail. Altschule did, testifying in detail (including presenting a radar map of precipitation) that on the day of the crime, it was raining and did not snow. In fact, it was raining enough to melt any snow—and Mosley was convicted of the two murders.

What is forensic botany?

Forensic botany is the study of plants used as evidence at a crime or accident scene. The forensic botanist is often an expert in not only the types and varieties of plants in an area (native or cultivated) but also the types of pollen, spores, seeds, and even soils. For example, if a certain plant material is found on a murder weapon, the forensic botanist may be able to determine the type of plant and/or where such plants are found. This can provide evidence that may link a perpetrator to a crime scene or help rule out a suspect. (For more about pollen and spores as evidence, see the chapter "In the Crime Lab: Trace Evidence.")

Ornithologists are scientists who study birds. Because birds exhibit distinctive behaviors based on the species, bird evidence at crime scenes can actually tell a lot about a crime scene. Forensic ornithologists also take cases involving the illegal bird trade.

What is a forensic ornithologist?

Forensic ornithologists are scientists who study birds, including the various species' feathers, beaks, wings, or any other part of an avian. Bird evidence is often useful, as most bird species have certain specific microscopic feather structures that can positively identify the bird involved. In terms of forensics, this knowledge of birds can be helpful to obtain evidence in a criminal or other case, including the illegal selling and trading of bird parts or accidents, such as if a bird strikes a plane, causing a crash. Feathers can even be used as evidence at a crime scene. For example, if the victim has a pet bird, a feather from the bird found on a suspect's clothes may link them to the crime scene.

What are some organizations specializing in forensic ornithology?

Several organizations specialize in forensic ornithology. For example, the Smithsonian Institution's Division of Birds has experts who identify feathers and feather fragments at the Feather Identification Laboratory (FIL). At this writing, they have six hundred thousand bird specimens and twenty thousand feather reference slides and analyze feathers using microscopes to understand the feather's microstructure. One famous case involved U.S. Airways Flight 1549 in January 2009, in which after taking off from New York's LaGuardia Airport, the plane collided with a flock of Canada geese at 2,900 feet (884 meters), disabling both engines. The plane landed safely in the Hudson River, thanks to the pilot's quick thinking—and the 155 people onboard survived, but it was important to determine just where the birds originated, as resident birds could cause even more problems with flights. The microscopic and other techniques from the FIL proved that the birds were migratory—not local birds—from Labrador, Canada. Another organization that has been instrumental in forensic ornithology is the U.S. Fish and

Wildlife Service's Forensics Laboratory in Oregon, considered to be the world's foremost facility dedicated to solving crimes against wildlife, including birds.

Do other countries have forensic ornithology laboratories?

Yes, many other organizations around the world need the expertise of forensic ornithologists, for example, the Feather Structure and Forensic Ornithology Lab in Canada, which is associated with the University of Windsor. Forensic ornithology experts are also at the Beaty Biodiversity Museum at the University of British Columbia, Canada.

What is wildlife forensics?

Just as the name implies, wildlife forensics deals with many scientific disciplines within the natural world to help with certain legal cases that involve nonhuman biological evidence. These disciplines include genetics, chemistry, morphology, pathology, wildlife behavior, and veterinary science. Wildlife forensics experts often help with investigations at an outdoor crime scene. For instance, if a body is found with bite wounds, they determine what species did the biting, or they determine whether hairs at a crime scene belonged to a human or animal. Wildlife forensic experts are also involved in cases, such as those that involve the illegal removal of plants or animals (especially poaching) for the black-market trade and animal cruelty cases.

What is the Convention on the International Trade in Endangered Species of Wild Fauna and Flora (CITES)?

The Convention on the International Trade in Endangered Species of Wild Fauna and Flora (CITES) was established in 1973 and, according to its mission, is an international agreement between governments aimed to ensure that the international trade in wild animal and plant specimens does not threaten the survival of such organisms. Because the trades in organisms cross borders between one or many countries, CITIES was formed primarily to safeguard those certain traded species from overexploitation. As of this writing, it helps to provide various degrees of protection to more than thirty-five thousand species of plants and animals—from live animal specimens to dried herbs.

How do several U.S. agencies help with wildlife crime?

In the United States, the U.S. Fish and Wildlife Service (FWS), the National Oceanic and Atmospheric Administration (NOAA), and several other state agencies all maintain forensic laboratories. These facilities help with wildlife crimes, including analytical services and expert witness testimonies when needed. The National Fish and Wildlife Forensics Laboratory (for more about the NFWFL, see below) of the FWS also is the analytical facility for the international INTERPOL Wildlife Crime Working Group along with the Convention on the International Trade in Endangered Species of Wild Fauna and Flora (CITES; see above).

What is the National Fish and Wildlife Forensics Laboratory?

The National Fish and Wildlife Forensics Laboratory is located in Ashland, Oregon, and is part of the U.S. Fish and Wildlife Service. Not only does it have experts in ornithology (see above), but it also conducts forensic investigations for such incidents as people illegally stealing timber from state or federal lands or determining who killed a certain animal for one of the creature's parts (poaching). It is also involved in the human aspect of forensics, too, including ballistics (in the case of poaching or shooting illegally on government lands), latent evidence (such as fingerprints at a poaching scene), pathology (such as determining how an animal died), and even DNA technology (in cases involving certain evidence, such as human blood at a wilderness crime scene).

What are some wildlife forensic groups located in the United States?

Numerous groups are involved in wildlife forensics in the United States on the state and federal levels—too many to mention them all here. For example, the Society for Wildlife Forensic Science (SWFS) was established in 2009 and supports wildlife forensic practitioners worldwide. On a more regional level, such groups exist as the William R. Maples Center for Forensic Medicine at the University of Florida's College of Medicine. All of these groups offer a range of resources and/or education in terms of wildlife forensics. For example, the William R. Maples Center offers crime scene analysts that help with federal, state, and local law-enforcement agencies and private organizations with wildlife crime investigations, with entomologists, botanists, anthropologists, toxicologists, and DNA analysts who specialize in wildlife crime.

What is forensic geology?

Simply put, forensic geology is the scientific application of earth science—including minerals, rocks, fossils, oil, petroleum, and other materials found in the Earth—to legal matters. A forensic geologist can analyze soil and rock samples from a suspected crime scene, such as using the soil on a suspect's shoe to place that person at the scene. Forensic geology also includes those geologists who understand the topography of an area (to determine how, for instance, an accident occurred based on the terrain); groundwater geologists who analyze the chemical degradation of substances in groundwater to pinpoint where a certain contamination originated); or mineralogists, who can help interpret a vehicle accident by analyzing the composition of a gravel road—and whether it influenced the event in any way.

THE CRIMINAL MIND

FORENSIC PSYCHOLOGY
AND PSYCHIATRY

What is forensic psychology and psychiatry?

Experts in forensic psychology and psychiatry deal with legal issues of criminal and civil cases (and sometimes family or domestic relations laws, such as child custody and juvenile delinquency issues). In general, forensic psychology is a branch of psychology related to the legal system; a forensic psychiatrist is also trained to work in the legal system, especially to help translate medical psychological information into legal language. People in both fields also help train (and even evaluate) law-enforcement personnel about criminal (and general human) behavior, such as providing criminal profiles of known and unknown criminals and possible responses of people who commit certain crimes. Experts in psychology also provide counseling for juveniles and adults who have been accused of criminal acts and counseling for those who have been convicted of a crime, those who are on probation, and even for victims of crimes (especially violent crimes).

In criminal cases, especially those that go to trial, forensic psychologists and psychiatrists concentrate on criminal issues, such as the competence of a person (suspect) to stand trial, to testify, or to waive legal representation. They also are often involved in assessing the mental illness of a criminal and just how a person's state of mind possibly contributed to a crime. For example, they are often called in to assess whether a criminal can be charged "not guilty for reason of insanity." In civil cases, forensic psychologists and psychiatrists address issues such as a person's competency to make medical decisions, the right of a person to refuse medical treatment, and whether a person needs to be committed for psychiatric reasons.

What education and training do forensic psychiatrists and psychologists need?

Psychiatrists are considered to be medical doctors, as they must complete twelve years of education and training similar to most doctors (undergraduate, medical school, and residency), but, of course, specializing in psychiatry. The branch of psychiatry that deals with forensics also means more education and experience in topics that may be relevant to a case, such as addiction or child psychiatry, along with training in certain aspects of the law. Forensic psychologists do not have to be medical doctors but still must complete several years of education and training (in general, undergraduate [usually majoring in behavioral science], one to two years for a master's degree, and graduate school for four to six years to obtain a PhD in psychology). Several paths exist to specializing in forensic psychology, including on-the-job or postdoctoral training. Certification in forensic psychology is usually presented (after an examination) by the American Board of Professional Practice in Psychology.

What is a forensic neuropsychologist?

A forensic neuropsychologist uses the assessment of brain functioning and behavior in legal settings or with legal applications. In general, this includes not just whether the patient has a certain dysfunction but whether that very dysfunction results from the event or crime under consideration. To determine this, neuropsychologists often use methods and studies from brain-damaged people that are scientifically reviewed and validated and compare them to the person in question, such as a defendant in a murder trial.

What do forensic psychologists and psychiatrists evaluate in terms of a criminal defendant?

No real "general evaluation" exists of a criminal defendant by a forensic psychologist and psychiatrist. If a forensic psychologist or psychiatrist is called upon to evaluate a criminal defendant in a trial, they usually try to determine several behavioral and mental functioning aspects of that specific person, which varies from crime to crime and person to person. (In fact, in most jurisdictions, it is the attorney, court, or legal system who/that is considered the psychologist's client, unlike in clinical psychology, in which a person is the client.) For example, they are often called in—many times by legal counsel—to determine whether a confession of a suspect (defendant) to a law-enforcement officer (or officers) was voluntary; whether the suspect (defendant) is a danger in the future if they are discharged into the community (or even if they will abide by the terms of their probation, if applicable); or whether the suspect (defendant) is incompetent to stand trial; for instance, if the defendant is determined to be actively psychotic or paranoid, they may be unable to work with the attorney in their best interest.

What is criminal psychology?

According to an article in *Psychology* journal, criminal psychology (also called criminological psychology) is the "study of the wills, thoughts, intentions, and reactions of

The fundamental task of a criminal psychologist is to determine whether a suspect in a crime is suffering from a mental health issue.

criminals and all that partakes in the criminal behavior." In other words, they help determine whether a criminal suspect has a mental health (some phrase this mental illness) issue. Experts in criminal psychology often work in prisons, police departments, law firms, schools and universities (juvenile crime), government agencies (that deal with crime investigation), and private practices.

What agencies and organizations employ forensic psychologists and psychiatrists?

A number of agencies and organizations employ forensic psychologists and psychiatrists, including U.S. Homeland Security, law-enforcement agencies, correctional institutions, and social services. For example, several government agencies employ psychologists. For instance, within the U.S. (or state equivalent) Department of Justice is the Bureau of Prisons, which is dedicated to prisons and the incarcerated. Psychologists are needed to counsel inmates and staff in the cases of such events as crisis activities (prison takeovers, escapes, etc.), drug abuse, suicide prevention, and so on. The Federal Bureau of Investigation (FBI) also has a Behavioral Science Unit. This unit is responsible for such tasks as profiling suspects of suspicious accidents or criminal activities and criminals (including terrorists)—and also helping to apprehend criminals based on the person's behavioral qualities and/or patterns. (For more about psychological profiling, see this chapter.)

Can forensic psychologists be expert witnesses in court?

Yes, in many court cases, a forensic psychologist is often called upon as an expert witness for many varied reasons. One of their major tasks is presenting their psychological findings in the legal language of the court so it can be understood by all and in legal terms. For example, in a child abuse case, the forensic psychologist may evaluate the defendant in order to identify certain psychological problems that underlie the criminal act, with the presenting of possible psychological treatments being part of the defendant's plea bargain agreement (if applicable). Forensic psychologists can also offer experimental data from their background knowledge or report on relevant studies they have conducted in relation to the same type of criminal case—or even offer verified (by their peers) psychological data that may give reasons for the certain event or circumstance in which the defendant was involved.

DEFINITIONS IN FORENSIC PSYCHOLOGY AND PSYCHIATRY

What is "insanity" in a criminal case?

Forensic psychologists (and psychiatrists) often have to assess a person in a *mens rea* (or insanity) case. For example, in the United States, a person cannot be held responsible for a crime if he or she did not possess a *mens rea*, or, literally, "guilty mind," when the crime was committed. No federal standard exists for insanity, and each state has its own rules as to whether a person can be declared insane (the term "insanity" is considered a legal term in such cases, not a psychological one). Overall, though, it is thought that if the person knew that they were doing wrong, it is not considered insanity, and it is often the task of forensic psychologists to make such a determination.

What does NGRI mean?

NGRI stands for "not guilty for reason of insanity"—an idea that dates back to the Roman Empire (or maybe before). In such cases, the person may be mentally ill and

Who was Kenneth Erksine?

British-born Kenneth Erksine (1962–) was a serial killer who was declared insane at his trial. Also known as "The Stockwell Strangler," he murdered seven elderly people at various times in London in 1986. In 1987, he was caught, and by 1988, he was convicted and sentenced to forty years in prison. He appealed in 2009, using an insanity plea (at age twenty-four, he was judged to have had the mental capability of an eleven-year-old; he was also eventually found to be schizophrenic among other behavioral problems). He won the appeal, and his sentence was changed to manslaughter on the grounds of diminished responsibility. He was being held at Broadmoor (previously known as Broadmoor Hospital for the Criminally Insane); in 2016, he was transferred to Thornford Park Hospital.

will not be imprisoned for the crime. This is based on the assumption that he or she was not capable of determining right from wrong when committing the crime. In today's world, the result is usually psychiatric treatment instead of jail time. Overall, the reason for this type of decision is clear: some mentally ill people will not be deterred by the threat of punishment (jail time), and the treatment will help the person and help protect society more than if the person was sent to jail without treatment. (For more about controversies surrounding NGRI, see the chapter "Controversies in Forensic Science.")

What does diminished capacity mean?

A criminal defendant is often psychologically evaluated for certain reasons. One in particular occurs if a person is found to be competent to stand trial, but they had a psychological disorder at the time the crime occurred. If so, it is thought that this prevented that person from forming the intent to commit a crime, a condition called diminished capacity. According to the Cornell Law School, the diminished capacity plea is based in the belief that "certain people, because of mental impairment or disease, are simply incapable of reaching the mental state required to commit a particular crime." For example, if a certain defendant is found to be incapable of intending to cause another person's death, then they must have caused the death recklessly. This translates to a plea of diminished capacity, resulting not in a charge of murder but reduced to manslaughter.

Who were some serial killers who were declared sane—or insane—at their trials?

Contrary to what many people think, not all serial killers are insane—even though it may seem so if someone can kill people repeatedly and usually in a certain manner. The idea is that a person is insane if they have no control over such behaviors, but very few serial killers have been declared insane. In other words, most serial killers are said to be sane at their trial, as no mental health issues appeared to have had a direct influence on their behavior and their reasons for such killings. Some of the more famous killers who were declared sane at their trials include Ted Bundy, John Wayne Gacy, and Jeffrey Dahmer. Of the very few serial killers who were declared insane, Kenneth Erksine is one of the most well known (see sidebar above).

Jeffrey Dahmer's 1978 high school yearbook photo provides no hint that he would soon begin a killing spree.

What is retrospective analysis?

When a forensic psychologist assesses a person being held for a crime, they must determine whether that person knew that what he or she was doing was wrong if they did commit a crime, and they must determine the accused person's mental state not only in the present but also in the past. This means that a forensic psychologist's analysis of the accused is retrospective and must rely on such past factors as information from others and written communications (such as statements made at the time of the crime).

What is psychopathology?

Psychopathology is often simply considered the study of mental illness. It is also, in terms of the individual, a mental or emotional disorder that has a great impact on the life of that individual. In forensics, especially in terms of criminal acts, psychopathology refers to the study of a person's mental illness or mental distress, a person's behavior or dysfunction because of mental illness, and/or experiences that may be indicative of a mental illness or psychological impairment—with all the factors that can contribute or be relevant to such manifestations of the disorders.

Who is Tom Sweatt?

Thomas Anthony Sweatt (1955–) is an American convicted serial arsonist who is thought to be one of the most prolific arsonists in American history. Since his incarceration, he confessed to having set more than 350 fires in and around Washington (many of which occurred between 2003 and 2004). In 2003, the Prince George's County, Maryland, and Washington, D.C., area experienced fourteen suspiciously similar incendiary house fires, with two resulting deaths and major destruction of personal property. The ATF became involved, and the agency's National Laboratory Center identified the arsonist's "signature" device that was always carried to a scene in a distinct, plastic bag. From there, Sweatt would fill a milk jug with gasoline and plug the opening with a piece of clothing. The cloth wick would burn the jug plastic (for about twenty minutes), with the fire starting when the container melted and gas fumes escaped. The final evidence linked Sweatt's DNA samples (he gave a sample willingly) to those biosamples found at various fire scenes, including fingerprints, skin, and hair samples. Sweatt, a former fast-food restaurant manager, was arrested in 2005 for the federal crimes of arson and arson resulting in death. (He told authorities he was "driven by demons" to set the fires; later, several reasons were found for his arsonist tendencies, including following people who he was sexually fascinated about—and setting fire to their home.) He was sentenced to a life term in federal prison.

What are projective and objective personality assessments?

A projective assessment (or test) is designed to allow a person to respond to several types of indistinct (also called "ambiguous") stimuli—such as looking at and interpreting certain shapes and colors—in order to reveal that person's hidden or subdued emotions and internal conflicts. An objective personality assessment (also called a self-report test) is based on an individual's responses based on the average person's response—or what is called a presumed universal standard (for example, a multiple-choice exam). Simply put, the responses to the projective tests are content analyzed for their meaning, whereas objective tests are based on presuppositions about the meaning.

What is the Personality Assessment Inventory?

The Personality Assessment Inventory (PAI) was created in 1991 and has been used in both forensic and correctional settings, especially in terms of certain crimes. It was developed to assess a person's personality (especially traits). It has twenty-two conditions within (nonoverlapping) four varieties of scales: validity, clinical, treatment considerations, and interpersonal scales. For example, the validity scales include the measurement of the person's approach to the test (whether they are exaggerating, defensive, etc.); the clinical scales include the measurement of the person's psychopathology (whether the person has physical complaints, has a high level of anxiety, has problems with drug use, etc.). The results of the PAI can be used for conditions, such as a child custody evaluation, to evaluate a person's fitness for duty, in a personal injury case, in the case of domestic violence, and many other circumstances.

What is victimology?

Victimology is a term used when a criminal profiler gathers and examines a victim's information in order to gain some insight into the perpetrator of the crime (and sometimes to verify or discredit that the person is truly a victim of the crime). In particular, in cases in which a victim's actions, history, or demeanor are relevant to the legal proceedings, forensic profilers can help assess the person's behavior. Unfortunately, this information is sometimes difficult to gather, as some information about the victim may be inaccurately reported, not documented correctly (or even collected), or even presented in a biased manner. All of this may impact the court proceedings, which is why victim information should be collected accurately, thoroughly, and without bias, giving a judge and/or jury the information they need to make decisions regarding the case.

What are some motives that cause an arsonist to start a fire?

According to several psychological references, many motives cause an arsonist to start a fire that may harm people and/or structures—some malicious, some psychological. They include insurance fraud (setting personal homes or businesses on fire to collect insurance); vandalism (forced entry by indigents, juveniles, or gangs, then starting a fire); revenge (including domestic, work-related, or other disputes); vanity (to gain attention, or, sadly, sometimes a firefighter committing arson to gain praise); domestic terrorism (fire used for political, religious, or social reasons, to harm people and/or their structures); and pathological reasons (someone who enjoys setting fires due to psychological issues). (For more about arson, see the chapter "Other Forensic Investigations.")

INTERPRETING THE CRIMINAL MIND

What is psychological profiling?

Psychological profiling is a method of linking an unknown offender's actions at a crime scene to their most likely behavioral, personality, and biographical characteristics. In particular, it can often provide an age range, type of employment, marital status, education, and possible behavioral (psychological) information about the offender. It is based on the idea that a person's behaviors are often connected to specific thought patterns and motives in a crime. This process (also called offender profiling, crime scene profiling, or personality profiling) is often used to help police and investigators narrow down the most likely suspect or suspects in a crime—and sometimes to determine the perpetrator from a group of suspects. As most investigative researchers agree, profiling is not intended to solve a crime but to be an investigative tool to use in the attempt to solve a crime.

What are descriptive and predictive profiling in terms of criminals?

Psychological (offender) profiling is often broken down into two methods that determine certain information about a suspect—present and future. Descriptive offender profiling is used to identify likely suspects in a crime, whereas predictive offender profiling uses the offender's patterns to predict possible future offensives (or types of victims) by the perpetrator.

What are inductive and deductive criminal profiling?

Criminal profiling of an offender has traditionally been examined in two ways. Inductive criminal profiling uses past information about certain crimes and known offenders who committed such crimes (especially the person's characteristics, personality type, and behavior) in order to understand a similar crime that the profilers are investigating. This method is based on the idea that even though similar crimes are committed by different criminals, the perpetrators may both share common personality traits. Deductive criminal profiling is one of the most well-known types of determining the characteristics of a perpetrator. In this case, the information about the offender is determined directly from the investigation and analysis of the crime scene.

Who is credited as one of the first modern criminal profilers?

More recently, former FBI special agent and unit chief John Edward Douglas (1945–) is credited as one of the first modern criminal profilers. Along with helping with profiling

When was criminal profiling first used?

Dr. Thomas Bond

No one truly knows when criminal profiling—at least a "crude" form of the method—was first used. The first recorded profiling apparently occurred in the 1880s by British physicians George Bagster Phillips (1835–1897; also a police physician) and Thomas Bond (1841–1901; also often thought of as the first offender profiler; tragically, mainly because of ill health, he committed suicide). They examined clues from the famous British serial killer Jack the Ripper's crime scenes and performed autopsies of some of his victims in order to determine the elusive murder's personality characteristics. (For more about Jack the Ripper, see the chapter "Famous (and Not-so-Famous) Crimes and Forensic Science.")

offenders for several high-profile cases—he also worked for the family on the JonBenét Ramsey murder case—he was also the inspiration for the character Jack Crawford in the movie *The Silence of the Lambs*. (For more about JonBenét Ramsey, see the chapter "Famous (and Not-so-Famous) Crimes and Forensic Science.")

Why do so many different terms exist for "profiling"?

Like many fields, terms often differ for certain methods. Profiling is no different, with most of the terms dependent upon the practitioners. For example, the FBI calls its type of profiling "criminal investigative analysis"; a forensic psychologist may call their work "investigative psychology"; and others use the term "crime action profiling." All of these are names for the same thing: to examine crime scene evidence and the reports from the victim or victims, along with interviews with witnesses to help determine the perpetrator's possible personality traits and behaviors—revealing a profile that can narrow down the field of possible suspects or even pinpoint the offender.

What is the mission of criminal profilers in, for example, the Bureau of Alcohol, Tobacco, Firearms, and Explosies (ATF)?

Although criminal profiler investigations go on at other government agencies, according to the ATF, the primary mission of the agency's behavioral profilers is to support arson and bombing investigations. This includes the identification, arrest, and eventual prosecution of the offender—all by analysis of the offender's behavior. ATF behavioral profilers are certified in criminal behavioral analysis and also provide training and presentations to other law-enforcement groups, including the police and fire personnel.

What criteria does the FBI often use to profile a criminal?

When the FBI does criminal investigative analysis, it often relies on information of the possible perpetrator's behavior in order to develop a criminal profile. For example, in a homicide case, FBI agents often look at a killer's behavior to give them a better idea of the person who committed the crime. For instance, such investigations are often broken down into four stages: the antecedent (what fantasy or plan, or both, did the murderer have in place before the act; what triggered the murderer to act some days and not others), the method and manner (what type of victim or victims did the murderer select; what was the method and manner of murder, such as shooting, stabbing, strangulation, or something else), the body disposal (did the murder and body disposal take place all at one scene, or multiple scenes); and postcriminal behavior (is the murderer trying to inject himself into the investigation by reacting to media reports or contacting investigators). In a rape case, the details of profiling are handled much in the same way, with additional information from a living victim (for instance, what were the forced sexual acts, in what order were they performed, etc.)—all of which give a general profile of the perpetrator.

PUTTING IT ALL TOGETHER

TERMS FROM THE COURT SYSTEM

What were some ancient ways in which guilt was determined?

Several methods were used in ancient countries to determine innocence or guilt—what many historians sometimes refer to as a precursor to a polygraph test. For example, one such method was used over two thousand years ago and involved a person's saliva and the examination of the mouth and tongue. In ancient China and India, a person accused of a crime would put rice powder or chew whole rice in their mouths. If the rice stuck in the accused's mouth, they would be considered guilty. This is because, they reasoned, if a person's mouth was so dry (less saliva) from guilt, they would have a hard time spitting out the rice. Although it seems harsh to modern ideology, ancient peoples attempted to detect lies in criminals in Medieval times in many ways: torture was used to detect a lie from an individual, with the assumption that an honest person would not succumb to the torture.

What are some Latin terms frequently used in association with law—and, often, forensic science?

Many Latin terms are used in association with forensic science. This is because the field developed side by side with the already established legal profession. Thus, as with the legal profession, Latin terms are often used. The following lists some of those terms, with most of them applying to criminal investigations (*note*: many of the Latin terms are loosely translated):

- *abet* (Latin for "to bait")—Used when one person encourages another person to commit a crime.
- *actus reus* (Latin for "guilty by act")—This is used when a person performs a wrongful deed with criminal intent.

- *compos mentis* (Latin for "of sound mind")—This is said when a person is legally responsible. In other words, they had control of their mind, or they are considered sane.

- *corpus delicti* (Latin for "body of the crime")—These are the fundamental facts that prove that a crime was committed.

- *de novo* (Latin for "new")—This is when a trial begins again without referring to previous trials.

- *flagrante delicto* (Latin for "while the crime is blazing")—Used when someone is caught in the act of a crime.

- *habeas corpus* (Latin for "that you have a body")—This is writ issued to bring a party (person) before a judge or court in order to release or continue to detain the party.

- *in loco parentis* (Latin for "in place of the parent")—The legal responsibility of a party (person) to take on parental responsibilities, usually of a minor.

- *in quaro* (Latin for "seeking into")—The word "inquest" comes from this Latin phrase, which is used for an inquiry into a death occurring under suspicious circumstances.

- *in situ* (Latin for "in its place")—This is used mainly for objects at a crime scene and means the object is in its original position.

- *indicia* (Latin for "to point out")—This is used when identifying marks or signs, usually at a crime scene.

- *mens rea* (Latin for "guilty in mind")—This is used when a person has the intent of knowledge of performing a criminal act.

- *modus operandi* (Latin for "method of operation")—This is usually abbreviated as "a person's M.O." or the particular way a crime is committed.

- *onus* (Latin for "burden")—This is often phrased as the burden of proof, or the responsibility of a governmental body or plaintiff to prove a case beyond a reasonable doubt.

- *postmortem* (Latin for "after death")—This term is used when an autopsy is performed after a person is dead; it is usually in reference to a victim of a crime.

- *prima facie* (Latin for "at first sight")—This is when evidence presented appears to be sufficient to establish proof.

- *pro se* (Latin for "on one's own behalf")—This is used when a person presents their own case before a court without the use of lawyers.

- *res judicata* (Latin for "the thing has been judged")—This means that a case before a court has already been decided by another court.

- *subpoena duces tecum* (Latin for "under penalty to bring with you")—This is used to help produce certain documents, papers, or tangible items of evidence that may be admissible before the court.

What is an arrest?

A person (suspect) who is arrested is taken into custody by law enforcement for breaking the law; they are no longer free to leave or move about. (Some define arrest as the person being taken into custody so their criminal activities are "at rest.") An arrest can occur if the arresting police officer observed the criminal activity by the person, if "probable cause" exists for the officer to arrest the person, or an arrest warrant for the person has been issued.

What is an interrogation?

An interrogation (also called questioning by some) is when a person is tenaciously interviewed to obtain useful information about an incident, person, or other concern or to obtain a confession from a suspect of a crime. It is usually conducted in connection with a crime, accident, or other event and most often by law-enforcement officers and investigators, military personnel, and intelligence agencies. A regular interview to obtain information is less formal than an interrogation, and, under many circumstances, the interrogation may include some intimidating methods. Police can use certain methods to persuade a suspect to talk (some reference mention lying and trickery) but are prohibited from using any type of strong-arm coercion (physical or psychological) when conducting interrogations. In fact, if a confession or incriminating evidence is from such coercive methods (for example, torture, threats, drugs, or inhumane treatment of the suspect), the results are not admissible in court.

What is an arraignment?

After the arrest, booking, and initial bail is set, a suspect usually attends an arraignment. In most cases, an arraignment is considered the suspect's (defendant) first appearance in court (whether the person is or is not in custody). In general, the defendant's attorney will receive the complaint, usually from the criminal court judge, starting with the charges made against the defendant, along with any police reports made about the event and the suspect's possible involvement. From there, the defendant is asked whether they plead guilty, not guilty, or no contest. Depending on the circumstances and the criminal charges (and even jurisdiction), the defendant is either released on their own recognizance or their lawyer will discuss bail, which will be set (or not) depending on the charges. The dates of future proceedings will then be announced, if applicable.

What is a trial?

A trial is a formal and extensive examination of evidence before a judge. Along with a judge, the evidence can also be presented before a jury. Most trials are conducted to determine guilt or innocence of a person in criminal or civil matters. Two common types of trials are a jury trial, when a panel of individuals determines a person's guilt or innocence, or a bench trial, in which the person waives their right to a jury and the judge makes the final ruling.

What are the general steps in a trial?

In general, the typical steps of a trial include selecting a jury, presenting the evidence to the jury, cross examining eyewitnesses and expert witnesses (if applicable), and the lawyers making closing statements. The jury then deliberates about the evidence presented and returns a verdict. In some states, a mistrial will be declared if the jury does not reach a unanimous verdict or if the jury is at a standstill (see hung jury, below).

There is no jury in a bench trial in which only the judge determines guilt or innocence.

What is an inquest?

An inquest—from the Latin *in* or "into" and *quaro* or "to look for"—is usually conducted by a judge, jury, or government official and is considered a legal or judicial inquiry. It is most often conducted to determine the cause of a person's death. If a person dies of natural causes, such as a heart attack of a person with heart trouble, no further investigation is required, but in the case of a suspicious or unattended death, for example, the death of a person on a trail in a park, then an inquest is made by a coroner or medical examiner to determine the cause of the person's death. Besides a coroner or medical examiner, others can request an inquest, including law-enforcement officers (for example, if a person dies while in custody) and magistrates.

What is the difference between a criminal and civil case?

A criminal case is one in which the local, state, or federal government is involved in if a violation of the law is suspected. In other words, an action by a person or persons is considered to be harmful to society as a whole. In criminal cases, the accused is generally charged in an indictment (a formal accusation for felonies or serious crimes) or information (for misdemeanors). Such cases also may involve a fine, jail sentence, or both. A civil case is most often brought by a person or people in the public, a corporation, or government (usually called the plaintiff) against other people or an entity, such as a corporation. In such cases, the plaintiff is usually asking for money owed or monetary damages because the other person or corporation did not carry out a legal duty owed to the plaintiff.

What are the prosecuting and defense lawyers' duties?

In general, the prosecutor is the lawyer who conducts a case against the defendant in a criminal court. The defense lawyer represents the defendant in a lawsuit or a criminal prosecution. They also cross-examine witnesses and are in charge of protecting the legal rights of the individual on trial.

What often swayed a jury's decisions about guilt around the 1700s?

Around the eighteenth century, a person's guilt in court (and often the actual criminal investigation that led to a trial) was often swayed by less evidence-based procedures. In particular, juries and judges were often swayed by forced confessions obtained by torture and even the "evidence" based on the court's or juries' beliefs in the occult or witchcraft.

What does "burden of proof" mean?

The "burden of proof" is different for a criminal and civil trial. In a criminal case, the burden of proving the defendant's guilt is the task of the prosecution. In such cases, they must prove beyond a reasonable doubt that the evidence against the accused is conclusive. In a civil case, the person with the complaint (plaintiff) has the "burden of proof" and must prove that their case is sound, usually by presenting evidence that verifies their claim.

What is a trial jury?

According to the judicial branch of the U.S. government, a trial jury, also known as a petit jury, consists of six to twelve people who decide whether the defendant committed the crime as charged in a criminal case or whether the defendant injured the plaintiff in a civil case. In most cases, trials are generally open to the public, but jury deliberations are private, and the defendants have the right to appear, testify, and call witnesses

In a jury trial, the accused's case is presented to a group of peers who then render a judgment as to guilt.

on their behalf. The final outcome of the trial is called the verdict, and it is either in favor of the plaintiff or defendant in a civil case and, in a criminal case, the accused is either guilty or not guilty.

What is a grand jury?

According to the judicial branch of the U.S. government, a grand jury is a group of sixteen to twenty-three people who are presented with evidence from the U.S. attorney, who is considered the prosecutor in federal criminal cases. (These jury proceedings are not open to the public.) The grand jury has the task of determining whether "probable cause" exists to believe that the individual has committed a crime and should be put on trial. If they determine that enough evidence exists, an indictment will be issued against the defendant. In this case, defendants and their attorneys do not have the right to appear before the grand jury.

What is a "hung jury"?

According to the American Bar Association, if the jurors cannot agree on a verdict, a hung jury results, leading to a mistrial. This also means that the case has not been decided and it may be tried again at a later date before a new jury. Another choice may be that the plaintiff or government may decide not to pursue the case further and, thus, no subsequent trial will occur.

What does "competent to stand trial" versus "insane" mean in a trial?

The term "competent to stand trial" means just what the phrase indicates—that the person is not suffering from any mental illness or incapacitation and therefore can stand trial. In order to be declared competent, they must be able to appear at the trial and understand the proceedings, but this is not the same as declaring a person sane. Sanity determines whether a defendant will be held responsible for their criminal actions. In fact, this means that a defendant who is competent to stand trial could still eventually be found "not guilty for reason of insanity." (For more about psychology and criminals, see the chapter "The Criminal Mind.")

What are "probative" facts or evidence?

A probative fact (or evidence) is when data is used to prove an issue or other information, especially as evidence. These facts often establish the existence of other facts and make the existence of something more probable—or less probable—than it would be without the probative facts. For example, in a motor vehicle accident, if a witness testifies that he saw a specific automobile drive through an intersection on a red light, it is a probative fact about whether the driver was at fault or not. In a trial situation, probative facts or evidence can be misleading. For example, sometimes the prosecutor in a trial (especially a criminal trial) offers probative evidence of something the defendant did that prejudices the minds of the jurors. This is because such evidence is often offered by the prosecution to show that the defendant has a tendency toward committing the crime charged. Thus, the trial judge often must weigh the probative evidence against prejudicing the jurors toward the criminal defendant and remind the court that the person be tried on the facts of the particular case, not on prior actions.

What is a proof hearing?

A proof hearing (also called a default judgment hearing) is a trial before a judge only—and no jury—in which only one side is present. In such hearings, the judge is the one who reviews the evidence, hears the testimony of the plaintiff, and often, based on the evidence and testimony, will enter a judgment concerning the plaintiff.

What is a decedent?

A decedent is a legal term meaning "the deceased" and is usually used in a court of law. The term is literally translated as "one who is dying," but in general, it is commonly used in a legal sense to mean one who has died, especially someone who has recently passed away. (It is also used in terms of a person's legal will. For example, a decedent can die intestate or testate, or without or with a will, respectively.)

What is culpability?

Culpability is defined as the responsibility of a person for a fault or wrong. In other words, a person is to blame for a certain crime or accident or having the responsibility for a fault or wrong. It also means a measure of the degree to which a person can be held morally or legally responsible for an action or inaction. It is from the Latin *culpa*, or "concept of fault." In law, it describes the degree of one's blameworthiness in the act of a crime or offense.

What is the "but for" principle?

The "but for" principle is when the question is asked about someone who has died: "… but for the inciting injury (or event), would the decedent still be alive?" In legal terms, and according to several legal dictionaries, it is phrased "In the law of Negligence, a principle that provides that the defendant's conduct is not the cause of an injury to the plaintiff, unless that injury would not have occurred except for ('but for') the defendant's conduct."

What is the difference between concurrent and consecutive sentences?

For an incarcerated criminal, concurrent and consecutive sentences are different. In a concurrent sentence, the person is incarcerated for their crimes concurrently. For example, if they are serving two years for larceny and one year for assault, they will serve two years total, and both sentences will be essentially meshed together. If it is a consecutive sentence, the crimes are "separated." For example, if a person is serving two years for larceny and one year for assault, they will serve a total of three years.

Does a "not guilty" verdict necessarily mean that the defendant is innocent?

No, just because a person's verdict is "not guilty," it does not mean that the defendant is innocent. A not guilty verdict is given for a variety of reasons (including that the person was truly not guilty), including that the evidence gathered was only circumstantial, that the prosecution did not prove "beyond a reasonable doubt" that the defendant was guilty, or that the evidence was contaminated or incorrectly handled, causing a question as to its validity. In most cases, a verdict of not guilty (also referred to as an acquittal) usually means that the prosecutor failed to prove their case beyond a reasonable doubt— not that the defendant was innocent.

ADMISSIBLE EVIDENCE

What is admissible evidence in court?

Although many times it depends on the jurisdiction, conditions, or other rules in a court of law, in general, admissible evidence is any document, testimony, or tangible evidence used in a court of law. Evidence is typically introduced to a judge or a jury to prove a point or element in a case. It can be the use of testimony (such as oral or written statements), documented evidence, items (such as physical objects found at a scene), or even demonstrative evidence (such as a digital video representing what is thought to have occurred at the crime scene). Items that are not admissible evidence in court include, for example, a person's opinions that are not based on facts.

What is a testimony?

In a criminal case, a testimony is the evidence given to support an assertion. For example, if a witness in a criminal trial stated that he saw the defendant shoot another person, it is a testimony and is considered direct evidence. Other testimonies can be circumstantial and are connected to a crime by inference, such as a suspect's fingerprints found at a crime scene. In other words, the person may or may not have had a part in the criminal act just because their fingerprints were found.

What is another name for "lie detector"?

Another name for "lie detector" is a polygraph. It measures the physiological changes in a person in order to determine their guilt or innocence. The theory is that when a person is lying, they will exhibit certain body changes, such as an increase in blood pressure and pulse rate. The use of a polygraph test once convicted many criminals in a court setting, but today, the results (in all but the rarest cases) are not admissible in court. (For more about controversies and polygraphs, see the chapter "Controversies in Forensic Science.")

What is eyewitness testimony?

An eyewitness testimony is just as the phrase sounds—the testimony of a person who has witnessed an event, such as a crime or an accident. The eyewitness's testimony is the account given by the eyewitness, for instance, of a bank robbery or a vehicular accident that they witnessed. The testimony includes details such as the identification of the people involved, the time of day, what the scene looked like when the event occurred, etc. (For more about controversies and eyewitness testimonies, see the chapter "Controversies in Forensic Science.")

Video from surveillance cameras is admissible in court, although the FBI has noted that time stamps on such recordings are often incorrect.

Can surveillance videos be used as evidence in a court trial?

Yes, but unless the original copy of the digital evidence is kept safe, in many cases, the video evidence's authenticity and reliability is questioned. Even if the video is kept safe, other concerns are present. For example, according to the FBI, more than half of all security camera systems have the wrong date and time stamp, mainly because of input error or not changing the clock to reflect such events as Daylight Saving Time. Or, if the video security camera is a "cheaper" model, it may also have low-cost imaging chips that can make it difficult to distinguish certain colors on the video, including the color of the alleged criminal's clothes. For instance, some camera brands have a difficult time distinguishing red and yellow colors when recording in daylight.

FORENSICS AND THE EXPERT WITNESS

What is an expert witness?

An expert witness is a person who is allowed to testify at a trial because they have special knowledge, training, educational background, or proficiency in a particular field—more than the average person—that is relevant to the case. For example, an expert witness in cutting weapons may be called in to give evidence if certain knives were found as possible evidence from a crime.

What are some positive aspects of expert witness testimonies?

Having an expert testimony at many trials is and always has been a positive thing. Whether for using laboratory simulations, having knowledge of certain types of environments, and/or having archival data that can support or contradict a claim, expert witnesses can be a crucial part of an investigation and litigation. For example, a weapons expert may be able to identify and provide details about a weapon that was used in a crime, including how it was used, and, thus, offer information that may (or may not) help the court identify the perpetrator.

What is a Frye (or frye) hearing?

A Frye hearing (also called a Frye standard, Frye test, or general acceptance test) is used to determine whether specific scientific evidence is admissible in a court or other case. It means that the expert opinion is based on a scientific test, method, or technique that has been generally or peer accepted in the scientific community. This acceptance of the scientific proof is important, especially in cases in which an expert witness brings forth evidence in a trial.

What types of expert witnesses are often asked to give evidence at a trial?

Expert witnesses come from a plethora of backgrounds. For example, in a trial involving firearms, an expert witness may be someone who understands the various types of ammunition, calibers, etc., that may have been found at a crime scene. Or, if an automobile accident has been deemed suspicious, the expert witness may be a meteorologist who would verify or negate the notion that the accident could have been caused by wet, slippery road conditions. Other experts include geologists, chemists, doctors, veterinarians, and so on.

What are direct and cross examinations?

A direct examination is when an attorney questions a witness to get an account of what happened during a crime, accident, or other event that triggered the need for a trial. The lawyers are not only trying to discern the facts but are also using testimonies to support their client's views of what occurred (this is usually done to help persuade the jury that the lawyer's client is telling the truth). After each witness has been questioned during a direct examination, the lawyers for the other side are allowed to question—or cross-examine—the witnesses. This is often done to make the lawyer's case "look better" and the opponent's case "look worse," but in reality, it is done to determine the truth of the situation.

What does "contempt of court" mean?

In most courts of law, contempt of court means that a person should not speak out of turn or interrupt others, especially during a trial or any judicial or court proceedings. If someone disrupts the court, the judge can hand down a "contempt of court" charge, which can result in fines and/or a jail sentence.

What happens to physical evidence after the trial is over?

Depending on the jurisdiction, when a criminal trial is over, the agency holding the physical evidence often disposes of it. For instance, in some cases, such as a lower-end offense, some items may be sent back to their rightful owner (such as a stolen car in which a crime occurred is given back to its owner), some evidence is destroyed (especially in the case of narcotics), or some is auctioned off (with the proceeds often going back into the local government general fund; this is why newspapers often run ads for a "police auction"). If it is a higher-end offense, and depending on the jurisdiction and crime, some physical evidence will be put into deep storage after the trial is over (and also, depending on the case, held for a certain number of years). For murders and other more serious crimes (again, depending on the jurisdiction), evidence can be stored for many decades (some say up to ninety-nine years). This is why some "cold cases" are taken out of storage, especially if new evidence is uncovered or advancement occurs in certain forensic techniques (such as DNA analysis).

Is the trial the culmination of the forensic science process?

In the majority of cases, the trial is the culmination of the forensic science process. Once such factors as the evidence being collected by investigators, the testimony of witnesses, and the prosecution of an individual is complete, usually forensic experts are no longer needed for that certain event, but this is not always the case. Even after a person goes to trial and is convicted, times have occurred when additional evidence is brought forth, either through new scientific techniques (such as a better understanding of DNA techniques) or other evidence being presented (such as a confession by another person for the same crime). In such cases, various forensic experts may be called upon again to review the new evidence and revisit the crime or accident details.

CONTROVERSIES IN FORENSIC SCIENCE

FINGERPRINT AND "LIE DETECTOR" PROBLEMS

Do fingerprints deteriorate over time?

The deterioration of fingerprints varies depending on where they are found (porous versus nonporous surfaces), the quality of the print (whether it is a partial print or even how much pressure was applied by the person's finger to make the print), and how the fingerprint is collected (whether it was treated with chemicals and/or whether it was contaminated at the crime scene). That being said, fingerprints have been reported to be found on certain items decades later. Other prints may rapidly deteriorate, especially under certain conditions, such as if it is hot or humid at a crime scene. If some of those fingerprints are of poor quality, misinterpretation often occurs—and that has erroneously sent many people to jail.

Why was the first "lie detector" or polygraph invented?

One of the earliest forms of lie detectors (polygraphs) was invented by British heart surgeon James MacKenzie (1853–1925) in the early 1900s. Using diaphragms and vibration detectors, his instrument recorded a boost in a person's breathing, pulse rate, and an increase in sweating. It was used mainly to detect irregular heartbeats. In particular, MacKenzie was the first to discover PVCs, or premature ventricular contractions, of the heart (also known as "extra heartbeats")—and used the device to determine whether the extra beats were harmless or harmful.

What was the evolution of the modern polygraph?

The polygraph as an instrument for use in forensics was invented by Canadian-born American inventor, criminologist, and forensic psychiatrist John Augustus Larson (1892–

1965) in 1921. He based his idea on William Moulton Marston's (1893–1947; Marston was also the creator of the comic book character "Wonder Woman") test for systolic blood pressure. Marston is often thought of as yet another inventor of the polygraph—but his device was not used in court, as it was not "generally accepted by the scientific community." Larson called his instrument a "cardio-pneumo psychogram" that tested for and relied on pulse, respirations, and skin conductivity in order to detect a lie. The polygraph was later improved upon by American inventor Leonarde Keeler (1903–1949; he is often called the co-inventor of the polygraph). He called his first instrument (1924) the "Emotograph." In 1935, he conducted the first criminal use of the "Compact Keeler

Leonarde Keeler, co-inventor of the early "Emotograph," is shown in this 1937 photograph giving a subject a polygraph test.

Polygraph" (or just "Keeler Polygraph") on two criminals in Wisconsin—who, based on their polygraph readings presented to the court, were both convicted of assault.

Are polygraph results admissible in court?

Yes and no, because it all depends on the court, but overall, in most courts, polygraph results are not considered to be admissible. In fact, according to the U.S. Supreme Court, no court has to admit polygraph tests, although a judge can decide to admit the lie detector test as evidence based on certain criteria, but for most cases, the results are usually ignored as evidence, as research has shown that the polygraph is not a good indicator of innocence or guilt. Even if a person is innocent and/or telling the truth, if they are nervous, the polygraph usually records a "negative" reading. In fact, certain courts, such as military courts, have banned the use of polygraphs outright.

CONTROVERSIES AND HAIR ANALYSIS

What scientific study led to questioning microscopic analysis of human hairs as evidence?

According to the FBI, before mitochondrial DNA testing—and nuclear DNA testing— was used to analyze hair in criminal cases, prosecutors throughout the country routinely relied on microscopic hair comparison to link a criminal defendant to a crime. In 2009,

Have mix-ups occurred when analyzing fingerprints from a crime scene?

Yes, problems have occurred with comparing fingerprints from a crime scene, even with the use of computer fingerprint-matching programs. One of the most famous occurred after the March 11, 2004, train bombings in Madrid, Spain. The nearly simultaneous, coordinated bombings of the commuter train system killed 192 people and injured two thousand. Officials discovered a bag that contained detonating devices in a stolen van at the train station, along with a partial fingerprint on the bag. The FBI, using its computerized Automated Fingerprint Identification System, examined close to five hundred million prints, discovering twenty possible matches, with one match being American attorney Brandon Mayfield (1966-; because he was once in the military, his fingerprints were on file with the Army and FBI). After more examination, several fingerprint experts had "absolute confidence" that the prints from the crime scene belonged to Mayfield (plus, he was said to have converted to Islam) and he was arrested, but the crime scene fingerprint was not perfect, and the print of Mayfield and that of the actual owner (an Algerian) were only *nearly* identical. Mayfield was exonerated, those responsible for the bombing were apprehended—and fingerprint analysis, especially using computer matching, has been scrutinized ever since.

the National Academy of Science examined the practice in a report, *Strengthening Forensic Science in the United States: A Path Forward*, in which they found that microscopic testing analysis of human hair was "highly unreliable." Even with this finding, many jurisdictions—mainly because of lack of funding or not having the time, means, or experts to conduct DNA tests—still use microscopic analysis of human hairs. (For more about hair examination and forensics, see the chapter "In the Crime Lab: Trace Evidence.")

Why have several agencies questioned microscopic human hair analysis used as evidence in criminal cases?

In early 2015, several agencies, including the U.S. Department of Justice (DOJ), the Federal Bureau of Investigation (FBI), the Innocence Project, and the National Association of Criminal Defense Lawyers (NACDL), reported that FBI examiners' testimonies in at least 90 percent of trial transcripts had erroneous statements based on microscopic human hair analysis. (These statements only included those looked at by the bureau as part of its Microscopic Hair Comparison Analysis Review.) All the cases reviewed were before 2000, which was before hair analysis using mitochondrial DNA testing became routine at the FBI. The FBI and the other agencies are, as of this writing, still reviewing many past criminal cases to determine other problems with analysis and testimonies based on microscopic hair analysis.

BITE MARK CONTROVERSIES

Why are bite marks controversial as evidence?

Although bite marks have been used in past criminal and injury cases, the use of them as evidence has recently become very controversial. The main reason is that bite mark interpretations can be extremely complex, as a bite does not just include the teeth but also the movement of a person's jaw, lips, and tongue. In addition, if the perpetrator or victim is moving, the bite mark will often look different than if the person was standing still. Bite marks also change over time (see sidebar), and if a person's skin has numerous bumps and indentations, it makes it difficult to interpret the actual shape and characteristics of the bite mark. Because of these controversies, if bite marks are presented as evidence in a court, they are offered in conjunction with other types of physical evidence. (For more about bite marks as evidence, see the chapter "In the Crime Lab: Analyzing a Body.")

What groups are responsible for questioning the use of bite marks as evidence?

In the past few years, several organizations have questioned the use of bite marks as evidence in criminal cases. For example, one of the first times bite marks were truly questioned as evidence occurred in 2009, when a report from the National Academy of Sciences stated, "The scientific basis is insufficient to conclude that bite mark comparisons can result in a conclusive match." Others followed, including studies that found no statistics to back up accurate comparisons between two or more sets of teeth. More recently, the Innocence Project Inc. of New York City has a history of challenging bite mark evidence in mainly criminal cases (for more about the Innocence Project, see this chapter). The President's Council of Advisors on Science and Technology, the Texas Forensic Science Commission, and many other academic researchers and scientists have stated that bite mark evidence is extremely unreliable and should not be used as evidence in a court of law.

What recently changed in the use of bite marks as evidence in a trial?

The use of bite marks as evidence in a trial was challenged again in 2016, when the American Board of Forensic Odontologists changed its guidelines (it certifies dentists as experts who identify remains based on teeth and bite mark comparisons to a suspect's teeth). The change was that members of the group could no longer conclude that a bite mark came from a certain individual or probably came from that person. The only mention a member could state was whether or not they could exclude a suspect—if they could make any conclusion about the bite marks at all. This was in response to the questions and wrong conclusions about bite marks that have occurred in the past few years.

What state no longer allows bite marks as admissible evidence in a trial?

In April 2016, the Texas' Forensic Science Commission recommended that bite mark comparison evidence "not be admitted" in criminal cases in the state until development of additional criteria was met. In addition, the Dallas County district attorney's office be-

Who is Steven Mark Chaney, and why is his case important to the field of bite mark analysis?

Construction worker Steven Mark Chaney (1956–) was convicted in the 1987 stabbing deaths of John (a drug dealer) and Sally Sweek in Dallas, Texas. According to the Innocence Project, Chaney was wrongly convicted based on a faulty interpretation of bite marks and in August 2016 was released. At the time of the trial, bite mark evidence linked Chaney to the crime by two expert witnesses in odontology (forensic dentistry), who testified that the bite marks were definitely from Chaney at the scene of the crime ("reasonable dental certainty" were the words used). It didn't seem to matter to the jury that Chaney had nine alibi witnesses who claimed that they had spent time with Chaney the day of the murders. Years later, when an affidavit was filed with the court, one of the expert witness odontologists at the original trial said that even an expert cannot truly and reliably match bite marks to teeth. Citing a Texas law passed in 2013—referred to as junk science law, which states that a review of the conviction can be done if new science contradicts the science used at a trial—the conviction was challenged, leading to Chaney's release.

came the first in the state to declare bite mark evidence "junk science." The main reasons were the many reports of false interpretation of evidence from such groups as the Innocence Project.

CONTROVERSIES AND DNA ANALYSIS

Why is the interpretation of DNA results so controversial?

DNA analysis results are often questioned for several reasons. For example, DNA technology has improved, making DNA analyses conducted a few decades ago suspect, as the tests may not have been as accurate. Others who question DNA results are concerned about several points, including the interpretation of the DNA analysis (whether the person interprets the results correctly), whether the methods being used are understood by the person doing the analysis, and whether the samples being tested are contaminated (by another person's DNA or possibly compromised by chemicals or other materials). (For more about DNA analysis, see the chapter "In the Crime Lab: DNA Analysis.")

How is the Frye test connected to controversies about DNA profiling and phenotyping?

The Frye test (or Frye Standard) is the legal standard that requires all scientific evidence to be widely accepted in its field—or, in other words, the test determines the admissibility of evidence based on whether the science behind it is accepted or not. When it comes to DNA profiling or phenotyping, some attorneys and judges (and some researchers) have suggested that neither passes the Frye test because of questions concerning an accurate analysis of certain DNA samples. Thus, both processes have caused a heated debate when it comes to accepting these types of DNA analyses. (For more about DNA profiling and phenotyping, see the chapter "In the Crime Lab: DNA Analysis.")

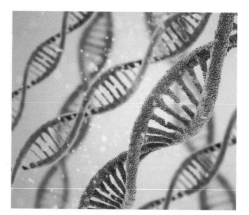

DNA testing is seen by the public as a miraculous way to positively link perpetrators to crimes and to exonerate the innocent, but some argue the tests can be flawed.

What is the Innocence Project?

According to its website, the Innocence Project was founded in 1992 and is a nonprofit legal organization committed to "exonerating wrongly convicted people through the use of DNA testing and to reforming the criminal justice system to prevent future injustice." As of this writing, it has exonerated 351 people who were wrongly imprisoned and has found close to 150 people who were the actual perpetrators.

Can a person be compensated for being incarcerated for years if DNA analysis eventually proves that they were innocent?

Yes, in many cases, DNA analysis can help prove that an incarcerated person was truly innocent. Overall, wrongful conviction compensation falls into two different types (as

Why has DNA analysis been questioned recently in New York City?

Not every town or city has a DNA analysis laboratory, but New York City's DNA laboratory in the office of the chief medical examiner is one of the more well known and fully equipped. The lab has had a reputation for two more complicated methods of DNA analysis that are beyond the standard practice of places like the FBI lab—the ability to identify DNA in tiny samples or in samples that are a mix of more than one person's genetic material. In 2017, the lab discontinued these two methods due to controversies that question the methods' validity, replacing them with newer, more broadly accepted methods of analysis (several criminal cases came into question, which led to the change in methods by the lab). As of this writing, because the two methods were used to analyze samples from hundreds (if not thousands) of cases, officials are concerned that such criticisms about the past DNA analyses may lead to retrials of certain incarcerated people—and many litigation headaches.

of this writing, as rules and regulations change or differ depending on various circumstances): federal and state. The federal wrongful conviction compensation statute is the only one that offers higher compensation for those who spent time on death row. Under this statute, a person can be awarded up to $50,000 per year of wrongful imprisonment and up to $100,000 per year on death row. In addition, states also have their own policies about compensation for wrongful conviction. For example, in Maine, if a person is convicted of a criminal offense and served time, received a pardon by the governor accompanied by a written finding of innocence, and the court finds the person innocent, they receive up to $300,000 per wrongful conviction (as of this writing). Other states, such as Alaska and Nevada, have no such statutes.

CRIMINAL BEHAVIORAL ISSUES

Why is NGRI, or "not guilty for reason of insanity," such an issue?

As with many problems with determining psychological profiles, many people who criticize NGRI have often cited that sane defendants use it to escape justice. In addition, not all people on a jury may understand the intricacies of the NGRI verdict—and how much weight it carries in terms of justice. In addition, some people who are insane may not get the legal counsel or help they truly need.

Do many criminals get away with NGRI?

Although it has been used as a defense in movies, television, and fiction stories, the use of NGRI is rare. It varies from state to state, but according to some legal resources, on the average, nationwide, less than 1 defendant in 100 actually raises the insanity defense. In fact, in several studies, it was shown that about 70 percent of all NGRI defendants withdrew their claim when an appointed expert was asked to evaluate the defendant—and found them to be legally sane. In the rest, the person was declared incompetent to stand trial, the court did not contest the claim of NGRI, or the charges were dropped.

What are some additional problems if a person is determined to be NGRI?

Several legal problems arise with the claim of "not guilty for reason of insanity." For example, regulations as to who can declare the sanity of a defendant is inconsistent from state to state. One survey noted that about 60 percent of states require that the expert witness retained to determine whether the defendant is insane has to be a psychologist or a psychiatrist, while around 20 percent wanted more certification to make such a decision. (The other 20 percent had even fewer rules for determining NGRI.) Problems with the person themselves is also an issue—some do not know, or are too mentally troubled, to even ask for such a defense from a lawyer, while some do not want to use such a defense, as they do not want to end up in a psychiatric facility. If they are determined to be NGRI, many times, the state has various treatments that do not help the person, such as a shorter duration than is truly needed or even a lesser quality of treatment.

What is neurocriminology, and why is it controversial?

Neurocriminology is a relatively new subfield of neuroscience, which includes looking at the different brain structures that may indicate that a person will exhibit criminal behavior. The idea is that the changes in the brain and its structure may point to why someone has a predisposition toward violence and aggressive behavior.

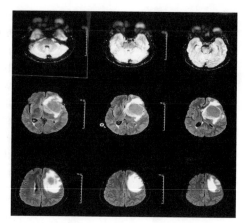

Neurocriminology is the study of how changes in brain structure—for example, damage to the frontal lobe—can lead to antisocial, even criminal behavior.

The controversy surrounding this field is nothing new. It is actually a well-known argument between behavioral scientists—or the case of nature versus nurture. In other words, does a person's brain structure (and genetics, for that matter) preclude them to violence and crime or is it more external factors, such as habits, lifestyle, a person's experiences and how they interpret them, abuse of drugs, problems with mental health, or exposure to violence? As always in such science discussions about human behavior, these ideas will remain controversial for a long time.

OTHER CONTROVERSIES

Why are eyewitness accounts not always reliable?

Not all eyewitness accounts are reliable. In fact, a great deal of research has been conducted regarding eyewitnesses and their "ability" to reliably remember what happened during an event, such as a bank robbery or accident. This is mainly because what humans view is always subjective. For instance, people view details differently, such as directions, heights, weights, sizes, shapes, colors, and other physical aspects of a scene. Or, the eyewitness may not realize that a perpetrator is in disguise, such as wearing a wig or mask, and therefore makes an inaccurate identification. Probably the most well-known problem with an eyewitness is the result of stress—most people are not as aware of what occurs when they witness a major event, such as a crime or accident. Most research indicates that when a person is under stress, it can lower their ability to recall various details of an event.

What conditions can often cause an eyewitness's testimony to be false?

Besides the stress of being on the witness stand, eyewitnesses can lead a jury to convict the wrong person. For example, leading questions from the attorneys and judge in the

What arson case led to a 2004 execution that now has questions about guilt?

In 2004, American auto mechanic Cameron Todd Willingham (1968–2004) was executed for murdering his three children by setting his house on fire in Corsicana, Texas. The conviction was mainly based on the testimony of an individual who testified that Willingham had confessed to the crime to him while they were both in jail, but by 2015, questions came up concerning Willingham's conviction, including whether the witness made up the testimony to lessen his own charges from another crime. In addition, before the execution (and several years after), numerous fire experts who looked at the evidence concluded that the fire had not been deliberately set, making the charges against Willingham even more questionable, and by 2017, the former state prosecutor at the Willingham trial was exonerated of a charge of misconduct in the trial. He had been accused by the Texas state bar of failing to disclose to Willingham's defense lawyer that the person who had given the testimony against Willingham was promised favorable treatment on an aggravated robbery conviction in return for the testimony against Willingham. As of this writing, the debate as to whether Willingham was truly guilty continues.

trial may make a witness (or victim as witness) recall things they never saw, events that never took place, and people who were never at the scene. Because most juries put a strong emphasis on the evidence of the eyewitness and the person's memory of the incident, the testimony may lead to a person being falsely convicted. In addition, the human memory is very vulnerable to bias and suggestions, especially from a third party. This could also cause the eyewitness to question—and often change their minds about—what they truly saw.

What are some reasons for controversies about arson fires?

Several questions have come up about interpreting the results of structural and other fires, including those that were thought to be caused by arson. In particular, fire investigators can often find certain evidence of accelerants used in a fire that often points to arson, but some fires have natural variability of burn patterns and damage characteristics—and even how they are affected by certain accelerants—that are naturally caused, even though they look as if it was arson.

FAMOUS (AND NOT-SO-FAMOUS) CRIMES AND FORENSIC SCIENCE

Note: Both famous and not-so-famous crimes in which forensic science has been used to investigate and analyze are numerous. What follows are some brief or very detailed looks at the more well-known crimes and how forensic science was used (or often not used) to gather evidence. Some of the crimes were solved; some were not....

LOOKING BACK: HISTORIC OCCURRENCES INTERPRETED WITH MODERN FORENSICS

Why is the death of Egyptian King Tutankhamen often called "the crime that wasn't"?

The death of the young Egyptian King Tutankhamen has been referred to as "the crime that wasn't," as it was once believed that the eighteen-year-old ruler died from a murderous blow to the skull, but several forensic examinations of the remains of the Egyptian pharaoh by scientists from Egypt and Germany around 2010 revealed otherwise. Through extensive DNA tests and CT scans, "King Tut" (as he is often called in the media) most likely succumbed to an infection in a leg that had recently been broken around the time he died. They also believe—because his parents were Pharaoh Akhenaten and one of the pharaoh's unnamed sisters (some references believe it may have been a cousin)—that Tutankhamen's incestuous birth weakened his immune system, and he was unable to fight off the infection. In addition, it appeared that King Tut also had several bouts of malaria that could have weakened his system and contributed to his demise. (It was also determined that the damage to King Tut's skull occurred after his death either during the embalming process or by the people who transported the mummified body when it was first found in 1922.)

How was forensic analysis used in the case of Napoléon Bonaparte's death?

Corsican-born French military and political leader Napoléon Bonaparte (1769–1821) gained prominence during and after the French Revolution. After leading several successful campaigns, including those in France, Italy, and Egypt, his name became well known by the aristocracy and French government. Such successes and military victories led to him becoming first consul (for life) and, eventually, led him to crown himself the emperor of France by 1812, but after being defeated in 1813 at the Battle of Leipzig, he was forced to renounce his throne. Exiled to the Mediterranean island of Elba for eleven months, he eventually made it back to France to claim the throne again, but fate would cause him to lose another battle—the Battle of Waterloo—in 1815. He was then exiled to the island of St. Helena in the South Atlantic Ocean, far from anywhere. In 1821, he became ill and died.

According to the American Museum of Natural History, a question has always surrounded his death, as studies of preserved samples of Napoléon's hair showed high levels of arsenic. In addition, when his body was exhumed in 1840 for reburial in Paris, France, his body was not as decomposed as it should have been for the amount of time he had been dead. (Arsenic creates a phenomenon called "arsenic mummification," as it slows down the decomposition of human tissue.) Many have speculated on his death, citing poisoning by his guards, stomach cancer, or foul play by a European government. Even certain pigments (for the bright green color) in the wallpaper (and the paste used to put up the wallpaper) at Longwood, where he spent his last days, had high arsenic lev-

What was usually the "poison of choice" in the 1800s?

According to the American Museum of Natural History, arsenic (and also often lead and mercury) was found in a plethora of items during the 1800s—from soaps, wallpaper, candles, and paper products to some popular medicinal tonics marketed as health supplements. Because of its easy access, it was also used by some unscrupulous people. For example, in France between 1835 and 1880, arsenic (called *poudre de succession* or "inheritance powder") was thought to have caused 40 percent of all the murders by poison in that country. Even in the United States between 1879 and 1889, in twelve counties in New York alone, around fifteen indictments for murder involved white arsenic. The reason for the use of arsenic to eliminate others was obvious. The chemical was difficult to discern in drinks or food, and, if given in small doses over time, the symptoms emulate many other types of natural diseases such as influenza or an ulcer, especially in the early stages of ingestion, but using this chemical is not so easy in modern times, as forensic techniques have dramatically improved and the effects are better understood, including how the poison spreads and affects the body.

els. This could have resulted in high amounts of the chemical in the former emperor—but it is thought that it was not enough to kill him.

In 2008, an Italian team at the Istituto Nazionale di Fisica Nucleare (Italian National Institute of Nuclear Physics) looked more deeply into Napoléon's death. Testing strands of Napoléon's hair from boyhood, his exile, the day of the death, and after—along with hair of his son, Napoléon II, and his wife Josephine—they found evidence of arsenic in all, and not only were Napoléon's arsenic levels from his boyhood and final days not any different, but the amounts were roughly one hundred times that of living people whose hairs were used for comparison. The researchers and toxicologists concluded that Napoléon probably wasn't poisoned by any person but died from the constant absorption of arsenic he and others were surrounded by every day. Since Napoléon had other ailments, doctors administered various potions that contained arsenic before he died to treat the various symptoms. It's no wonder the former emperor succumbed.

How did U.S. president Zachary Taylor die according to forensic analysis?

Zachary Taylor (1784–1850) was the twelfth president of the United States and served for just over a year in that capacity (March 1849 to July 1850), but what made him a study in forensics is the claim from some people that Taylor had died of unnatural causes, in particular, that he had been killed by arsenic poisoning, not because of gastroenteritis (or *cholera morbus*, a term usually used for those who died from unknown causes in the nineteenth century). This theory had several motivations—especially that the United States was in turmoil and on the brink of the Civil War. His alleged stance on slavery made him especially a target by disgruntled Southerners.

In 1991, upon the urging of a retired humanities professor who believed that Taylor's symptoms before he died were similar to arsenic poisoning, the former president's body was exhumed (after permission was granted by his distant relatives). Dr. Clara Rising (1923–2010) procured permission to have the body examined, and the Kentucky State medical examiner collected the samples to be analyzed from the corpse, including various dental, bone, and hair samples. The samples were sent to three different facilities, including the State Toxicology Laboratory (for colorimetric analysis, or a coloring agent used to detect trace elements), the University of Louisville (to scan

Was it gastroenteritis or arsenic poisoning that killed President Zachary Taylor? Forensics determined that it was natural causes and not foul play that killed him.

the samples with an electron microscope that was equipped with an x-ray diffraction spectrometer to show close-up views), and the Oak Ridge National Lab (for neutron activation analysis, or when a sample is bombarded with neutrons that cause the elements to form radioactive isotopes). The results showed that, indeed, former President Taylor had died from gastroenteritis and not arsenic poisoning—and no foul play had taken place.

Where is outlaw Clell Miller buried?

The U.S. Wild West had its share of killings and murders, and most of them are not even footnotes in history, but some killings caught the attention of many people. One was the outlaw and member of the notorious James–Younger gang (Jesse James and Cole Younger), Clell Miller (1849 [or 1850]–1878). Miller was shot and killed while attempting to rob the First National Bank of Northfield, Minnesota, along with gang member Bill Chadwell (alias Bill Stiles). Henry Wheeler, a medical student from the University of Michigan—and who had actually killed Miller during the robbery—was given permission to take the corpses of both gang members for dissection and study (a common practice in those days at medical schools), but the Miller family asked for Clell's body. The medical school student eventually became a doctor. Some believe he may not have given Miller's body to the family but rather Chadwell's body, as Wheeler displayed the skull of "Clell Miller" at his practice—some believe because he was the one who shot Miller and wanted a trophy.

After several others "owned" the skull after Wheeler, the skull eventually was examined in 2013 by a specialist. He used craniofacial superimposition, or comparing a skull's facial features (using a CT, or computed tomography, scan) with other evidence—in this case, postmortem photos of Miller and Chadwell. The expert concluded that based on similarities between bone structure of the skull and the men's images, the skull was not Chadwell's and may have been Miller's, but it was still doubtful. The researchers failed to obtain a bone sample from the Miller family grave of "Clell" (the skeleton's upper leg bone or femur or teeth) for DNA testing, and when an exhumation was granted, it was cancelled when a ground-penetrating radar showed four bodies in the grave—and no one could determine which one was "Clell's." Thus, who is buried in Clell's grave—and the location of Clell's true remains—remains a mystery.

What happened to the RMS *Titanic*?

The RMS (Royal Mail Steamer) *Titanic* was a British passenger ocean liner built between 1911 and 1912 and meant to be "virtually unsinkable." Contrary to that claim, on its maiden voyage, at 11:40 P.M. (ship time) on Sunday, April 14, 1912, the *Titanic* collided with an iceberg about ten times its size while crossing the North Atlantic Ocean on its way from Southampton to New York City. It was 375 miles (600 kilometers) south of Newfoundland. The collision sliced a gash into the vessel's hull between 220 to 245 feet (67 to 75 meters) long. The strike opened five or six of its alleged "watertight" compartments (the sixteen in total compartments were not watertight but open at the top) to ocean water—and the vessel sank within two and a half hours. Although the RMS

Carpathia arrived at the scene just under two hours after the collision—it rescued around seven hundred people—the total loss of life was over fifteen hundred people (references range from 1,503 to 1,517). The dead were a mix of passengers and crew, many of whom died of hypothermia in the cold North Atlantic waters (the water temperature was around 31 degrees Fahrenheit [–0.6 Celsius]) and drifted away with their life jackets on, while very few went down with the *Titanic*.

How were forensic techniques used to investigate the sinking of the *Titanic*?

The wreck of the RMS *Titanic* was discovered on the ocean floor in two pieces on September 1, 1985, by an expedition headed by American oceanographer Robert Ballard (1942–). The studies of the wreck—either through images or examination of items, such as steel and iron wrought rivets from the vessel—have since been conducted. One in particular was conducted in 2008. By using certain forensic analyses, experts examined the rivets under a microscope, tested the rivets mechanically, and created computer simulations to see how the rivets would respond to a similar iceberg collision. In this way, they reconstructed what may have truly happened when the vessel struck the iceberg that April night in 1912.

It took two years and around three thousand men to build the *Titanic*. The massive hull—the vessel was 882 feet (269 meters) long—was held together using around three million rivets. Many parts of the hull were triple riveted with steel rivets and some double riveted using wrought iron (handmade at the time). It was later discovered that the

Who are some well-known dead people who have been disinterred?

Not every famous person has been left alone after they died. Many have been disinterred, or dug up, to undergo additional analysis, including autopsies, toxicology examinations, and to move to a different cemetery (usually at the descendants' request). For example, a number of disinterments occurred to the remains of President Abraham Lincoln's assassin, American actor John Wilkes Booth (1838–1865). After being shot and killed, he was first buried in a storage room at a prison at the Washington Arsenal. When the prison was demolished in 1867, his remains were moved to a warehouse. In 1869, his remains were once again dug up and given to the family. Booth's remains are now in the family burial plot in Baltimore, Maryland. When American actor Charlie Chaplin died of natural causes in 1977, he was buried in Switzerland. In 1978, robbers dug up his body to hold for ransom, but they were quickly caught, and the body was recovered. (Chaplin is now buried in concrete to deter anyone from stealing his remains again.) Even more recently, the body of artist Salvador Dali was exhumed for a paternity suit in mid-2017. Subsequent DNA tests on the body proved a woman's claim that she was Dali's daughter was false.

six-inch rivets in the bow and stern were made of wrought iron, not steel. Thus, in the area of the hull that experienced the most damage, the seams had double rows of the wrought iron rivets. The forensic study of the steel used for certain rivets indicated that they were able to provide the necessary strength to hold the hull together, but the wrought iron rivets had up to three times the amount of slag in them than was acceptable—and the slag was in larger pieces within the rivets. It is thought that the poor quality was due not only to negligence of the people preparing the rivets (they may not have had the skills to make good rivets or were obtained from suppliers who were not certified to make quality rivets) but also because of the pressure to finish the *Titanic* and save money, causing the ship's parent company to order wrought iron that was below standards. The experts concluded that if the rivets had been better quality and stronger, fewer compartments would have been opened to the ocean waters and the vessel could have stayed afloat in time for the RMS *Carpathia* to rescue the passengers and crew.

How were Adolf Hitler's teeth once connected to the identification of his body?

It is known that Chancellor of Germany and Fuhrer of Nazi Germany Adolf Hitler (1889–1945) had very bad teeth, with only about five of his own teeth left in his mouth by the last year of World War II. Because of this, he needed an elaborate collection of gold crowns and bridges with porcelain veneers made by his dentist, Hugo Blaschke (1881–1959), and his dental assistants. One report used "forensic dentistry" to look at some teeth and jaw bones that eventually were thought to be from Hitler's body. The U.S.S.R. (Union of Soviet Socialist Republics) or the Soviet Union (today's Russia and environs) finally obtained what it thought were Hitler's teeth and jaw parts from the Reich Chancellery Garden, where Hitler's body was burned and buried (and allegedly exhumed and buried and exhumed again, depending on the reference) after he committed suicide. In an effort to verify the death of the dictator, the Soviets eventually found and interrogated Blaschke's assistants (Blaschke had escaped to the South and was captured by the Americans). Hitler's dental records were lost just before he died, but the dental assistants remembered much of the dental work they performed on Hitler. For

Some conspiracy theorists have suggested that Adolf Hitler staged his suicide with Eva Braun and actually escaped to South America. This idea was compounded by the lack of a body and dental records to confirm the teeth that were found were the Fuhrer's.

300

> ## What were the "Hitler Diaries"?
>
> In the early 1980s, it was claimed that German politician, dictator, and head of the Nazi Party Adolf Hitler (1889–1945) left behind sixty-two volumes of diaries, reportedly lost since a plane crash in 1945. Although the diaries were pronounced authentic by many (and rejected as fake by some), it took a short time to discover that they were merely fakes. The diaries were all forged by a prolific forger from Germany named Konrad Kujau (1938–2000) between 1981 and 1983, and they were miraculously "found" (not all at once) by German journalist Gerd Heidemann (1931–). In the end, it was mainly the paper and ink that proved that the documents could not have been written by Hitler—especially since the chemical compounds in the book's paper cover were not available when Hitler was alive.

example, they remembered what they called the "telephone bridge" that spanned a crown in Hitler's lower jaw. Sketches from memory also seemed to verify that the teeth and bones that the Soviets held were indeed Hitler's.

Why does doubt surround the death of Adolf Hitler?

After World War II, the Cold War between the Soviet Union and the United States halted any information exchange between the two countries, leading to several theories about Hitler's death, including that Hitler was alive and living in South America. At the end of the Cold War, papers were released that allegedly confirmed that Hitler had indeed died on April 30, 1945, but some doubt the authenticity of the bones held by the Soviets. In fact, a DNA analysis of certain bones claimed to have been Hitler's were analyzed in 2009 and found to actually be from a woman younger than forty years old. Thus, where Hitler's bones exist—and even whether he truly died in the bunker—will no doubt always be questioned.

DETAILS ON MORE FAMOUS CRIMES

LIZZIE BORDEN

Who was Lizzie Borden?

American Lizzie Andrew Borden (1860–1927) was the daughter of businessman Andrew Borden and stepdaughter of Abby Borden. Both parents were bludgeoned to death at their home in Fall River, Massachusetts, on August 4, 1892, Andrew in the parlor and Abby in the upstairs bedroom. Both were killed with a hatchet, and Lizzie Borden was arrested on August 11—then eventually acquitted—for their murders.

Why do some people think Lizzie Borden killed her father and stepmother?

After the police arrived at the Borden home, many discrepancies were found in Lizzie's answers to certain questions. The police also found her seemingly too calm for such a calamity. Days after the murders, other indications arose that Lizzie could have killed her parents. After all, Andrew Borden was frugal to the point of denying certain conveniences to his family, such as indoor plumbing. This, and his marrying of Abby Borden (Lizzie's mother had died), broke his relationship with Lizzie and her sister, Emma, even more—and offered a good reason for Lizzie to kill them. Lizzie was also seen by a friend burning a blue dress in a kitchen fire on August 7, 1892. When questioned, Lizzie said that it was stained with paint while doing housework. Because of her strange answers and what the police believed was

While many people strongly suspected Lizzie Borden killed her parents with a hatchet in 1892, investigators did not do a great job collecing evidence. Without a convincing case, Lizzie was acquitted.

"destruction of evidence" (the dress—she was allegedly wearing a blue dress the day of the murders), Lizzie was indicted for the murders on December 2, 1892.

How was the investigation of the Borden murders hampered?

The investigation of the Borden murders was hampered in several ways—especially by the lack of evidence. Initially, the investigators made several mistakes, including not checking Lizzie for bloodstains at the crime scene and agreeing not to search Lizzie's room too much after the murder, as she told them she "wasn't feeling well" that day. The hatchet allegedly used for the crime was found in the basement but could not be used as evidence (fingerprinting was in its infancy and was never used in the evidence search). It was also not proven that it was the instrument used to kill the Bordens. The blade was clean and the handle broken off and it looked as if dust had been added to the hatchet, making it appear to have been untouched in the basement for a while.

Why do some people think that Lizzie Borden couldn't have killed her father and stepmother?

Not everyone believed that Lizzie killed her father and stepmother. Andrew Borden was an extremely wealthy businessman and was not popular in Fall River, making many enemies on his rise to power and money. Other suspects could have killed the Bordens, including the maid, Bridget Sullivan; Andrew Borden's illegitimate son, William Borden; and even Lizzie's older sister, Emma.

Was Lizzie Borden ever convicted of the murders?

The newspapers of the time printed literally hundreds of stories about the gruesome murders, and by the time the trial started on June 5, 1893, Lizzie Borden was a media sensation (even without Facebook or the Internet!). It is said that when the damaged skulls of her parents were brought into the courtroom, she swooned. The defense argued that her contrary statements in the original inquest were justifiable, and, thus, those statements were ruled inadmissible. She never took the stand during the entire trial, and in ninety minutes, twelve men of the jury decided that she was not guilty. On June 20, she was acquitted of the murders. It is often said that one of the great advantages Lizzie and her defense team had was that, in 1893, few people believed that a woman—especially of her background—would commit such a brutal crime.

THE LINDBERGH KIDNAPPING

What was the Lindbergh kidnapping?

A crime that stunned the world occurred on March 1, 1932, when the twenty-month-old Charles A. Lindbergh Jr. was kidnapped. He was the son of the famous American aviator, Charles Lindbergh (1902–1974; he made the first solo nonstop flight from New York to Paris in 1927) and American aviator and writer Anne Morrow Lindbergh (1906–2001). According to the Federal Bureau of Investigation (FBI) archives, the child was kidnapped from his home in East Amwell, New Jersey, between 8 and 10 P.M. The child's disappearance from his second-floor bedroom was discovered just after 10 P.M. by the child's nurse, Betty Gow. The Lindberghs and Gow searched the premises and did not find the child, but they did find, on the windowsill of the nursery, a ransom note demanding $50,000. The local police were notified, and the New Jersey State Police assumed charge of the investigation. After the police arrived at the kidnapping scene, they began to find evidence of the crime—but nothing to incriminate anyone. The footprints on the floor of the nursery were not conclusive enough to trace, and no evidence of blood or fingerprints was found. A two-section ladder was used to reach the nursery, but it was split in two.

How many ransom notes were sent in the kidnapping?

The Lindberghs and many other local, state, and government officials made widespread appeals for more negotiations from the kidnapper (or kidnappers—no one knew at that time how many were involved), and the police asked the public for any clues in solving the case. A second ransom note was received on March 6, 1932, asking for $70,000. A police conference was held in which various theories and further procedures were discussed. The Lindberghs began negotiating through their attorney, Henry Breckenridge, and on March 8, a third ransom note was received by Breckenridge. This time, the kidnapper did not approve of the Lindberghs' "go-between" and requested a note in the newspaper. The same day, John Condon, a retired school principal, published a note in the *Bronx Home News* offering to be a go-between and pay an extra $1,000 for the return of the child. The next day, another ransom note was received by Condon, agreeing that he would be the go-between. About March 10, Condon received $70,000 in cash as ransom and started negotiations in the newspaper using the code name "Jafsie."

By March 12, a fifth ransom note was received, explaining where a sixth ransom note could be found, which led Condon to meet with an unidentified man in the Woodlawn Cemetery. The man who called himself "John" said that he would provide evidence of the child's identity. Still negotiating via the newspapers, on March 16, Condon received a seventh ransom note and the Lindbergh baby's sleeping suit. An eighth ransom note was received by Condon on March 21, insisting on complete compliance to the kidnapper's wants (and the note also mentioned that the kidnap-

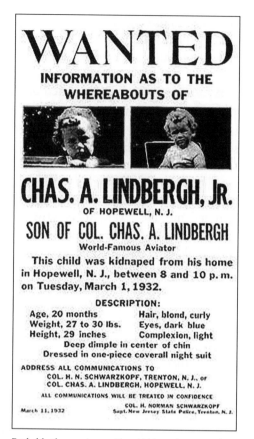

Probably the most sensational kidnapping case of the twentieth century, the disappearance of aviator Charles Lindbergh's infant son in 1932 led to a conviction. Sadly, the boy's lifeless body was found just a few miles from his house.

ping had been planned for a year). On March 30, a ninth ransom note was received, threatening to increase the ransom to $100,000. The tenth note came on April 1, telling Condon to have the money ready the following night. The eleventh ransom note was received on April 2, which led Condon to find the twelfth note in front of a certain greenhouse in the Bronx. That note lowered the ransom amount to $50,000. Condon met and gave "John" the money in exchange for a receipt and the thirteenth note, which indicated that the child could be found on a boat named *Nellie* near Martha's Vineyard, Massachusetts, but, as most people suspected, their search was unsuccessful.

How was the Lindbergh baby kidnapper found?

The investigation of the Lindbergh baby kidnapping was long and arduous, with many leads and false starts. Hundreds of photographs and data of known criminals were examined, along with other suspects, in trying to find the elusive "John" who made contact with John Condon several times. Thousands of leads were collected from across the country. Banks in New York were also notified to watch for the ransom money, and rewards were offered for information resulting in the apprehension, arrest, and conviction of the kidnapper or kidnappers. Even the president became involved: besides eventually giving the FBI jurisdiction in the case, in 1933, President Franklin D. Roosevelt made a proclamation requiring the return to the U.S. Treasury of all gold and gold certificates. This helped, as about $40,000 of the ransom money was in gold certificates.

The kidnapper of Charles A. Lindbergh Jr. was eventually found because of two attentive people. On September 15, 1934, service station manager Walter Lyle asked for 98 cents for gas from the driver of a dark blue Dodge sedan. The driver said he only had a $10—and it was a gold certificate, too. Because the certificates had been out of circulation for a year and his company warned that counterfeiters might attempt to make fake gold certificates, Lyle wrote the driver's New York license plate number—4U13-41—on the margin of the bill. When Lyle deposited the bill three days later, the bank teller noted the unusual bill. Checking the bill's serial number with the Lindbergh list, they found a match—it was part of the $70,000 paid to the kidnapper. Authorities were called, and the license plate number search indicated that the car belonged to German-born carpenter Bruno Richard Hauptmann (1899–1936).

How was forensic evidence used in the court case against Bruno Hauptmann?

A good deal of evidence led to the conviction of Bruno Richard Hauptmann. After tracking the carpenter down in a residential neighborhood in the Bronx, police and federal investigators discovered around $13,750 in ransom money hidden inside a dirty oil can. They also found a plank with the address and phone number of John Condon. Hauptmann was also identified by Condon as the person who he met to deliver the ransom money. Forensic experts also examined the wood found in Hauptmann's attic, verifying that it was the same wood as the ladder used in the kidnapping. Hauptmann was also identified by several eyewitnesses, including people who had seen him around the estate and those merchants who had accepted some of the Lindbergh gold certificates as payment. The most intriguing evidence was based on handwriting analysis. In particular, examination of the ransom notes by handwriting experts led them to believe that the person was probably German by birth but had spent some time in America. When they compared some of Hauptmann's handwriting to the ransom notes, the matches were undeniable.

What was the outcome of the Lindbergh kidnapping case?

Unfortunately, on May 12, 1932, the decomposed body of the kidnapped baby was accidentally found partly buried about four miles southeast of the Lindbergh home. The baby was around 45 feet (13.7 meters) from the highway near Mount Rose, New Jersey, found by an assistant, William Allen, to a truck driver. The coroner ruled that the child had been dead for two months and died of a blow to the head. After all the evidence was presented, Hauptmann was convicted of murder and kidnapping. He died in the electric chair in the New Jersey State Prison in Trenton on April 3, 1936.

JonBenét Ramsey Murder

What was the JonBenét Ramsey murder?

JonBenét Patricia Ramsey (1990–1996) was a Boulder, Colorado, child beauty pageant queen who was murdered in her family's home on December 25, 1996. Present were JonBenét's father John (a wealthy businessman), mother Patsy (former beauty queen and former Miss West Virginia), and nine-year-old brother Burke.

Where was JonBenét Ramsey found?

JonBenét Ramsey's body was found by her father in the basement of their home on December 26, 1996, several hours after her mother discovered a ransom note for $118,000. The girl had been hit on the head, strangled with a nylon rope and crude garrote, her wrists tied, and tape was over her mouth.

Why was the ransom note evidence so confusing?

Of the many questions concerning the murder, investigators could not understand why someone would murder JonBenét in her own home and leave a ransom note that she was kidnapped. It was also noted that the paper used for the ransom note came from a notebook in the family home, which investigators believe meant that it was written at the scene of the crime (thought of as strange not only because the family was upstairs, but in a very tense situation like a kidnapping, most people would not stop to write such a note). In addition, according to former Boulder police chief Mark Beckner, who headed the murder investigation, experts were puzzled as to why the ransom note was two and a half pages long.

What was the problem with the evidence found in the investigation?

The biggest problem with the gathering of evidence at the Ramsey home was that the house was not treated as a crime scene that morning. It took until the afternoon to declare the crime scene, and by then, people—including friends and family—had walked in and out of the house, possibly destroying a great deal of evidence. In addition, John Ramsey, after finding his daughter in the basement, allegedly brought her upstairs from the basement and covered her with a blanket, destroying any possible evidence at the crime scene. Thus, many events led to a lack of certain evidence in the entire case.

What conclusions came from the evidence collected?

One set of evidence came from DNA found on the clothing JonBenét was wearing that night. Several DNA tests have been made on various items since the murder—some analyzed years after JonBenét was killed. So far, according to most sources, no DNA evidence connected any family member to the murder (including JonBenét's mother, father, and older brother Burke), or several other suspects, such as a person who was a known pedophile in the area (although some still disagree as to whether the DNA evidence, including the DNA found on the clothes of JonBenét, were from one or multiple people). In addition, no connection was found between the father's and mother's—both were initially suspects—handwriting and the ransom note.

Has any new evidence been brought forth in the murder investigation?

In the past two decades-plus, little new evidence has been brought forth concerning the murder of JonBenét Ramsey. Numerous investigative reports and television documentaries have brought up all the theories, but no one has been arrested for the murders. JonBenét's parents were initially suspected, along with her brother Burke, but DNA evidence cleared the Ramseys of any criminal charges in the death in 2008 (Patsy Ramsey had died of ovarian cancer in 2006). Even today, with all the experts and forensic analysis, along with the more advanced DNA tests—everything still appears to be inconclusive, and the case has never been solved.

WOOD CHIPPER MURDER

What is often called the "Wood Chipper Murder"?

Helle Lorck Nielsen Crafts (1947–1986) was a former Danish flight attendant killed by her husband, airline pilot Richard Crafts (1937–), in 1986—a murder in Newtown, Connecticut, that is often called the "Wood Chipper Murder" (also seen as "Woodchipper Murder"). Crafts was thought of as a philanderer, and Helle had told some of her friends that he had had numerous affairs. One report stated that Helle told her friends in late 1986 that if anything happened to her, "don't assume it was an accident."

What was some of the forensic evidence Richard Crafts left behind?

One reason why Richard was found guilty of murder is because of a snowplow driver. In the middle of a severe snowstorm in November 1986, a snowplow driver noticed a wood chipper on the back of a U-Haul box van he had to swing around while plowing near Lake Zoar. He also noted that more than a foot of snow had covered the ground so tree branches would be difficult to reach, the area was nowhere near a wood source, and almost everyone was off the road. In addition, wood chips were around the chipper. It didn't make sense, but when the story of a missing woman—Helle Crafts—was brought out, he contacted authorities.

After several leads, including the snowplow driver's information, investigators began to find evidence of Richard Crafts's involvement in the crime. Further evidence included a rented wood chipper (not only was it strange to rent such a machine in the winter, but it came back to the commercial rental store in pristine condition—almost too clean); a chainsaw—with the serial number filed off—near the lake where the wood chipper was used (Crafts used it to cut up the body); and even more incriminating, investigators found thousands of bits of evidence (teeth, bones, blonde hair, tissue fibers, and pieces of a letter addressed to Helle) at the lake around the chipper site.

Was Richard Crafts ever convicted?

Yes, Richard Crafts was eventually convicted of murdering Helle Crafts. His first trial ended in a mistrial because of one juror who held out, but Crafts was found guilty and sentenced to fifty years in prison after his second trial. He will be eligible for parole in 2021.

FAMOUS SERIAL KILLERS

JACK THE RIPPER

Who was "Jack the Ripper"?

"Jack the Ripper" was the self-proclaimed alias of the serial killer—some suggest killers—who murdered at least five prostitutes in London from August to November 1888 (and more murders may have occurred after 1888, but investigators did not have enough evidence that it was Jack the Ripper). The killer mutilated the women's bodies in an unusual manner, indicating that he had knowledge of human anatomy. This is why many historians who have examined the case have pointed to someone who had a background that included anatomy, including physicians, morticians, and, some even say, butchers.

Where did the name "Jack the Ripper" originate?

Not everyone agrees about the origin of "Jack the Ripper," with some historians suggesting that it may have even been a journalist who wanted to sell more newspapers! The first time the enigmatic serial killer of five prostitutes in London's East End allegedly called himself "Jack the Ripper" was in a letter forwarded to the Scotland Yard in September 1888 (some claim another letter first used the title, but others say the letter was faked). This note, called the "Dear Boss" letter, threatened to "cut the ladys (*sic*) ear off"; the latest victim had her ear nicked—and, thus, the letter was not considered a hoax. (Once again, still other historians suggest that this letter was written by a journalist.) Another letter thought to have come from the killer was called the "From Hell" letter, or the "Lusk Letter," as it was received

The "From Hell" letter from Jack the Ripper declared that he ate a victim's kidney and saved the other one for the police. Many misspellings indicate a low education level, while police suspected the real Ripper was from the gentry.

by George Lusk, the leader of the Whitechapel Vigilance Committee, or volunteers who patrolled the streets of the Whitechapel district during the "Jack the Ripper" murder spree. The letter was posted in 1888, along with half a human kidney (one of the latest victims had had her kidney removed), by the person claiming to be "Jack the Ripper."

Who were the suspects in the Whitechapel ("Jack the Ripper") murders?

After the nicknaming of the killer (and massive amount of coverage) in the newspaper of the day, the public's interest in the case was overwhelming. As a result, the police received hundreds of letters claiming to be "Jack the Ripper," but no one was ever arrested or found guilty of the murders. Over the past century since the murders, numerous speculations have come up as to the true identity of Jack, with a plethora of suspects "investigated." Most don't fit the murderer profile, while others are outlandish (such as author Lewis Carroll [*Alice in Wonderland*] and Prince Albert Victor, eldest son of King Edward VII). Trying to determine the true identity of Jack the Ripper will probably always be debated. In particular, in the nineteenth century, collection of evidence was not as advanced as modern times, making it difficult to narrow down a true suspect. More recent examinations of the evidence have also led to several guesses about Jack the Ripper's true identity, but such educated guesses are difficult to prove, as the evidence is no longer available (and some of it contradictory)—and the possible person or persons responsible are now long dead.

BELLE GUNNESS

Who was Belle Gunness?

Belle Sorenson Gunness (1859–1908?; some references believe c. 1930) was a Norwegian-born American who eventually became one of the country's most prolific serial killers. It is thought that she murdered over two dozen people—men, women, and children (including some of her own)—something a strong, six-foot, over-two-hundred-pound woman could do. Her crimes were only discovered when the Gunness farmhouse burned down in 1908 in La Porte, Indiana, when the remains of three of her children and a headless woman were discovered along with the unearthing of other butchered remains.

Why was the Gunness farm called the "Murder Farm"?

After the fire burned down the farmhouse on the Gunness farm, investigators found

Belle Gunness's murder spree was only discovered after her farmhouse burned in 1908, revealing several bodies, including three of her own children.

many human remains, all of whom were thought to be murdered, thus, the nickname for the farm became the "Murder Farm." Authorities unearthed three bodies of Gunness's children and a headless woman's body in the house and at least eleven people buried near the hog pen. Because the authorities never searched the property thoroughly, it is thought that more remains were probably buried elsewhere on the property. Based on reports of missing people who reportedly had some contact with Belle Gunness, it is estimated (it varies by each report) that she murdered between twenty-five and forty-nine people.

How did Belle Gunness lure her victims to her home?

Belle Gunness had several different ways of luring her victims, including her own children. For example, Belle married Mads Sorenson and had two biological children who survived infancy and a foster child.

- *Husbands*—Her first male victims may have been her first and second husbands, Mads Sorenson and Peter Gunness. Sorenson died on July 30, 1900, the only day his two life insurance policies overlapped (his doctor ruled his death as heart failure). Belle moved to La Porte, Indiana, after that, purchasing the farm on McClung Road. She eventually married local butcher Peter Gunness in 1902, and only one week later, Peter's infant daughter died (Belle was watching her). Peter died when a sausage grinder and jar of hot water (allegedly) accidentally fell on him less than a year later. Although the coroner ruled his death suspicious, Belle was not convicted—and she collected on yet another life insurance policy.

- *Men*—Belle Gunness attracted men by advertising in the matrimonial columns of several Midwestern Norwegian-language newspapers. She also advertised for handymen to help work on the farm. Several men answered both types of ads, traveling to see Belle in La Porte, and many were never seen again.

- *Women*—Although more men than women were reported missing after contact from Belle, some victim reports were of women. In particular, it is thought that the woman's body found in the burned farmhouse was probably someone Belle had found who looked the same physically. She left the body without a head, so the authorities would think it was Belle who died in the fire. (This has never been proven.)

- *Children*—Belle Gunness had three children—all of whom either died in the farmhouse fire or were killed by Belle earlier. Her foster child was found with the bodies of at least eleven people near the hog pen, which included three adolescents, an infant, and a woman.

Was the investigation of the Gunness farm mishandled?

Yes, possibly because of the inexperience and crude recovery methods of the investigators—it was a horrific discovery for such a "small town"—the search of the Gunness farm was not as informative as it could have been. One of the only ways information was uncovered about the Belle Gunness murders was when, in 1910, a Gunness farm worker, Ray Lamphere, made an alleged deathbed confession that he had only helped Belle bury the dead, but he did not kill anyone. He also gave some details of Belle's methods: she would have the man who answered one of her ads to dinner, drug them, and hit them over the head with a meat cleaver, or she would just feed the unsuspecting victim strychnine. She would then get rid of the body, either feeding the remains to the hogs or just have Lamphere help her bury the body near the hog pen. In that confession, too, Lamphere swore that Belle Gunness had not died in the fire but was still alive. He also mentioned that Belle was a rich woman, stealing a total of close to $250,000 from her victims over several years.

Was Belle Gunness ever found?

It is unknown whether Belle Gunness truly died in her farmhouse's fire. After the fire, numerous reports came up of someone resembling Belle Gunness in places around the country. In 2007, a team of forensic anthropologists from the University of Indiana had permission to exhume Belle's coffin, but instead of just finding an older woman's bones, they also found the remains of two children. This seemed to be more evidence that the investigation was mishandled. In 2008, the forensic team returned to exhume the remains of the three children found in the basement after the farmhouse fire. They also hoped to extract DNA from an envelope and stamp known to have been sent by Belle Gunness, but the DNA was too old to get a viable sample, and the other tests were inconclusive—and Belle's final days are still a mystery.

TED BUNDY

Who was Ted Bundy?

American Theodore Robert Bundy (1946–1989) was a serial killer thought to be responsible for assaulting and murdering an estimated thirty or more young women and girls during the 1970s (and possibly earlier). He was known as a kidnapper, burglar, rapist, and necrophile. Most of his victims seemed to resemble a woman who once severed a relationship with Bundy, with most of his victims from college campuses in Washington, Utah, Colorado, and, finally, Florida.

Rapist, serial killer, and necrophiliac Ted Bundy (1946–1989) was judged sane, found guilty, and executed for his crimes after he confessed to killing thirty women.

When was Ted Bundy arrested?

He was arrested in 1975, but he was only convicted of kidnapping, as no evidence connected him to any murders. In 1977, while he was preparing to stand trial for murder in Colorado, he escaped to Florida, where he killed three more people in early 1978. By February 1978, he was captured (he was stopped in Florida for a traffic violation). He was finally convicted of several murders because certain evidence was finally connected to him. He was put to death in the electric chair in 1989.

How did forensic methods lead to the arrest and conviction of Ted Bundy?

Ted Bundy was finally convicted of several murders based on forensic evidence. One piece of evidence was in the form of a bite mark on the buttock of one of his victims (Lisa Levy). In this case, a bite mark proved to be good evidence, as the mark matched Bundy's crooked and chipped teeth. Another piece of evidence also convicted Bundy of the murder of twelve-year-old Kimberly Leach, as a fiber found in his van matched the girl's clothing.

THE GREEN RIVER KILLER

Who was the "Green River killer"?

American serial killer Gary Leon Ridgway (1949–) was eventually found to be the "Green River killer," a person who murdered at least forty-nine people (and claimed to have murdered about seventy-one people, although some experts believe it was closer to ninety). Most of his victims were strangled. They were mostly prostitutes, as he once stated that he "hated most of them" and were "easy to pick up," or runaways, women in vulnerable circumstances, and drug addicts. He did most of the killings near Tacoma and Seattle, Washington, dumping many of the bodies along the banks of the Green River. Others, in order to throw off suspicion by the police, would be disposed of in other places, such as Oregon. He also used other items from people that would have DNA evidence, such as gum or cigarettes near the crime scenes (which many people say is why he was not caught for close to two decades). It was not for lack of trying on the police's

---

How was Ted Bundy connected to the "Green River killer"?

In a bizarre twist, serial killer Ted Bundy (see above) helped to capture the "Green River killer" by offering his ideas about the killer's motives. In the 1980s, a task force was created (the Green River Task Force) in order to find and arrest the Green River killer. Two of the people on the task force—Robert Keppel and Dave Reichert—also interviewed Ted Bundy while he was in prison (Bundy originally contacted the task force, volunteering to help). Bundy suggested that the Green River killer was returning to his victims' bodies in order to perform acts of necrophilia. He also speculated that if the police found a fresh grave, they should wait for the killer to return to the scene of that crime. Although this information was correct, the police would never find a fresh grave, and it took until 2001 for Ridgway to be caught.

part—in 1984, Ridgway took and apparently passed a polygraph test. Later investigation of that test proved that he had failed, but no one caught it at that time (for more about the problems with polygraphs, see the chapter "Controversies in Forensic Science").

How was Gary Ridgway caught?

In 2001, investigators finally collected the DNA evidence they needed to arrest Ridgway based on a saliva swab collected from him in 1987: DNA analysis of the semen found on several of the victims matched the DNA in the saliva. This connected him to four of the victims, while three more murders were connected to Ridgway after spray paint traces were found on the bodies. The paint was the same used at the Kenworth Truck factory where Ridgway worked. Ridgway agreed to a plea bargain (admitting to killing more people) in order to avoid the death penalty and led the police to the bodies of many of his other victims. He was eventually convicted of killing forty-eight people between 1982 and 1998 and pleaded guilty to a forty-ninth victim in 2011 after being connected to the body. As of this writing, he is serving forty-eight consecutive life sentences without parole.

FAMOUS BOMBINGS

What were some famous bombings in the United States?

A large number of bombings have occurred in the United States by both domestic and foreign terrorists. Several are well known for not only the bombing but for the search—and often discovery—of the bombers using forensic techniques. The following lists only a few of the more well-known bombings in the United States:

- *The Boston Marathon Bombing*—The Boston Marathon bombing took place at 2:49 P.M. Eastern Daylight Time on April 15, 2013, near the finish line of the Boston Marathon. Two homemade bombs detonated twelve seconds and 210 yards apart on Boylston Street, killing three people and injuring around 264 people (sixteen who lost limbs). The suspects were identified through the registration records on their Honda, which was left at the scene—two brothers whose family immigrated to the United States around 2002 from Chechnya: then-twenty-six-year-old Tamerlan Tsarnaev and nineteen-year-old Dzhokhar "Jahar" Tsarnaev. The evidence against the two brothers not only included traces of the bomb and detonation items but also documents, such as evidence of the use of a credit card by Dzhokhar for items to remotely detonate bombs and the purchase of two backpacks used to carry the bombs. Tamerlan died in a shootout with police after the bombing. His brother was captured and given the death penalty in 2015 for the bombing. (A Massachusetts Institute of Technology [MIT] police officer was also killed as well as two others injured by the brothers during the manhunt, one of whom died from his injuries a year later.) As of this writing, appeals are being made, and Dzhokhar is still on death row.

313

- *Atlanta Olympic Bombing*—Two people died (one from a heart attack) and 111 people were injured when a pipe bomb exploded in the Centennial Olympic Park in Atlanta, Georgia. It occurred on July 27 at the 1996 Summer Olympics and was set by Eric Robert Rudolph (1966–), a former U.S. Army explosives expert. Rudolph called the police to warn them of the bomb. A temporary security guard, Richard Jewell, noticed a green backpack, alerted authorities, and, after starting to clear the area, the bomb went off, but because of the warning, many lives were saved. Rudolph was identified as the perpetrator because of two eyewitnesses who saw Rudolph leaving the scene in his truck. For five years, he was on the run. (The FBI and other law-enforcement agencies are said to have spent $24 million to catch Rudolph—also wanted by then for several abortion clinic bombings and antigay-motivated bombings.) He was finally caught in Murphy, North Carolina, in 2003. He agreed to a plea bargain; he was sentenced in 2005 to two consecutive life terms without parole for the murder of a police officer in 1998 and, for the bombing, another two consecutive life terms.

- *First World Trade Tower Bombing*—The terrorist attacks on the World Trade Center Towers in New York City on September 11, 2001, was preceded by a bombing—on February 26, 1993. A Ryder rental truck with a bomb detonated beneath the North Tower's parking garage (the bomb was reported to be a 1,200-pound (544-kilogram) nitrate-hydrogen gas-enhanced bomb stuffed with cyanide). The blast caused a hole 200 feet (61 meters) by 100 feet (30.5 meters) wide and several stories deep and caused the ceiling of the train station underneath the tower to collapse. Six people died, and more than a thousand people were injured. The evidence found included vehicle parts with identification numbers (tracing back to who rented the truck) and bomb-making chemicals in a rented shed of the suspects. In 1994, Mohammed Salameh, Nidal Ayyad, Mahmud Abouhalima, and Ahmad Ajaj were arrested, convicted, and sentenced to prison terms of 240 years each for the bombing (although in 1998, the sentences were vacated, and in 1999, they were all resentenced to terms of more than one hundred years). In 1995, the mastermind of the bombing was captured, Ramzi Ahmed Yousef, who received a sentence of 240 years in prison. Eyad Ismoil, who drove the truck, was sentenced in 1998 for a term of 240 years.

- *Oklahoma Federal Building Bombing*—The Oklahoma City bombing was carried out by ex-Army soldier and security guard—and a homegrown terrorist and antigovernment militant—Timothy McVeigh (1968–2001). On April 19, 1995, McVeigh drove a truck bomb outside the Alfred P. Murrah Federal Building in downtown Oklahoma City, Oklahoma. The explosion—a bomb made of around 4,800 pounds (2,200 kilograms) of ammonium nitrate fertilizer, nitromethane, and diesel fuel mixture—killed 168 people, and more than six hundred people were injured. The evidence found that led to McVeigh's capture and conviction included pieces of the truck with an identification number, which was then traced to a body shop where employees helped to put together a sketch of the person who rented the van. Around ninety minutes after the bombing, McVeigh was already in prison—but not because of the bombing. A state trooper noticed that McVeigh's car was missing a license plate, and McVeigh was found to have a concealed weapon. Additional evidence included chemicals used in the explosion that were found on a business card and his clothes, and a friend, Terry Nichols (1955–), who helped build the bomb (he was convicted of coconspiring with McVeigh and sentenced to life in prison without parole). McVeigh was convicted and executed for his crime in 2001.

What were some well-known bombings in other countries?

A very large number of bombings have occurred in countries other than the United States. The following lists only a few of the more well-known ones:

Domestic terrorist Timothy McVeigh nearly completely destroyed the Oklahoma Federal Building in 1995, killing many innocent people, including women and children.

- *Lockerbie Bombing of Pan Am Flight 103*—In 1988, at 31,000 feet, Pan Am Flight 103 (a Boeing 747) in a flight from London to New York exploded over Lockerbie, Scotland, thirty-eight minutes after takeoff. The explosion and subsequent crash killed all 259 people on board and eleven people on the ground. The evidence included fragments of a suitcase believed to have held the bomb and pieces of a circuit board of a certain radio cassette player. Pieces of baby clothes from the suitcase were found to have been made in Malta—which were traced back to a merchant who claimed he sold them to a Libyan man eventually identified as Abdelbaset Ali al-Megrahi (1952–2012). Based on other evidence found at the scene, al-Megrahi was arrested, convicted, and indicted on 270 counts of murder in November 1991. He was sentenced to life in prison, and although he always proclaimed his innocence, he was unsuccessful in an appeal against his conviction. He was eventually allowed to return to Libya, where he died of cancer in 2012.

- *Japan Subway Gassing*—On March 25, 1995, during the morning rush hour in Tokyo, Japan, five two-men terrorist groups riding on separate subway trains on three different lines converged at the Kasumigaeki station, secretly releasing lethal sarin gas into the air. The attack killed thirteen people and left more than six thousand sick or injured. To spread the sarin, the cultists, members of the Aum Shinrikyo religious doomsday cult, left plastic bags filled with the nerve gas on the floors of the trains and punctured them with sharpened umbrellas. Because sarin had already been released elsewhere in Japan a few years prior to the Tokyo attack, authorities were able to act fast, as the symptoms of the people in the Tokyo attack were similar. Newspapers, containers, and other items from the crime scene were quickly taken to a lab to be analyzed, and sarin was detected. It was determined that the attack was masterminded by half-blind Japanese guru Shoko Asahara, whose real name is Chizuo Matsumoto. (Asahara told his disciples that the reason for such attacks was a holy attempt to elevate the doomed souls of this world to a higher spiritual stage.) Asahara and several others in the cult were eventually arrested; in 2012, the two last wanted suspects in the bombing were arrested. As of this writing, Asahara remains on death row, while many of the others arrested were given life in prison sentences.

• *Madrid Train Bombing in Spain*—On March 11, 2004, a commuter train was rocked by three powerful explosions. Then, in the next two minutes—between 7:37 and 7:39 A.M. precisely—another seven bombs went off in three different trains, the explosions killing a total of 192 people and injuring around two thousand. It was the worst terror attack in Spain's history and occurred just three days before a highly contested general election. The evidence eventually pointed to 116 suspects. Of that number, twenty-nine went to trial; twenty-one were found guilty on a range of charges from forgery to murder, with two of the defendants sentenced each to more than forty thousand years in prison. The findings indicated that the bombings were the work of a radical Jihadist cell that was loosely linked to al-Qaeda. (At one point, the discovery of a fingerprint on a plastic bag from the scene led authorities to accuse Brandon Mayfield, an Oregon lawyer; they were later found to be from an Algerian national. Mayfield was released two weeks after his arrest—with an official apology from the FBI who accused him.) Even after the trial, though, the topic of just who the actual perpetrators were continues to be a highly debated subject. (For more about Mayfield, see the chapter "Controversies in Forensic Science.")

THE MEDIA AND FORENSIC SCIENCE

FORENSIC SCIENCE IN THE MOVIES AND ON TELEVISION

Do any movies portray forensic science?

It all depends on what a person calls "forensic science"! In particular, a 1938 black-and-white program of "Sherlock Holmes" could be considered a portrayal of forensic science, as Holmes and Dr. Watson both search for clues (as do crime scene investigators) and find certain evidence (such as fingerprints or a jimmied window). If that is the definition, then hundreds, if not thousands, of movies involve forensic science—too many to mention them all in this text.

What are some popular fictional movies that include crime?

Many popular fictional movies include a criminal element—but few with true forensic science. Some of the more well-known ones (that actually had some forensic science in them) include the following:

- *Murder by the Numbers*—This 2002 movie was about two gifted high school students who performed the "perfect" murder, but a seasoned homicide detective got the best of the murderers. It starred Sandra Bullock, Ben Chaplin, and Ryan Gosling.

- *The Bone Collector*—In this 1999 movie, a quadriplegic ex-homicide detective, along with his female partner, track down a serial killer in New York City. It starred Denzel Washington, Angelina Jolie, and Queen Latifah.

- *Se7en*—This 1995 movie was about two detectives, a rookie and veteran, who look for a serial killer who uses the "seven deadly sins" as his motives. It starred Morgan Freeman, Brad Pitt, and Kevin Spacey.

> ## Why are people fascinated with forensic science?
>
> **D**epending on the study, the researcher, or law-enforcement officer, people are fascinated with forensic science for many reasons. Some believe it is because many people believe in justice and putting "the bad guy" behind bars. Others want to believe that they are clever enough to solve a crime—a kind of forensic puzzle to determine just what the criminal was thinking. Still others believe that deep down inside, everyone is a born detective. All of this—along with the character development of the people on the show—is no doubt why television programs such as *CSI: Crime Scene Investigation* (and the spin-offs that are "located" in various cities) are very popular with viewers.

- *Taking Lives*—This 2004 movie involves a serial killer who takes on the identity of each new victim—and a FBI profiler who is called in by the French Canadian police to hunt the killer down. It starred Angelina Jolie, Ethan Hawke, and Kiefer Sutherland.

- *The Silence of the Lambs*—This 1991 classic movie was about a young FBI cadet who must confide in an incarcerated and manipulative killer—who skinned his victims—in order to get his help to catch another killer with the same tactic. It starred Jodie Foster, Anthony Hopkins, and Lawrence Bonney.

What are some examples of true crime shows on television?

True crime shows on television usually depict either a crime that was committed (and the resolution) or a crime that has been committed and not solved. The following lists some of the more popular true crime shows to date:

- *Crime 360*—This series from the A&E network involves actual criminal investigations as they unfold. This includes the moment the detectives are called in on a case until it is ultimately solved. (2008–)

- *Cold Justice*—This reality series follows former prosecutor Kelly Siegler and crime scene investigator Yolanda McClary as they solve cold cases across the United States. (2013–)

- *Trace Evidence: The Case Files of Dr. Henry Lee*—Although not a "true crime" series like the others, this one does include real-life information. It is about Dr. Lee, a renowned forensic scientist, who reconstructs some of his cases from his forty years of forensic experience. (2004–)

What is the television show *Secrets of the Dead*?

In this series, experts use modern forensic techniques to shed new light on historical mysteries. Not everything is about a crime, but most are looked at through the eyes of a forensic analyst, such as how the *Andrea Doria* sank, identifying some of the *Titanic*'s victims, looking for Nero's sunken city, and the riddle of whether a weather or geological event of some kind might have triggered the Dark Ages. The series started in 2000.

Why do some experts believe that "forensic science," as it is portrayed on television, may be affecting the real criminal court system?

The "CSI effect" is a term used by many real crime scene investigators—in other words, that television dramas that rely on their definition of "forensic science" are affecting certain aspects of the real criminal court system (for more about television CSI, see sidebar). For example, according to several forensic science experts, CSI-type dramas have made it so jurors expect more cate-

Actor Ted Danson plays D. B. Russell in the popular television series *C.S.I.* Although the show centers on forensics solving many of the cases, it has been criticized for being unrealistic.

gorical proof than modern forensic science is often capable of delivering. In one study, it was found that jury selection was taking longer than it used to—mainly because the legal teams had to be sure perspective jurors were not judging scientific evidence based on television programs. Some in the legal profession have presented a "negative witness"—or a person who can explain to a jury that investigators in real life often do not find any (or very little) evidence at a crime scene as they do in the movies or on television.

Does any evidence exist that crime shows have influenced criminals?

Undoubtedly, criminals watch television crime shows, and some officials believe that this may be changing some of the criminals' behaviors. For example, the wearing of gloves seems to be more common, and they are even using certain chemicals (like bleach that can destroy DNA samples) to erase evidence. On the other hand, incorrect methods are also sometimes used in a crime show—which can lead the investigators of a true crime to the perpetrator.

To date, what are some fictional television shows that include forensics?

Many television shows include what is thought of as forensic science. The following lists some of the more well-known past and present crime shows (to date):

- *CSI: Crime Scene Investigation*—An elite team of police forensic evidence investigation experts work their cases in Las Vegas. (2000–2015)

319

- *Bones*—Forensic anthropologist Dr. Temperance "Bones" Brennan and FBI special agent Seeley Booth and their forensic team investigate murders—even when they only have rotten flesh or mere bones to examine. (2005–2017)

- *Sherlock*—A modern-day update of Sherlock Holmes (along with a "new" Dr. Watson) solves crimes in twenty-first-century London. (2010–)

- *Dexter*—This former program was about a blood-splatter analyst (Dexter) for the Miami Police Department who, at night, was a serial killer who only targeted other murderers. (2006–2013)

- *Rizzoli & Isles*—Jane Rizzoli is a detective, who, along with Chief Medical Examiner Dr. Maura Isles, team up to solve crimes in Boston, Massachusetts. The show was based on the Tess Gerritsen book series. (2010–2016)

- *Law & Order: Special Victims Unit*—This program is a spinoff of the *Law & Order* series about the Special Victims Unit. The unit is a specially trained squad of detectives in the New York Police Department involved in investigating sexually related crimes. (1999–)

What are some examples of major inaccuracies in television shows that involve forensic science?

We hate to burst everyone's bubble, but … many myths have been perpetrated about forensic science on television shows. In some cases, the shows reveal a crime that is solved with an exaggerated fact or (very) little true science. The following lists some of those myths based on information from forensic analysts and investigators:

- *Testing time*—It is impossible for a forensic lab to get a sample from a crime scene, prepare the sample, and test it—all in a few hours. In particular, television crime shows tend to make the viewer believe that DNA tests can be run in less than a day. In reality, DNA tests (if a DNA analysis lab is even nearby the crime scene or in the law enforcement's jurisdiction) commonly take weeks or even months—mainly because of backlog.

- *Investigation time*—On television, the crime scene investigators often finish their task, grab the "bad guy," and conclude with a pithy comment at the end—all within a few days. A real criminal investigation takes weeks, months, years, and is often never solved (and becomes a "cold case").

- *Suspects*—Many myths abound about suspects from the clothes they wear at a crime scene and during an interrogation to the conclusive tests made on the clothes that come back in a few hours. Not only that, the television investigator will often not identify the actual sample they are testing. Differences definitely exist in the time it takes to test hair, blood, saliva, etc., in the real crime lab—but apparently not on television!

- *Blood tests*—Bloodstains are often the main way a television criminal is caught, but the discovery of the blood is usually not quite correct. For example, in a CSI television show, blood shows up in an unknown place just by pointing an ultraviolet light at the crime scene. While it is accurate that ultraviolet light can be used to make blood fluoresce, it first needs to be sprayed with a certain chemical before it can be seen.

- *Contamination*—Probably one of the most interesting television misconceptions is the snacking, eating, drinking, etc., of crime scene investigators and analysts while obtaining and testing certain samples, especially DNA. At a real-life crime scene, investigators and technicians take extra care not to contaminate samples, and in the lab, they are even more careful, as contamination from food, drink, or even putting on hand cream and handling samples can affect the results of the tests.

- *High heels*—Although a female television crime scene investigator may look great in high heels, any real-life female investigator will agree that high heels are definitely impractical at a crime scene. Most wear heavy boots or sneakers, as they often have to climb over objects, walk over uneven or textured floors, and go up and down stairs many times.

How are DNA tests often misconstrued on television shows?

DNA tests are misconstrued on television shows in many ways. For example, DNA is found everywhere, but in some cases, it can be difficult to obtain a sample from certain surfaces, especially slippery or highly textured objects. On television, DNA seems to be collected from any surface. In addition, even if a DNA sample is found, it does not mean that a person is guilty or not guilty—it may only mean that the possible age, gender, and other characteristics of the DNA from a certain person have allegedly been determined. Another problem on television is that a person's DNA sample is always matched in a database. In reality, not everyone in the world, or in the United States for that matter, is in the real-life DNA databases.

FORENSIC SCIENCE IN NONFICTION MAGAZINES AND JOURNALS

Are any magazines dedicated to forensic science?

Yes, several magazines are dedicated to forensic science—some in print, some only on the Internet (called e-zines or webzines), and almost all with some representation on the Internet. The following lists only a few of those publications and a brief description of each:

- *Forensic Magazine*—This publication looks at everything from forensic facility issues to forensic safety, along with the latest news in forensic science. Although it is for forensic science professionals, law enforcement, and vendors of products and services that are forensic related, it has some interesting and useful information for those who are interested in the field. (http://www.forensicmag.com/)

- *Crime Magazine*—This magazine was launched in 1998 and covers all aspects of true crime. This includes organized crime, serial killers, assassinations, historical crimes, and celebrity crimes. (http://crimemagazine.com)

- *Science Daily: Forensic News*—This popular science e-zine was started in 1995, and besides offering up-to-date information on almost every aspect of science, it also includes forensic news. (http://www.sciencedaily.com/news/health_medicine/forensics/)

- *Digital Forensic Magazine*—This quarterly print (and Internet) magazine features news from the world of cybercrime and digital forensics. It includes such topics as cyberterrorism, investigation technologies and procedures, tools and techniques, and hardware, software, and network forensic information. (http://www.digital-forensicsmagazine.com)

Are any journals dedicated to forensic science?

Yes, many journals are dedicated to forensic science. The following lists a few, along with a brief description:

- *Journal of Forensic Sciences*—This is the official publication of the Academy of Forensic Sciences. It offers research and education information in a peer-reviewed publication. (http://onlinelibrary.wiley.com/journal/10.1111/(ISSN)1556–4029)

- *Journal of Forensic Research*—This scholarly journal is also a peer-reviewed publication that serves the international forensic science community. The topics include forensic genetics and DNA analysis, forensic clinical medicine, criminal cases, fingerprinting and techniques, and environmental forensics. (https://www.omics online.org/forensic-research.php)

- *Open Access Journal of Forensic Psychology*—A peer-reviewed journal created by and for forensic psychologists. (http://www.oajfp.com)

- *Journal of Forensic & Investigative Accounting*—This is an open-access journal that publishes articles concerning forensic accounting issues, such as fraud and litigation, forensic accounting research skills, tools, and techniques, and encourages discussion about the field of forensic accounting. (http://www.nacva.com/jfia-current)

- *The American Journal of Forensic Medicine and Pathology*—This peer-reviewed journal is one of the foremost in forensic medicine and pathology, including case reports. (http://journals.lww.com/amjforensicmedicine/)

- *Forensic Toxicology and Pharmacology*—This peer-reviewed scholarly forensic journal publishes information on the discoveries and current developments in forensic toxicology and pharmacology by such means as articles, case reports, and short communications. (http://www.scitechnol.com)

- *Journal of Forensic Anthropology*—This open-access, peer-reviewed journal deals with criminal investigations that have forensic anthropology connections. (https://www.omicsonline.org/forensic-anthropology.php)

What magazines that are not dedicated to forensic science often have articles on the subject?

Several magazines that are not dedicated to forensic science often offer articles about crime and forensics. (Some newspapers also carry information about forensics but only occasionally, such as the *New York Times*.) The following are some of the more popular magazines (both print and Internet or both):

- *National Geographic*—*National Geographic* covers a great deal about forensic science on its website and occasionally in print. Its extensive listing includes such topics as people in forensics, advances in forensic techniques, the history behind forensics (and some crimes), and crime scene information. (http://www.na tional-geographic.com)

- *Popular Science*—This magazine is mainly about science and technology and often includes articles about forensic science and the latest (and future) techniques in the field. (http://www.popsci.com)

- *Smithsonian*—*Smithsonian* magazine is known for its in-depth articles about certain subjects—including forensics. In particular, it often has articles about forensics, including certain historical crimes, forensic anthropology, cyberforensics, and even the Smithsonian Institution's past cooperation with the FBI in forensics. (http://www.smithsonianmag.com; there is also a Smithsonian channel at http://www.smithsonianchannel.com)

- *Discover*—*Discover* magazine is mainly a science magazine and will often carry articles about forensic science, including the latest in criminal investigation techniques and DNA analysis and forensics. (http://www.discovermagazine.com)

- *The Atlantic*—Although this is not the usual venue for forensic science, the *Atlantic* often covers topics in forensics, such as recent criminal investigations, and how certain fields within forensics help to solve crimes. (http://www.theatlantic.com)

NONFICTION FORENSIC SCIENCE BOOKS

Do any nonfiction books present early forensic methods?

Although not as popular as fiction books, some nonfiction works include early forensic methods. The following lists only two of them:

- *The Father of Forensics: The Groundbreaking Cases of Sir Bernard Spilsbury, and the Beginnings of Modern CSI*—This book explores the person who is thought to have brought criminal investigations into the modern age—Sir Bernard Spilsbury, considered to be a medical detective in early twentieth-century Britain. (Coin Evans, 2006, Berkley Trade)

- *The Sherlock Holmes Handbook: The Methods and Mysteries of the World's Greatest Detective*—This book walks a somewhat nonfiction and fictional edge, presenting some real-life how-to skills of the fictional character created by Sir Arthur Conan Doyle, Sherlock Holmes of nineteenth-century England, along with some trivia about the famous detective. (Ransom Riggs with illustrator Eugene Smith, 2009, Quirk Books)

Do any nonfiction books specialize in forensic science?

Yes, because forensic science is so popular—not to mention the topic so vast—many nonfiction books are written in the field. The following lists several such books:

- *Bodies We've Buried: Inside the National Forensic Academy, the World's Top CSI Training School*—This book presents the inside workings of the National Forensic Academy and presents the real world of forensic science with firsthand stories of the students, along with how crime scene investigation has solved several famous forensic cases. (Jarrett Hallcox and Amy Welch, 2006, Berkley Hardcover)

- *Forensic Detective: How I Cracked the World's Toughest Cases*—This book was written by the deputy scientific director of the U.S. government's Central Identification Laboratory and forensic anthropologist and presents an in-depth and behind-the-scenes portrait—including some past examples—of how a real forensic anthropologist carries out his or her tasks. (Robert Mann, 2007, Ballantine Books)

- *Blood Secrets: A Forensic Expert Reveals How Blood Splatter Tells the Crime Scene's Story*—This book reveals how forensic experts determine certain criminal cases—mainly of murder—based on the traces of blood left behind. (Rod Englert and Kathy Passero, 2010, Thomas Dunne Books)

- *The Anatomy of Motive: The FBI's Legendary Mindhunter Explores the Key to Understanding and Catching Violent Criminals*—A former FBI profiler and cowriter present some insights into the complexity of the criminal mind—including possible motives behind such criminal acts as serial, mass, and spree killings, poisonings, and even individuals who send bombs through the mail. (John E. Douglas and Mark Olshaker, 2000, Pocket Books)

- *Criminalistics: An Introduction to Forensic Science* (12th edition)—This book is considered an introduction for students of forensic science and crime scene investigation. (Richard Saferstein, 2017, Pearson)

- *Forensics: What Bugs, Burns, Prints, DNA, and More Tell Us About Crime*—This book is written by a well-known fiction crime writer and goes behind the scenes with some of the top forensic experts. It offers some information about the history of the field to today's cutting-edge forensic science. (Val McDermid, Grove Press, 2016, reprint edition)

- *The 20 Most Psychologically Intriguing Legal Cases*—This book, although dated a bit (so many more criminals would have been interesting to read about psychology-wise since 2006), is authored by a University at Buffalo law professor and a clinical psychologist. It looks at twenty of the most psychologically interesting legal cases of the past fifty years, such as Lee Harvey Oswald's troubled adolescence and Mike Tyson's violent outbursts and tantrums. It not only explores the often bizarre workings of the human mind but also how the practice of psychology fits into the legal system. (Charles Patrick Ewing and Joseph T. McCann, 2006, Oxford University Press)

What is the definition of "true crime"?

True crime is just as the name implies: nonfiction books (and often movies, documentaries, or in-depth news stories) that are based on true or real-life crimes. (In many cases, not everything is known about the actual crime—even if it is deeply researched. This often leads to filling in the unknown parts of the story with the writers' interpretation of the events.) For example, true crime books include Truman Capote's *In Cold Blood* (about a 1959 home invasion and murder in rural Kansas) and Anne

Author Truman Capote wrote the first true crime novel, *In Cold Blood* (1966), which slightly fictionalized the real-life case of two men who murdered an entire family in Kansas.

Rule's *The Stranger Beside Me: Ted Bundy, the Shocking Inside Story* (about how she once sat by seemingly friendly Bundy while they worked together at a suicide hotline center).

FORENSIC SCIENCE IN FICTION BOOKS

What are some fictional series of early detectives and amateur sleuths?

Literally hundreds of fiction novels involve early detectives and amateur sleuths—including many crime solvers going back a few centuries in both the United States and Europe. The following lists some of the fictional portrayals of those who solved earlier crimes—without the help of modern-day techniques:

- *Sherlock Holmes*—One of the most famous fictional detectives is Sir Arthur Conan Doyle's fictional character Sherlock Holmes. Doyle's books about Holmes were not only a hit in his time (the late 1800s) but have endured for over a century as "everyone's" favorite detective. Holmes is the iconic figure, thought of as brilliant, observant, eccentric, and with amazing deductive reasoning. He is assisted by Dr. John Watson, who is also the narrator of the Holmes novels. Some of Doyle's more famous Holmes stories are *A Study in Scarlet, The Hound of the Baskervilles, Memoirs of Sherlock Holmes*, and *The Return of Sherlock Holmes*. (The "return" was written after Doyle "killed off" his famous detective; the public response was so great, he brought Holmes back to life and continued the series.)

- *Sir John Fielding Mysteries*—This series was written by Bruce Alexander (real name Bruce Alexander Cook, 1932–2003) and is a fictional account of Sir John Fielding, the blind magistrate who was the cofounder of the 1800s Bow Street Runners with his half-brother Henry Fielding. The series is set in eighteenth-century England and includes the magistrate and the fictional character Jeremy Proctor, the narrator—once a penniless, thirteen-year-old orphan whom Sir John took into his household and who helps to solve certain crimes as Sir John's "eyes."

Sherlock Holmes (right) with his faithful friend, Dr. John Watson, in a classic 1892 illustration by Sidney Paget.

- *Lord Peter Wimsey series*—This well-written series was penned by scholar and essayist Dorothy Sayers. The stories take place in the early 1920s to the late 1930s and are about the rich and oftentimes witty Wimsey, who solves mysteries (not always murder) and other crimes as an amateur detective.

- *Charlie Chan Mysteries*—The Charlie Chan series was written by American novelist Earl Derr Biggers (1884–1933) and has been represented in books, movies, and comics. Chan's character speaks in broken English, always seems to be smiling, and has plenty of aphorisms. When the first book came out in 1925 (*The House without a Key*)—the time period in which the books are set—Chan became the most positive Chinese character ever introduced to American and European audiences. In addition, he was loosely based on a real-life American detective working in Hawaii, Chang Apana (who was said to be smart when it came to solving crimes and even carried a bullwhip).

- *Hercule Poirot series*—This series of stories by Dame Agatha Christie take place in the early 1920s and are about the famous fastidious and eccentric Belgium detective Hercule Poirot, known for his suspense-filled speeches (usually with all the suspects in one room at the end of the book when he makes his accurate accusations). One of her most famous books in the series is *Murder on the Orient Express*.

The list continues, and no shortage exists of fictional detectives: for instance, Theodore Roosevelt, the police commissioner in New York City in the 1890s (by Lawrence Alexander); the Inspector Witherspoon and Mrs. Jefferies series in the Victorian era (by Emily Brightwell); Maggie Maguire, the ex-Pinkerton agent in 1870s San Francisco (by Kate Bryan); or even Timothy Wilde, the ex-bartender and police officer in the newly formed New York City police force in 1845 (by Lyndsay Faye).

What are some nonserial fiction novels with a forensic basis?

Literally hundreds of stand-alone fiction novels depend on real-life aspects of the field of forensics to tell a story. For example, one recent such fiction novel is *The Poisoner's Handbook: Murder and the Birth of Forensic Medicine in Jazz Age New York* by Deborah Blum (2010, Penguin Press). This book relays the untold story of how poison played a part in New York City's Jazz Age—tracking early forensic scientists as they fought to end an era when untraceable poisons were used for many crimes, with Blum doing a great deal of real-life research for the fiction book.

What are some modern series books with a forensic basis?

Numerous—too many to mention here—fiction series books are based on modern forensic science. The following is a good cross-section of several fictional characters who perform a wide range of tasks in the forensic field, listed by the author and their series:

- Patricia Cornwell is a crime writer who has written many fiction books with Kay Scarpetta as a medical examiner. For example, the first in the series, *Postmortem* (1990), is about a serial killer on the loose in Richmond, Virginia, and *The Body Farm* (1994) brings out information from the actual studies done at the real-life Body Farm in Tennessee.

- Kathy Reichs is a crime writer of the Tempe Brennan series, which is about a forensic anthropologist who investigates human remains at crime scenes that are usually too degraded for a coroner to obtain evidence. The first in the series is titled *Déjà Dead* (1997).

- Jon Jefferson has written several novels in his *Body Farm* series under the name Jefferson Bass. The books are written in consultation with William Bass (1928–), who is the founder of the Body Farm in Tennessee (for more about the Body Farm, see the chapter "In the Crime Lab: Analyzing Older Remains"). The first in the series is titled *Carved in Bone* (2006).

- Sarah Andrews is a real-life geologist who writes about a fictional forensic geologist, Em Hansen. The first in the series is titled *Tensleep* (1994).

- Tess Gerritsen's *Rizzoli & Isles* series is about Jane Rizzoli, a detective, who, along with Chief Medical Examiner Dr. Maura Isles, solve crimes in Boston, Massachusetts. It was also a television series, which was based on the book. The first in the series is titled *The Surgeon* (2001).

- Robin Burcell writes a series based on FBI special agent and forensic artist Sydney Fitzpatrick. The first book in the series is titled *Face of a Killer* (2008).

- Lori Andrews is the author of the Dr. Alexandra Blake series, a geneticist at the Armed Forces Institute of Pathology in Washington, D.C. The first book in the series is titled *Sequence* (2006).

- Ridley Pearson is the author of the Boldt/Matthews series, which is about police detective Lou Boldt and forensic psychologist Daphne Matthews in Seattle's homicide bureau. The first book in the series is titled *Undercurrents* (1988).

RESOURCES IN FORENSIC SCIENCE

(Note: Although all website addresses were current as of this writing, they frequently change; the authors regret any inconvenience caused by such changes.)

FORENSIC SCIENCE WEBSITES: INFORMATION FOR STUDENTS

What websites have forensic information for young people (and teachers)?

Many websites offer information and activities for young people who are interested in forensic science. Many of them are commercial, and some are run by certain groups or organizations, most of them associated with teaching. The following are only some of the many offerings for students:

- *STEM-works*—This site is sponsored by Southern Methodist University (SMU) and offers teaching kits for young people about forensic science, such as a tour of a forensic biology lab and handwriting analysis activities. (STEM is an effort to bring activities and projects in science, technology, engineering, and mathematics to young people in schools, to those who are homeschooled, or just to young people interested in learning more about the STEM fields.) For more websites, just put the keywords "students forensic science" into your search engine. STEM-works can be found at http://www.stem-works.com.

- *National Law Enforcement Museum's "The Forensic Detectives Summer Camp"*— This site includes information about "The Forensic Detectives," a weeklong summer camp that exposes students to the "messy and meticulous world" of forensic science. Students get hands-on training in the basics—from fingerprints to DNA and interpreting toolmarks to trace evidence—and get to meet with professionals working in the field today. This camp gives young participants a greater understanding of forensic science, its role in the criminal justice system, and especially gives them exposure to STEM-related careers in law enforcement. It can be found at http://www.nleomf.org/museum/education/programs-activities/forensics/the-forensic-detectives/.

- *American Academy of Forensic Sciences*—This site (AAFS; at https://www.aafs.org/) has several offerings for students. This includes the Young Forensic Scientists Forum (https://yfsf.aafs.org/) and the CSI Summer Camps (https://www.aafs.org/students/csi-summer-camps/). It is also one of the foremost forensic science organizations in the United States.

- *CSI: Web Adventures*—This website from Rice University's Center for Technology in Teaching and Learning presents information for students and teachers about forensic science. This includes online activities (such as testing a person's skills at solving certain virtual "crimes"), videos, and educational activities. It can be found at http://www.forensics.rice.edu.

Do any companies have forensic kits for teenagers to young adults?

Yes, one of the first companies to offer forensic studies to the classroom is Ward's Scientific. The company offers Ward's Forensic Science Kits, including those that involve forensics of skeletal remains, fingerprint identification, and blood splatter analysis. For kits and information, link to https://www.wardsci.com/store/content/externalContentPage.jsp?path=/www.wardsci.com/en_US/Wards_Forensic_Kits.jsp.

GENERAL INTEREST FORENSIC SCIENCE WEBSITES

What are some websites that offer forensic science information to the public?

Many websites give out information to the general public about forensic science, and most are run by former forensic scientists. The following lists a few of those websites:

- *Reddy's Forensic Page*—This all-encompassing website is the creation of a retired forensic scientist with the New York City Police Laboratory. It can be found at http://www.forensicpage.com.

- *Zeno's Forensic Site*—This is a website with many forensic links and has been written since 1994 by a senior forensic scientist at the Netherlands Forensic Institute of the Ministry of Justice. It can be found at http://forensic.to/.

- *Crimes & Clues: The Art and Science of Criminal Investigation*—This is a listing of forensic science articles compiled by two former law-enforcement officers. It can be found at http://crimeandclues.com/.
- *Crime Scene Investigator Network*—This site covers a great deal of ground when it comes to forensic science—from articles and information about careers and training to crime scene response and evidence collection. It can be found at www.crime-scene-investigator.net.
- *National Clearinghouse for Science Technology and the Law* (NCSTL)—The NCSTL offers a searchable database of legal, forensic, and technology resources, along with a reference collection of law, science, and technological materials (and many other forensic-connected offerings). This database is said to be the only free compilation of forensic resources in the world and can be found at http://www.ncstl.org.
- *National Forensic Science Technology Center*—The NFSTC is located in Largo, Florida, and is dedicated to supporting the forensic, justice, and military communities through training for analysts and law enforcement, technology test and evaluation, needs assessments and efficiency studies, and laboratory quality reviews. This site can be found at http://www.nfstc.org.
- *National Center for Forensic Science*—This center is supported by the University of Central Florida in Orlando. It is not a crime lab but does support research in the field of forensic science. Much of its research focuses on the analysis of physical and biological evidence. This site can be found at https://ncfs.ucf.edu/.

Do any foundations contribute to the field of forensic science?

Yes, several foundations contribute to forensic science, especially education. For example, the Frederic Rieders Family Foundation offers programs to educate and train current and future forensic science professionals at all stages in their careers. They also sponsor the Center for Forensic Science Research and Education (http://www.forensic scienceeducation.org). Another group is the Ellis R. Kerley Foundation (http://www .elliskerleyfoundation.org/), which develops and encourages the science of forensic anthropology, including scholarships and enrichment programs for students in the field.

Is it possible to access WinID, a forensic odontology database, over the Internet?

Yes, it is, but it is mostly offered to those in the forensic odontology field. WinID is a database that assists forensic odontologists in the identification of human remains, mainly from an accident or victim of a crime (assaulted for a short or long time before found). It can be found at http://www.abfo.org/winid at the American Board of Forensic Odontology website. (For more about WinID, see the chapter "In the Crime Lab: Trace Evidence.")

What are some museums in the United States that are dedicated to law enforcement?

Several museums in the United States are dedicated to law enforcement or forensic science. The following lists only a few of those places:

- *International Police Museum*—One of the more interesting law-enforcement museums is the International Police Museum in Rockaway Beach, Oregon. It offers exhibits and educational information about police around the world. (http://www.internationalpolicemuseum.org)

- *National Law Enforcement Museum*—This museum is currently being built in Washington, D.C., near the National Law Enforcement Memorial. It will offer information about American law enforcement through high-tech, interactive exhibits and a collection of artifacts from past law-enforcement events and provide extensive resources for research and educational programs. The museum is set to open in fall 2018, and updates and information can be found at http://www.nleomf.museum/.

- *The American Police Hall of Fame and Museum*—This museum was founded in 1960 in Titusville, Florida. It was the first national police museum and memorial in the United States dedicated to American law-enforcement officers killed in the line of duty. To date, the marble wall of the memorial lists the approximately nine thousand officers who were killed in the line of duty. Its website is at http://www.aphf.org/.

The American Police Hall of Fame and Museum in Titusville, Florida, is dedicated to officers killed in the line of duty.

- *The Texas Ranger Hall of Fame and Museum*—This museum in Waco, Texas, is dedicated to the over-a-century-old law enforcers known as the Texas Rangers—past (the first Texas Rangers in 1823) and present. It can be found at http://www.texasranger.org/.

FORENSIC SCIENCE WEBSITES: U.S. AND INTERNATIONAL PROFESSIONAL ORGANIZATIONS

UNITED STATES

What are some specialized U.S. organizations involved in forensic science?

Many U.S. organizations support specialized fields within forensic science. The following lists only a few of the specialties and their associated organizations:

- *Crime Scene Investigators*—The Association for Crime Scene Reconstruction (ACSR) was established to exchange information between crime scene reconstruction analysts, including how to gain explicit knowledge of the series of events that surround a crime—all using deductive and inductive reasoning, physical evidence, scientific methods, and their interrelationships. It can be found at https://www.acsr.org/.

- *Medical Examiners and Medicolegal Death Investigators*—The National Association of Medical Examiners (NAME) is a national professional organization of physician medical examiners, medicolegal death investigators, and the death investigation system. NAME was founded in 1966 to foster the professional growth of physician death investigators and the exchange of professional and technical information vital to improving the medical investigation of violent, suspicious, and unusual deaths in the United States. It can be found at http://www.thename.org/.

- *The American Board of Medicolegal Death Investigators*—ABMDI (at http://www.abmdi.org/) is a voluntary, national, not-for-profit, independent professional certification board that promotes the highest standards of practice for medicolegal death investigators. The board also certifies individuals who prove they have the knowledge and skills necessary to perform medicolegal death investigation—all as set forth in the National Institute of Justice 1999 publication *Death Investigation: A Guide for the Scene Investigator* (2011 updated version).

- *Crime Lab Directors*—The American Society of Crime Laboratory Directors (ASCLD; at http://www.ascld.org/) is a nonprofit professional organization of crime laboratory directors and forensic science managers. According to the society, the purpose of the ASCLD is to foster professional interests, assist in the development of laboratory-management ideas and techniques; acquire, preserve, and disseminate forensic-based information; maintain and improve communications among crime laboratory directors; and promote, encourage, and maintain the highest standards of practice in the field.

- *Trace Evidence Examiners*—The American Society of Trace Evidence Examiners (ASTEE; at http://www.asteetrace.org/) is an international professional organization whose members specialize in trace evidence. The 350 (to date) members include students, academics, forensic practitioners, and others interested in the field of trace evidence.

- *Firearms and Toolmarks*—The Association of Firearm and Toolmark Examiners (AFTE) is an international professional organization for practitioners of firearm and/or toolmark identification. It has been dedicated to the exchange of information, methods and best practices, and forensic firearm and toolmark research since its creation in 1969. It can be found at https://afte.org/.

- *DNA Analysis*—The Association of Forensic DNA Analysts and Administrators (AFDAA) is a nonprofit organization composed of professionals engaged in forensic DNA analysis for the judicial system. Members include forensic DNA analysts, supervisors, and administrators, with the association providing a forum for the exchange of ideas and information among forensic DNA scientists. It can be found at http://afdaa.org/2013/.

What are some U.S. organizations that specialize in forensic odontology?

Several organizations specialize in forensic odontology. The American Society of Forensic Odontology (ASFO) specializes in odontology, for instance, in analyzing bite marks or teeth of individuals for identification at a crime scene. It can be found at http://www.asfo.org. The American Board of Forensic Odontology's goal is to establish, enhance, and revise (as necessary) the standards of qualifications for those who practice forensic odontology and to certify as qualified specialists those voluntary applicants who comply with the requirements of the board. Link to this organization at https://abfo.org/.

What are some U.S. organizations in forensic toxicology?

Several organizations in the United States specialize in forensic toxicology. The following lists three of the most well known:

- *Society of Forensic Toxicologists, Inc. (SOFT)*—The Society of Forensic Toxicologists is a nonprofit professional organization composed of practicing forensic toxicologists and those interested in the discipline. The society also provides a forum for the exchange of information and ideas among toxicology professionals and sponsors programs, such as workshops, newsletters, and SOFT-sponsored technical publications. It can be found at http://www.soft-tox.org/.

- *The American Board of Forensic Toxicology (ABFT)*—The purpose of the American Board of Forensic Toxicology is to help establish standards for the practice of forensic toxicology and for the examination and recognition of scientists and laboratories providing forensic toxicology services. It can be found at http://www.abft.org/.

What are a few U.S. organizations that highlight forensic engineering?

Several organizations highlight forensic engineering and offer students and professionals information, conferences, and contacts in the field. For example, the National Academy of Forensic Engineers (NAFE) was organized to improve the practice, elevate the standards, and advance the cause of forensic engineering. It can be found at http://www.nafe.org/. The American Society of Civil Engineers (ASCE) covers many topics and also includes forensic engineering, including analysis of structural failures or what occurred in a transportation accident. It can be found at http://www.asce.org/forensic-engineering/forensic-engineering/.

- *Society of Toxicology (SOT)*—The SOT was founded in 1961 and specializes in toxicology, not only in terms of forensic science but also in other types of toxicity in the United States and around the world. This site provides information about such concerns as pollutants in the air and water, toxic waste dumps, product safety (especially foodstuff), and toxic elements that can affect human and environmental health. It can be found at http://www.toxicology.org/.

What are some U.S. organizations that deal with questioned documents?

Several organizations deal with forensic document examiners, or questioned documents. Here are only a few:

- The American Board of Forensic Document Examiners, Inc.® (ABFDE) organization was established in 1977. Its objectives include to establish, maintain, and enhance standards of qualification for those who practice forensic document examination and to certify applicants who comply with ABFDE requirements for this expertise. This ensures that anyone who claims to be a specialist in forensic document examination possesses the necessary skills and qualifications to do such work. It can be found at the website https://www.abfde.org/index.html.

- The American Society of Questioned Document Examiners (ASQDE) is the oldest and largest organization in the world dedicated to the profession of forensic document examination. The beginnings of ASQDE were in 1913, when Albert S. Osborn initiated a program for the interchange of ideas and research in document examination. In 1942, Mr. Osborn and fourteen other prominent document examiners formally organized the American Society of Questioned Document Examiners. It can be found at http://www.asqde.org/.

- The Scientific Working Group for Forensic Document Examination (SWGDOC) develops standards and guidelines for the field of forensic document examination and is composed of private examiners and government examiners from local, state, and federal laboratories throughout the United States. According to its website, the group started in 1997 as the TWGDOC (Technical Working Group for Questioned Documents), renamed SWGDOC in 1999, then reorganized in 2001. From 2000 to 2012, SWGDOC published their standards through the American Society for Testing and Materials International (ASTM). By 2012, SWGDOC stopped publishing its standards through ASTM and began self-publishing its standards, as is the practice for nearly every other SWG group. It can be found at http://www.swgdoc.org/.

INTERNATIONAL

What are some specialized international organizations and certification boards in forensic science?

Many international organizations specialize in a certain field within forensic science. The following lists only a few of those groups:

- *International Association of Crime Analysts (IACA)*—This organization was founded in 1990 to help crime analysts around the world improve their skills and make valuable contacts, to help law-enforcement agencies make the best use of crime analysis, and to advocate for standards of performance and technique within the profession itself—all through training, networking, and publications. It can be found at http://www.iaca.net/.

- *International Association of Forensic Toxicologists (TIAFT)*—Nowadays, TIAFT comprises about two thousand members from all regions of the world who are actively engaged in analytical toxicology or allied areas. The aims of this association are to promote cooperation and coordination of efforts among members and to encourage research in forensic toxicology.

  TIAFT members come from the police force, medical examiners and coroners' laboratories, horse-racing and sports-doping laboratories, hospitals, departments of legal medicine, pharmacology, pharmacy, and toxicology. It can be found at http://www.tiaft.org/.

- *Federation of European Toxicologists & European Societies of Toxicology (EUROTOX)*—This group is the Federation of National Societies of Toxicology in Europe, which together have approximately seven thousand members. EUROTOX itself has more than two hundred individual members who come from fifty countries (mostly Western Europe) and provide scientific toxicology education, networking, and training. It can be found at http://www.eurotox.com/.

- *International Association of Bloodstain Pattern Analysts (IABPA)*—The IABPA is an organization of forensic experts specializing in the field of bloodstain pattern analysis. The organization encourages and promotes the science of bloodstain pattern analysis and informs its members of the latest techniques, discoveries, and developments in the field. It can be found at http://www.iabpa.org/.

- *International Association for Craniofacial Identification (IACI)*—This association was formed in 1987 as a special research group focusing on all areas of craniofacial identification. The IACI is now an international organization with a worldwide membership, with members from fields such as physical anthropology, forensic odontology, forensic art, anatomy, facial image analysis, psychology, computer science, biometrics, and law. It can be found at http://www.craniofacial-id.org/.

- *Canadian Society of Forensic Science (CSFS)*—This is a professional nonprofit organization whose aim is to maintain professional standards in the field and to promote the study and enhance the stature of forensic science. Members join sections representing certain areas of forensic science, including anthropology, medical, odontology, biology, chemistry, questioned documents, engineering, firearms, and toxicology. It can be reached at http://www.csfs.ca/.

FORENSIC SCIENCE WEBSITES: U.S. GOVERNMENT

What are some U.S. government agencies that offer general information about forensic science to the public?

Several U.S. government agencies offer forensic science information to the public. The following lists two of the more popular sites:

- *Federal Bureau of Investigation (FBI) Laboratory Services*—Created in 1932, the FBI Laboratory is one of the largest crime labs in the world and is located in Quantico, Virginia. The scientific experts and special agents who work in the lab often have global assignments and support law enforcement, intelligence, military, and forensic science partners. It can be found at https://www.fbi.gov/services/laboratory.

- *National Institute of Justice, Forensic Science*—The National Institute of Justice is the research, development, and evaluation agency of the U.S. Department of Justice. Its main mission is to improve knowledge and understanding of criminal and justice issues through science, along with offering tools and knowledge to the criminal justice community, particularly at the state and local levels of law enforcement. Its website is found at http://www.nij.gov/topics/forensics/Pages/welcome.aspx.

What is the FBI's Criminal Justice Information Services?

The law-enforcement, national security, and intelligence community partners with the criminal justice information they need to protect the United States while preserving civil liberties. The Criminal Justice Information Services (CJIS) is the largest division in the FBI. The CJIS Division was established in February 1992 out of the former Identification Division to serve as the focal point and central repository for criminal justice information services in the FBI. Programs initially consolidated under the CJIS Division included the National Crime Information Center (NCIC), Uniform Crime Reporting (UCR), and Fingerprint Identification. In addition, responsibility for several ongoing technological initiatives was transferred to the CJIS Division, including the Integrated Automated Fingerprint Identification System (IAFIS), NCIC 2000, and the National Incident-Based Reporting System (NIBRS). It can be found at https://www.fbi.gov/services/cjis.

What is NamUs?

NamUs, or the National Missing and Unidentified Persons System, is a centralized national repository and resource center database for missing persons, unidentified persons, and unclaimed persons under the U.S. Department of Justice's Office of Justice Programs. It is a free online system that can be searched by medical examiners, coroners, law-enforcement officials, and the general public from all over the country in hopes of resolving these cases. It includes missing persons, unidentified persons, and unclaimed persons databases. It can be found at www.namus.gov. (For more about NamUs, see the chapter "In the Crime Lab: Analyzing Older Remains.")

What is the Defense Criminal Investigative Service?

The Defense Criminal Investigative Service is the criminal investigative arm of the Office of the Inspector General, U.S. Department of Defense. DCIS's duties are protecting military personnel by investigating cases of fraud, bribery, and corruption; preventing the illegal transfer of sensitive defense technologies to proscribed nations and criminal elements; investigating companies that use defective, substandard, or counterfeit parts

Why is the National Institute of Standards and Technology important to the future of forensic science?

The National Institute of Standards and Technology (NIST) is truly important to the future study of forensic science, as it is one of the "watchdogs" of public justice and safety, including when forensic science is used inappropriately—leading to innocent people being wrongfully convicted and criminals remaining free to commit more crimes. Thus, the NIST is involved in strengthening forensic science research and improving standards in the field, including DNA, ballistics, fingerprint analysis, trace evidence, and digital, among others. In addition, the NIST provides physical reference standards and data that help forensic laboratories validate their analytical methods and ensure accurate test results. According to its website, the NIST cochaired (with the Department of Justice) the National Commission on Forensic Science, which formulates recommendations for the U.S. Attorney General about matters such as accreditation requirements for forensic science service providers, and also administered the Organization of Scientific Area Committees (OSAC), which facilitates the development of science-based standards and guidelines for a broad array of forensic disciplines. Information about the NIST and forensic science can be found at https://www.nist.gov/topics/forensic-science.

in weapons systems and equipment used by the military; and stopping cybercrimes and computer intrusions. It can be found at http://www.dodig.mil/INV_DCIS/index.cfm.

What are the duties of the Naval Criminal Investigative Service (NCIS)?

The (real, not television version) Naval Criminal Investigative Service (NCIS) is a team of federal law-enforcement professionals dedicated to protecting the people, equipment, technology, and infrastructure of the U.S. Navy and Marine Corps. It is part of the Department of Navy (DON) and includes more than two hundred military members and nine hundred civilian crimi-

The Defense Criminal Investigative Service's purpose is to protect military personnel in cases of corruption and fraud.

nal investigator specialists. Its work includes helping to prevent global terrorism and reducing crime, with a presence in the United States and around forty countries. It also works with state or local law-enforcement agencies on crime affecting the Department of the Navy. It can be found at http://www.ncis.navy.mil/Pages/public default.aspx.

What are some government websites that deal with explosives in association with forensics?

A few government websites deal with forensics and explosives. For example, the Terrorist Explosive Device Analytical Center (TEDAC) contributes to the eradication of the IED (improvised explosive devices) threat worldwide. The group informs its partners, who disrupt those individuals and networks responsible for the design, development, purchase, assembly, and deployment of IEDs. It can be found at https://www.fbi.gov/services/laboratory/tedac. Another explosives website is called "Tools of the Trade: Special Agent Bomb Technicians," which talks about the special agent bomb technicians—"bomb techs"—including the use of a variety of tools (from robots to x-ray machines) to identify, diagnose, and disrupt suspected or real explosive devices. The details of these brave technicians can be found through the FBI site at https://archives.fbi.gov/archives/fun games/tools_of_the_trade/tools-of-the-trade-bomb-technicians-text-version.

What are some government websites that deal with biometrics?

Several government websites deal with the field of biometrics as it applies to forensic science. For example, the Federal Bureau of Investigation (FBI) has a number of connections to the field of biometrics (for more about biometrics, see the chapter "Other Forensic Investigations"). For instance, it developed the Next Generation Identification (NGI) system, which provides the criminal justice community with the world's largest and most efficient electronic repository of biometric and criminal history information. In addition, the Bureau's Science and Technology Branch created the Biometric Center of Excellence (BCOE) to combat crime and terrorism with state-of-the-art biometrics technology. In addition to the BCOE, its Criminal Justice Services Division has a repository of fingerprints and biographical data. (For other connections between the FBI and biometrics, link to https://www.fbi.gov/services/cjis/fingerprints-and-other-biometrics.)

Still another government agency involved in biometrics is Homeland Security (or the Department of Homeland Security, or DHS). According to its website, this group provides biometric identification services to protect the nation through its Office of Biometric Identity Management (OBIM), which supplies the technology for matching, storing, and sharing biometric data. OBIM is the designated lead provider of biometric identity services for DHS and maintains the largest biometric repository in the U.S. government—the Automated Biometric Identification System or IDENT (operated and maintained by OBIM). IDENT currently holds more than two hundred million unique identities and processes more than three hundred thousand biometric transactions per day. (To find out more, link to https://www.dhs.gov/biometrics.)

FORENSIC SCIENCE WEBSITES: INTERNATIONAL

What is the Chartered Society of Forensic Sciences?

The Chartered Society of Forensic Sciences (CSFS) is an international professional body for forensic practice both in the United Kingdom and abroad and claims to be the voice for forensic practitioners, individuals, and organizations related to professional work in the forensic sciences. It currently has chartered status in the United Kingdom but provides representation, guidance, and support worldwide, including in sixty countries across Europe, North and South America, the Middle East, Asia, and the Pacific Region. Currently, the CSFS has several divisions, including the Forensic Imagery Analysis Group and the Fingerprint Division (formerly the Fingerprint Society). It can be found at http://www.csofs.org.

What does the Virtual Museum of Canada offer about forensics?

The Simon Fraser University's Museum of Archaeology & Ethnology offers an online interactive exhibit from the Virtual Museum of Canada. In this exhibit, the viewer becomes a forensic investigator at a scene where bones have been discovered. The viewer looks for clues and learns about forensic science at the same time. It can be found at http://www.sfu.museum/forensics/.

What is the FBI National Academy Associates?

According to its website, the FBI National Academy Associates, Inc. (FBI NAA) is a nonprofit, international organization located in Virginia. The nearly seventeen thousand

What website specializes in the "Old Bailey" in England?

A website that explains the "Old Bailey" (the Central Criminal Court) in England covers the court from 1674 to 1913 and includes, in its words, a "fully searchable edition of the largest body of texts detailing the lives of non-elite people ever published, containing 197,745 criminal trials held at London's central criminal court" in cooperation with several universities. It can be found at www.oldbailey-online.org.

senior law-enforcement professionals are dedicated to providing communities, states, countries, and professions with the highest degree of law-enforcement expertise, training, education, and information. The members are graduates of the FBI's National Academy Program and represent all the states in the United States, 170 countries, and over 7,500 law-enforcement agencies. To date, over fifty thousand graduates have completed the FBI NAA Program. It can be found at https://www.fbinaa.org/.

What is the International Association for Identification?

International Association for Identification (IAI) is the oldest (started in 1915) and largest forensic association in the world. It represents a diverse, knowledgeable, and experienced professional membership who educate, share, critique, and publish methods, techniques, and research in the physical forensic science disciplines. It also offers certification to people interested in becoming crime scene investigators. To date, over 6,500 people from seventy-seven countries are members. It can be found at https://www.theiai.org/.

What is the International Forensic Program?

The International Forensic Program (IFP) at Physicians for Human Rights (PHR) is dedicated to providing independent forensic expertise to document and collect evidence of human rights violations and of violations of international humanitarian law. Starting in the 1980s, PHR has mobilized forensic scientists (and other experts) worldwide to respond to inquiries by governments, organizations, families, and individuals. Experts come from such disciplines as forensic pathology, forensic anthropology, forensic laboratories, and firearm examiners. It can be found at http://physiciansforhumanrights.org/justice-forensic-science/ifp/.

What is the International Institute of Certified Forensic Investigation Professionals?

The International Institute of Certified Forensic Investigation Professionals, Inc. (IICFIP) is called the world's premier forensic investigation professional organization. It not only brings together forensic investigators but also provides forensic investigation skills training to everyone who is interested in forensic investigations. IICFIP has members in 142 countries, including South America, Asia, Europe, North America, Australia/Oceania, and Africa. It can be found at http://iicfip.org/.

OTHER FORENSIC WEBSITES

What is the *Handbook of Forensic Services*?

The *Handbook of Forensic Services* is the official Federal Bureau of Investigation's guide detailing the procedures for a crime scene (for example, collecting, preserving, packaging, and shipping evidence). It provides guidance and procedures for safe and efficient methods of collecting, preserving, packaging, and shipping evidence, along with describing the forensic examinations performed by the FBI's Laboratory Division. It can be viewed at https://www.fbi.gov/file-repository/handbook-of-forensic-services-pdf.pdf/view.

What are a few websites that offer information about crime scene investigations?

Many websites offer information about crime scene investigations. The following are only a few:

- *Crime Scene and Evidence Photography*—This website offers a comprehensive listing of links to articles and sites about crime scene photography. It can be found at http://www.crime-scene-investigator.net/csi-photo.html.

- *Tread Forensics*—This is a website dedicated to providing footwear and tire resources to the forensic community. The site went live in April 2017 and was created to perpetuate the online resources that were available at the Scientific Working Group for Shoeprint and Tire Tread Evidence (or SWGTREAD; for more information, see the chapter "In the Crime Lab: Patent, Latent, and Plastic Prints"). Tread Forensics can be found at http://treadforensics.com/index.php.

- *Scientific Working Group on Bloodstain Pattern Analysis (SWGSTAIN)*—In the spring of 2002, the FBI Laboratory coordinated a meeting to explore organizing a scientific working group in bloodstain pattern analysis. It organized a core group of sixteen recognized bloodstain pattern analysis experts from federal, state, and local governments as well as private practitioners in the United States and Canada—eventually forming the Scientific Working Group on Bloodstain Pattern Analysis (SWGSTAIN). It can be found at http://www.swgstain.org/Home.

What are some websites that deal with autopsies and forensic pathology?

Several websites deal with autopsies and forensic pathology. The following gives a brief listing in these forensic fields:

- *Visible Proofs: Forensic Views of the Body*—This website is from the National Institutes of Health and is about the history of forensic medicine. Designed for students and educators, it offers activities that introduce forensic medicine, anthropology, technology, and history. (According to its website, the activity's name is based on the idea that over the centuries, physicians, surgeons, and other professionals have struggled to develop scientific methods that translate views of bodies and body parts into "visible proofs" that can persuade judges, juries, and the public.) It can be found at https://www.nlm.nih.gov/visibleproofs/index.html.

- *Interactive Autopsy*—This website is from the Australian Museum in Sydney and is a step-by-step demonstration of what happens during an autopsy procedure. (*WARNING*: This site could be disturbing for some people.) It can be found at https://australianmuseum.net.au/interactive-tools/autopsy/.

What are some websites that deal with DNA analysis?

Several websites give insight into the field of forensic DNA analysis. One can be found at the Scientific Working Group on DNA Analysis Methods (SWGDAM) website. This group serves as a forum to discuss, share, and evaluate forensic biology methods, protocols, training, and research to enhance forensic biology services as well as provide recommendations to the FBI director on quality assurance standards for forensic DNA analysis. It can be found at https://www.swgdam.org/. Two more are the Combined DNA Index System (CODIS) and the National DNA Index System (NDIS), which blend forensic science and computer technology into a tool for linking violent crimes. They enable federal, state, and local forensic laboratories to exchange and compare DNA profiles electronically, possibly linking serial violent crimes to each other—and possibly to known offenders. More information about CODIS can be found at https://www.fbi.gov/services/laboratory/biometric-analysis/codis (for more information about CODIS, see the chapter "In the Crime Lab: DNA Analysis").

Do any websites look at the forensic field of questioned documents?

Yes, a few websites look at questioned documents in association with forensics, for example, the website of certified document examiner Emily J. Will, a board certified forensic document examiner, who specializes in handwriting identification and suspect documents. At her site, she offers an overview of the subject through areas exploring the theories and applications of questioned document examination, the external tools used in examination, and a presentation of famous cases. It can be found at http://www.qdewill.com.

What is the American Forensic Nurses?

One of the lesser-known forensic organizations deals with forensic nursing: the American Forensic Nurses (AMRN), founded in 1983. It serves Southern California, providing specific mobile forensic evidence connection services for federal, state, and local law enforcement in that area. The nurses are on call at all hours, seven days a week, and perform such tasks as body fluid collection (such as blood, urine, saliva), sexual assault examinations, and sampling for DNA evidence. Its website can be found at http://www.amrn.com/.

Are any organizations that are dedicated to forensic science associated with certain states?

Yes, many organizations dedicated to forensic science are associated with a certain U.S. state. For example, the New Jersey Association of Forensic Scientists (http://www.njafs .org/) supports forensic science in New Jersey (with its headquarters in Trenton), including support, education, and information for its members who are scientists, academics, and students in the field of forensics. Another is the California Association of Criminologists (http://www.cacnews.org/membership/lab_directory.shtml#nevada) that not only provides a listing of crime labs in the state (and also other state labs and law-enforcement agencies) but offers education and information to its members.

CAREERS AND EDUCATION IN FORENSIC SCIENCE

Do any resources exist to help a young person know more about becoming a forensic scientist?

Several resources can help a young person know more about becoming a forensic scientist. For example, the American Academy of Forensic Sciences (AAFS; http://www.aafs .org) has extensive resources for aspiring forensic scientists, including "Choosing a Career" (https://www.aafs.org/students/choosing-a-career/) and a "Student Career Resources" section on its website (https://www.aafs.org/students/choosing-a-career/student-career-resources/), along with a "Young Forensic Scientists" forum.

What organization often offers workshops for young people in forensic science?

A special program that offers forensic science lessons is called "Q?rius for Teachers" (pronounced "curious") for teachers and students (grades K–5 and 6–12) at the Smithsonian Institution's National Museum of Natural History in Washington, D.C. (link at http://qrius.si.edu/teachers/school-programs-at-museum#/–1/). For example, one forensic science lesson includes "The Mystery at Yorktown Creek." In this study, the students learn that a human skeleton has been exposed by erosion along a creek. It is up to the students to examine the evidence collected by an archaeologist using forensic tools and techniques from the Smithsonian scientists to determine the details about that person.

What was the first university in the United States to offer criminology and criminalistics?

According to the University of California at Berkeley, that university was the first in the United States to offer criminology and criminalistics. In 1916, the then-chief of police at Berkley, August Vollmer, who needed training in preparation for police service, joined with Alexander M. Kidd, professor of law, to create a summer session program in crim-

The first American university to offer a program in criminology was the University of California at Berkeley.

inology. Funds were found to establish an actual criminology program in 1931; in 1939, the Bureau of Criminology was organized in the Department of Political Science; and in 1950, the School of Criminology was established. A master's program was added in 1947 (first awarded in 1949) and a Ph.D. program in 1963.

Do any organizations exist that accredit colleges and universities in the disciplines of forensic science?

The Forensic Science Education Programs Accreditation Commission (FEPAC; an affiliate of the American Academy of Forensic Sciences, or AAFS), under its "Policies & Procedures," has the task of conducting ongoing and comprehensive reviews of its accreditation standards for forensic science. It is in charge of the evaluation of educational institutions—both undergraduate and graduate forensic science programs— and making sure the institution offers quality education to students seeking a career in forensic science. It can be found at the website http://www.fepac-edu.org/.

What are some possible undergraduate degree programs available to a person interested in forensics?

Numerous degree programs are available to a person interested in the field of forensic science. The following lists some of those programs (both bachelor's and master's [graduate] degrees):

• Bachelor of Arts in Criminal Justice

345

What are the differences between criminology, criminalistics, and criminal science?

Majors in criminology, criminalistics, and criminal science have small differences—and, many times, these terms are used synonymously. In general, criminology is the study of crime and its prevention, along with the examination of criminals and their treatment. Typical courses include punishment, criminological theory, social research, and juvenile delinquency. Criminalistics is the application of scientific principles to provide evidence in a criminal case. The person usually has a background in science, often with a bachelor's degree in chemistry (for instance, drug analysis and/or organic chemistry), biology (for instance, genetics), or forensic science. They apply certain scientific methods and techniques to analyze items and are often used as expert witnesses in a trial. A person studying criminal science learns how to reconstruct crimes and analyze physical and/or biological evidence. Studies include lab science and procedures, criminology, police science, and evidence handling.

- Bachelor of Science in Criminal Justice
- Bachelor of Science in Criminology and Criminal Justice
- Bachelor of Science in Cybersecurity
- Bachelor of Science in Organizational Leadership (Criminal Justice Administration)
- Master of Arts in Forensic Psychology and Psychiatry
- Master of Forensic Science
- Master of Science in Criminal Justice
- Master of Science in Criminal Justice Administration
- Master of Science in Applied Criminology

What does a student need to study in order to specialize in a particular field of forensics?

A student needs to take certain courses in order to specialize in a particular field of forensic science. The following lists a few specialty fields and the courses that are most helpful according to the American Chemical Society:

- *Toxicology*—If a student is interested in toxicology, they need to have at least an undergraduate degree in toxicology or a related field (such as chemistry, biology, or biochemistry). Laboratory experience is always good to have too, as well as courses in statistics and mathematics. A bachelor's or master's degree will help a person get work in a lab, while a Ph.D. will enable the student to direct and manage studies in the field. Those interested in the toxicological aspects of trace evidence (see below), such as obtaining and interpreting toxicology reports, are advised to study physiology, biochemistry, and chemistry.

- *Forensic Chemistry*—If a student is interested in forensic chemistry, they should have a good background in chemistry and instruments used for analysis, along with a strong grounding in criminalistics. An undergraduate degree in forensic science or a natural science is required to work in crime laboratories, with extensive coursework in mathematics, chemistry, and biology. For the more advanced positions, such as a lab manager, a master's degree may be required, and a Ph.D. is often preferred for positions such as a lab director and is almost always required if the person wants to do research in academic institutions.

- *Trace Evidence (Physical) Specialist*—For a student who wants to become a trace evidence specialist, such as an expert in glass or shotgun residue, it is advised that they concentrate on instrument skills used to analyze such evidence. In addition, courses in geology, soil chemistry, and materials science are useful when examining trace evidence.

- *Trace Evidence (Biological) Specialist*—Those interested in working with trace evidence in terms of biology, such as hair or DNA analysis, should also focus on instrument skills. In addition, courses in microbiology, genetics, and biochemistry—depending on what type of specialty is desired—will also help to obtain a job in a forensic lab.

What are some examples of accredited U.S. universities or colleges in forensic science?

At this writing, thirty-four colleges and universities are accredited through FEPAC (Forensic Science Education Programs Accreditation Commission; see above). The following lists some of those institutions, along with the program offered, address, and website (for a complete list of FEPAC accredited colleges and universities, go to http://www.fepac-edu.org/accredited-universities):

Albany State University
Full Accreditation for the Bachelor of Science in Forensic Science Degree
504 College Drive
Albany, GA 31705
http://www.asurams.edu/academics/college-of-science-health-professions/natural-sciences/

Boston University School of Medicine
Full Accreditation for the Master of Science Degree in Biomedical Forensic Science
Biomedical Forensic Sciences Program
Department of Anatomy and Neurobiology
72 E Concord Street
R806
Boston, MA 02118
http://www.bumc.bu.edu/biomedforensic

Duquesne University
Full Accreditation for the Master of Science in Forensic Science Degree
Master of Science in Forensic Science and Law
Bayer School of Natural and Environmental Sciences
600 Forbes Avenue
Pittsburgh, PA 15282
http://www.duq.edu/academics/schools/natural-and-environmental-sciences/academic-programs/forensic-science-and-law

The George Washington University
On Probation for the Master of Forensic Science Degree, Concentration in Forensic Chemistry, Molecular Biology, Forensic Toxicology
Department of Forensic Science
2100 Foxhall Road, NW
Washington, DC 20007
http://forensicsciences.columbian.gwu.edu

John Jay College of Criminal Justice
Full Accreditation for the Master of Science Degree in Forensic Science
Department of Sciences
524 West 59th Street
Room 05.66.20 NB
New York, NY 10019
http://www.jjay.cuny.edu/master-science-forensic-science

Michigan State University
Full Accreditation for the Master of Science Degree, Forensic Biology and Forensic Chemistry Tracks
560A Baker Hall
East Lansing, MI 48824-1118
http://www.forensic.msu.edu

The Ohio University
On Probation for the Bachelor of Science Degree in Forensic Chemistry
Department of Chemistry and Biochemistry
249A Clippinger Laboratory
Athens, OH 45701
http://www.ohio.edu/chemistry/forensic

The Pennsylvania State University
Full Accreditation for the Bachelor of Science in Forensic Science Degree
On Probation for the Master of Professional Studies in Forensic Science Degree
Forensic Science Program
107 Whitmore Lab
University Park, PA 16802

http://www.forensics.psu.edu

Texas A&M University
Full Accreditation for the Bachelor of Science in Forensic and Investigative Sciences
Degree
Department of Entomology
MS 2475
College Station, TX 77843-2475
http://forensics.tamu.edu

West Virginia University
Full Accreditation for the Bachelor of Science Degree in Forensic and Investigative
Sciences
Full Accreditation for the Master of Science Degree in Forensic and Investigative
Sciences
1600 University Avenue
208 Oglebay Hall
PO Box 6121
Morgantown, WV 26506-6121
http://forensics.wvu.edu/

Does another listing exist of colleges and universities that offer education in forensic science?

Yes, besides FEPAC (Forensic Science Education Programs Accreditation Commission), the American Academy of Forensic Sciences (AAFS) lists many colleges and universities that offer education in the forensic sciences. This searchable list includes both those institutions accredited by FEPAC and those that are not, along with colleges and universities that have "on-campus" and/or "online" courses. These lists can be found at https://www.aafs.org/students/college-university-listings/, which includes a link to FEPAC.

Further Reading

(Note: Along with the books mentioned in the "The Media and Forensic Science" chapter, this list has only a few books that highlight forensic science or a certain subdivision within the field. To uncover more, just go to your local library or favorite bookseller.)

Englert, Rod, and Kathy Passero. *Blood Secrets: A Forensic Expert Reveals How Blood Spatter Tells the Crime Scene's Story.* New York: Thomas Dunne Books, 2010.

Fisher, Barry, and David Fisher. *Techniques of Crime Scene Investigation,* 9th edition. Boca Raton, FL: CRC Press, 2018.

Hallcox, Jarrett, and Amy Welch. *Bodies We've Buried: Inside the National Forensic Academy, the World's Top CSI Training School.* New York: Berkley Hardcover, 2006.

James, Stuart H., Jon J. Nordby, and Suzanne Bell. *Forensic Science: An Introduction to Scientific and Investigative Techniques,* 4th edition. Boca Raton, FL: CRC Press, 2014.

McCrery, Nigel. *Silent Witnesses: The Often Gruesome but Always Fascinating History of Forensic Science.* Chicago: Chicago Review Press, 2014.

McDermid, Val. *Forensics: What Bugs, Burns, Prints, DNA, and More Tell Us about Crime,* reprint edition. New York: Grove Press, 2016.

Osborn, Albert S. *Questioned Documents.* Wolcott, NY: Scholar's Choice, 2015.

Owen, David L. *Hidden Evidence: 40 True Crimes and How Forensic Science Helped Solve Them.* Richmond Hill, ON: Firefly Books, 2000.

Rafter, Nicole, and Michelle Brown. *Criminology Goes to the Movies: Crime Theory and Popular Culture.* New York: NYU Press, 2011.

Reddy, K. S. N. *The Essentials of Forensic Medicine and Toxicology,* 34th edition. New Delhi, India: Jaypee Brothers Medical Publishers, 2017.

Rosewood, Jack, and Rebecca Lo. *The Big Book of Serial Killers.* Amazon Digital Services, 2017.

Saferstein, Richard. *Criminalistics: An Introduction to Forensic Science,* 12th edition. London, England:Pearson, 2017.

Samenow, Stanton. *Inside the Criminal Mind.* New York: Broadway Books, 2014.

Sharma, B. R. *Forensic Science in Criminal Investigation and Trials.* Universal Law Publishing Company, 2015.

Starr, Douglas. *The Killer of Little Shepherds: A True Crime Story and the Birth of Forensic Science.* New York: Knopf, 2010.

Glossary

ACE-V—This is an acronym for analysis, comparison, evaluation, and verification. It is most often used to describe the process of comparing a latent print to a known print.

Associative evidence—Evidence that can link a person or item to the scene of a crime.

Ballistics—The study of the motion of projectiles. In particular, it is often used to describe the study of bullets from the time the projectile is shot from a firearm to the time it impacts an object or a person. (Note: Ballistics is NOT the study of firearms identification.)

Binary explosive—When two substances that are not explosive in and of themselves are mixed together and become explosive.

Biological evidence—Physical evidence that is biological in nature (such as blood or body fluids) that originates from a human, animal, or plant.

Black powder—A low explosive that is commonly made from potassium (or sodium) nitrate, sulfur, and charcoal.

Bloodstain pattern—These are stains of blood that have a regular pattern, order, or repetitive form deposited on objects, walls, the ground, etc., and that are often used as evidence at a crime scene. They are most often from a victim who has been murdered by an object, gunshot, or even at an accident scene in which a person is struck by a vehicle. (See also "drip pattern.")

Capture—In photographing a crime scene, the process of recording the data of the scene, such as with images from a camera, a video sequence of the site, or an audio stream.

Cartridge—A cartridge is the unfired round of ammunition consisting of the cartridge case (usually made of brass, steel, or nickel), the bullet (or projectile), the primer, and a smokeless powder. It is also referred to in many other ways (some erroneous), including a round, ammo, bullet, or projectile.

Cipher—A cipher is a form of code in which numbers or letters replace the plain text message. This prevents others from interpreting the information unless they are the recipient of the message and know how to translate the cipher. (See also "codes" and "encryption.")

Class characteristic—A characteristic (such as physical shape or size) of shoes or tires that are intentional or unavoidable and that repeats during the manufacturing process. This often allows forensic experts to examine and trace back certain physical characteristics of shoes or tires to use as evidence. (See also "individual characteristic.")

Codes—A code is a way of using words, numbers or symbols to replace plain text in order to obscure the meaning of a message. Not every code is a cipher. And in some codes even a single symbol may represent an entire message or idea. (See also "cipher" and "encryption.")

Contamination (or evidence contamination)—When there is an unwanted transfer of material—biological or not—from a source to a piece of evidence at a scene. For example, if a person picks up a gun upon discovering a body at a crime scene their fingerprints will contaminate the weapon.

Cryptography—A way of using and interpreting codes and ciphers to communicate something that was once in plain text. It is often used in forensics in relation to questioned documents.

Detonator—A device that is used to start (or create an internal reaction within) certain types of high explosives.

Disguised writing—Writing that is deliberately altered to conceal the identity of the writer. (See also "distorted writing.")

Distorted writing—Writing that does not appear to have been the natural way a person wrote. It can include disguised writing or be indicative of a physical illness or uneven writing surface. (See also "disguised writing.")

Drip pattern—This is a bloodstain pattern that results from liquid that dripped into another liquid—at least one of which is blood. (See also "bloodstain patterns.")

Dud—An explosive device that does not explode even though it has gone through the entire arming and firing cycle. Even though it has failed to explode, it is a dangerous condition in which, if tampered with, it may explode.

Encryption—A procedure that converts plain text into symbols, letters, or numbers and prevents others—other than the intended receiver of the text—from understanding the information. (See also "cipher" and "codes.")

Evidence—Evidence is the information or objects that are accepted in court when presenting a case. Evidence can include microscopic and macroscopic items and materials from a variety of sources, such as impressions, fingerprints, genetic material, or dental records.

Evidence quality photos—The images—usually of a scene—that are of good quality and sufficient size to allow comparison and examination by a qualified forensic expert.

Explosion—Rapid expansion of gases that is caused by a chemical or physical action. It also produces a pressure (or shock) wave.

Explosive—A chemical substance or a mix of chemicals and/or compounds that produce an explosion.

Forensic document examiner—An expert in the details and elements of questioned documents, mainly to determine the authenticity of a document.

Fracture match—A fracture match (or physical match) is examining two or more objects that helps experts conclude that the object(s) was/were once on an original piece or were held or bonded together in a unique way.

Friction ridge—On a person's fingertip, it is the raised portion of the skin that forms the fingerprint pattern. The fingerprint consists of one or more collected ridges. (See also "furrow.")

Furrow—A furrow is the division between a person's friction ridges in their fingertip that help form a fingerprint. These are often referred to as the valleys or depressions of the friction ridges. (See also "friction ridge.")

Gunpowder—Gunpowder has many different formulations, but its main purpose is to create oxides of carbon, especially carbon dioxide gas that propels the projectile (bullet) down through a barrel of a firearm to the target.

Individual characteristic—The unique characteristic of footwear or tire treads that is not shared by any other shoe or tires—even if they are from the same manufacturing process. Most often it is from some mechanical change in the footwear or tire, such as a wearing down of a part of a shoe or a stone caught in a tire tread. (See also "class characteristic.")

Inked fingerprint—An inked fingerprint is one way to record a person's fingerprints—or the friction ridges/furrows of a person's fingers—most often for identification. In most cases, it is conducted in a law enforcement station. The person's finger(s) is rolled in black printer's ink, then "rolled" on special paper with the impression of the ridges and furrows imprinted on the paper.

Intermediate range shot—An intermediate range shot is one fired at a close enough distance to produced powder stippling on a victim's skin or particles deposited on an object. (See also "range shot or range of fire.")

Media—Media are objects on which data is stored. They include flash drives, hard drives, CDs, DVDs, SIM cards from mobile devices, etc. Such media is often used by forensic analysts to collect possible evidence from a suspect in a crime.

Medicolegal—Medicolegal involves not only medicine but the legal aspects involving medicine—in other words, how medicine and law interact. It is often thought of as a subset of forensic medicine.

Munitions—The term for all and any military explosives. The term "ordnance" is also used in this sense.

Pistol—A pistol is another name for a handgun. It is usually in the form of a semi-automatic pistol.

Primary high explosive—A high explosive that is extremely sensitive to friction, shock, spark, or heat. Depending on the type of primary high explosive, this sensitivity causes the explosive to detonate and/or burn rapidly.

Primary transfer—The direct transfer of trace evidence from one object to another, such as a visible fingerprint to a glass.

Print—A print is the mark that is made by a fingertip, foot, ear, or other body part on a hard surface or soft material. Prints are divided into patent (visible), latent (mostly invisible), and plastic (thought of as a three-dimensional impression in soft material).

Range shot or range of fire—The range shot, or range of fire, is the distance a shot is fired from the gun's muzzle to the target, which is usually a victim of a crime. (See also "Intermediate range shot.")

Reference sample—A material or substance that has a known composition or physical characteristic. These samples are authenticated and documented, and they are often used to compare found evidence—for example, a bullet found in a wall at a crime scene.

Report—A loud noise that is produced by an explosion.

Revolver—A revolver is a firearm with a rotating cylinder that holds ammunition for firing. Unlike a semi-automatic firearm (see "pistol"), a revolver does not eject spent cartridge cases automatically. Instead, the cylinder rotates after each firing, moving a new round to be fired to the barrel. It also fires fewer rounds than most semi-automatics.

Satellite stain—A smaller bloodstain that forms when the parent stain from a person impacts a surface.

Secondary high explosive—A high explosive that is less sensitive to shock, heat, or friction and is initiated by another explosive.

Semi-automatic—A semi-automatic is a shortened term for most pistols. A semi-automatic commonly uses a magazine—a container (clip) in which the ammunition (or rounds or cartridges) are inserted. Unlike a revolver, the cartridge cases in a semi-automatic are automatically ejected after the handgun is fired.

Shotgun—A shotgun is a firearm usually fired from the shoulder and that has a long, smooth barrel.

Shotshell—A shortened version of the term "shotgun shell" that is used to describe an unfired round of ammunition. It consists of the shotshell (shotgun shell) casing (which is usually made of plastic with a thin brass base), the projectile (or projectiles, either shot or slug), wadding, a primer, and smokeless powder—all of which together form the ammunition fired from the shotgun.

Slug—A single shotshell projectile.

Smokeless powder—Smokeless powder is a major component of ammunition. It is composed of several chemicals that, when ignited by a cartridge's primer, generates a gas that forces the projectile out of the cartridge casing.

Transient evidence—Because of its nature or the conditions at a scene, it is evidence that will lose (or eventually lose) its value as evidence. For example, if there is blood on a sidewalk and it begins to rain, the blood becomes transient evidence.

Wadding—Wadding is the paper or other material in a shotshell (shotgun shell) that forms the seal between the smokeless powder and the shot.

Index

Note: (ill.) indicates photos and illustrations.

first municipal police forces in America, 20
first organized police force in Paris, 15, 16
first uniformed policemen, 16
forensic, 17
"forensic" as word first used, 17
forensic science experts, 30–31
forensic toxicology, 28
Hebenstreit, Joannes Ernestus, 18
Henry, Sir Edward Richard, 25–26
Henry System of Fingerprint Classification, 25–26
Herschel, Sir William James, 23–24
high-definition digital imagery, 30
INTERPOL, 33–34
law enforcer, 14, 15
Locard, Edmond, 28
Lombroso, Cesare, 19 (ill.), 19–20
Malpighi, Marcello, 17–18, 18 (ill.)
North American Indian trackers, 14
Peel, Sir Robert, 21 (ill.), 21–22
Peelers, 21–22
Peelian Principles, 22
physical matching, 18
police, 17
Purkinje, Jan Evangelista, 23, 23 (ill.)
questioned document analysis, 21
as "real" science, 17
scientific discipline, 24
Scotland Yard, 23, 32
Shadow Wolves, 34
technology's role in, 29
U.S. Department of Homeland Security, 32–33
U.S. law enforcement officers, 31
Vidocq, Eugène François, 20–21
forensic science cases
arsenic in 1800s, 296
Atlanta Olympics bombing, 314
bombings, 313–16
Borden, Lizzie, 301–3, 302 (ill.)
Boston Marathon bombing, 313
Bundy, Ted, 311 (ill.), 311–12
famous disinterrments, 299
Green River Killer, 312–13
Gunness, Belle, 309 (ill.), 309–11
Hitler, Adolf, 300 (ill.), 300–301
Jack the Ripper, 308 (ill.), 308–9
Japan subway gassing, 315–16
Lindbergh kidnapping, 303–5, 304 (ill.)

Lockerbie bombing of Pan Am flight 103, 315
Madrid train bombing, 316
Miller, Clell, 298
Napoléon Bonaparte, 296–97
Oklahoma City bombing, 134, 314–15, 315 (ill.)
Ramsey, JonBenét, 306–7
serial killers, 308–13
Taylor, Zachary, 297 (ill.), 297–98
Titanic, 298–300
Tutankhamen, King, 295
Wood Chipper Murder, 307–8
World Trade Center tower bombing, 314
Forensic Science Education Programs Accreditation Commission (FEPAC), 345, 349
forensic science resources
books, fiction, 325–27
books, nonfiction, 323–25
careers and education, 344–49
degree programs, 345–49
education in, 347
foundations, 331
international organizations, 336–37, 340
journals, 322
magazines, 321–22, 323
museums, 332–33, 343
public, 330–31
students, 329–30
U.S. government, 337–40, 342
U.S. organizations, 333–36
WinID, 331
forensic serology, 97–98
forensic toxicology, 9, 10, 28, 104, 334–35, 336, 346, (ill.). *See also* autopsy—toxicology
Forensic Toxicology and Pharmacology, 322
forensics, 1–2
Forensics: What Bugs, Burns, Prints, DNA, and More Tell Us about Crime (McDermid), 324
forgeries, 233
Foster, Jodie, 318
foundations, 331
France, 15–16
fratricide, 7
Frederic Rieders Family Foundation, 331
Freeman, Morgan, 317
friction ridges, 166–67, 168–70
Frye hearing, 282
Frye test, 289–90
fungi, 68
fur, 121
furrows, 166–67, 168–70

G

Gacy, John Wayne, 135, 267
Gall, Franz Joseph, 19
Galton, Sir Francis, 24, 25, 167
Galton's details, 167
gang signs, 236
gastric juices. *See* autopsy—gastric juices and body organs
gastrointestinal tract contents, 101, 102
Gaye, Marvin, 11
genome, 176
geology, 148
geology, forensic, 11, 149, 262
George Washington University, 348
Gerritsen, Tess, 327
glass, 82–84, 83 (ill.), 150–51, 151 (ill.)
Goddard, Calvin Hooker, 203
Goddard, Henry, 26–27
Gosling, Ryan, 317
Gow, Betty, 303
grand jury, 278
Green River Killer, 312–13
Grew, Nehemiah, 167
grid search, 39
Gross, Hans Gustav Adolf, 9, 149
gun, 196
Gunness, Belle, 309 (ill.), 309–11
Gunness, Peter, 310
gunpowder, 200–201
gunshot residue (GSR), 154 (ill.)
    analysis of, 154, 201
    challenged as evidence, 154–55
    definition, 82, 154
    formation of, 201
    gunpowder vs., 200–201
    lead in, 201–2
    misinterpretation of, 202
gunshot wounds, 111–12, 112 (ill.). *See also* autopsy—contusions, bruises, and gunshot wounds
gymnosperms, 157

H

habeus corpus, 274
hair, 121. *See also* autopsy—nails and hair
    analysis of, 144, 144 (ill.)
    animal, 146
    color, 145–46
    controversies about analysis, 286–87
    DNA (deoxyribonucleic acid), 146, 180–81
    drug use, 145
    evidence, 60–61
    found at crime scene, used against suspect, 144–45
    human remains, 130

I

J

K

cryptanalysis, 233–34, 236
cryptography, 233
cryptology, 233–36
damaged, 224–25
databases, 225–26, 232–33
definition, 223
digital analysis, 224
Enigma machine, 234–35, 235 (ill.)
examples of, 223
famous cases, 235–36
faxes, 226
forensic accounting, 226–27
Forensic Information System for Handwriting (FISH), 232
forgeries, 233
gang signs, 236
handwriting, 231–33
indented impressions, 229
ink, 229–31
International Ink Library, 230–31
investigation of, 223–24
invisible ink, 229–30
legal document, 228
limitations in analysis of, 225, 225 (ill.)
paper age, 228–29
paper analysis, 227–28
Stewart, Martha, 231, 231 (ill.)
tools used to examine, 224
trace evidence, 225
U.S. organizations, 335–36
watermarks, 229
websites, 343

R

race, 145
radial loop, 169
radiocarbon dating, 135–36
Ramsey, Burke, 306–7
Ramsey, John, 306–7
Ramsey, JonBenét, 31, 271, 306–7
Ramsey, Patsy, 306–7
range shot/range of fire, 111
rapid-result DNA testing, 184
ray search pattern, 39–40
Reddy's Forensic Page (website), 330
Reference Firearms Collection, 209
Reichert, Dave, 312
Reichs, Kathy, 327
remains. *See* human remains
res judicata, 274
retinal scan, 241, 241 (ill.)
retrospective analysis, 268
revolver, 196 (ill.), 196–97
Reynie, Gabriel Nicolas de la, 16
ribs, 113, 114 (ill.)
Richard III, King, 189–90, 190 (ill.)

ricin, 109
Ridgway, Gary Leon, 312–13
rifle, 196
rigor mortis, 57–58
Rising, Clara, 297
Rizzoli & Isles, 320
Robert C. Williams Museum of Papermaking, 228
Rojas, Francisca, 25
Roman gladiators, 127
Romanov family, 190, 191 (ill.)
Roosevelt, Franklin D., 305
Roosevelt, Theodore, 32, 326
Rowan, Sir Charles, 23
Rudolph, Eric Robert, 314
Rule, Anne, 325

S

Saferstein, Richard, 324
Salameh, Mohammed, 314
Sayers, Dorothy, 326
scenes of crime officers (SOCOs), 47
Scherbius, Arthur, 234
Science Daily: Forensic News, 322
Scientific Polymer Products, Inc., 150
Scientific Working Group for Forensic Document Examination (SWG-DOC), 335–36
Scientific Working Group for Shoeprint and Tire Tread Evidence (SWGTREAD), 172
Scientific Working Group on Bloodstain Pattern Analysis (SWGSTAIN), 342
Scientific Working Group on DNA Analysis Methods (SWGDAM), 343
Scotland Yard, 23, 32
scratched-out serial number, 207–8
search and rescue dogs, 53
seat of the explosion, 212–13
secondary crime scene, 36
Secrets of the Dead, 318–19
semen, 64–65, 100–101
September 11, 2001, World Trade Center tragedy, 191
serial killers, 267, 308–13
serology, forensic, 97–98
Se7en (1995), 317
sex-determining chromosomes, 178
sexual assault kit, 64 (ill.), 65
Shadow Wolves, 34
Sherlock, 320
The Sherlock Holmes Handbook: The Methods and Mysteries of the World's Greatest Detective (Riggs), 323–24
Sherlock Holmes series (Doyle), 317, 325, 326 (ill.)
shoe prints, 77–79, 78 (ill.), 155, 173–74, 342

short tandem repeats (STR), 185–86
shot patterns, 82
shoulder, 170
shredders, 225, 225 (ill.)
Shroud of Turin, 136, 136 (ill.)
Siegler, Kelly, 318
The Silence of the Lambs (1991), 318
Simpson, O. J., 31
Sir John Fielding mysteries (Alexander), 326
skeleton. *See* bones
skull, 140
Smith, Eugene, 324
Smithsonian, 323
Snow, Clyde, 134–35
Society for Wildlife Forensic Science (SWFS), 262
Society of Forensic Toxicologists (SOFT), 334
Society of Toxicology (SOT), 335
soda-lime-silica glass, 150
soils, 148, 148 (ill.)
SoleMate, 155
Song Ci, 14
Sorenson, Mads, 310
sororicide, 7
Spacey, Kevin, 317
speaker recognition, 242–43
speaker verification, 242–43
Spectra Library for Identification and Classification Engine (SLICE), 157
speech recognition, 243
spent casing, 198
Spilsbury, Bernard, 323
spinal cord, 114–15
spiral search, 39
spoliation, 37
spores, 157–58
Spurzheim, Johann Gaspar, 19
State DNA Index System (SDIS), 189
Steenkamp, Reeva, 7
STEM-works, 329
Stewart, Martha, 231, 231 (ill.)
Stiles, Bill, 298
Stockwell Strangler, 266
stomach contents, 101, 103
straight line search, 39
The Stranger Beside Me: Ted Bundy, the Shocking Inside Story (Rule), 325
strip search, 39
subpoena duces tecum, 274
substantive animation, 247
suicide bombers, 221
Sullivan, Bridget, 303
superglue, 164
suppressor, 197
surveillance videos, 281, 281 (ill.)
Sutherland, Kiefer, 318
Sweatt, Tom, 268

X, Y, Z